Pharaohs of the Sun

Akhenaten · Nefertiti · Tutankhamen

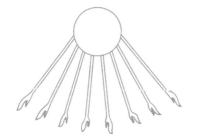

Pharaohs of the Sun

Akhenaten • Nefertiti • Tutankhamen

EDITED BY

Rita E. Freed, Yvonne J. Markowitz
and Sue H. D'Auria

Museum of Fine Arts, Boston

IN ASSOCIATION WITH

Bulfinch Press / Little, Brown and Company

Boston   New York   London

This exhibition was organized by the Museum of Fine Arts, Boston.

NATIONAL ENDOWMENT FOR THE **HUMANITIES** This exhibition is supported by the National Endowment for the Humanities, dedicated to expanding American understanding of history and culture.

The Museum is on the Web at www.mfa.org.

Exhibition dates:
Museum of Fine Arts, Boston: November 14, 1999–February 6, 2000
Los Angeles County Museum of Art: March 19–June 6, 2000
Art Institute of Chicago: July 17–September 24, 2000
Rijksmuseum van Oudheden, Leiden: November 23, 2000–February 18, 2001

Design and production by Cynthia Rockwell Randall
Manuscript edited by Marsha Pomerantz
Printed and bound at Arnoldo Mondadori, A. M. E. Publishing Ltd., Verona, Italy

Front cover:
Colossal statue of Amenhotep IV with *nemes* and double crown (cat. 23)

Back cover: (left to right)
Sculpture of Akhenaten (cat. 85)
Youthful Nefertiti (cat. 42)
Tutankhamen wearing a *nemes* headdress (cat. 240)

Frontispiece:
Stela of the royal family, detail (cat. 53)

Bulfinch Press is an imprint and trademark of Little, Brown and Company (Inc.)

PRINTED IN ITALY

Contents

Director's Preface

Visionary, zealot, dreamer, iconoclast: the pharaoh Akhenaten has been called all of these. Some credit him with the introduction of monotheism. Others have labeled him a criminal and a heretic. All agree that he revolutionized Egyptian art and religious practice. In a reign lasting only seventeen years (1353–1336 B.C.), he rejected Egypt's age-old traditions and institutions, building a new capital city in a remote region of the Nile Valley to serve his personal ideology. At the center of his beliefs was Aten, the sole god, the light emanating from the sun. Akhenaten's queen, Nefertiti, enjoyed unprecedented power and may have reigned both with and after him. Her compelling image appears throughout the city and is lasting testimony to her influence. With the eventual accession of Tutankhamen —perhaps Akhenaten's son—to the throne, the old gods and practices were reinstated and Akhenaten's experiment was abandoned.

For us, the fascination and the mystery remain. It is therefore with great pleasure that the Museum of Fine Arts, Boston, presents the exhibition *Pharaohs of the Sun: Akhenaten, Nefertiti, Tutankhamen*. Organized by the Museum, it includes nearly three hundred objects from more than thirty institutions and private collections. Most dramatic are the colossal statues of Akhenaten from Thebes. These extraordinary images, recently conserved and seen here for the first time, are signature pieces from the period.

The Museum of Fine Arts is particularly grateful to the Supreme Council of Antiquities of Egypt for giving generously of its time and resources to help make this exhibition possible. Ambassador Ahmed Maher el-Sayed of the Embassy of the Arab Republic of Egypt, Washington, D.C.; Dr. Gaballa Ali Gaballa; Dr. Mohamed Saleh; and Dr. Mohamed el-Shemy were especially helpful. To the National Endowment for the Humanities, a federal agency, the MFA owes a special debt of gratitude for the award of both planning and implementation grants.

In addition, I would like to express my appreciation to Rita E. Freed, the Norma-Jean Calderwood Curator of Ancient Egyptian, Nubian, and Near Eastern Art, for proposing this exhibition of exceptional breadth. Special thanks go also to Yvonne J. Markowitz and Sue H. D'Auria, who worked with Dr. Freed as exhibition coordinators, and without whom there would have been no show.

We extend our gratitude to the exhibition's other venues, the Los Angeles County Museum of Art, the Art Institute of Chicago, and the Rijksmuseum van Oudheden, Leiden.

MALCOLM ROGERS
Ann and Graham Gund Director

Royal hand (cat. 58)

With its elegant and expressive gesture, the hand exemplifies Akhenaten's innovative style.

Acknowledgments

Recognizing both the broad popular appeal of ancient Egyptian art and the allure it holds for scholars, Malcolm Rogers, Ann and Graham Gund Director, four years ago gave his enthusiastic endorsement to the idea of a comprehensive exhibition devoted to the age of the revolutionary pharaoh Akhenaten.

Many individuals and institutions have contributed to the success of this endeavor. For their continued help and encouragement, we are grateful to His Excellency Ahmed Maher el-Sayed, Ambassador of the Arab Republic of Egypt; Gaballa Ali Gaballa, Secretary General of the Supreme Council of Antiquities; Zahi Hawass, Undersecretary of State for the Giza Pyramids; Mohamed Saleh, former Director General of the Egyptian Museum; Mohamed el-Shemy, current Director General of the Egyptian Museum, and his staff, especially Adel Mahmoud, Selwa Ahmed Abd el Rahman, Ibrahim Abdel Gawad, May Trad, and Makram Farag; Mohamed el-Sogheir, Director of the Egyptian Sector; Mohamed Nasr, General Director of Antiquities of Upper Egypt; Madeline el-Malakh, Director of the Luxor Museum, and her staff, especially Sanaa Mohamed Ali; Bekhit Mahmoud Ahmed, Director of Antiquities for Karnak and Luxor; and Fadiya Hanna, Director of the Abu'l Good Storeroom, and her staff. To Nadia Lokma and Awatif Abdel Aziz, special thanks for their unparalleled hospitality and friendship. We are also grateful to Farouk el-Baz for his assistance and sage advice.

Pharaohs of the Sun: Akhenaten, Nefertiti, Tutankhamen would not have been possible without the generosity of many lenders in Europe and the United States. The Ägyptisches Museum, Berlin, contributed more than forty objects—many of them masterpieces of Egyptian art. Our sincere thanks to Dietrich Wildung and Karl-Heinz Priese for their cooperation and kind assistance. We would also like to thank Angela Thomas (Bolton Museum and Art Gallery); Luc Limme (Musées Royaux d'Art et d'Histoire, Brussels); Elena Vassilika and Penelope Wilson (Fitzwilliam Museum, Cambridge); Mogens Jørgensen (Ny Carlsberg Glyptotek, Copenhagen); Rosalyn Clancey (National Museums of Scotland, Edinburgh); Rosalie Drenkhahn (Kestner-Museum, Hannover); Michael Maass (Badisches Landesmuseum, Karlsruhe); Hans Schneider and Maarten Raven (Rijksmuseum van Oudheden, Leiden); Piotr Bienkowski and Joanna Hayward (National Museums and Galleries on Merseyside, Liverpool Museum); Vivien Davies, Morris Bierbrier, Carol Andrews, and John Taylor (The British Museum, London); Barbara Adams, Sally MacDonald, and Lucia Gahlin (Petrie Museum of Egyptian

Two men and a boy (cat. 174)

By the end of the Amarna Period, the exaggerated rendering of the human figure had given way to a softer, more relaxed style.

Raising Pharaoh

In the Egyptian Museum, Cairo, a colossal sculpture of Akhenaten is prepared for conservation before its journey to Boston.

Archaeology, University College London); Kevin Johnson (The National Museum of Science and Industry, London); Rosalie David (The Manchester Museum); Sylvia Schoske (Staatliche Sammlung Ägyptischer Kunst, Munich); Helen Whitehouse (Ashmolean Museum, Oxford); and Christiane Ziegler and Marc Etienne (Musée du Louvre, Paris).

Many American institutions generously agreed to lend objects to the exhibition. For their enthusiastic cooperation and support, we would like to express sincere thanks to Ellen Reeder and Stephen Harvey (The Walters Art Gallery, Baltimore); Richard Fazzini, Edna Russmann, and James Romano (Brooklyn Museum of Art, New York); Glenn Markoe (Cincinnati Art Museum); Arielle Kozloff and Lawrence Berman (The Cleveland Museum of Art); Robert Cohon (Nelson-Atkins Museum of Art, Kansas City); Dorothea Arnold, Marsha Hill, and Elena Pischikova (The Metropolitan Museum of Art, New York); David Silverman and Denise Doxey (University of Pennsylvania Museum of Archaeology and Anthropology, Philadelphia); Rose Tyson (San Diego Museum of Man); Christine Kondoleon, Elizabeth de Sabato Swinton, and Larry Becker (The Worcester Art Museum).

Loans from private collectors add a special dimension to the exhibition and catalogue. We are indebted to the Fritz-Behrens-Stiftung, Theodore and Aristea Halkedis, Pamela and Benson Harer, Jack Josephson, and Thomas Lee for their generosity.

For sharing information about their Amarna material, we thank Evelyn Klengel (Vorderasiatisches Museum, Berlin); Janice Klein (The Field Museum, Chicago); Kurt Luckner (The Toledo Museum of Art); Biri Fay (Berlin); and William Kelly Simpson (Katonah, New York).

Funding in the form of planning and implementation grants from the National Endowment for the Humanities, a federal agency, helped make the exhibition and its accompanying catalogue possible.

The patience, encouragement, and efforts of our colleagues at the Museum were evident from the project's inception. Jennifer Cooper was instrumental in assembling grant-related material; Katie Getchell helped expedite arrangements with the Egyptian government and applied her extensive organizational skills to the exhibition; Paul Bessire developed a dynamic marketing strategy; Valerie McGregor fine-tuned the exhibition design; Arthur Beale, Pamela Hatchfield, Jean-Louis Lachevre, Marie Svoboda, and Will Jeffers addressed the often complex conservation issues; and Jill Kennedy-Kernohan cheerfully served as registrar for the project. Cynthia Randall designed the elegant catalogue, and managed its production with the relentless assistance of Dacey Sartor; David Sturtevant gathered images for the catalogue from around the globe; Tom Lang facilitated their preparation; Greg Heins and John Woolf took superb photographs, and John performed his special artistry on the computer.

The Museum's Department of Education and Public Programs developed several exciting and innovative programs for the exhibition, including a video, an interactive website, a series of teacher workshops, and a public symposium. Our thanks for this go to William Burback, Barbara Martin, Peggy Burchenal, and Gilian Wohlauer. For their help in forging a liaison between the Museum and the Boston Public Schools, we extend our gratitude to two friends of the Department, Eric Collins and Barbara Fields.

We would like to thank our colleague Barry Kemp for his scholarly input and overall support of the exhibition. We are indebted to Core Committee members Michael Mallinson, William Murnane, and Edna Russmann, who gave tirelessly of their time and expertise, answering queries and sharing academic insights. Michael Mallinson also provided installation drawings and graphic material for the exhibition. He worked closely with London-based model maker Andrew Ingham, supplying detailed information as needed to produce an accurate re-creation of the city of Amarna in miniature.

The catalogue has benefited tremendously from the careful scrutiny of Marianne Eaton-Krauss, doyenne of Amarna studies. We are indebted to her for her many additions and comments. We were fortunate in having Marsha Pomerantz to edit the text. The result, we feel, reflects her special talent and diligent efforts. For creating compelling photographs of Amarna and objects in Cairo and Luxor, we are grateful to Gwil Owen, Sherif Sonbol, and Mohamed Gabr.

We would like to thank Peter Lacovara for his expertise and selfless commitment of time; Peter Der Manuelian for creating graphics and solving countless imaging and database problems; Natasha Whitestone for tending the endless correspondence and administrative details; Brigit Crowell for providing hard-to-find references; Diana McDonald for advice on cuneiform images; Margy Faulkner for painstaking work on the bibliography; and Sheila Shear for her reconstruction of our Amarna beaded collar.

Last, but not least, we would like to express our appreciation to the volunteers and interns whose sunny dispositions and contagious energy helped make the exhibition a reality: Ann Cogswell, Melissa Dean, Gary Freeman, Nancy McMahon, Diana Nickel, Meg Robbins, and Sophia Yanakakis.

RITA E. FREED
YVONNE J. MARKOWITZ
SUE H. D'AURIA

Lenders

Baltimore, The Walters Art Gallery
Berlin, Ägyptisches Museum
Bolton, Bolton Museum and Art Gallery
Boston, Museum of Fine Arts
Brussels, Musées Royaux d'Art et
  d'Histoire
Cairo, The Egyptian Museum
Cambridge, Fitzwilliam Museum
Cincinnati, Cincinnati Art Museum
Cleveland, The Cleveland Museum of Art
Copenhagen, Ny Carlsberg Glyptotek
Edinburgh, National Museums of
  Scotland
Hannover, Kestner-Museum
Kansas City, The Nelson-Atkins Museum
  of Art
Karlsruhe, Badisches Landesmuseum
Leiden, Rijksmuseum van Oudheden
Liverpool, National Museums and
  Galleries on Merseyside
London, The British Museum
London, The National Museum of Science
  and Industry
London, Petrie Museum of Egyptian
  Archaeology, University College London
Luxor, Abu'l Good Storeroom
Luxor, The Luxor Museum
Manchester, The Manchester Museum

Munich, Staatliche Sammlung
  Ägyptischer Kunst
New York, Brooklyn Museum of Art
New York, The Metropolitan Museum
  of Art
Oxford, Ashmolean Museum
Paris, Musée du Louvre
Philadelphia, University of Pennsylvania
  Museum of Archaeology and
  Anthropology
San Diego, San Diego Museum of Man
Worcester, The Worcester Art Museum

Private Collections

Anonymous
Fritz-Behrens-Stiftung
Pamela and Benson Harer, The Harer
  Family Trust
Josephson Collection
Thomas H. Lee Collection
The Thalassic Collection, Ltd.

Chronology of Ancient Egypt

Predynastic Period	4800–3100 B.C.		**New Kingdom**		
Dynasty 0	3100–3000 B.C.		Dynasty 18		
Early Dynastic Period			Ahmose	1539–1514 B.C.	
			Amenhotep I	1514–1493 B.C.	
Dynasty 1	3000–2800 B.C.		Thutmose I, II	1493–1479 B.C.	
Dynasty 2	2800–2675 B.C.		Hatshepsut	1478–1458 B.C.	
			Thutmose III	1479–1425 B.C.	
Old Kingdom			Amenhotep II	1426–1400 B.C.	
Dynasty 3	2675–2625 B.C.		Thutmose IV	1400–1390 B.C.	
Dynasty 4	2625–2500 B.C.		Amenhotep III	1390–1353 B.C.	
Dynasty 5	2500–2350 B.C.		Amenhotep IV/Akhenaten	1353–1336 B.C.	
Dynasty 6	2350–2170 B.C.		Nefernefruaten/Smenkhkara	1336–1332 B.C.	
Dynasties 7–8	2170–2130 B.C.		Tutankhamen	1332–1322 B.C.	
			Ay	1322–1319 B.C.	
First Intermediate Period	2130–1980 B.C.		Horemheb	1319–1292 B.C.	
Middle Kingdom			Dynasty 19	1292–1190 B.C.	
Dynasty 11 (after reunification)	1980–1938 B.C.				
Dynasty 12	1938–1759 B.C.		Dynasty 20	1190–1075 B.C.	
Dynasties 13–14	1759–1630 B.C.				
			Third Intermediate Period	1075–656 B.C.	
Second Intermediate Period	1630–1539 B.C.		**Late Period**	664–332 B.C.	
			Greco-Roman Period	332 B.C.–A.D. 642	

Based on William J. Murnane, "The History of Ancient Egypt," in Civilizations of the Ancient Near East, *ed. Jack M. Sasson (New York, 1995), vol. 2, pp. 712–14.*

Geography

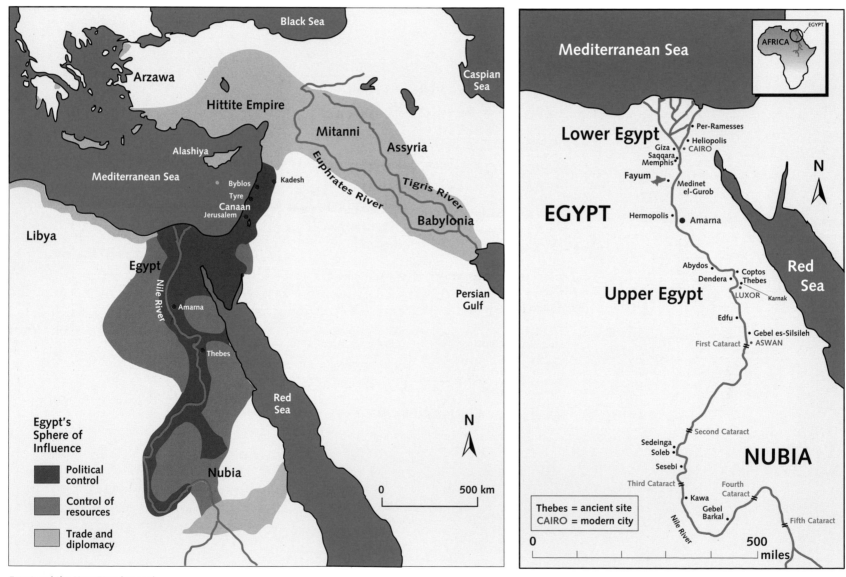

Egypt and the Near East during the
Amarna Period

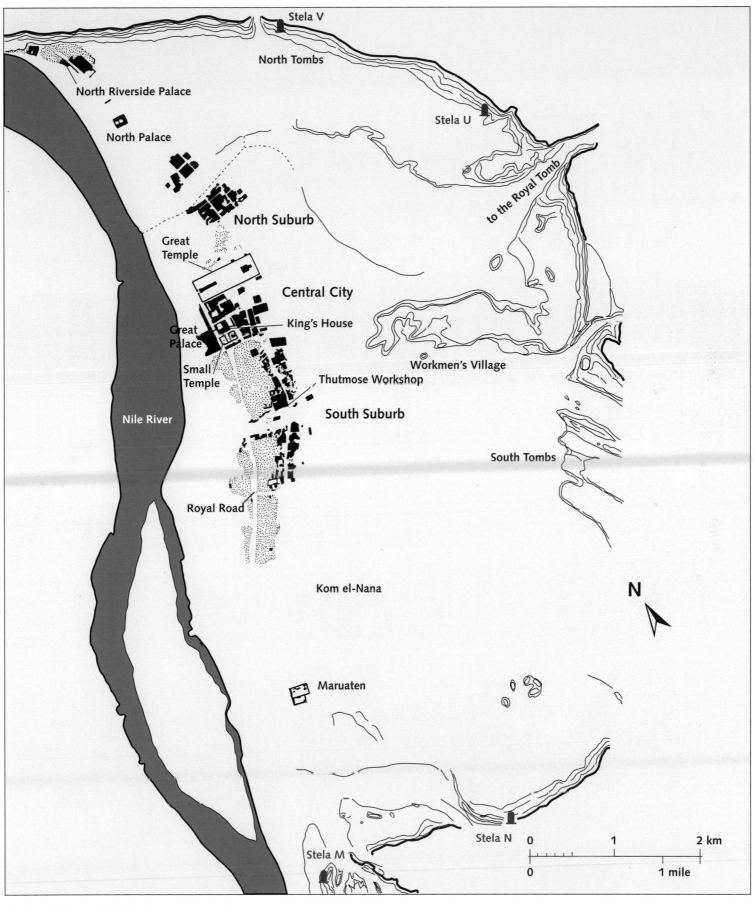

Stela V

North Tombs

North Riverside Palace

North Palace

Stela U

to the Royal Tomb

North Suburb

Great
Temple

Central City

King's House

Great
Palace

Workmen's Village

Small
Temple

Thutmose Workshop

South Suburb

Nile River

South Tombs

Royal Road

Kom el-Nana

N

Maruaten

Stela N

0   1   2 km

0   1 mile

Stela M

The City of Amarna (Akhetaten)

Introduction

Rita E. Freed

Dramatic changes in art and religious thought make the Amarna Period one of the most tantalizing in Egyptian history.

Fig. 1 Sculpture of Akhenaten (cat. 85)

In the art style Akhenaten introduced, faces became elongated, arms spindly, and bellies flaccid. Scholars wonder whether the distortions had symbolic meaning.

ew figures in history evoke the curiosity or command the attention that Akhenaten, Nefertiti, and Tutankhamen do. Although they lived 3,500 years ago, their impact on religion, history, art, and literature reverberates to this day. The international intrigue, politics, romance, and mystery that marked their lives seem familiar to us. Because a wealth of new information has emerged—about these luminaries, the people who served them, the monuments they erected, and the world they influenced—it is fitting and timely that their period be explored and celebrated in *Pharaohs of the Sun: Akhenaten, Nefertiti, Tutankhamen.*

The time span from the apex of Egypt's empire under Thutmose III (1479–1425 B.C.) to the end of the 18th Dynasty was less than two hundred years. But, for a country that took strength from its dogged adherence to age-old principles and pride in its ability to resist change, those two centuries encompass dramatic experiments in nearly all aspects of culture.

One of the things that makes this period so intriguing to lay people and Egyptologists alike is the number of unanswered, and perhaps unanswerable, questions that arise when these pharaohs and their world are discussed. Who was Akhenaten, really (fig. 1)? He has been called everything from a genius to a heretic. What motivated him to abandon the worship of Egypt's traditional gods in favor of a single god, Aten, and remove himself and his court to a city he built midway between Egypt's traditional capitals of Memphis and Thebes? Was it religious fervor? Politics? Psyche? He is shown with an emaciated upper torso and swollen lower body (fig. 4). Why were his depictions so grotesque? Did he have some disease—Froehlich's and Marfan's syndromes have been suggested—or was he expressing his religious beliefs by means of his art? Was he truly a monotheist? Could he even have influenced Moses, as a person no less illustrious than Sigmund Freud suggested?

And who exactly was Nefertiti, his wife (fig. 3)? Where did she come from? Her names were written in cartouches, as were the names of kings, and she was shown in the traditional pharaoh's role of smiter of enemies and officiant at temples. What role did she play in Akhenaten's court? It has been suggested that she ruled as king after Akhenaten's death. What was her eventual fate? What about Kiya, the "other woman" in Akhenaten's life, who is described as his "greatly beloved"? And who was Tutankhamen (figs. 11, 12)? Who were his parents? How did he die? These are only

17

Fig. 2 The Nile
Nile floods spread fertile silt through the river valley and made farming possible.

Fig. 3 Youthful Nefertiti (cat. 42)
Found in a sculptor's workshop, this head of Nefertiti, when finished, would have formed part of a composite sculpture.

a few of the many issues scholars have debated for more than one hundred years.

In this catalogue, a number of today's top scholars in the field of Amarna studies propose solutions to some of these mysteries. The opinions they present are their own, and theories differ from essay to essay. All, however, shed light on a fundamental question pervading this volume and the exhibition it accompanies: was the Amarna Period a revolution, or simply evolution?

Early Egypt

The story really begins around 6000 B.C., when ancient people were drawn to the banks of the Nile because of the reliable food source the river offered them and their animals (fig. 2). In about 3000 B.C. a number of city-states were amalgamated under one ruler, heralding the beginning of Dynasty 1. Dynasties 3 through 8, known as the Old Kingdom, saw the building of Egypt's largest pyramids. After an intermediate period (Dynasties 9 and 10) when Egypt's central government collapsed, Egypt was reunited in Dynasty 11 by a ruler from Thebes, then a provincial area but soon to assume a central position on the world stage. The ensuing period, known as the Middle Kingdom, was a time of relative prosperity and growth, when some of Egypt's finest literature was written.

After a succession of weak rulers, Egypt was infiltrated through the eastern Delta by Canaanites, whose leaders were known as the Hyksos. Again Egypt's salvation came from Thebes, as Ahmose and his brother Kamose, outmaneuvering and outwitting the Hyksos, reunited Egypt. The army that had been built and trained to expel the Hyksos did not stop there. In the next four and a half centuries, the period known as the New Kingdom, Egypt's rulers succeeded in extending its borders from the Fifth Cataract of the Nile in the Sudan to northern Syria. This expansion enabled them to exact tribute and control trade as far east as Persia, northward around the Levantine coast, and southward into sub-Saharan Africa.

Egypt's empire reached its greatest size under King Thutmose III, who, like rulers of the New Kingdom before him, gave thanks to the god Amen for his victories by embellishing the great temple at Karnak in Thebes. Amen's prosperity—as well as that of his priesthood—grew. The empire was consolidated under Thutmose III's son, Amenhotep II, and grandson, Thutmose IV. Tribute and trade not only filled Egypt's

treasuries, but also brought new products and fresh ideas. With prosperity came the freedom to experiment, and two prime areas of experimentation were religion and art.

Egypt had always been a polytheistic society. In addition to certain national gods, including Atum, Ra, and Osiris, each city had its own local gods, usually a trinity consisting of father, mother, and son. When a city gained special importance, as Thebes did in the New Kingdom, its local gods, in this case Amen, his consort Mut, and their son Khonsu, were elevated to national prominence and worshipped accordingly. In addition to these inaccessible state deities, Egyptians had their own more personal gods for key activities and rites of passage, such as the harvest and childbirth.

From the very first, the sun god, known as Ra, played a significant role. As early as Dynasty 2, kings incorporated Ra into their names, and rulers of the 5th Dynasty built sun temples in the god's honor. Aten, the sun's disk and one of the manifestations of the sun god, first appears in literature of the Middle Kingdom. By the reign of Thutmose IV, nonroyal individuals were offering to the gods images of themselves embracing stelae inscribed with hymns to the sun. The sun god was elevated to special prominence by Amenhotep III, the son and successor of Thutmose IV, who added Ra to his name at the time of his jubilee festival celebrating thirty years of rule. He associated Aten with Ra and honored the former by naming his large and opulent boat "Radiance of Aten."

Fig. 4 Colossal statue of Amenhotep IV/Akhenaten from Karnak (Egyptian Museum, Cairo)

The material wealth and political stability of Amenhotep III's reign made an
elaborate construction program possible,
and in the course of his thirty-eight-year
rule he built more and larger monuments
than any king before him. Notable
among these were two 720-ton statues
of himself in radiant golden quartzite
(fig. 6), which marked the entrance to
his vast funerary temple on the west
bank of Thebes. Passersby could not but
marvel at these awesome, godlike images
of their monarch. (We know them today
as the Colossi of Memnon, thanks to
early Greek travelers who named them
after the legendary Ethiopian king killed
by the Greek hero Achilles in the Trojan
War.) Amenhotep III was, in fact, divine
in his own eyes, and even so bold as to
depict Amenhotep III, the man, worshipping Amenhotep III, the god. Although
earlier kings had been deified after
death, never before had a king so
brazenly proclaimed himself a god in his
own lifetime. The manner in which he
was depicted also broke the rules, when
the trim and idealized royal figure took
on a decided plumpness. Clearly change
was in the air.

With his Great Royal Wife, Queen
Tiye, Amenhotep III had at least six
children: two sons and four daughters.
When his young son Thutmose (V) died,
his second son, Amenhotep (IV), became
heir apparent, and it was he who later
changed his name to Akhenaten.

Certain events during the last years of
Amenhotep III's rule remain controversial. It is possible that either in his thirtieth regnal year, the time of the jubilee
festival honoring his longevity, or some

**Fig. 5 Colossal statue, possibly
Nefertiti, from Karnak** (Egyptian
Museum, Cairo)

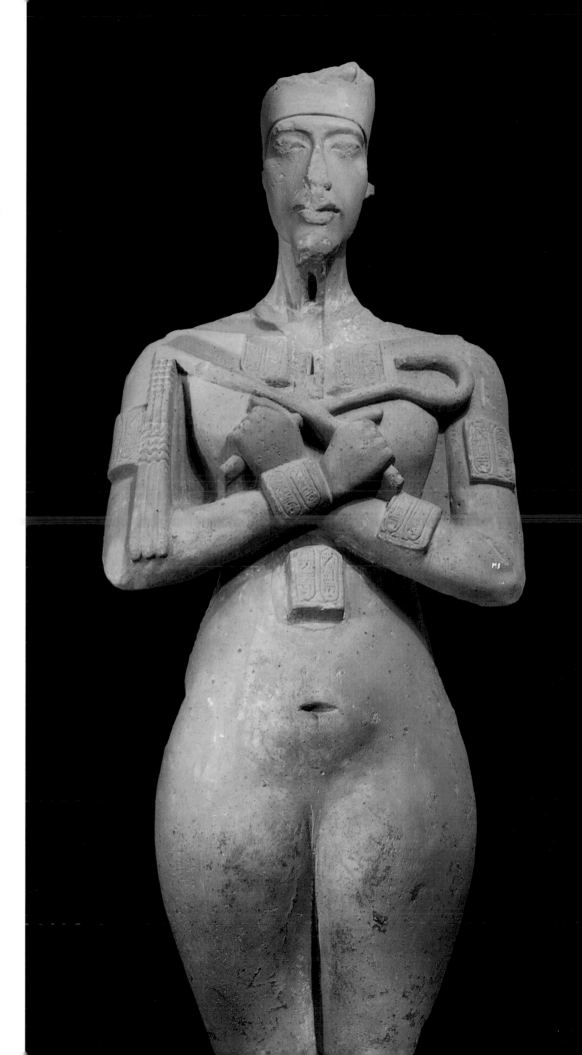

years later, when his health began to fail, the king placed his surviving son on the throne beside him as coregent. This had been an occasional practice in Egypt since the Middle Kingdom: it gave experience to the future monarch and ensured a peaceful succession. But many scholars do not believe such a coregency occurred.

Amenhotep IV at Thebes

Whether Amenhotep IV was ruling jointly with his father or on his own, the earliest record we have of him is at Thebes, where, in his first regnal year, he completed the decoration of the Third Pylon, begun by his father in the great temple of Amen at Karnak. At that time he was already married to his chief wife, Nefertiti, and may have fathered a daughter. Five more were to follow. Nefertiti's origins are unknown, but because she never tells us so, it seems unlikely that she came from within the royal family. Amenhotep IV extols her beauty. Yet since she is shown, in all but a few instances, with the eccentric hallmarks of every other Amarna family member, we really do not know what she looked like. The few exceptions include the famous bust of Nefertiti in the Ägyptisches Museum in Berlin, a work of art that in contemporary society has become synonymous with elegance (fig. 57).

Within five years, Amenhotep IV had erected at least four giant temples in the Karnak precinct, in addition to finishing some of his father's work there. All of Amenhotep IV's building activity at Karnak was dedicated to Aten, who is first depicted as a falcon-headed god on the pylons and later in a much more abstract way. The god is shown simply as a disk with oblique lines, symbolizing the sun's rays, terminating in human hands that embrace whatever the sun shines upon (fig. 70). In at least one of the temples, wall scenes show, it was not Amenhotep IV, as would be expected, but Nefertiti who officiated as Aten's high priest. Another of the four temples included a colonnaded court in which the pillars were fronted by colossal images of the king with arms crossed, a pose reminiscent of Osiris, traditional god of resurrection (fig. 4). Like his father, Amenhotep IV broke with tradition in the portrayal of the pharaoh's body. But he went much further: in a startling departure from the millennium-old

Fig. 6 Colossi of Memnon

A single block of quartzite nearly eighteen meters (sixty feet) high was used to make each of these statues of Amenhotep III. They were restored by the Roman emperor Septimus Severus.

canon of proportion that governed the representation of the human figure, he had himself depicted with an elongated head and facial features, skinny upper torso, voluptuous hips, and overhanging belly. In the same temple from early in his reign, the king is shown celebrating his own jubilee festival of renewal, an event that traditionally did not take place before regnal year thirty.

The Move to Amarna

Clearly, this king's ideologies represented a dramatic break with the past, a break too dramatic to fit comfortably into Amen's stronghold of Thebes. Within a few years, Amenhotep IV had resolved the conflict by establishing a new capital, which he named Akhetaten, "Horizon of Aten." Known today as Amarna or Tell el-Amarna (from the name of the nearby Arab village and its inhabitants), the site was ideal. On the east bank of the Nile an arc of limestone cliffs approaching the river in two places approximately ten miles apart set off an area that was defensible as well as secluded. It had never been occupied and therefore belonged to no god. On fifteen stelae carved into the cliffs on both the east and west banks, Amenhotep IV not only defined Amarna's boundaries, but also described his vision for the new city and listed some of its features:

Fig. 7 Princess nibbling a roasted duck (cat. 56)

The artist sketched the entire scene but carved only part of it.

> *As to what is inside these four stelae, starting*
> *with the eastern (var. western) mountain of Akhet-Aten*
> *as far as the western (var. eastern) mountain, it is Akhet-Aten in*
> *its entirety. It belongs to my father, HOR-ATEN—given life forever continually—*
> *consisting of hills, uplands, marshes, new lands, basin lands, fresh lands, fields,*
> *waters, towns, banks, people, herds, groves and everything that the Aten, my father,*
> *causes to come into existence continually forever.*[1]

Construction must have proceeded at a feverish pace to complete a massive temple to Aten and several lesser ones, as well as the palaces, administrative buildings, barracks, granaries, food-preparation areas, roads, houses, estates, formal gardens, and tombs that ultimately made up the city. Exactly when the king, his family, and the court moved to Amarna is not certain, but it must have been between his sixth and ninth years of rule. By this time Amenhotep IV had further emphasized his break with

the god Amen and its priesthood by changing his name to Akhenaten ("One Who is Effective for Aten"), thereby honoring his new god. It may have been at this time that he also authorized the destruction of the name and images of Amen, wherever and whenever they appeared. Statues and temples as far away as Nubia fell under the blow.

The move to Amarna must have been quite a sight to see, as Akhenaten, his chief wife Nefertiti, their daughters (who then probably numbered three), lesser wives including his beloved Kiya, trusted officials, Egypt's citizenry, and the army made their way, probably by both land and river, to occupy their new home. Even Akhenaten's mother came to visit, if not to live. It has been estimated that between twenty thousand and fifty thousand people called Amarna home.

Today only tantalizing traces remain of this once-splendid city. Nevertheless, for archaeologists, it is a dream come true, because it presents a pristine picture of a planned city from the middle of the second millennium B.C. Excavations begun in the nineteenth century (see "The Exploration of Amarna," page 289) continue today under the leadership of Barry Kemp, for the Egypt Exploration Society. Our present understanding of Amarna is based upon these excavations as well as representations of the city's institutions carved in relief on tomb and temple walls. With the exception of some of the boundary stelae, virtually all of its structures were laid out on the east bank of the Nile, the place where the sun rose and traditionally where houses of both men and gods were built. Tombs were generally located in the west, but at Amarna this bank seems to have been reserved for farming, since Amarna's tombs lay in the eastern cliffs.

The Worship of Aten

Two temples in the Central City were at the very heart of Amarna, and they were, understandably, among the first structures built. Like earlier New Kingdom temples, they consisted of successively smaller courtyards leading to a holy of holies. In traditional temples, this innermost sanctuary was a tiny, dark shrine, accessible only to the king and his high priests, which housed the god's statue. But although Aten could be represented as an abstract sun disk, it had no tangible idol and by its very nature could not be enclosed. Aten's sanctuaries, therefore, were open to the sky so the sun's rays could shine in, and they had no closed doors. (A serpentine entrance passage, however, prevented the casual viewer from seeing what transpired inside.) The areas around the sanctuaries were carefully landscaped with groves of trees, yielding the same interplay of light and shadow as the more traditional hall of columns the groves replaced, and making the transition to the brightness within even more dramatic.

Every god demanded offerings, and Aten was no exception. In the Great Temple, so called because of its enormous size (about 750 by 230 meters, or 2,500 by 750 feet), hundreds of mud-brick altars adorned each side of the central axis. They would have been piled high with fruits, vegetables, birds, and other animals that had been conse-

Fig. 9 Plaster head of an older woman (cat. 139)

Life-size heads found in the studio of the sculptor Thutmose show that artists experimented with depictions of age.

Fig. 8 Royal torso (cat. 49)

The narrow upper torso, high waist, and voluptuous hips are emphasized by the sculpted folds of the diaphanous garment this royal woman wears.

crated to the god. The Great Temple even had its own slaughter yard and adjacent areas for food production. The royal couple and their daughters were frequently depicted in relief on walls and columns, making offerings to Aten in their function as the god's high clergy. After the god was satiated, these vast food resources were distributed to Amarna's citizenry.

Akhenaten also paid homage to his god by means of the liturgy he created. It is through "The Great Hymn to Aten," found in the tomb of the Commander of Chariotry, Ay, that his religious philosophy is revealed to its fullest extent.

Fig. 10 Ancient paths to the tombs of Amarna's elite

Just over two dozen tombs of Akhenaten's officials have been found in the eastern cliffs. Virtually all were unfinished and may never have been used.

Let your holy Light shine from the height of heaven,
  O living Aten,
        source of all life!
From eastern horizon risen and streaming,
  you have flooded the world with your beauty.
You are majestic, awesome, bedazzling, exalted, overlord over all earth,
  yet your rays, they touch lightly, compass the lands
        to the limit of all your creation.
. . . .
How various is the world you have created,
  each thing mysterious, sacred to sight,
O sole God,
  beside whom is no other!
. . . .
And you are in my heart;
  there is no other who truly knows you
        but for your son, Akhenaten.
May you make him wise with your inmost counsels,
        wise with your power,
  that earth may aspire to your godhead,
        its creatures fine as the day you made them.[2]

Whether Akhenaten was the world's first monotheist has been and will continue to be debated by theologians for years to come. Whatever the case, it cannot be denied that Akhenaten believed in one god and saw that god as an all-powerful creator. It is harder to argue that the citizens of Amarna practiced monotheism, however. In all likelihood they still worshipped a trinity of gods, now represented by Aten, Akhenaten, and

Nefertiti. As a further symbol of their close association, the names of all three were enclosed in cartouches, a designation previously restricted to royalty.

Although figural images of the sun god were not a part of the Amarna repertoire, countless images of Akhenaten and Nefertiti must have more than made up for the lack. Thousands of fragments of such statues, large and small, in granite, limestone, sandstone, jasper, and quartzite—seated, standing, and kneeling, but for the most part smashed beyond recognition—were ignobly tossed in a heap outside the enclosure wall of the Great Temple. Evidence of their original placement around the temple and palace courts, pavilions, and altars comes from the discovery of statue pedestals *in situ* as well as representations of statuary on Amarna tomb walls. As the years progressed, the eccentricities of style so characteristic of Akhenaten's relief and sculpture at Karnak gave way to a softer, more naturalistic treatment of the human figure (fig. 18). Throughout, the representations maintained their characteristic vitality and spirituality. Some of Amarna's later works rank among the world's finest artistic achievements.

Since, after Aten, the king and queen were Amarna's most important inhabitants, it is no surprise that Amarna's landscape should include several sumptuous palaces. One, the so-called "King's House," was probably where the king conducted his official business, conferring with his ministers, architects, and priests. From a balcony known as the "Window of Appearances" the king and queen greeted their subjects and tossed favors down to them. Perhaps these gifts included the faience rings and necklaces that have been found in such profusion at Amarna, and even gifts of food from the royal storerooms.

A bridge across the Royal Road linked the King's House with the Great Palace, a massive formal residence where the king would have received large delegations. There was also a North Riverside Palace, away from the Central City and within a walled

enclosure, where the royal family probably spent most of its time, and a North Palace, which was built originally for someone else but given to the king's eldest daughter when she came of age. Reception rooms, throne rooms, altars, outdoor courtyards, living rooms, bed-

Fig. 11 Tutankhamen wearing a *nemes* headdress (cat. 240)

Amarna's artistic impact may be seen in the fleshy features of this later king, who is probably Tutankhamen. The top of the headdress—the combined crown of Upper and Lower Egypt—was most likely a separate piece of stone, now missing.

Fig. 12 Tutankhamen wearing a blue crown (cat. 241)

Tutankhaten changed his name to Tutankhamen and restored Amen to prominence. The hand behind the king's head was probably the god's.

rooms, kitchens, bathrooms, *harim*s, nurseries for the royal daughters, servants' quarters, and storerooms were found in all the palaces. Wall paintings of domestic life, floor paintings that reproduced Amarna's plants and wildlife, and vibrant faience tiles inlaid in stone walls and columns would have added bright splashes of color. A sophisticated irrigation system in the North Palace, the royal residence best preserved, brought water from a large sunken pool to what must have been elegant formal gardens.

Representations of Akhenaten and Nefertiti fondling and even kissing their daughters provide intimate glimpses into the life of the royal family, something quite unheard of with previous pharaohs (fig. 13). Yet it is still hard to imagine what daily life was like for them within the confines of Amarna. The pageantry previously reserved for religious festivals now focused on the royal family. Amarna was ideally laid out for the purpose, with the broad, straight Royal Road that connected all the city's institutions providing the perfect stage for pomp and circumstance. Making offerings at Aten's many altars, conferring with state bureaucrats, receiving foreign delegations, greeting and gifting subjects from the Window of Appearances, or riding in a great state chariot along the Royal Road must have been among the family's official activities, while privately it undoubtedly enjoyed the shade and comfort of its elegant private quarters, lavish gardens, and pools. From tomb representations it is clear that the royal family was the object of reverence during its frequent public appearances.

Fig. 13 Akhenaten kissing a child
(Egyptian Museum, Cairo)

Although the right-angle composition of these two figures harks back to a much earlier era, the theme of a king kissing his child is unprecedented.

Private Homes

Amarna's private citizens lived in suburbs to the north and south of the Central City. Mud brick was the primary domestic building material, but those who could afford it used stone selectively for support elements such as door jambs, lintels, or window gratings. Not surprisingly, houses varied in size according to the wealth of their owners; the larger ones might have more than forty rooms on a plot of nearly nine hundred square meters (ten thousand square feet) enclosed by a mud-brick wall. These estates were laid out first, and then smaller houses, some with only a few rooms, were clustered around them. Larger estates included gardens, separate outbuildings for servants' quarters, granaries, kitchens, storerooms, and an open-air altar.

Most houses were square in plan, with a square living room at the center. Taller than the rooms around it, it was lit by means of clerestory windows and furnished simply, with built-in platforms and portable wooden or stone seats and tables. For private worship a small shrine was set into one wall. Leading into the living room from one side was a columned reception room; on the other three sides were more private quarters. A wealthy homeowner at Amarna could boast of a master bedroom suite that included not only a room for bathing but a toilet as well.

The sun, the life it fostered, and the vibrancy of nature were key to Amarna religion, and these elements were recreated inside the most lavish houses. Walls might be gaily painted with swags of flowers, fruit, and birds. Painted dadoes, columns, and floors added even more color.

Was the god of Akhenaten the god of his citizenry? Evidence suggests that the objects of their reverence differed. Only Akhenaten and Nefertiti are shown offering to Aten at Amarna and flourishing under its life giving rays; nowhere do ordinary people worship the disk directly. Officially, they worshipped the king and queen worshipping the disk, as stelae and statues found in the house shrines show.

As far as their unofficial beliefs are concerned, the archaeological material tells another story. Tiny amulets and ostraca (fragments of painted limestone or pottery) depicting some of the old gods are found in profusion in domestic contexts. This was particularly true for gods that could be counted on to oversee the welfare of the household, such as the leonine dwarf Bes, or Taweret (fig. 15), the pregnant hippopotamus goddess of childbirth. Even the hated Amen made his appearance (fig. 14). Clearly, although it might have been simple for Akhenaten to worship a new god, others found it more difficult to make the change.

When people abandoned Amarna after Akhenaten's death, they took almost everything of value with them; remarkably little of a personal nature has been found there. Such items as a pair of worn-out sandals, bits of linen from garments, razors, hair curlers, earrings, beer jars, food-storage vessels, a toilet seat, and tools provide hints of what life was like at Amarna 3,500 years ago.

Administering City and Empire

Fortunately, the remains of Amarna's bureaucracy are much richer. One of the administrative buildings in the Central City, the "House of the Correspondence of the Pharaoh," yielded nearly four hundred tablets written in cuneiform: diplomatic letters sent by kings and overlords from throughout Egypt's sphere of influence, including Babylon, Mitanni, Assyria, Canaan, and Hatti, to Amenhotep III, Akhenaten, and Tutankhamen. Most of these were relatively standard in form (figs. 117–19). After politely inquiring about Pharaoh's well-being and that of his family, they went on to

Fig. 14 Unfinished statuette of a ram representing Amen (cat. 183)

Fig. 15 The goddess Taweret (cat. 180)

Although Aten was the official deity at Amarna, some private citizens still worshipped the gods of old. Taweret, the pregnant hippopotamus goddess, protected women in childbirth.

Fig. 16 Relief of female musicians
(cat. 145)

Orchestras made up of women
entertained on state occasions.
A harp, two lutes, and a lyre
may be seen here.

solicit quantities of gold and military aid in exchange for loyalty. Unfortunately, no responses are preserved, but, judging from what happened to Egypt's empire in later years, it seems unlikely that Akhenaten filled many of these requests.

In many respects, the bureaucracy it took to run Amarna was not substantially different from what was required to run any other city in Egypt. Scribes, army officers, police, temple personnel, courtiers, stewards, and artisans were all in attendance, many of them known to us by name thanks to inscriptions on their houses, tombs, or personal possessions. One of the most exciting discoveries at Amarna was the house and adjoining workshop of the Overseer of Works and Sculptor Thutmose, which remained just as its owner had abandoned it nearly three and a half millennia ago. Found by German archaeologists in 1912, it not only yielded a pristine example of such an institution, but also provided a rare opportunity to identify a sculptor with his work. The famous bust of Nefertiti now in Berlin was just one of Thutmose's masterworks. About two dozen other busts, made of limestone or plaster, portray realistic faces in extraordinary detail—young and old (fig. 9), distinguished and homely, royal and nonroyal. Perhaps more than any other individual, the sculptor Thutmose has made Amarna come alive again.

Amarna must have been quite a noisy, bustling city. Construction was constant as suburbs grew, temples were altered or expanded to correspond with Akhenaten's developing religious beliefs, and new state buildings were required. In addition to fostering cottage industries such as spinning and weaving, which could be found in many households, Amarna appears to have been a leading center internationally for the manufacture of glass. Kilns yielded many types of pottery, both utilitarian and more decorative painted wares, and bakeries produced enormous quantities of bread for Aten.

Fig. 17 Grieving scene from the Royal Tomb at Amarna

The royal family and their attendants grieve at the death of Akhenaten's second daughter, Meketaten. She is depicted in a kiosk whose flowers symbolize fertility and rebirth. (Line drawing from a relief.)

Although archaeology helps reconstruct a general picture of life at Amarna, it is regrettably silent about the timing of most specific events. One notable exception is documentation in tomb reliefs of a grand celebration that took place in Akhenaten's twelfth regnal year, perhaps coinciding with another jubilee festival. Ambassadorial delegations came from the outermost reaches of Egypt's sphere of influence, bearing tribute and extolling Akhenaten and his god. For the general populace, it must have been quite a splendid event to see: dignitaries colorfully attired in their native dress and laden with gifts from their homelands. Feasting, favors, and a general carnival-like atmosphere would have added to the fun. Akhenaten, Nefertiti, and their six daughters observed the foreign guests and accepted their tribute from a public reviewing stand (fig. 60). As fate would have it, this was also the last time that Akhenaten would be depicted with Nefertiti and all six daughters.

Tragedy struck Amarna. Sometime after year 12, Akhenaten's second daughter, Meketaten, died. Like most pharaohs before him, Akhenaten had begun the preparation of his tomb early in his reign, perhaps even before his move to Amarna. This assumption is based on the presence in the tomb of the early form of an epithet for Aten (though it is accompanied by the later form), the fact that the tomb is mentioned on the early boundary stelae, and the extreme style of the reliefs. Located due east of the Small Temple, in a narrow wadi (dry river bed) nearly two miles into the eastern cliffs, the site Akhenaten chose was strategic, beautiful, and distant—not unlike the Valley of the Kings at Thebes. A series of side rooms in the rock-cut tomb was prepared for his beloved daughter. The burial chamber is now empty except for bits of wall relief—most notably a poignant scene that shows the grieving parents bidding farewell to their child (fig. 17). It is an emotional scene even in its fragmentary state, and, for royalty, unprecedented.

The End of Amarna

The final years at Amarna may well not have been happy ones. By regnal year 15, inscriptions cease to mention Akhenaten's mother, Tiye. By around year 16, representations of his greatly beloved Kiya have been recarved into images of his eldest daughter, Meretaten. Had misfortune struck additional family members? It has been suggested that they succumbed to a plague introduced into Egypt inadvertently by the tribute-bearing foreign delegations. Akhenaten's general neglect of the empire and his lack of attention to cities other than Amarna must have contributed to a general feeling of unrest. Was Amen's old priesthood capitalizing on this or stirring it up? Some have associated an increasingly intense effort to desecrate names and images of Egypt's old gods, particularly Amen, with this period of Amarna's history.

Even Akhenaten's own fervent worship of Aten could not alter the inevitable, and sometime during the king's seventeenth regnal year, he died. In stark contrast to the old order, which provided specific directions for the treatment of the body after death and a precise funerary liturgy, Aten's precepts included no such provisions; his sun hymns dealt only with life. But what little is left of Akhenaten's tomb and its remains indicate how cleverly Akhenaten succeeded in reconciling his own beliefs with those of the past. Although the tomb was apparently never finished, its architectural components are similar to those of his royal predecessors' tombs, despite its location in the eastern, rather than western, cliffs. His burial equipment included the traditional sarcophagus; canopic chest (for the preservation of internal organs); *shabti*s, or servant figures (fig. 19); storage vessels; and miscellaneous supplies.

Where Akhenaten's tomb differed so dramatically (and predictably) was in its decoration. Tiny bits of relief preserved in Akhenaten's burial chamber feature themes from the standard Amarna repertoire—namely, the king and queen making offerings to Aten. On each side of the royal sarcophagus, a central image of Aten with its rays presenting *ankh* signs replaces the traditional funerary deities. Figures of Nefertiti stand at the corners as if to protect the king's body within, just as the goddesses Isis, Nephthys, Selket, and Neith had stood at the corners of Amenhotep II's canopic chest. Akhenaten's *shabti*s lack the standard formula dedicated to Osiris, god of resurrection, although Osiris is invoked on some magical bricks of Akhenaten's found elsewhere. Most likely the king was mummified. Over the years, some have suggested that fragmentary human remains found in the vicinity of the Royal Tomb are those of Akhenaten. Others believe the body of a young man found in a problematic Theban tomb known as KV 55 is Akhenaten's. Nevertheless, at the time of this writing, his body has yet to be conclusively identified.

Who else, besides Akhenaten and his second daughter, Meketaten, might have been buried in the Royal Tomb at Amarna? A fragment of a *shabti* of Nefertiti's was found there, but nothing else of hers. The evidence that Akhenaten's mother, Tiye, was interred there at one time is a little stronger, thanks to the identification of fragments

Fig. 19 Upper part of a *shabti* of Akhenaten wearing a bag wig (cat. 220)

Excavations in the vicinity of the Royal Tomb at Amarna have turned up hundreds of fragments of *shabti*s of the king, in a variety of materials.

Fig. 18 Princess with a side lock (cat. 46)

The princess, probably a teenager when this sculpture was carved, displays the elegant sensuality characteristic of the later years of Akhenaten's rule.

of her sarcophagus in the tomb. However, the situation of her burial is far from clear-cut. Akhenaten's father, Amenhotep III, had already prepared a chamber for her in his tomb in the Valley of the Kings at Thebes, where a few of her *shabti*s have been found. Her gilded-wood shrine, on the other hand, was found in the enigmatic KV 55 mentioned above. In a bizarre twist, what may be her body—identified on the basis of cranofacial morphology, ion etching, and scanning electron microprobe analysis—turned up, together with sixteen other royal burials, in the tomb of Amenhotep II in the Valley of the Kings, where priests of the 22nd Dynasty had reburied them in an effort to protect them. Recently, however, the identification of the body has been questioned.

Akhenaten's highest officials, like their king, had tombs constructed in the eastern cliffs at Amarna (fig. 10), although most were never finished. Just over two dozen have been identified, in two groups, one north and one south of the royal wadi. In these private tombs as well, traditional funerary motifs were replaced by images of the king and royal family at worship. The substitution of scenes from the daily life of the royal family for scenes from the daily life of the tomb owner further highlights the centrality of Akhenaten in the lives of Amarna's citizens. Moreover, it vividly demonstrates that even for these not-so-average citizens, Akhenaten and the royal family were the vehicle for access to and worship of Aten.

Apprehension mingled with a wary curiosity must have dominated the mood at Amarna upon Akhenaten's death, more so than upon the death of any previous monarch. What would happen, now that the chief advocate of Aten was gone? All indications are that Akhenaten's chief wife, Nefertiti, had no sons, since they are neither shown nor mentioned. Who would the next pharaoh be? Would the old order be restored? If so, what would be the status of Akhenaten's followers, and what would be their fate?

What happened immediately before and after Akhenaten's death remains a subject of great speculation, and theories abound. Some suggest that, in an attempt to resolve the question of his succession, Akhenaten appointed a coregent, and that the two ruled jointly for several years. But was Akhenaten's coregent male or female? Here, too, the evidence is ambiguous. It is not out of the question that Nefertiti ruled as pharaoh with Akhenaten until his death. Others propose that the coregent was an ephemeral king named Smenkhkara, possibly a son of Akhenaten and the greatly beloved Kiya, whose claim to the throne would have been strengthened by his marriage to Akhenaten's (and Nefertiti's) eldest daughter. Still others propose that both figures were involved—namely, that Nefertiti ruled as coregent with Akhenaten and that Smenkhkara then took over as sole ruler after Akhenaten's death. Yet another theory (see the essay "The Royal Family") is that Nefertiti and Smenkhkara were one and the same! In any case, Smenkhkara's reign was brief, and, assuming a coregency with Akhenaten, no more than a year after Akhenaten's demise, Smenkhkara, too, was gone.

Restoration under Tutankhamen

A boy named Tutankhaten became Egypt's next pharaoh. Although he was less than ten years of age when he assumed the throne, he was already married to Akhenaten's third daughter, Ankhesenpaaten. Because of his youth, it seems clear that others decided the momentous events that followed.

Amarna and Aten had run out of mature advocates. Aten's remaining priesthood would have been no match for what remained of Amen's empire. The army, one of the main vehicles Akhenaten had employed for controlling the country, probably had no particular interest in Aten, but gave service to the ruler who paid its wages. Countless bureaucrats who had worked in previous reigns for temple properties throughout the land or benefited from temple largesse would hardly have lent their support to the god who was responsible for the loss of their livelihood. The populace outside of Amarna must have mourned the end of the feasting and bounty that had been part of the grand celebrations honoring Egypt's traditional gods and under Akhenaten were limited to Amarna. Politically, therefore, there was no advantage in lending support to Aten, and the choice must have been straightforward for the powers behind the throne.

As a result of suggestion or coercion, the young Tutankhaten changed his name to Tutankhamen early in his reign and authorized the abandonment of the city of his birth. By decree, he reinstated Amen (fig. 20), returned power to the god's extensive priesthood, and began the long process of restoring Amen's temples, desecrated and neglected during Akhenaten's rule. The words of the young king are preserved on a large granite stela (fig. 140) now in the Egyptian Museum in Cairo:

> *(Tutankhamen) ... the good ruler who performs benefactions for his father and all the gods, having repaired what was ruined as a monument lasting to the length of continuity, and having repelled disorder throughout the Two Lands, so that Maat rests [in her place] as he causes falsehood to be abomination and the land to be like its primeval state.*[3]

Memphis and Thebes were to regain their status as Egypt's political and religious capitals, respectively. Statues of Tutankhamen as Egypt's savior were erected throughout the land, and particularly in Thebes (figs. 11, 12). Because they still showed the influence of the artistic style of Amarna's artisans, his face and physique were unmistakable. Other statues bore Tutankhamen's physiognomy but sported Amen's crown.

What emotions greeted Tutankhamen's edict? Were Amarna's citizens confused by the sudden change of religious allegiance, or relieved? What went through their minds as they packed everything of value in what had been their homes and businesses for more than a dozen years? Did most leave at once, in a grand and joyous procession, or did they exit gradually, in stunned silence? Archaeological evidence shows that at least some people remained at Amarna well into the reign of Tutankhamen. How were the

Fig. 20 Amen with gold inlays
(cat. 242)

The corselet and crown identify this bronze as a figure of the god Amen. Yet he still exhibits the high waist and pendant belly characteristic of Akhenaten.

people from Amarna received wherever they went? Were they considered apostates? Or enterprising opportunists? Surprisingly, in all but a few instances, the records are silent.

Ay, the Commander of Chariotry, was one of the few officials known to have served both Akhenaten and Tutankhamen. His elegant but unused tomb at Amarna is proof that he expected to end his days there. He reappears, however, in a dramatically new role. After less than a decade of rule, Tutankhamen died without living heirs. In an unprecedented move, his widow Ankhesenamen (née Ankesenpaaten) solicited a prince from the ruler of the Hittites to be her new husband and to rule Egypt, but he never arrived. (According to another view, it was Nefertiti who wrote the letter on her own behalf.) In Tutankhamen's tomb, Ay is shown performing funerary rites that, in private tombs, a son is usually shown performing for his father; Ay had taken over as king.

After a brief reign, Ay was buried in regal splendor in the Valley of the Kings. He was followed on the throne by yet another military personality, General Horemheb. Whether Horemheb had served Akhenaten is unclear, but his splendid tomb at Saqqara, the age-old necropolis of Memphis, shows him lavishly rewarded under Tutankhamen (fig. 136). With all the heirs of Akhenaten—male and female—gone, he asserted his power and demonstrated his devotion to Amen by inaugurating a wholesale desecration of what was left at Amarna.

Judging by the fragmentary condition of the remains, Horemheb's legions must have unleashed a fury matched only by Akhenaten's against Amen. Statues were toppled, names and faces of Akhenaten and his family were hacked out of reliefs; Aten's cartouches were defaced and its rays slashed. Of the hundreds of sculptures of the royal family and the myriad architectural elements of Amarna's temples and palaces, hardly any sizable fragment survives. Horemheb and then Ramesses the Great of the next dynasty continued the destruction when they used Amarna's reliefs as core blocks for their buildings across the river at Hermopolis. Sand covered what was left. Over time, the city of Amarna was forgotten.

In retrospect, had Akhenaten and his achievements been a revolution, or simply evolution? Akhenaten's god, the sun, had been revered since the beginning of Egypt itself, but never previously as the sole object of worship. Artistic canons in fact changed constantly in Egypt, even with regard to depiction of the king. But never before had they changed so rapidly and so drastically. Many elements in the city of Amarna, including its layout, replicated those of other cities, especially Thebes. But never before had a king so specifically designed and tailored so many institutions to accommodate the worship of a deity. The answer, it seems, is that the Amarna Period represents both revolution and evolution.

The legacy of Amarna lived on long after its inhabitants and advocates had disappeared, and long after the physical remains of the city were gone. In many respects

Amarna is still with us today: in the concept of a single god, man's intimacy with his deity, naturalistic expression in art, and the ability of a single individual to dramatically influence the lives of so many.

Fig. 21 Amenmose and Depet, parents of General Amenemonet (cat. 258)

Resplendant in their elaborate wigs and fine pleated garments, the parents of the general were featured in his tomb. This relief is characteristic of post-Amarna works from Saqqara, which recall works made during the reign of Amenhotep III.

---

1. Murnane 1995b, p. 84 (§4).
2. Foster 1992, pp. 5–10.
3. Murnane 1995b, pp. 212–13 (§99).

Fig. 22 Osiris with the features of
Amenhotep III (cat. 4)

The Setting: History, Religion, and Art

W. Raymond Johnson

The art of the Amarna Period, even
with its extremes and innovation,
was rooted in traditional canons of
proportion and composition.

Egyptian art is noteworthy for an extraordinary homogeneity of style over its 3,500-year history. Whether it is from the Old, Middle, or New Kingdoms, from its Predynastic beginnings to its late-Roman eclipse, the work is always instantly recognizable by its distinctive style.

What perhaps gave it such consistency for so long was the ancient Egyptians' unique sense of time. Unlike Westerners, who perceive time as essentially a straight line, with the future stretching ahead into infinity and the past receding behind, the Egyptians believed in two fundamental dimensions of time. One was eternal, or *djet*, time, which was the realm of the gods and the state of being people entered at death. The other was the cyclical time dictated by nature.

In *djet* time, all things were happening simultaneously and creation was constantly occurring. When people entered an Egyptian temple, they passed into this dimension of eternity as they walked between the twin entrance pylons, or towers, that represented the mountains of the horizon. The papyrus-columned halls, screened from profane view, represented the great papyrus swamp that existed before creation and the birth of light. In the back sanctuary, where the creator god dwelled, creation began anew every morning at dawn. To pass into this realm of the gods and the dead one had to be ritually purified, a rite that imitated death and mummification, requiring the individual to shave all body hair, gargle with natron,[1] and be sprinkled with the sacred water of Nun, from which the world was created.

Although the Egyptians did have a sense of the past, and referred to "the time of the ancestors," they saw normal time as a circle that described an endlessly repeating present. This dimension of time was the product of Egypt's natural environment, with its clockwork seasons and the annual flooding of the Nile. Survival depended on keen observation of the natural indicators that signaled these changes: the rising and falling of certain stars and constellations, and the shifting position of the sun. In some ways, even the gods were subject to cyclical time. Each year during the festival of Opet in Thebes, the creator-god Amen-Ra was required to leave his great temple-palace at Karnak and travel back to the temple at Luxor, the site of his birth and the creation of the world. There, assisted by the king, who was the creator god's firstborn, he would return to his uncreated state and be born again, the king and all of creation with him.

Ancient Egyptian art functioned as a mechanism for bridging normal time and eter-

nity. Carved and painted ritual scenes on the walls of temples and tombs served to thrust those rituals from normal time into eternal time, thus ensuring their efficacy forever. Statuary functioned in the same way, as eternal "bodies" for the spirits of gods, kings, and ordinary individuals. Temple and tomb scenes emphasized timeless, programmatic acts of offering to the gods and receiving from them, rites the Egyptians believed were crucial for the perpetuation of all life. The basic elements of these scenes varied little over time because deviation could have disastrous consequences for the world.

The adherence to a perpetual present might appear to have allowed for little change in the habits and traditions of the Egyptian population. Indeed, it is commonly assumed that ancient Egyptian society was morbidly static and rigorously conservative on all levels, from religion to politics to art. It is the paradox of Egyptian culture, however, that within seemingly rigid parameters there was constant flux, with art often modified to reflect changes in other areas. But the parameters did preclude extreme shifts: even Akhenaten's artistic styles, among the most radical deviations from the norm in Egyptian history, were solidly grounded in traditional canons of proportion and composition.

The Old Kingdom

The style that became the model for ancient Egyptian art was developed at Memphis, the political and administrative capital from about 3100 B.C., when Upper and Lower Egypt were united by kings from the south. By Dynasty 3, about five hundred years later, the Memphite tradition was fully developed and was the official artistic canon for both royalty and the nobility ("private" art)[2] through most of the Old Kingdom. This style idealized the human body and physiognomy, but often rendered enough characteristics of face, and sometimes body, to allow for the identification of specific individuals. Thus portraiture existed from the very beginning of Egyptian art, but was idealized in varying degrees from one period to another. In some private tombs astonishingly naturalistic stone and wood statuary depicting the deceased as middle-aged and fat might be found alongside idealized, youthful statues of the same individual. The two contrasting styles tell us that the Egyptians attributed significance to both natural and ideal states of being.

Recent research has documented a major shift in artistic style at the end of the Old Kingdom, in Dynasty 6 sculpture (almost a thousand years before Akhenaten's time) with antecedents in late Dynasty 5.[3] The human figure in royal and some private art becomes noticeably attenuated, with overlarge heads and exaggerated features, particularly the eyes. Although scholars traditionally view the change as a decline in style symptomatic of the deteriorating central authority at this time, Edna Russmann points out that it should be seen instead as "the earliest documented occurrence of deliberate stylistic change in ancient art."[4] The new style spread throughout Egypt during Dynasty 6. The fact that it is found outside the Memphite area, in Coptos, Dendera,

Edfu, and elsewhere, suggests that the state indeed had mechanisms for ensuring the homogeneity of the official court style throughout the land, even during a period of political fragmentation.

One wonders what prompted the change in style. Russmann suggests that it reflected a shift in the religious attitudes of the time: with its emphasis on the head and eyes at the expense of the body, the new style was perhaps an attempt to externalize the inner spiritual life of the subject.[5]

The Middle Kingdom

The second Old Kingdom style persisted throughout the period of political breakdown and the Dynasty 11 rule of Nebhepetra Mentuhotep in Thebes—until he reunited Egypt in about 1980 B.C., and the Middle Kingdom began.[6] At that point the official art style reverted to the older Memphite tradition, which became the official model for Dynasty 12 and the rest of the Middle Kingdom. The revival of this "classic" court style of Dynasties 4 and 5—the term most commonly used is "archaizing"—was an attempt to restore the order and stability associated with that style.

This is not to say that the Middle Kingdom did not see artistic change. There is nothing quite as dramatic in Egyptian art as the increasingly naturalistic royal portraiture from the latter part of Dynasty 12, particularly during the reigns of Sesostris III and Amenemhat III, which together spanned about 1836 to 1772 B.C.[7]; every indication is that the style was manipulated for political reasons. It is no accident that the lined, almost haggard faces of Sesostris III appear at the same time he was suppressing the powerful local governors and revamping Egypt's administrative system—undoubtedly not the most popular moves in some quarters. Texts from the period stress the king's role as good shepherd to his flock, Egypt, with the cares of the world on his shoulders. Literary and sculptural propaganda of this sort suggests that a media blitz was under way throughout the land to generate sympathy and support for the king who had been "forced" to act for the good of the nation. It worked: Sesostris III ruled for eighteen years, and his administrative reforms outlived him by centuries.

The New Kingdom: Dynasty 18

The Second Intermediate Period, a span of about one hundred years between the Middle and New Kingdoms, was dominated by Hyksos rulers, "shepherd kings" who invaded Egypt from the north. Egypt overthrew its foreign overlords and was once again united by a Theban family between 1539 and 1523 B.C. The kings of Dynasty 18 revived the Memphite tradition of Dynasty 12 as the official court style, tangible evidence that the old order had been restored. In the temple of Amen-Ra at Karnak, Amenhotep I (about 1514–1493 B.C.) even went as far as to erect a limestone shrine that was directly inspired by the White Chapel built by Sesostris I almost four hundred years earlier. But recent analysis has detected significant, politically motivated changes

Fig. 23 Head of Amenhotep III wearing a solar diadem (cat. 8)

The head was probably part of a kneeling figure of the king made during the late years of his reign.

in the art styles of Hatshepsut and Thutmose III that reflect shifts in the distribution of power during their overlapping reigns (about 1478–1458 and 1479–1425 B.C., respectively).[8] Under Thutmose III alone there were four distinguishable artistic styles: the first, at his accession, continued the tradition of his predecessors Thutmose I and II; the second, appearing when the young king's regent, Hatshepsut, became his coregent, made her facial characteristics dominant and patterned his after hers; the third, after Hatshepsut's death, marked the beginning of his sole rule, but was still influenced by her style; and the fourth harked back to the first, in deliberate rejection of the style associated with Hatshepsut.[9] This final change was part of the program of Hatshepsut's proscription, which appears to have been prompted by the accession of Thutmose III's son Amenhotep II, and Thutmose III's desire to discredit any rival claimants.

Hatshepsut's art had its own consecutive phases: When she was queen, her style was associated with that of her husband, Thutmose II; when she became coregent with Thutmose III, her style closely matched his. Finally, she adopted a style of her own that reflected her physical traits.

Within its seemingly rigid parameters, then, Egyptian art could be quite malleable when religion or politics was involved. With both factors at play, the results could be remarkable indeed. By the time of Thutmose IV (about 1400–1390 B.C.), the Egyptians were casting their eyes back to the Old Kingdom solar cults. A growing preoccupation with the sun god and the king's role as his representative on earth can be perceived in the art and literature of the time. Before the end of Thutmose IV's nine-year reign, the official style—in private as well as royal art—featured a face dominated by large, oblique, almond-shaped eyes.[10] The trend was cut short by the king's premature death, though it continued somewhat into the reign of his son, Amenhotep III, whose own style changed several times during almost thirty-nine years of rule.

The Deification of Amenhotep III

By the time Nebmaatra Amenhotep III came to the throne (about 1390 B.C.), the Aten, or sun's disk—with which the king unites at death, according to texts going back at least to Dynasty 12—had become a god in its own right, strongly associated with the king. One of Amenhotep III's epithets is "Dazzling Sun-Disk (Aten)," which equates the king with that god. For the first three decades of his reign, Amenhotep III's Thutmoside art style, grounded in the classical Memphite tradition, was largely characterized by an austerity of detail and formal simplicity of costume that makes the period one of the high points in Egyptian art, unequaled for refinement and taste. Amenhotep's Luxor temple was executed largely in this style, as were the great private tombs of his high officials in Thebes.

Artistic style and iconography changed radically after the first of three jubilees (sedfestivals) Amenhotep III celebrated in his last decade, in years 30, 34, and 37. These festivals of kingly rejuvenation, generally celebrated after a king's first thirty years of rule and every three years thereafter to ensure his continued well-being, go back to the dawn of Egyptian history. Amenhotep III apparently took great pride in claiming that he had consulted "writings of old" for guidance in planning his own.[11]

The relief work in the new style, while still superbly carved, was either very highly raised or very deeply cut. Figures of the king in relief and sculpture were dominated by large, youthful faces with overlarge, oblique eyes (fig. 23), and the royal costumes were almost jarringly baroque, festooned with solar and funerary iconography. Elements of dress included *wah* collars, shaped like flower petals and associated with Osiris, who ruled the realm of the dead; gold-disk-bead *shebyu* necklaces and accompanying armbands (fig. 24), usually presented to high officials who had performed exceptional service for the king; sporrans, or elaborate aprons decorated with falcon-tail designs and associated with the sun god; crimped, free-hanging, and looped sashes; sun-diskcrowned cobras suspended from elaborate crowns and sporrans; long, pleated kilts and sheer cloaks; heraldic sedge-plant and papyrus-umbel cords hanging from wide, sometimes pleated, belts[12]; and panther heads at the tops of the sporrans. Even the posture of the king had changed; the formerly ramrod-straight Thutmoside-style royal figures were now bent forward at the waist, sometimes slightly, often radically, and the figures were often noticeably stockier. The contrast between the old and new styles was dramatic. Were the changes prompted by politics, or religion, or both?

It has recently been demonstrated that the elaborate, pleated costume of the king, with long kilt and sheer cloak, replaces the traditional jubilee cloak in sculpture after Amenhotep III's first jubilee and becomes standard thereafter.[13] Multiple sashes on the king's sporran usually accompanied the bowing posture in earlier examples, but only in scenes where the king was embracing/assimilating with the creator god, or was about to do so.[14] Other finds reinforce evidence of a change in the king's status. Texts from Amenhotep's last decade, found at the jubilee palace at Malqata, on the west bank of the Nile at Thebes, refer to it as the "Palace of Nebmaatra-is-the-Dazzling-Sun-Disk (Aten)," and a rebus (hieroglyphic pun) of the king's prenomen, Nebmaatra, found on documents and seal impressions all over Egypt, identifies the king with the sun-god Ra. An autobiographical inscription from Amenhotep III's High Steward of Memphis, "Amenhotep called Huy," describes his building for his lord a "temple of millions of years" called "Nebmaatra-is-United-with-Ptah," where the king was identified and

Fig. 24 Amenhotep III offering
(cat. 10)

The king's armbands and *shebyu* necklaces, and the uraei on his lap, are all solar symbols.

worshipped as the Memphite creator god. At the same time an extraordinary number of statues of Amenhotep III in kingly and divine form were set up throughout the country (figs. 22, 25), including many examples—some quite colossal—in quartzite, a stone associated with the sun god.

Both the texts and the iconography of the costumes on figures of the king proclaim an extraordinary event: Amenhotep III's deification while alive, through assimilation with Ra, Ptah, Aten, and all the other gods of Egypt. Among the costume elements emphasizing the king's dramatic elevation in status, the most significant is probably the *shebyu* necklace. Only in private-tomb scenes, beginning at the time of Amenhotep II, had the king ever been shown wearing that necklace and its associated arm bands, symbolic of a rise in status, and in those scenes he was depicted after death, in the eternal realm of the afterlife and the gods, merged with the sun-god Ra. The depiction of this necklace on figures of the living Amenhotep III in his non-funerary monuments was a way to show that the king had been uplifted in life, had entered this divine realm as a result of his jubilee rites, nine years before his death.[15] There is evidence that his mortuary temple, which would normally have been activated only to serve the cult of the dead king, was inaugurated after his jubilee; statues of the living, deified Amenhotep III were dedicated in it and dispersed throughout the land to commemorate his apotheosis.[16]

One must ask, why? Was Amenhotep III's deification a shrewd political and religious strategy designed to temper the power of the Amen cult and its priesthood, which, since Amen was introduced by the Dynasty 11 family that joined Upper and Lower Egypt, had become pre-eminent?[17] Was the king's personification of all of Egypt's gods designed to act as a great leveling device, equalizing their status and raising his own? Whether or not it was intentional, this is exactly what happened: by the Ramesside period, beginning about 1292 B.C., Amen was no longer dominant in Egypt, but shared his throne with Ptah, Ra-Horakhty, and all the other gods. And the cult of the king was now equal to the cult of the gods.[18]

The identification of Amenhotep III as the sun's disk, the Aten, and the preoccupation of his son, Amenhotep IV, later called Akhenaten, with that same deity, cannot have been a coincidence. Akhenaten's religious revolution had to have been greatly influenced by his father's deification, and may even have been a vital part of that deification program. The two kings' styles of sculpture and decoration followed parallel lines: Amenhotep III's shifted from the traditional to a new style that exaggerated his rejuvenation and assimilation with the creator/sun god. Akhenaten's style shifted from the traditional, in which he was represented with the features of his father (just as Thutmose III had been shown with the features of the senior coregent, Hatshepsut) to a style that exaggerated his individuality and his special role as the firstborn of the creator god, male and female in one. The two kings' different theological natures were expressed through intentional modifications in art—the kind of change that first occurred in the late Old Kingdom—and there is good reason to believe that the two styles were concurrent.

Fig. 26 Detail of Amenhotep III on a sledge (Luxor Museum, Luxor)

This statue of the deified king represents his rejuvenated body and perhaps depicts him in the guise of the ever-youthful creator-god Atum, whose hieroglyphic name is spelled with the sledge sign.

Fig. 25 Ptah-Sokar-Osiris with the features of Amenhotep III (cat. 6)

This is one of a number of sculptures of deities set up in temples throughout Egypt at the time of Amenhotep III's deification and first jubilee.

The Coregency Problem

Concurrent artistic programs suggest concurrent reigns. Scholars have pondered the coregency question since Akhenaten was first "rediscovered": did he begin his rule alone, or did he rule jointly with his father, Amenhotep III? The evidence can often be interpreted either way, and Egyptologists are still split down the middle over the question. If the reigns were consecutive, Akhenaten came to the throne after his father's death, ruled alone, and was solely responsible for the Amarna episode. In the coregency model, the senior king was present during the formation and evolution of his son's new solar cult.

The deification of Amenhotep III and his subsequent identification with the sun's disk, Aten, may well have been the event that launched the entire Amarna episode. A coregency of the two kings, inaugurated shortly before Amenhotep III's first jubilee, could have been part of the mechanism by which the father achieved his deified state. The rationale can be found in the creation myth that originated at Heliopolis. The Egyptians believed that creation occurred when the creator-god Atum "gave birth to," or separated from, his firstborn, Shu. At that moment Atum himself became conscious, heaven separated from earth, and Shu, who represented life-giving air and light, separated from his twin-sister Tefnut, who represented moisture. Akhenaten's art style and iconography emphasize his role as Shu (fig. 30) while underscoring his principal wife Nefertiti's role as Tefnut. In order to rule as deified king/Atum, Amenhotep III may have required a junior coregent/firstborn son/Shu nearby, since Atum cannot exist without Shu. Akhenaten's famous cult of his "father," the living Aten, over which he presided as high priest, may well have had as its focus Akhenaten's real, deified, living father, Amenhotep III. He was worshipped at Amarna as the sun's disk, but this was only one of his many deified forms throughout the land.

The youthful "deification style" of Amenhotep III's last decade existed side by side with statuary and relief work carved in a totally different style, that of Old Kingdom private sculpture. Two torsos made of an igneous rock called granodiorite, which were excavated in his mortuary temple, and a reused granodiorite head (fig. 27) that probably came from one of these bodies and was excavated at Medinet Habu nearby, display a severe naturalism that must have been influenced by the great Dynasty 12 sculptures of Sesostris III (that haggard shepherd of his Egyptian flock) and Amenemhat III. But Amenhotep III went one step further than his royal predecessors, having his body as well as his head portrayed naturalistically: unidealized and fat (fig. 28). One might wonder if the portly bodies—which, according to the inscriptions, probably date back to the first jubilee—are symbolic, with the swelling midsections representing fecundity in this king who was all gods and goddesses in one. But a series of red-granite and plaster portrait heads in the same style depict him growing fatter and older, as if great care was being taken to commemorate the king's aging body at the same time he was being depicted in the deification style as eternally youthful.

Most of these heads, though purchased in Thebes, probably came from Amarna, where one can watch Akhenaten's family literally grow up, grow old, and even die in its art. The tradition of representing the royal family exclusively in timeless, eternal fashion was rejected at Amarna (fig. 29). Again one must ask, why?

Reaction or Revolution?

This preoccupation with the present rather than the eternal is one of the hallmarks of Amarna art.[19] It is almost as if the two dimensions of Egyptian time—the eternity of the gods and the endlessly repeating present of nature and humanity—had converged. Heaven and earth had also converged, for had not the royal family taken on the identities of the gods themselves, and taken their places on the temple walls? Amenhotep III was Atum, Queen Tiye was the love-goddess Hathor, Akhenaten was Shu, Nefertiti was Tefnut: the deities of creation had come back to earth, and the whole world was in jubilee. Dated events in the life of the king and his family now replaced the timeless scenes in temple and tomb; living, in its myriad aspects, was celebrated. But similar scenes graced the walls of the great solar-temple complexes of the Dynasty 5 kings, which were dedicated to Ra. Was Akhenaten being original here, or was he trying to revive the past? Was his "revolution" radical, or one of the most reactionary episodes in Egyptian history?

Toward the end of his reign, Akhenaten proscribed the Amen cult throughout the land. All images of Amen and his pantheon were destroyed during a period of short-term but furious iconoclasm. What prompted this act? If it was a reactionary effort to purge and purify the sun cult, why was Amen expunged so viciously? The god's figures and name were literally hacked out of the painted walls, leaving deep, ugly holes. The brutality of Akhenaten's program is quite in contrast with the thoughtful orders of Thutmose III, who had figures of Hatshepsut carefully excised and/or modified.

The emotional element in Akhenaten's suppression of Amen is perplexing, and difficult to explain away simply as religious zeal; after all, Akhenaten himself did not wield

Fig. 29 Stela featuring Amenhotep III and Queen Tiye (cat. 169)

On this private stela found at Amarna, the royal couple embrace as they sit before a pile of offerings presented to the king and the rayed disk above him.

Fig. 27 Head of Amenhotep III wearing the crown of Upper Egypt (cat. 11)

Fig. 28 Torso of a corpulent Amenhotep III (cat. 12)

the chisels, the Egyptian populace did. Might the unexpected death of his coregent father have triggered such a reaction? If the older king's plan was indeed to equalize all of Egypt's cults in an effort to temper Amen's power, Amenhotep III's sudden death just might have caused Akhenaten, and the devastated population, to lash out at the god in their grief. From the look of the enormous building projects that Amenhotep III had barely begun at the time of his death and that were left unfinished forever, one suspects that his death caught everyone, even him, by surprise.

An extraordinary new clue, enigmatic but perhaps significant, has recently emerged. In one monument and one monument alone, Akhenaten's iconoclasts modified Amen's figures rather than destroying them. Limestone blocks from the northern entrance to Amenhotep III's gigantic mortuary complex, dismantled and reused by Merneptah (about 1213–1204 B.C.) in his own mortuary temple nearby, have recently been documented and analyzed, with some surprising results.[20] In the scenes of this gateway and other monuments within Amenhotep III's mortuary precinct, figures of the god Amen were recarved by Akhenaten's men into figures of the deified Amenhotep III, the creator-god Ptah, and the god of the dead Ptah-Sokar-Osiris. Later the figures were restored as Amen by Tutankhamen, who left inscriptions proclaiming the restoration of that god in at least two scenes. Major traces of all phases of decoration remain, and the sequence is clear.

Among the implications of this discovery: Akhenaten's religion was not monotheism, but something far more complex, embracing not only Aten, but also the deified Amenhotep III, and the gods Ptah and Ptah-Sokar-Osiris. A review of monuments to gods other than Amen elsewhere in Egypt, particularly in Memphis and Abydos, reveals no proscription by Akhenaten; his destruction was highly selective, focusing on Amen and his associates only.

The fact that of all the temple complexes in Egypt, the mortuary complex of Amenhotep III alone was singled out for this special treatment underscores the close, albeit enigmatic, theological relationship between the two kings. At the very least, Akhenaten and the Amarna episode were greatly influenced by the theological event of Amenhotep III's deification and assimilation with Aten. At the most Akhenaten was active in implementing that program. As more material surfaces, perhaps questions about their unusual relationship will be answered conclusively. Until then, we will continue to spill much ink, and sometimes blood, in our efforts to understand this perplexing period, so original and yet so grounded in Egypt's past.

---

1. An absorbent mineral found in Wadi Natrun and used in the preservation of mummies.

2. Private art was influenced by the art of the court, but not necessarily identical to it, partly because the finest craftsmen were utilized by the palace first and nobility second. An exception was made in cases of royal favor, when the king allowed a court craftsman to execute tomb reliefs or sculpture for a dignitary as a reward for service to the crown. In the case of provincial private art, there might also have been a stylistic "lag" because of distance from the court.

3. Russmann 1995.

4. Ibid., p. 271.

5. Ibid., p. 278.

6. Ibid.

7. Polz 1995.

8. Lipinska 1966.

9. Laboury 1998.

10. Bryan 1991, p. 175.

11. Epigraphic Survey 1980, p. 43, pl. 24.

12. The sedge-plant flower is the symbol of Upper Egypt (the south) and the papyrus umbel, or flower, is the symbol of Lower Egypt (the northern, Delta region). By wearing cords around his waist that were decorated with these devices, Amenhotep III showed himself to be the living embodiment of the union of the Two Lands. The *shebyu* collar and sun-disk–crowned cobras appear once each in at least two separate, nonfunerary monuments of Thutmose IV, who was the first to experiment with this iconography.

13. Sourouzian 1994.

14. Such scenes are found in Thutmose III's bark sanctuary (where a model of the boat that transported the god from one temple to another was housed) in the small temple of Amen at Medinet Habu, west exterior wall; and the back sanctuary area, room III, west wall; also Luxor temple, antechamber to the bark sanctuary, south wall, west side, first register; and the inner east jamb of the portal leading to the bark sanctuary.

15. W. R. Johnson 1996, pp. 67–72.

16. Betsy M. Bryan in Kozloff and Bryan 1992, pp. 200–202.

17. Amen-Ra was king of the gods from the Middle Kingdom on. Amen was a southern interloper, an invisible sky deity ("Amen" = hidden) who fused with the traditional king of the gods, the sun-god Ra, when Nebhepetra Mentuhotep, who revered him, united Egypt. Since the king of the gods traditionally had to be the sun god, the Egyptians simply fused the two deities into one.

18. Habachi 1969.

19. J. Allen 1996.

20. Bickel and Jaritz 1994.

Fig. 31 Colossal statue of
Amenhotep IV with *nemes*
and double crown (cat. 23)

The Beginning of the Heresy

Donald B. Redford

Amenhotep IV's new religious
beliefs were first manifested in the
Theban monuments he built early
in his reign.

Amenhotep IV's short residence at Thebes at the outset of his reign proved revolutionary for the belief systems of Egypt and the artistic canon used for religious expression. His five to six years there were a time of experimentation in which he rationalized and perfected his devotion to the Aten, or sun-disk of Ra-Horakhty. His father, Amenhotep III, had claimed to be that very "Dazzling Sun-Disk": now the son exulted in this occasion for filial celebration. The single most far-reaching ramification of this obsession was the king's conviction that all other gods "had ceased," and that the sun-disk, his father, was now the sole god.[1]

When Amenhotep IV ascended the throne there were two temple complexes in Thebes dedicated to the prevailing god Amen-Ra: Karnak and, about a mile and a half to the south, Luxor. Amenhotep IV added his own monuments to the great temple at Karnak, but these were subsequently either effaced or recycled, and their recovery in modern times has invariably involved dismantling or excavating later structures. As early as the 1840s, fragments of inscribed masonry began to appear in the vicinity of the Ninth Pylon (tower) of the Karnak temple (fig. 32). Many of the fragments bore a sun-disk and references to Amenhotep IV, and were characterized by an eccentric style of art, exaggerated in its naturalism and wholly different from the conventional hieratic reliefs, with their numerous anthropomorphic gods and sacred plants and animals. When the French-run antiquities service undertook a major project to clear and restore the ruins at Karnak, between the late 1890s and World War II, tens of thousands of similar blocks were found. Very soon a pattern emerged: these blocks—named *talatat* by excavation workers, from the Italian *tagliata*, "cut masonry"—had been recycled as filling for the Second, Ninth, and Tenth pylons; as foundation material for the temple's hypostyle (pillared) hall; and as part of the structure of the Luxor temple. Scattered *talatat* elsewhere at Karnak and at the neighboring site of Medamud all proved upon inspection to have emanated from Amenhotep IV's Karnak buildings as well.

For the first two decades of the restoration project, none of the material from the period of Amenhotep IV was found in its original position. It was not until 1925 that *in situ* remains were located and identified, and the discovery was a dramatic one. Excavating a drainage canal for the local municipality, workers stumbled upon a line of fallen colossi of Amenhotep IV (figs. 31, 34). A formal clearance of the site, direct-

Fig. 32 The Ninth Pylon

Many inscribed and decorated blocks
from Amenhotep IV's buildings at
Karnak were recycled as fill material
for building projects of later pharaohs.

ed by Henri Chevrier, then inspector of antiquities at Karnak, uncovered additional fragmentary statues, but failed to identify any associated structure.

The study of Amenhotep IV's construction program at Thebes received impetus from the founding in 1965–66 of the Centre Franco-Égyptien and the Akhenaten Temple Project, both of which focused their work on Karnak (fig. 33). The Centre assumed responsibility for retrieving *talatat* from the still-uninvestigated core of the Ninth Pylon, and in the event tens of thousands of additional blocks were brought to light. The Akhenaten Temple Project, working from photographs, was able to assemble nearly nine hundred scenes from fragments of the temple walls. In 1975 the Project initiated excavations in East Karnak, where the fallen colossi had been found. Over a period of sixteen seasons a major portion of the Gempaaten, the largest of the sun temples, was unearthed. It is chiefly because of these projects that the following sketch of Amenhotep IV's residency at Thebes can be drawn and confirmed.

In the first year of his reign, the evidence suggests, the king completed monuments left unfinished at the death of his father. Several scattered blocks at Karnak, clearly from the reign of Amenhotep III, contain texts or reliefs that could only have been added by his son. The best example is a cluster of large blocks from a gate that were recycled as core material for the Tenth Pylon, on the south side of Karnak, under Horemheb, the fourth pharaoh in succession after Amenhotep IV. Here we see Amenhotep IV, in a traditional mode of representation, offering to the falcon-headed sun god identified by the unwieldy epithet "Live Ra-Horakhty, He Who Rejoices in the Horizon in His Name: 'Light-That-is-in-the-Disk.'"[2]

Very soon, however—probably in the second year of his reign—the king devised a program of his own that would transform the environs of the temple of Amen and ultimately denigrate its divine proprietor. This program and the construction work involved were motivated primarily by the resolve to orchestrate a grandiose jubilee, apparently in emulation of his father, who had celebrated no fewer than three jubilees late in his reign. In anticipation of this festival, which occurred late in year 3, a nationwide corvée, or forced-labor campaign, was

Fig. 33 Plan of Karnak

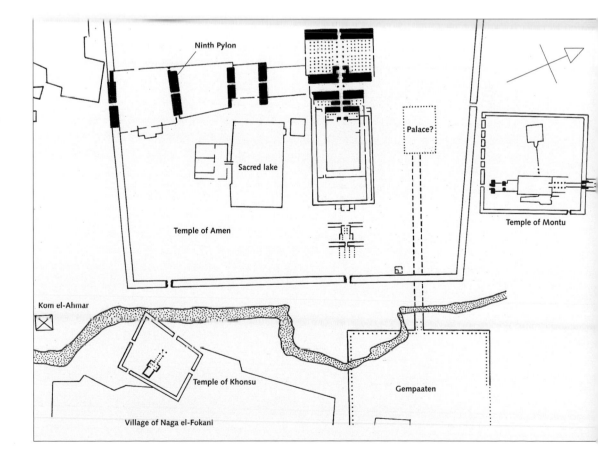

Ninth Pylon

Sacred lake

Temple of Amen

Palace?

Temple of Montu

Kom el-Ahmar

Temple of Khonsu

Village of Naga el-Fokani

Gempaaten

inaugurated, and vast quantities of sand-stone were quarried at Gebel es-Silsileh. Undoubtedly in an effort to speed up the construction, Amenhotep IV opted for blocks of standard size—52 by 26 by 24 centimeters (20 by 10 by 10 inches)—which were small enough for a single worker to carry. These *talatat* were hacked out at the quarry and intended to be finished at the construction site. Under pressure of time, however, the rough face was in many cases simply plastered over rather than smoothed with a chisel.

The new construction techniques involving *talatat* cannot be separated from the other revolutionary aspects of the king's program. The reliefs used to decorate buildings made of *talatat* centered upon a portrayal of the king that abandoned the traditional athletic form in favor of a potbelly, spindly legs, sunken chest, and elongated skull. (Debate continues in the scholarly world as to whether Amenhotep IV really looked like this or was grasping after some abstruse symbolism.) Dispensing with all anthropomorphic and, slightly later, theriomorphic (animal-like) representations of the divine, the art of the new *talatat* structures permitted the depiction only of the sun-god Ra-Horakhty in the guise of the sun-disk icon with stick-like "arms"—rays ending in hands. Amenhotep IV had turned his back on all cultic ritual and its underpinning mythology, save for the divine offerings and the ceremonial of kingship. Consequently the temple-wall scenes are devoid of the varied acts of worship formerly pictured. In their place artists substituted events from everyday life (figs. 35, 36), all under the extended rays of the sun-disk.

The texts of the early years of Amenhotep IV refer to four major buildings constructed by the king at Thebes. Photographs of the inscribed surfaces have made possible the jig-saw-style reconstruction and identification of relief scenes coming from each of these buildings. The clues are the captions that accompany the ubiquitous sun-disk and state specifically in which structure the scene stood. Thus it has proven possible to appreciate the variety of scene types peculiar to each building and to identify the style,

Fig. 35 Dancing women (cat. 30)

Fig. 36 Workers carrying heavy loads (cat. 34)

Painted reliefs from the walls of Amenhotep IV's temples at Karnak often depicted palace entertainments or scenes from everyday life. These *talatat* blocks show fragments of the sort that have been retrieved from pylon fill. A small proportion of them have been reassembled.

Fig. 34 Colossi fragments *in situ*, as discovered by Henri Chevrier in 1925.

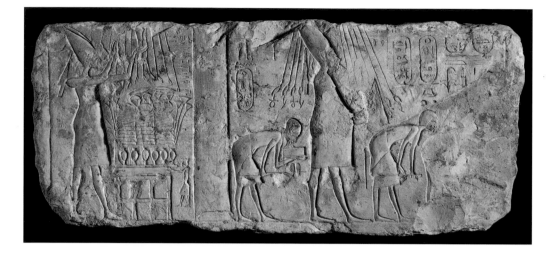

purpose, and relative date of each.

By far the largest of the four buildings, accounting for nearly half the *talatat* recovered to date, is the Gempaaten (Emperaten), provisionally translated as "The Sun-Disk is Found (in the House of the Sun-Disk)." The Akhenaten Temple Project excavations have located the site of this building east of the temple of Amen and south of the temple of Montu,[3] with an east-west axis parallel to that of the Amen temple. A recently discovered inscription by Amenhotep IV from the site states that the temple was built on a vacant "mud-flat," and excavation has demonstrated that, at the beginning of the king's reign, East Karnak was indeed unoccupied alluvial land. Oriented toward the east, the Gempaaten was 210 meters wide and more than 600 meters long (700 by 2,000 feet), with a simple series of open courts along its axis. A perimeter wall built of *talatat*, two meters (six feet) thick and possibly nine meters (thirty feet) high, enclosed this vast space; its

Fig. 37 *Heb-sed* (jubilee) representation (cat. 25)

Although this example may come from Memphis, it resembles *talatat* originating in the Gempaaten at Karnak. It shows two figures of Akhenaten (upright). The figure on the right, in a jubilee cloak, is flanked by two bowing priests, one of them carrying a papyrus scroll and the other, sandals.

Fig. 38 Amenhotep IV censing an altar (cat. 21)

inner face was carved with brightly colored reliefs. A colonnade of rectangular piers, obviously designed to protect the painted surfaces, ran around the inside of this wall. On the south side of the temple these piers were adorned with colossal statues of the king, some of which had been chanced upon in 1925 (fig. 34). On the north side, however, life-size statues of red quartzite were set between the piers, the inner faces of which bore reliefs showing the king gesticulating before the sun-disk. To judge from a scene in the Theban tomb of Amenhotep IV's Royal Butler, Parennefer,[4] the focal point of the temple—the cella, or chamber, at the eastern end—was dominated by a large altar dedicated to Ra-Horakhty.

The scenes on *talatat* identified as coming from the Gempaaten focus on the jubilee or *sed*-festival celebrated in the third year of the reign, and it is a virtual certainty that the Gempaaten was the venue for the performance. The festival, a royal ritual as old as the monarchy itself, re-enacted the king's coronation, and a major part of the original celebration involved offerings to all the gods of Egypt in conclave, each in his own small guest shrine. Amenhotep IV modified the service only slightly to suit his incipient monotheism. In the Gempaaten the wall scenes show the vast courts full of small kiosks with open roofs, now the preserve of the sun god alone. The king, perambulating among the kiosks, gives an offering in each at an altar laden with food and drink. He is accompanied by three priests: the chief priest of the sun god; the chief lector-priest, who carries the written order of service; and the king's personal priest, who carries his master's stool and sandals. At other points in the enormous enclosure the king is shown censing (fig. 38) and libating toward a forest of large, canopied stands, all stocked with food and wine. Servants and officials stand among them, libating toward the king and intoning benedictions. Royal symbolism in the reliefs is governed by geographic orientation: reliefs on the south side of the courts portray the king in the white crown of Upper Egypt, while those on the north show him in the red crown of Lower Egypt.

The *sed* festival took many days to perform, with a gala parade from palace to temple each day and a return at nightfall. The reliefs dwell heavily on these processionals. We see the king in jubilee costume leaving the palace as incense is wafted before him. He mounts his palanquin with the queen and "royal children" (as the text refers to them) in tow, and is borne along on the shoulders of his porters. Lining the parade route are cheering crowds, including officials, courtiers, foreign ambassadors, and even the prime minister. In the evening, back in the palace, the king and queen feast to the accompaniment of an orchestra of Egyptian women and a band of Hittite male musicians who appear to be wearing women's clothing. Occasionally the royal couple can be seen in the palace's "Window of Appearances," waving to the crowd dining at the king's expense in the court below.

Excavation has now cast light on the processional avenue depicted in reliefs as leading from the palace to the temple. The only access to the Gempaaten unearthed so far lies in the middle of the west side, and consists of a colonnaded corridor about four meters (thirteen feet) wide, decorated with scenes of men kissing the earth at the approach of the king (fig. 39). A projection westward of the excavated portion leads to an unexcavated space due north of the Fourth Pylon of the Amen temple, which was, according to textual evidence from earlier in Dynasty 18, the location of a palace. Amenhotep IV was thus apparently utilizing an existing installation for his performance.

Excavations have not yet provided information to positively situate the other three structures erected by the king. For one of them, however, it is possible to propose a site. This is the Hutbenben, or "Mansion of the *Benben* Stone," a building clearly inspired by a shrine at Heliopolis. Originally in the shape of a conical or stepped stone, the *benben* was an icon associated with the sun; but in the hieroglyphic script at Karnak it is represented by the sign of a single obelisk. Since a single obelisk, dedicated to Ra-Horakhty by Amenhotep IV's grandfather Thutmose IV, once stood adjacent to the Gempaaten at the eastern end of the temple of Amen, it is tempting to identify that object as the structural focus of the Mansion. If this is the case, the proximity of the Mansion to the Gempaaten would explain why it is sometimes said to be "in" that

Fig. 39 Bowing foreigners (Egyptian Museum, Cairo)

Foreigners were often depicted in scenes at court, their dress and hairstyle revealing their origins. This relief fragment shows, from left, a Libyan, a Canaanite, a Syrian, and a Nubian.

building. The Mansion was unexceptional in design and decoration except for three features. First, it was provided with tall, slender pylons and thin partition walls—graceful, perhaps, but structurally weak. Second, it shows Nefertiti the queen as celebrant in all offering scenes—to the exclusion of her husband, who is nowhere to be found in the decoration. Third, it seems to be the only building in which the two eldest daughters of the king, Meretaten and Meketaten, are depicted with their mother. The purpose of the shrine is not apparent.

The two remaining buildings, Rewedmenu and Tenimenu (respectively, "Sturdy are the Monuments ..." and "Exalted are the Monuments [of the Sun-Disk Forever]") have not been located or assigned a purpose. Their decoration, however, is striking, and may suggest that they, like the Mansion, represent a later stage than that of the Gempaaten. Although cultic scenes of offering to the sun-disk appear on *talatat* from these buildings as well, the decoration includes a varied selection of domestic and agricultural themes. The Rewedmenu has a number of scenes showing king and court traveling in chariots toward a mass of braziers set on tall stands. The braziers contain meat and ducks for roasting, and servants are seen lighting the fires.

The entire period of construction reviewed above reflects the rapid, almost *ad hoc* evolution of the king's thinking in theology, art, and architecture. At the outset of the reign, reliefs and texts, especially those of private sponsorship, continued traditional themes and style. But already in the months following his father's death, Amenhotep IV was conceiving of the "cessation" of the gods and of the supernatural as a monad. The most far-reaching changes were effected in anticipation of the jubilee: anthropomorphic representation of the god was interdicted, mythology and its use in art became obsolete, and the eccentric depiction of the king fostered a new artistic canon. By the third year artists were replacing the forbidden scenes with a repertoire taken from life; the sole unifying thread appears to have been the beneficent influence of the sun-disk on all living things. Finally, in the fourth year, facing criticism from unnamed groups—perhaps the priesthood of Amen, perhaps high-ranking bureaucrats or nobility—Amenhotep IV decided to relocate to a new capital in Middle Egypt, a site that is modern Amarna. At that point much more stringent changes presaged the iconoclasm to come. The antipathy toward Amen, the "King of the Gods," that had been latent in the king's thinking from the start now broke out in an orgy of desecration. Amen's temple was closed, his name and likeness everywhere hacked to pieces, and his high priest sent to the quarries in the Eastern Desert. Throughout Egypt, but especially at Thebes, construction of buildings for the sun-disk was halted and all labor and revenues diverted to the new capital. The traditional cultic establishments, already impoverished, ceased operation entirely. The king changed his name from the hated Amenhotep ("Amen is Placated") to Akhenaten ("One Who is Effective for Aten"), and with his wife, three daughters (the youngest a babe in arms), and a purged court, repaired to his dream city, Akhetaten, the "Horizon of the Sun-Disk."

1. This writer prefers the "high" chronology for the period, which would put the death of Amenhotep III and the accession of Amenhotep IV at 1374 B.C. There persists in some quarters the mistaken notion that Akhenaten enjoyed a coregency with his father. This has long since been disproven to the satisfaction of the present writer and the vast majority of the scholarly world.

2. "Live" in the subjunctive mood, as in "May Ra-Horakhty live …"

3. A falcon-headed war-god of Thebes who became prominent around 2000 B.C.

4. Theban Tomb 188.

The City of Amarna

Peter Lacovara

Akhenaten founded a sprawling city in Middle Egypt to serve as both the new capital of Egypt and the center of worship for his new religion.

Our most important source of evidence for understanding Akhenaten's period is the ephemeral capital the pharaoh built at the site known today as Tell el-Amarna.¹ Two hundred miles north of the Theban heartland, Akhetaten, the "Horizon of Aten," was conceived as a showplace for the cult of the Aten and the radical new art style that accompanied it.

Akhenaten's architects made the most of the local topography to underscore the symbolic nature of the urban plan: the site chosen for the city, virgin ground, was ringed by sheer limestone cliffs and divided approximately in half by the Nile, its north-south axis. The west bank was used for cultivation, and the east, except for fields on the river bank, was used for building, with the main royal palaces and temples of the Central City occupying the center of the semicircle described by the cliffs (map, page 15). The city stretched about eight miles along the Nile and was about three miles wide at its midpoint, a swath of construction that formed its east-west axis. A broad avenue now known as the Royal Road ran parallel to the river. Based on a circle divided into quadrants, the plan was the ideal urban order for the ancient Egyptians, whose hieroglyph for city was ⊗ (*niwt*).

In its heyday, Amarna may have served as home to twenty thousand or more individuals living in clusters of large and small houses north and south of the Central City. In addition to these residences, the grand scheme included planned housing for the workmen engaged in construction projects, as well as offices for diplomatic correspondence and for the bureaucracy associated with the royal court. At the periphery of the site, cut into the forbidding cliffs to the east, were the tombs of the king, his family, and his most trusted courtiers. These, too, were carefully aligned with the city plan.

Although such royal cities—built as magnificent settings for the king and his court, not unlike Versailles—had long been a feature of Egyptian society,² both the scale and the location of Akhetaten were unprecedented. Most earlier royal cities had been close to, or within, the traditional hubs of power—Thebes and Memphis—and could draw on the resources of those established communities. Situated approximately midway between the two, in remote Middle Egypt, Amarna had to be self-sustaining and perform all the functions of a major urban center.

The design of Akhetaten, although unique in many ways, most closely followed the plan of the palace city of Malqata and other projects built by Akhenaten's father,

Fig. 40 Fragment of a boundary stela with Nefertiti and two princesses (cat. 38)

Akhenaten used more than a dozen such stelae to mark the limits of his city and describe his projected buildings.

Fig. 41 Plan of the Great Temple

The plan shows the pylons flanking the entrance (at left), the columned portico ("pavilions") called the Per Khai, and the series of courts that formed the Gempaaten.

Amenhotep III, at Thebes, the city Akhenaten abandoned in the fifth year of his reign (see the essay "The Sacred Landscape").

The Founding of Akhetaten

Akhenaten carefully recorded his intentions for the new city on a series of boundary stelae set into the cliffs ringing Amarna (fig. 40).[3] Two of the stelae he erected after his first visit to the site describe the city's location and parameters. To judge by surviving fragments, they seem to have borne the same declaration:

> ... I shall make Akhet-Aten for the Aten, my father, in this place. I shall not make Akhet-Aten for him south of it, north of it, west of (it) or east of it. I shall not go past the southern stela of Akhet-Aten toward the south, nor shall I go past the northern stela of Akhet-Aten downstream, in order to make Akhet-Aten for him there. Nor shall I make <it> for him on the western side of Akhet-Aten; but I shall make Akhet-Aten for the Aten, my father, on the orient (side) of Akhet-Aten—the place which he himself made to be enclosed for him by the mountain, on which he may achieve happiness and on which I shall offer to him. This is it![4]

The Temples

Texts on the boundary stelae also mention the projected buildings, whose names hint at some of their functions and their organization. "The House of the Sun-Disk" and "The Mansion of the Sun-Disk" were the two main cult buildings at Amarna.[5]

The "House," or Great Temple, was a massive structure about 750 meters long and 230 meters wide (2,500 by 750 feet), unique in its design (fig. 41). Unlike traditional Egyptian temples, which were partly shadowed by their own forests of columns and had a succession of increasingly constricted shrines, chapels, and chambers leading to the dark inner recesses of the holy of holies, the Amarna temples were spacious enclosures open to the sky and full of light. The entrance to the Great Temple, on the Royal Road, was flanked by two huge pylons leading to a columned portico known as the Per Khai ("The House of Rejoicing"). Most of the interior of the temple was a vast court filled with offering tables. Extending down its center, toward the east, was a long, rectangular structure appended to the portico and known as the Gempaaten ("The Sun-Disk is Found"), which was similar but not identical in design to the temple of the same name that Akhenaten had built in Thebes (see the essay "The Beginning of the Heresy"). It consisted of a series of open courts separated by pylon gates and filled with more offering tables which, in depictions of the temple in tombs and elsewhere, were piled high with food. Surrounding the court was a series of storage magazines for additional provisions, and beyond these, more courts for offering tables. The food placed on these hundreds of tables would later have been distributed to the residents of the city, emphasizing the importance of the king and his cult to the community. Traditionally, people without priestly functions had no access to the temples; it is not clear whether Atenism departed from tradition in this respect.

Figs. 42, 43 Painted pavements from the Maruaten

Lively scenes of plants and animals were rendered in painted plaster in a structure believed to have been dedicated to Princess Meretaten. Illustrated here are fragments of a floor painting with bird and marsh plants (left, cat. 83) and a floor painting with marsh plants (cat. 82).

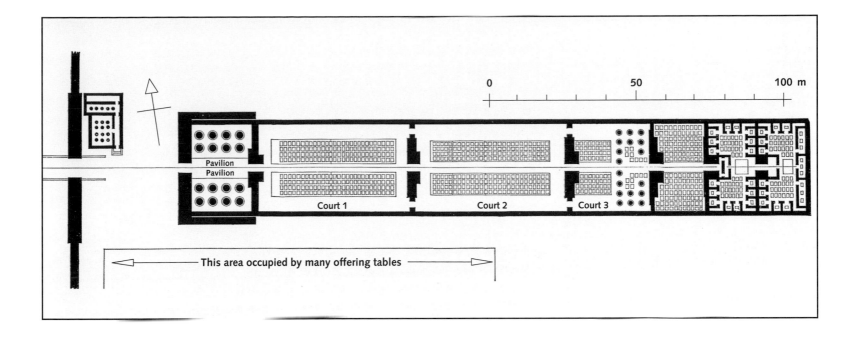

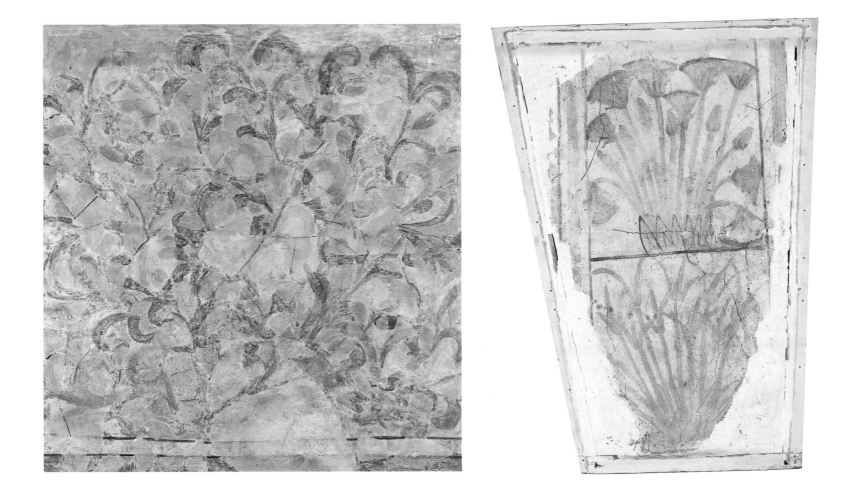

The odd, narrow design of these structures may be explained by their possible use as a processional route that led to an earlier construction at the rear of the enclosure. That construction was a sanctuary composed of a series of courts fronted by a massive pylon gate, which was in turn flanked by two columned kiosks.

"The Mansion of the Sun-Disk," identified on stamped bricks found at the site, was an abridged version of the Great Temple sanctuary. Known as the Small Temple, it was attached to the "King's House" (see below), and may have served as a chapel royal. The "Sunshade of the Great Royal Wife" referred to in the foundation text is less easy to identify. Barry Kemp, director of the current excavations at Amarna, has suggested that a number of temples at the periphery of Amarna were dedicated to the royal women: the Kom el-Nana, to Nefertiti; the Maruaten, to Akhenaten and Nefertiti's eldest daughter, Meretaten; and a temple located by Richard Lepsius in the nineteenth century but now lost, to Akhenaten's mother, Queen Tiye.[6] Other constructions—isolated, raised platforms on the margins of the city, which excavators have called desert altars—may have been dedicated to the other princesses. The Maruaten, the most complete example of these temples honoring royal women, was a vast enclosure surrounding a water-garden that looked like an enormous lily pond bordered by lush plantings, garden kiosks, and open-air altars (figs. 42, 43). Kemp has noted the propaganda value of these establishments, with which "Akhenaten and the women of his family gave themselves important territorial markers scattered over the Amarna plain, well beyond the limits of the residential city. Wherever the … ordinary city-dwellers went, there, shimmering in the distance, was a royal enclave claiming attention."[7]

The Palaces

Amarna's multiplicity of palaces may have been as much of a departure from the tradition of palatial architecture as the Amarna temples were from earlier cult buildings. Because of their unique design, it has been difficult to establish which of the three main palaces—the Great Palace, the North Palace, or the North Riverside Palace—was the pharaoh's chief residence; there has even been debate about whether the Great Palace (Per Aten) was some form of temple. Drawing on Kemp's observation that movement from one palace to another may have been a way of publicly marking the king's progress during the day, we may find it useful to regard these structures as an "exploded" version of the traditional palace, with its parts set at intervals along the Royal Road.

The Great Palace was the largest residential structure in the Central City and the most extensive of all the palaces at Amarna. It was a long, rambling building to the west of the Royal Road, and its remains are now partially obscured by cultivation. The palace complex probably covered an area of more than 15,000 square meters (162,000 square feet). The northernmost section consisted of open courts, storerooms, and several parallel rows of contiguous houses, possibly residences and offices for palace officials. The section just to the south, known as the North *Harim* and probably used as the royal women's quarters, had, among its columned halls and spacious courts, a large garden with a pool at its center. Suites of rooms were grouped around a hall opening onto a columned portico with a painted pavement depicting a pool surrounded by marshes.

Among the features of the Great Palace were also a vast open court (in the northwest section) that was once bordered by statues of the king and queen, and a spacious, square, pillared hall flanked by six narrow, rectangular halls—a cluster of rooms that resembled the pillared Festival Hall in the Malqata palace of Amenhotep III.

Fig. 44 Palace scene featuring the Window of Appearances (cat. 66)

The Window was an elaborate balcony where the royal family was seen on special occasions. It is shown set in a columned courtyard in which attendants sweep the ground and carry water. A guard with stick in hand stands beside the entrance gate next to a pile of shields and weapons.

Opposite the Great Palace and connected to it by a bridge spanning the Royal Road was another complex sometimes known as the King's Estate, a large enclosure containing a garden, pool, storerooms, courts, and the King's House, a residential structure occupying the southwest quarter. The King's House has been likened in plan to the Amarna villa discussed below, but was much larger and contained a court with an altar. There were also groups of storage chambers, a wing believed to be servants' quarters, and residential *harim*-style suites. The interior of the King's House was decorated with mural paintings, including depictions of the royal family and a dado of panels on which heraldic plants of Upper and Lower Egypt alternated.

The most prominent feature of the Egyptian royal palace was the "Window of Appearances" (fig. 44), the balcony from which the royal family greeted and rewarded its subjects. Although earlier excavators thought the Window was on the bridge overlooking the Royal Road, Kemp has suggested that it was in the Great Palace and noted that there was a smaller Window of Appearances in the King's House. Despite the presence of this traditional feature, however, Kemp believes that neither the Great Palace nor the King's House served as the principal residence of the king: "there is nowhere in the centre of the city," he writes, "where one can seriously imagine the royal family permanently residing." He goes on to point out that the "King's House, even if part of it possessed an upper story, is far too small to have served as anything but a reception suite" and that the "Great Palace, if palace it is, is manifestly non-residential, though one might argue that the domestic part lay beside the waterfront and is now buried beneath the cultivation."[8]

The North Palace (fig. 45), beyond the Central City, is also unlikely to have been the primary royal residence. Although it, too, had some features of a traditional palace—it was planned around two large central courts with smaller pillared halls leading to a throne room—it had vast facilities for animal keeping, along with a number of store-

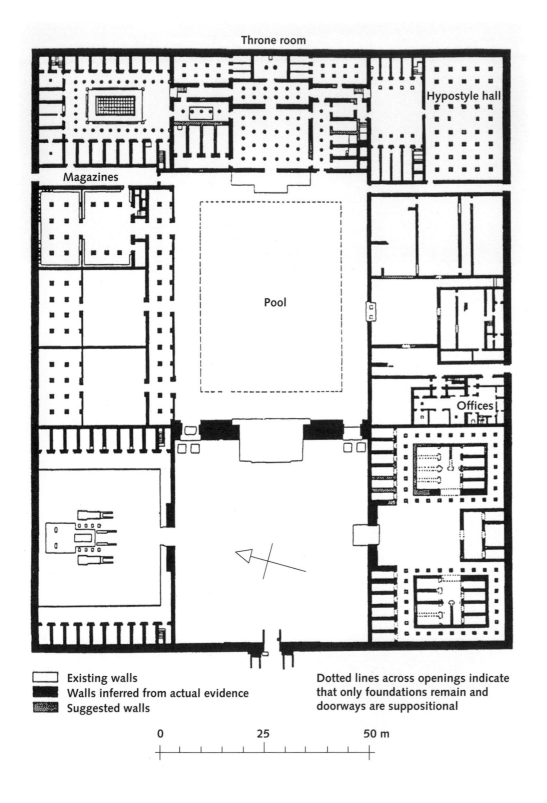

Throne room

Hypostyle hall

Magazines

Pool

Offices

Existing walls
Walls inferred from actual evidence
Suggested walls

Dotted lines across openings indicate
that only foundations remain and
doorways are suppositional

0   25   50 m

Fig. 45 Plan of the North Palace

rooms and a large court containing altars. Its mural decoration consisted of depictions of birds, fish, and other animals. The "palace" part of the structure was limited to the eastern end of the building and was laid out in an abbreviated form.

The North Riverside Palace, one of the most enigmatic buildings at Amarna, has been only partially excavated, and the results have never been fully published. It was enclosed by a monumental wall and contained a number of large storerooms and pillared halls. Across the Royal Road from its enclosure wall was a group of residences. One in particular,[9] described as the largest "private" house at the site, has been suggested as a residence of Nefertiti. I would suggest, rather, that this house and the North Riverside Palace mirror the juxtaposition of the King's House and the Great Palace in the Central City. Besides the villa, there was a vast garden, a large lake, a series of storerooms, a chapel, several large open courts, and a series of clerks' houses—again similar to the King's Estate.

It is the North Riverside Palace that Kemp has proposed as the main residential quarters of Akhenaten. Indeed, the very fragmentary plan of that palace suggests similarities to the palace of Amenhotep III at Malqata. Kemp believes that the North Riverside Palace, far removed from the center of the city, was incorporated into a routine "royal progress" that ended at the Great Palace in the Central City:

At intervals—how frequently we cannot tell—the king drove to the city centre along the Royal Road, making this an occasion for a public display of the monarchy. His duties on arrival would have been primarily threefold: worship at the temple, contact with officials for policy decisions and for audiences and for the distribution of rewards, and the occasional reception of a foreign prince or envoy. Since, for the latter, a fine and impressive display was an important adjunct ... it may be that the Great Palace was used for this, amongst other roles.... This separation between palace and government, between the domestic life of the king and his official duties as head of state, would be a striking illustration of the extent to which the role of the king had been rationalized by the mid-New Kingdom.[10]

If the Amarna palaces are seen as an "exploded" version of the traditional palace, the North Riverside Palace was most likely the sleeping quarters of the king. The North Palace functioned as a ceremonial palace that, with its animals—some painted on pavements as in the palaces of Amenhotep III at Malqata in Thebes and Merneptah (19th Dynasty) at Memphis but others fully alive—placed the king at the center of all living things. The Great Palace and the King's House served the official needs of the pharaoh in his capacity as head of state. The passage of the king through the city not only evoked the transit of the sun through the sky, but also the traditional procession of cult images to various temples, which had been a facet of Egyptian religion before the Amarna revolution (see "The Sacred Landscape").

Official Buildings

The palaces and temples at Amarna did not exist in splendid isolation, but within a sea of administrative offices, nonresidential structures for the production and storage of goods, and housing for the community (fig. 46). Among the specific buildings identified at Amarna are a records office, barracks for the police and/or military, granaries, and bakeries. Like the architecture of temples and palaces, the structure of Amarna's varied administrative buildings suggests the manner in which the city functioned.

Although it is unusual to have direct confirmation of the specific nature of an administrative building, the records office at Akhetaten—the "House of the Correspondence of the Pharaoh"—was identified, like the Small Temple, by stamped bricks bearing its name.[11] An expedition of the Egypt Exploration Society of London in the 1930s found the remains of some of the famous Amarna clay tablets here, and presumably this was the source of the original cache of diplomatic correspondence, discovered in 1887.

Many of the buildings in the Central City seem to have been designed for domestic purposes, but may also have been used in connection with palace records or storage. Throughout the city there are long blocks of storehouses built with one central corridor flanked by long, narrow chambers perpendicular to it. Their narrow rooms and thick walls were apparently intended to support arched roofs made of unbaked mud brick, which presumably offered better protection than flat, thatched roofs. Fairly elaborate shrines or offices were often incorporated into these storage units.

Fig. 46 Aerial view of the Central City

The dark area (bottom) is the cultivation at the western edge of the city. East of it is the Great Palace, then the Royal Road, where a bridge links the palace to the King's Estate. Farther east are the records office and clerks' houses, with the military and police barracks extending into the desert. In the north are faint traces of the Great Temple; south of the King's Estate is the Small Temple (see figs. 52, 53).

J. D. S. Pendlebury, excavating in the twenties and thirties, identified military and police quarters at Amarna southeast of the Central City. These consisted of two rectangular blocks set at right angles to each other. The smaller of the two buildings was presumably residential, with grain silos, a garden, and pillared halls. Beside it was a great enclosure that apparently contained horse stables and a large well: though it is difficult to differentiate between barracks, stables, and storerooms, since all are composed of long, rectangular cells of brickwork, the excavators identified the eastern section, with a sloping stone floor, as the stables. The barracks, along with storerooms, granaries, and offices, occupied the western part of this building and the building immediately to the west.[12]

Since grain was not only food, but a principal form of currency, capacious silos associated with the large villas were displays of private wealth. Throughout Egypt grain was stored in rectangular brick or wood compartments, cylindrical brick silos, wattle-and-daub structures (made of mud-plastered reeds), or open yards. The cylindrical silo seems to have been more common in the New Kingdom, particularly at Amarna, but there appears to have been open storage there as well. Barley and wheat would also, of course, have been used for making beer and bread. According to Kemp, the bakery/brewery complexes found adjacent to the Great Temple and other official structures (beer was made from partially baked bread) were designed as "simply a repetition … of the basic domestic kitchen until the necessary capacity was obtained."[13]

The Workmen's Village

An element unique to ancient Egyptian urban design was the workmen's village, a group of small, contiguous dwellings, often designed on an orthogonal plan and usually bounded by a perimeter wall. The village at Kahun associated with the pyramid of Sesostris II is generally regarded as the earliest of these (Middle Kingdom, about five hundred years before the Amarna Period), although they are all related in design as well as function to the pyramid cities of the Old Kingdom. The best-known is the village at Deir el-Medina for the craftsmen who worked on the royal tombs of the New Kingdom in the Valley of the Kings at Thebes.[14]

The Workmen's Village at Amarna, also known as the Eastern Village, was square in plan, with a thick enclosure wall 70 meters (about 230 feet) square. Within it were six rows of houses built along five streets running north-south. The individual houses were built to a uniform standard, 10 meters long and 4 meters wide (33 by 13 feet), in three sections divided by two transverse walls. As at Deir el-Medina (where the village plan was not as geometrically rigid), each house had a forecourt or hall and a central living room with a central post or column. There were two smaller rooms at the rear, one presumably a bedroom, and a kitchen with a cylindrical oven,

open hearth, and storage bins. A stairwell at the back of the house provided ventilation for the kitchen and access to the roof. There may also have been an upper story, as suggested by recent fieldwork at the site.[15]

When the Deir el-Medina Workmen's Village was expanded in the late 18th Dynasty, there seems to have been a conscious attempt to repeat the pattern of the Amarna village. The later additions have the effect of squaring off the village and giving it a substantial enclosure wall. Since Amarna artisans may have lived at both places, it could well be that there was influence from Amarna on the redesign of Deir el-Medina.

Associated with the workmen's villages at both sites were clusters of small votive chapels built outside the perimeter walls to the southeast (fig. 47). It has been suggested that most of the Amarna chapels were the kind called *henu*, or "resting place," used for family gatherings on feast days. These structures frequently had domestic features such as kitchens, benches, and even animal pens. Though the chapels at Amarna seem similar to the poorer tomb chapels of the early 18th Dynasty, they do not appear to have been constructed as tomb chapels, since there are no accompanying graves.[16]

The votive chapels are highly variable in plan, often consisting of one or more courts with stairs or ramps and having thick walls or small pylons at the rear. They also incorporate the local topography in their design: cut into hillsides, they gradually rise toward the rear of the structure as if imitating traditional temple architecture in which the raised inner sanctum symbolized the primeval mound in Egyptian creation mythology.

Fig. 47 Reconstruction of a chapel outside the Workmen's Village

Chapels associated with the village at Amarna are similar to those found near the Workmen's Village at Deir el-Medina (Thebes) and elsewhere, although at Amarna they appear to have been for private worship rather than for funerary purposes.

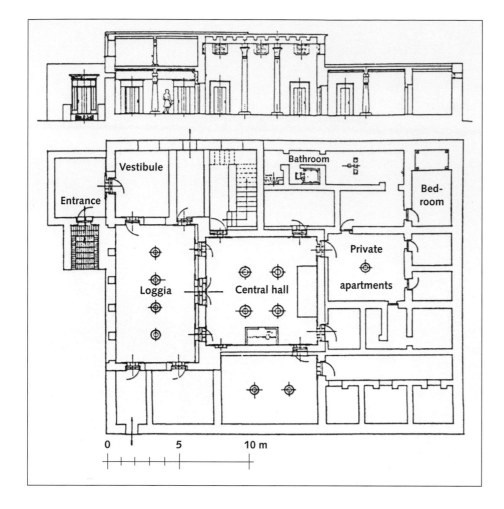

Fig. 48 Plan of Amarna house T.36.11

Private Houses

Egyptologists have often cited the "standard Amarna villa" as the quintessential pre-Roman example of domestic architecture from the Mediterranean world,[17] suggesting that it was "fully in keeping with tradition."[18] But there is good evidence that the villa was in fact as radical a departure from the norm as other Amarna architecture.

The villa in question was a square house with three sections, two of them public and one private (fig. 48)[19]: Its front section contained an entrance, usually approached by a ramp or stairway; a vestibule; and a long hall (loggia). Its middle section had a square central hall that usually incorporated a dais along the back wall. Adjacent to the central hall were a rectangular side hall and a stairway for access to the second story. The rear of the house was occupied by private apartments, which in the larger houses were replicated many times. However, there was usually only one master-bedroom suite, which consisted of a bedroom with a raised sleeping niche, a bathroom, a short hall, and a square room with a central column. Smaller guest, servant, or *harim* quarters were sometimes grouped in this section of the house, along with storerooms.

The interior and exterior appearance of this house has been debated considerably. One of the earliest discussions was by Seton Lloyd, who attempted to build a three-dimensional scale model, drawing on data from several hundred excavated examples[20] but basing the plan mainly on a large house in Amarna's North Suburb. The house was located at the center of a large square plot of ground in a walled enclosure, among workshops, storage magazines, a well, grain silos, an oven, and a small chapel set in a garden. Seton described the villa in detail (the main elements as in the outline given above) and posited that it had had a second story over its north room and central hall, since column bases were found in and around those areas.[21]

It is the Lloyd model that has too often been used as an exemplar of an ancient Egyptian house. Evidence that this villa was in fact relatively rare, even at Amarna, comes from Christian Tietze, who has recently analyzed more than five hundred houses from the German excavations of 1911–14 in Amarna's South Suburb. He notes eight types of private home,[22] which he classifies according to wall thickness and number of rooms. Using this classification, Tietze divides the inhabitants of Amarna into three groups: the lowest social stratum, comprising 54 to 59 per cent of the population, a "middle class," making up about 34 to 37 per cent, and an "upper class," comprising

7 to 9 per cent. It is this last group that is associated with the villa Lloyd described.

Although that villa was much too elaborate to be called standard, it was in some ways typical of Amarna houses, quite distinct from the seemingly random design of houses outside Amarna during the same period and private dwellings during other periods in the history of ancient Egypt. As Kemp notes:

> The plans of the individual Amarna houses are remarkably uniform, irrespective of size. Although it is rare to find two identical houses, the same elements are constantly repeated in slightly different combinations.... Houses of rich and poor are distinguished more by size than design, although larger houses did possess features, such as an entrance porch, which denoted status in themselves.[23]

The Amarna villa can be seen not as the result of the evolution of the standard Egyptian house, but—with its off-axis entrance and tripartite plan including vestibule and central hall—as a deliberate borrowing from traditional New Kingdom palatial architecture.[24] Given the remarkable uniformity of Amarna houses, even across social classes, it might be said that at Amarna every man's home was his castle. Both the uniformity and the radical departure from the norm in domestic architecture are indicators of how far Akhenaten went to "micromanage" his new capital.

The End of Amarna

After the death of Akhenaten in his seventeenth regnal year, the court moved back to the traditional centers of Thebes and Memphis, and Amarna was gradually abandoned. With wooden elements such as doors and roofs removed, the buildings, largely of unbaked mud brick, quickly crumbled. Although some occupation continued into the reign of Tutankhamen, by the end of the 19th Dynasty (about 1190 B.C.) the temples had been demolished, and the remaining residents had left. The city was forgotten for more than thirty centuries.

Fig. 49 Statuette of a king (cat. 170)
Amarna residents kept figures of the royal family in their household shrines.

1. The name "Tell el-Amarna" combines the name of a nearby village, El-Til, and that of a local tribe, the Beni Amram. "Tell" here does not mean the mound at a site of settlement as it does in the rest of the Near East. See Aldred 1982, p. 89.

2. Lacovara 1997, pp. 68–80.

3. Murnane and van Siclen 1993.

4. Murnane 1995b, pp. 76–77 (§4).

5. Pendlebury 1951, pp. 189–212.

6. Another interpretation is that Tiye's sunshade temple was incorporated into the Great Palace. See "The Sacred Landscape."

7. Kemp 1995, p. 461.

8. Kemp 1976, p. 92.

9. House U.25.11.

10. Kemp 1976, p. 99.

11. Pendlebury 1951, pp. 113–30.

12. Ibid., pp. 131–38.

13. Kemp 1989, p. 291.

14. See Romer 1984.

15. Kemp 1987.

16. Bomann 1991, pp. 57–79.

17. Kemp 1977b.

18. Fairman 1949.

19. For an enumeration of the three sections of the house, see Ricke 1932.

20. Lloyd 1933.

21. Ibid., p. 7.

22. Tietze 1985 and Tietze 1986.

23. Kemp 1989, pp. 294, 298.

24. Lacovara 1997, p. 60.

**Fig. 50 Sanctuary of the Great
Temple** (cat. 96)
The altars are heaped with food
offerings to Aten.

The Sacred Landscape

Michael Mallinson

The city of Amarna can be seen
to embody Akhenaten's religious
beliefs, through the use of natural
features and the location and orientation of buildings and monuments.
The sun, rising from the direction of
the Royal Tomb, enveloped all.

Amarna, unique in the history of ancient Egypt, was laid out to be both a political capital and a ceremonial city, the embodiment of a new religion. Its
uniqueness can be understood only in relationship to its urban precedents and
the history that brought it about. Akhenaten, who came to the throne as Amenhotep
IV, at first ruled Egypt from the two traditional capitals, Memphis and Thebes. His
father, Amenhotep III, had been one of the most successful kings of the 18th Dynasty,
and had, in the traditional role of the pharaoh, rebuilt and enlarged all of the main
religious structures at the two capitals. At Thebes in particular he had built a series of
works on an unprecedented scale, culminating in his mortuary temple (dedicated to his
funerary cult) and the palace city of Malqata on the west bank of the Nile.

During his reign of nearly thirty-eight years, Amenhotep III used elements of his
extensive building program to elevate his position in the divine order and to reformu-
late worship within the city. He gave special emphasis to the annual Opet festival, celebrated during the flood season, when images of the god Amen, his consort Mut, and
their son Khonsu were taken from Karnak to Luxor in a procession of bark shrines on
the river or litters over land.[1] The Luxor temple was associated with the divine birth of
Amenhotep III: Amen-Ra was pictured there as his father, approaching his mother, and
the king was shown in a birth scene, being created on a potter's wheel by the god
Khnum.[2]

Amenhotep III celebrated his reign's achievements in three jubilee festivals held at
Malqata,[3] at the edge of a giant rectangular lake, Birket Habu, which he created and
which in retrospect seems to have been an important precedent for the conception of
Amarna.[4] The lake was the length of the processional route from Karnak to Luxor and
had a processional route along its western side leading from Malqata to a group of
shrines[5] and residential palaces[6] to the south. The Nile had been the reference point for
orientation until Birket Habu was created; temples had been built perpendicular to the
river and the direction of religious processions gauged in relation to it.[7] Even some
hieroglyphs related to direction derived from the Nile: "traveling north" was a boat
symbol with its sails lowered (going downstream) and "traveling south," a boat with
its sails raised. But there is evidence that Birket Habu (whose axis was in fact forty-five
degrees off north-south) was built to symbolically alter the orientation of the Nile—or
at least that the creation of the lake and the shift in orientation were associated. The

72

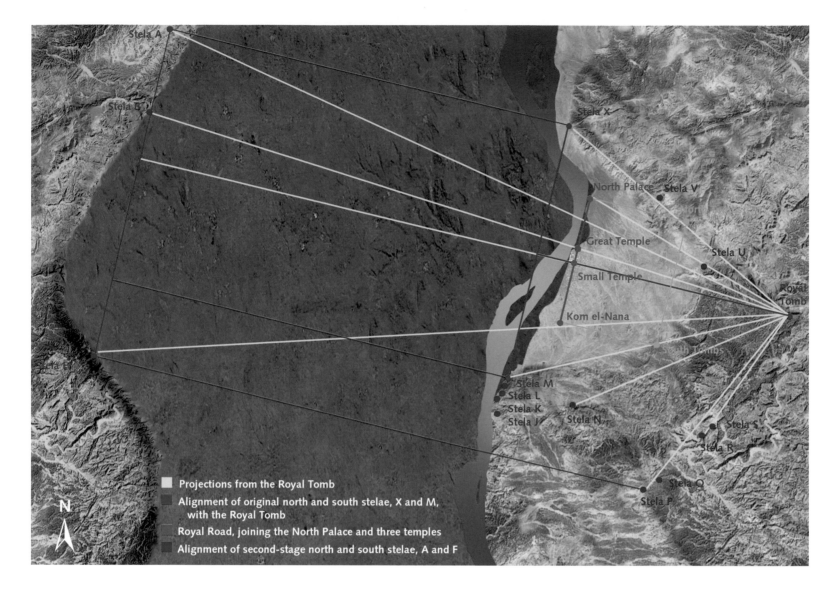

Projections from the Royal Tomb

Alignment of original north and south stelae, X and M, with the Royal Tomb

Royal Road, joining the North Palace and three temples

Alignment of second-stage north and south stelae, A and F

Fig. 51 Plotting out the city

Among the alignments that seem to have had significance in Amarna are north-south parallels (see key) and ray-like projections from the Royal Tomb in the east. One ray links the tomb to the Great Temple and Stela B across the river. Another goes through the Small Temple and bisects the line joining the two original stelae. A third goes through the North Tombs and Stela X. A fourth links the South Tombs and Stela M.

jubilee temple of Amenhotep III was built perpendicular to the lake rather than the river, and all later pharaohs building in western Thebes used the new orientation. Birket Habu thus seems to have been the first instance of a large-scale topographical element modified by man for symbolic use in orientation. Although pyramids were an earlier example of man-made structures symbolically associated with natural features (mountains), Birket Habu extended the association of structure and topography out into the wider landscape.

Akhenaten was clearly influenced by his father's works. Their link to Akhenaten's new cult is shown by the Colossi of Memnon, the golden quartzite statues of Amenhotep III that flanked the entrance to his mortuary temple and were a focal point of his "new" Thebes. Amenhotep III described these images of himself as "rays … in people's faces like the sun-disc ('Aten') when it shines in the morning."[8] Emphasizing his own divinity, he called the boat he sailed on Birket Habu at its opening "Radiance of Aten"[9] and gave the same name to a palace at Malqata.[10]

In the first few years of his reign, Amenhotep IV assumed the traditional role of the pharaoh, but, apparently inspired by his father's emphasis on Aten, he elevated this manifestation of the divinity of Amen-Ra,[11] making the sun-disk sole god. He built on a massive scale with great speed,[12] developing a new unit of construction, the *talatat* block, which not only allowed rapid construction but also ensured that all buildings would have royal scale and proportion. The block was a "royal cubit" in length (fifty-two centimeters, or twenty inches), and half as wide and deep. Palaces and temples had previously been measured in royal cubits, but the blocks had been of irregular size—whatever the quarry produced. Now, since only whole blocks were used, buildings would have proportions based on the royal unit of measurement.

Amenhotep IV's early buildings were extensions of his father's key monuments in Memphis/Heliopolis (on opposite sides of the river), as well as in Thebes. The new god's temples at Karnak, including one dedicated by Nefertiti, were unique not only in their elevation of other members of the royal family to priestly roles, but also in their external decoration, which featured images of the city and everyday life. Akhenaten's understanding of Aten as the animator of all living things may have united different segments of society, at least conceptually.

The Symbolism of the Site

Despite the colossal scale of these works at Thebes, Akhenaten seems not to have been satisfied with his efforts to rededicate Egypt to his new god. In Egyptian belief, even if a temple was neglected, as long as it was still standing and still decorated, its cult retained its symbolic power. At Thebes this must have been inescapable. So Akhenaten decided to lead his people to a new site, away from the corrupting influence of the past.

He needed a site suitable for celebration of his new religion in a form comprehensible to his followers—but also one that had symbolic power equal to that of the religious foundations he was leaving behind. His choice of a location halfway between Memphis/Heliopolis and Thebes was apparently an effort—from a safe distance—to unite the capitals of the Two Lands (Lower and Upper Egypt) in a new center dedicated to a new, centralized religion (map, page 14). To achieve his own city's authenticity he had to recreate aspects of theirs, which he did by incorporating elements of their scale and architecture. The name he gave the city, Akhetaten, refers to the *akhet*, or horizon, where the sun took its final form before rebirth in the morning; it was traditionally represented by an image of the sun cradled between two mountain peaks.[13] From the site Akhenaten chose, his people could witness the enactment of this symbolic event: on certain key days of the year, the rising sun emerged from a break in the cliffs.

Akhenaten's first act at Amarna was one of dedication, orientation, and the establishment of proportion; it is here that he seems to have drawn on the precedent of modifying a topographical feature for orientation. He had two boundary stelae (X and M; see fig. 51) carved into the cliffs[14]—one in the north and one in the south, as if addressing the old capital cities. The two stelae, which list buildings, recall a stela his father had erected in Thebes[15]—except that his father's summarized the works he had completed, and dedicated them to Amen-Ra, whereas Akhenaten's, uniquely, listed the buildings he was planning, and dedicated the city to Aten.[16] Proportion was achieved by making the distance between the stelae four times the distance between Karnak and Luxor, the processional route established by his father for the Opet festival. Although the significance of four is unclear, the fact that it is a whole number suggests that the relationship was intentional and not coincidental.

Orientation was achieved by drawing a line between the two stelae and ensuring that all temples and other ceremonial structures within the city would be aligned with it. At the midpoint between the stelae a perpendicular center line was created: an axis on which Akhenaten erected his first altar. Here again, the temple is perpendicular to the defining orientation. At the center line's eastern terminus, the same distance from the midpoint as the two original boundary stelae are from each other—in the wadi that formed the cleft in the cliffs—the king built his tomb.

The first altar could not lie directly between the stelae, as the river was in the way, so its location was shifted one-sixth of the distance (again, apparently an intentional measure) toward the Royal Tomb. It became the center of the "House of Rejoicing of Aten,"[17] a name that referred to the Central City (map, page 15). In the first stage there was a simple sacred grove around the altar, and a small palace on the northern side. A second temple, dedicated as the main temple to Aten, was also erected to the north, and two important palace complexes were established, one to the north and one to the south.

The distances between some of the new buildings were based on the processional routes from Karnak. The Great Temple is the same distance from the Small Temple as Karnak's Amen temple is from its temple of Mut. Amarna's North Palace is the same distance from the Small Temple as the Small Temple is from Kom el-Nana, a temple possibly dedicated to Nefertiti[18]—the distance from Karnak's Amen temple to Luxor. The Royal Road that connects the complexes seems to have become the route for Akhenaten's procession—not statues of the god sailing down the Nile in boats or carried in litters over land, but the king himself, god's appointed, riding in his chariot to the temple. This elevation of his and his family's status, first seen in Karnak, continued at Amarna: the outlying temples were dedicated not to other gods but as "sunshades" honoring his wife and daughters.

The second stage of work on the Great and Small temples saw the original shrines replaced with stone sanctuaries and the enclosure walls redefined.[19] The sanctuaries were simplifications of the small stone temples Amenhotep III had developed at Karnak, combined with a hypaethral (roofless) architecture reminiscent of early sun temples at Abusir (near Memphis) and smaller solar-cult rooms elsewhere. The huge wall around the main Heliopolitan temple may have been the inspiration for the Great Temple's enclosure, which was about 750 meters, or 2,500 feet, in length. The Small Temple's enclosure wall (figs. 52, 53) was the same size as that of the Karnak Amen temple at this time. The Great Temple was the main cult building and the Small

Temple, adjacent to the King's House, probably served as chapel royal. They were also symbolic substitutes for the two main Ra temples—Ra-Horakhty at Heliopolis and Amen-Ra at Karnak, respectively. Amarna thus united the two earlier cult centers in its spatial order.

Whereas the larger elements of the city appear to have been scaled by processional distance, smaller elements may have been dictated by the pragmatic considerations of construction. For some of the smaller elements, however, there does seem to have been a measure worked out in advance. The distance between the Small Temple's axis and the outer enclosure of the Great Temple, for instance, is also the length of the Great Temple's enclosure wall.

Extending the Boundaries

The final stage in the founding of the city extended the symbolic nature of its structure. Thirteen more stelae were carved into the cliffs to establish the final boundaries. Their texts describe the process of measuring the city and extending its limits across the valley and into the desert. This was similar to the "stretching of the cord" ceremony used to establish the limits of a temple and trace out right angles. The placement of the new stelae was determined through a kind of projective geometry, or plane-table surveying, used traditionally to enlarge a plan into a building. Stela A, which marks the northwestern boundary, is at the spot where a projection west from the original northern stela, parallel to the city's axis, meets a projection from the center of the eastern (back)

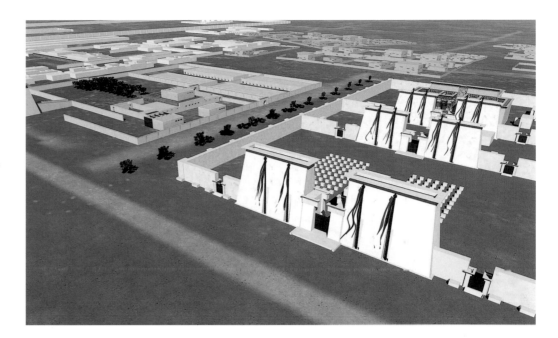

Figs. 52, 53 Small Temple, computer reconstruction and aerial view

The reconstruction shows the entrance pylons fronting the Royal Road and two more pairs of pylons to the east. The aerial view, looking west, shows the back of the temple and vestiges of the three pairs of pylons. The dark area (top) is cultivation along the Nile.

wall of the Small Temple out through its northwestern corner. Stela B, the middle stela of the three on the western side of the river, is not, as one might expect, on the city's central east-west axis, but north of it, on a line projecting out from the Royal Tomb through the sanctuary of the Great Temple (fig. 50). Thus the city can be seen as a unified whole, with the royal tomb linked through the religious structures to the boundary stelae, in a sequence that follows the narrative on the first stelae.

That this projective geometry had taken on a symbolic role may be seen in the Royal Tomb's relief of the sun being worshipped: the sun rises on the horizon, its rays projecting out through the temple, which is shown here with no enclosure wall, touching and invigorating the temple and the surrounding city.[20] The symbolic measurement of the city, radiating from the Royal Tomb, may have been a celebration of this idea. It also connected the Royal Tomb, which would be Akhenaten's place of unification with Aten on his death, with the place where Aten gave life to the city, the *akhet* where the sun was reborn every morning.

The role of the palace in the new city became that of mediation between man and god, and is symbolized in the image of the "Window of Appearances," where the king rewarded his courtiers. Though no such structure has been found for certain in the city, it is represented on wall reliefs of the city in the tombs—either in use at reward ceremonies, or closed, as part of palace architecture. From that Window the king gave his followers gold—a symbol of the divine light of the sun. But Akhenaten rewarded his followers with more than that: he provided houses for them, designed, with minor variations, on a standard plan, and tombs for the nobility (as promised in the foundation decrees on the early boundary stelae to these "God's Fathers of Aten"),[21] decorated with images of the new city. The city itself was to include all his people as part of its dedication to his god. From recovered *talatat* blocks, it seems that the two temples, like those at Karnak, were decorated with images that included everyday life and people participating in the king's worship in the temple.[22]

A summation of the king's role may be seen in the Great Palace, which was finished later in the reign and is situated between the two temples but on the opposite side of the Royal Road. It may have incorporated the sunshade temple of Akhenaten's mother, Tiye, and so been important as a celebration of the kingly authority Akhenaten inherited from Amenhotep III. But it clearly also was connected—physically and symbolically—to the King's House, an early building, which held the audience chamber and may have had a small Window of Appearances.[23] The King's House was joined to the Great Palace by a bridge that also formed a triumphal gate and pylon on the Royal Road when the palace was finished: a link that suggests the Great Palace was an enlarged version of the King's House. This palace, which may have had a hypaethral roof to let the midday sun shine in its central hall, this colossal building with an enormous forecourt surrounded by statues of the king and his family—the largest stone building in Amarna—was perhaps a temple dedicated to the living king and his divine role as mediator with the sun god.

Though the mediator was denounced soon after his death, and the city of Amarna forgotten for millennia, Akhenaten's influence in urban planning lived on. A number of later cities were laid out using processional distance as an ordering device. One of these was the Delta capital of the Ramesside kings, Per-Ramesses, which also had a processional route, apparently the distance between Karnak and Luxor, linking the main temple groups in the city. Though Akhenaten's perhaps more pragmatic successors destroyed his vision, it may have been the source of subsequent attempts to develop the city as an icon for a unifying order under a single god—in cultures influenced by Egyptian thinking but less bound by its conventions. The New Jerusalem of the Book of Revelation is certainly closer to Amarna than to the thoroughly measured "rational" Greek city. But whereas Akhenaten sought to make divinity and light immanent in his city, the architect of the New Jerusalem seems to have built no home for his god, who is transcendent: "I saw no temple in the city; for its temple was the sovereign Lord God and the Lamb. And the city had no need of sun or moon to shine upon it; for the glory of God gave it light, and its lamp was the Lamb."[24]

1. Wolf 1931, pls. 1–2, and Murnane 1981.

2. L. Bell 1985.

3. Hayes 1951, p. 163.

4. The lake is referred to on a commemorative scarab dated year 11, third month of the inundation, during the Opet festival. It was 3,700 cubits long and 600 cubits wide, created for Queen Tiye in her town of Djaruku, where the king was carried on his barge. See B. G. Davies 1992, no. 579, A, p. 36; and Sethe and Helck 1927–58, IV, 1737.

5. Watanabe and Iseke 1986; Daressy 1903, p. 170.

6. Kemp 1977a.

7. Moret 1902 and O'Connor 1989.

8. B. G. Davies 1992, no. 562, p. 2; Sethe and Helck 1927–58, IV, 1648.

9. B. G. Davies 1992, no. 579, A, p. 36; Sethe and Helck 1927–58, IV, 1737.

10. Hayes 1951, p. 178.

11. Assmann 1995, p. 148.

12. D. Redford 1973, p. 80, table, and Saad 1976, p. 69.

13. Aldred 1976.

14. N. de G. Davies 1903–8, vol. 5, pp. 20–27, pls. XXVI–XLIII.

15. B. G. Davies 1992, no. 562, p. 1; and Sethe and Helck, IV, 1648–55.

16. Murnane and van Siclen 1993, p. 37.

17. Pendlebury 1951, appendix A, pp. 189–212. ("House of Rejoicing" is a traditional name for a palace. There is some debate about whether the name "House of Rejoicing of Aten" applies to a building or a precinct.)

18. Barry Kemp suggests this possible identification of the temple with Nefertiti. See Kemp 1995, pp. 456–57.

19. Mallinson 1995.

20. Martin 1974, 1989, vol. 2, pl. 34.

21. Murnane 1995b, p. 78 (§4).

22. Many of the people depicted are servants and soldiers accompanying the royal family. Given the presence of hundreds of altars in the forecourts of the two main temples, some scholars have suggested that large numbers of people entered with offerings.

23. Kemp 1976.

24. Rev. 21:22–23 New English Bible.

The Royal Family

Nicholas Reeves

The leading personalities of the Armarna Period seem more familiar to us than those of any other period in ancient Egypt. Akhenaten, the radical king, was called the first individual in history by the Egyptologist James Henry Breasted. And Nefertiti, that classic beauty, enjoyed a degree of power that was exceptional for a queen.

The young prince Amenhotep, son of Amenhotep III (fig. 54), was raised to the status of heir-apparent only by the premature death of an elder brother, Thutmose[1] (fig. 56)—of whom, beyond a brief text recorded by Auguste Mariette (the French founder of the Egyptian Antiquities Service), the testimony of a limestone cat-sarcophagus, and other minor items, we know next to nothing. For Egypt, Thutmose's early demise was to prove a disaster of epic proportions: with the accession to the throne of Neferkheprura-Waenra Amenhotep (IV)—better known today by his later name, Akhenaten—the country would be plunged into a period of ruthless dictatorial rule, divisive experiment, and fear. The repercussions of the next twenty years would be felt for generations to come.

Amenhotep IV first tasted power with his formal appointment as coregent to his father. The nature and extent (in some quarters, even the existence) of this period of joint rule are still disputed[2]—which is unfortunate, given that the question is fundamental to our proper understanding of many aspects of the period, not least the family relationships. A relatively limited coregency of less than two years[3] still seems most likely—the principal (but not sole) evidence for this restricted span being the controversial "year 2" notation, in hieratic, on a letter addressed to the newly independent Amenhotep IV (as Napkhurreya) by Tushratta, king of Mitanni.[4] It is characteristic of the ambiguities and contradictions of the period, however, that this same docket is occasionally restored as "year [1]2," and offered in support of a long coregency.

Amenhotep III "joined the gods" in the thirty-eighth year of a reign that had witnessed three jubilees, in years 29/30, 33?/34 and 37/38.[5] The age at death of Amenhotep III's mummy, recovered from the cache in the Valley of the Kings tomb of Amenhotep II (KV 35), has been estimated at thirty to thirty-five years.[6] Such estimates of age at death, based upon modern maturation formulae, are now seen as improbably low;[7] nevertheless, it is unlikely the king was of any great age when he died.

The tomb in which the son, Amenhotep IV, buried his father is that now designated WV 22 in the western annex of the Valley of the Kings (fig. 123), a sepulcher begun by the late king's own father, Thutmose IV. As the design of this sepulcher clearly indicates (with its two subsidiary suites of rooms attached to the principal burial chamber), Amenhotep III had made provision to be buried here with two of his queens—the Great Royal Wife Tiye and, most probably, his daughter Sitamen, who functioned as

Fig. 54 Detail from a relief of Amenhotep III, tomb of Khaemhat (Ägyptisches Museum, Berlin)

Great Royal Wife at a later stage in the reign (see below). Since Pharaoh was survived by both women, he would enter the underworld alone—though Tiye was to dedicate a number of *shabti*-like images to the burial,[8] as later would her daughter-in-law, Nefertiti, to the funeral equipment of Amenhotep IV/Akhenaten sometime before the latter king's death.[9]

Tiye (fig. 55) was the principal of Amenhotep III's several queens; the king's lesser (named) "consorts" included his previously mentioned daughter Sitamen, as well as Henuttaneb and Isis, who were evidently his offspring also. The arrival in Egypt of yet another queen, the Mitannian princess Gilukhepa, daughter of Shuttarna II and sister of Tushratta, is mentioned in another Amarna letter,[10] and was marked by the issue of a commemorative scarab dated to year 10 of Amenhotep III's reign. This lady disappears from the records with the arrival of a second Mitannian bride, Tadukhepa, a daughter of this same Tushratta, who followed in Gilukhepa's footsteps before year 36 and was inherited by the son, Amenhotep IV.[11] Lesser members of the *harim* of Amenhotep III—apparently named on the basis of their sexual specialities—are known from a cache of canopic-jar fragments brought to light on the Theban west bank early this century.[12] Except for Tiye, Sitamen, and conceivably Tadukhepa, none of Amenhotep III's women are today remembered by anything more substantial than a name and occasional image.

Tiye herself was of nonroyal birth, daughter of the chariotry-officer Yuya and his wife Tjuyu (whose partially robbed double burial was brought to light in Valley of the Kings tomb KV 46 in 1904).[13] The family hailed from Akhmim in Middle Egypt; claims for an ultimately foreign origin have perhaps been overstated. Tiye's brother was the high priest of Ra, Aanen,[14] destined, perhaps, to be a significant influence on his nephew, Amenhotep IV; the future king Ay, who shared Yuya's principal titles, may well have been another sibling. The alliance between the royal house and the Yuya family was celebrated on a scarab issued at the start of the reign, and the proclamation of the queen's nonroyal (but clearly powerful) parentage would be repeated on the above-mentioned Gilukhepa scarab series of year 10.

Tiye was evidently a dominant force during her husband's reign, her enhanced status reflected in the fact that her name is consistently incorporated into the full pharaonic titulary, while her appearances in both sculpture and relief are frequent and imposing. As another commemorative scarab records, a lake was dug in her honor, perhaps in the vicinity of Akhmim, in year 11. At Sedeinga in Nubia she was worshipped as a manifestation of the goddess Hathor, divine consort of her deified husband whose own cult was celebrated *ante mortem* at nearby Soleb; elsewhere she was identified with other goddesses, including Maat (the personification of cosmic order) and the hippopotamus deity Taweret. Tiye's continuing influence following the death of Amenhotep III and the accession of Amenhotep IV as sole ruler is clear both from scenes in the tomb of Kheruef, Steward of the Great Royal Wife, where she is shown as her son's sole companion,[15] and from the diplomatic correspondence that is addressed to her by the Mitannian king Tushratta.[16] (The tone of Tushratta's above-mentioned missive to Amenhotep IV himself on the same matter hints at not only the successor's inexperience in the pharaonic role but also his relative youth.)

A supposed visit by Tiye to Amarna, Amenhotep IV/Akhenaten's newly founded city where a temple ("sunshade") had been erected in her honor, is recorded in the tomb of Huya, her Steward at that time.[17] It is evident that Tiye died shortly after this visit, following the mid-reign change in the name of the Aten (below). Despite Amenhotep III's plans for her interment with him in WV 22, she

Fig. 55 Queen Tiye wearing a Hathor headdress (cat. 39)

Fig. 56 Prince Thutmose ("Thutmose V") on a bier (cat. 15)

If Prince Thutmose had survived, the Amarna interlude might never have taken place.

appears, from the surviving traces of wall decoration, to have been interred in the principal (if *ad hoc*) burial chamber of the extensive tomb Akhenaten had prepared for himself in the desert cliffs to the east of Amarna (tomb plan, fig. 127); her body would be contained within a splendid granite sarcophagus of Amarna style presented by the king for his mother's use.[18] Following the official abandonment of Akhetaten under Tutankhamen, when the principal cemeteries were evacuated the queen's body was removed from Amarna for reburial at Thebes. Here, within tomb KV 55 in the Valley of the Kings, Tiye's corpse was reinterred, accompanied by a selection of her original grave goods (including a marvellous shrine of gilded wood,[19] another gift from Akhenaten)—only to be transferred from this second tomb during the reign of Ramesses IX.[20] Although the identification has not gone unchallenged,[21] it has been proposed (on the basis of hair samples and craniofacial morphology) that we are to recognize the queen's mortal remains in the mummy of the so-called "Elder Lady"[22]—a stripped and otherwise unidentified corpse that was eventually deposited in the Amenhotep II cache (KV 35) during the early years of the Third Intermediate Period.

Of Sitamen, Amenhotep III's eldest surviving daughter, latterly (by year 30)[23] functioning in the ritualistic role[24] of Great Royal Wife, we know very little. Like Tiye, she perhaps lived on into the reign of her brother, Amenhotep IV, though unlike the mother she drops from view soon after (her latest mention is on a jar label from Malqata of Amenhotep III's year 37).[25] Sitamen's presumed sisters, Henuttaneb and Isis, have already been mentioned; a fourth daughter, Nebetah, perhaps died young. Another supposed daughter of Amenhotep III and Tiye was the enigmatic Baketaten, who appears in the celebratory scenes recording Tiye's year 12 Amarna visit in the tomb of Huya; she *may*, in fact, be none other than Sitamen herself, sporting a Late-Egyptian name change, or even a daughter of this princess.

One suggestion sometimes put forward by those espousing a long coregency between Amenhotep III and his eldest surviving son is that the "King's Bodily Son Tutankhuaten [*sic*]" (as Tutankhamen is described on a reused block from Hermopolis)[26] was a child of this former king and a younger brother both to Amenhotep IV and to the mystery king Smenkhkara (below). A carefully preserved lock of Tiye's hair found in the boy-king's tomb, though probably indicating lineal descent, nevertheless offers no clear support for direct filiation, and, in the event of a shorter period of joint rule between Amenhotep IV and his father, the proposed relationships are difficult to maintain. The question of Tutankhamen's likely parentage is considered further below.

Virtually nothing is known of Amenhotep (IV) as a prince. When he first enters upon the world stage (on blocks from the Tenth Pylon in the temple of Amen at Karnak) during the period of coregency with his father, Amenhotep III, Amenhotep IV is represented in a wholly traditional style; not long after year 2 of his reign the tendency toward physical exaggeration that is today the hallmark of the art of this period (but would in fact wane as the reign developed) begins to make itself felt. The change

Fig. 58 Stirrup ring featuring Akhenaten and Nefertiti as Shu and Tefnut (cat. 98)

Fig. 57 Bust of Queen Nefertiti (Ägyptisches Museum, Berlin) This now-famous image of the queen was found in the sculptor Thutmose's workshop (reconstruction, fig. 84) by German excavators in 1912.

came with the erection, at East Karnak and elsewhere, of a series of shrines dedicated to the Aten, or solar disk—visible manifestation of Ra and the consuming object of Amenhotep IV's personal devotion. In large part, as the Gempaaten temple clearly shows, the Karnak structures were intended for the celebration of the junior coregent's first *sed*-festival, which took place at a date subsequent to year 2/3.[27] Further jubilees are postulated as having been celebrated by the younger king at intervals thereafter.[28]

Amenhotep IV assumed full pharaonic powers upon the death of his father, whose burial arrangements may have been finally concluded in the successor's year 3;[29] the dead king, already regarded as a god during his lifetime, now became one with the Aten. Work at Karnak evidently ceased a short time after the burial of Amenhotep III (though it perhaps resumed toward the end of the reign) as, coincident with Amenhotep IV's adoption of the new nomen Akhenaten—conventionally translated "He Who is Beneficial to the Aten"—the king's efforts were transferred to the building of a new capital at a virgin site in Middle Egypt. The boundaries of this new city— Akhetaten, "Horizon of the Aten," the site better known today as Amarna—were demarcated by a series of large stelae, each inscribed with versions of the king's decrees of years 5, 6, and 8 that outlined in general terms his intentions for the future.[30] The name of the Aten itself—"Ra-Horakhty Who Rejoices on the Horizon/ in His Name of Shu [Light] Which is Aten"—enclosed in a pair of cartouches since the time of the first jubilee, was "purified," perhaps in (or after) year 11,[31] to exclude all allusions to the old religion: "Ra, Horizon Ruler, who Rejoices on the Horizon/ in His Name of Ra the Father Who Has Returned as Aten."[32] Conceivably this change was prompted by the formal installation of the god in his new capital. It almost certainly marked the high point of Akhenaten's fanaticism,[33] when the names and images of Amen and other deities belonging to the traditional pantheon were ruthlessly and systematically expunged throughout Egypt; clearly, in the case of small, private objects such as scarabs, this was a form of fearful self-censorship by the owners themselves. The persecution was followed soon after by the formal divinization of Akhenaten and the appointment of his coregent, Nefernefruaten (below), to rule the earthly domain in his stead.

Akhenaten died in or after his seventeenth regnal year, and was interred, as his boundary stelae had decreed, within the Amarna family vault, by the side of his mother. It was to prove a tight fit, with two of the four rock-cut supports having to be removed to accommodate the large royal sarcophagus of pink granite, the calcite canopic chest, and the huge wooden shrines in which these two sets of burial equipment would have been separately nested. As already observed, the Amarna dead were destined to remain in the Royal Tomb for a relatively short time only: the dismantling of the burials would be carried out by Akhenaten's successor but one, Tutankhamen, some time after the official abandonment of Akhetaten. The body of the king apparently followed that of his mother, Tiye, to Thebes for reburial within tomb KV 55, utilizing one of the coffins, hastily adapted, that had originally been employed by his lesser wife Kiya (see below). The burial equipment from the Amarna Royal Tomb, it is clear, had been appropriated and pooled; much of it—far more than is apparent today— would go for almost immediate reuse, suitably adapted, in the burial of Tutankhamen himself.[34]

Amenhotep IV/Akhenaten's principal wife was Nefertiti (fig. 57), whose image is well-known from her famous colored portrait-bust[35] found by the Deutsche Orient-Gesellschaft in the abandoned workshop of the sculptor Thutmose at Amarna in 1912. The parentage of Nefertiti is a mystery. Given the royal couple's persistent identification with the divinities Shu and Tefnut[36] (fig. 58), offspring of the creator-god Ra-Atum, it would perhaps be logical to see the queen (who adopts Tefnut's flat-topped headgear for almost universal use after year 4) as the king's twin;[37] but neither she nor her sister, Mutbenret, anywhere employ the title "King's Daughter." Some have seen Nefertiti's name—which is conventionally translated "The Beautiful One is Come"—as reflecting her foreign origin; an identification with the Mitannian princess Tadukhepa is clearly one possibility. Others, perhaps with better reason, have speculated that Nefertiti was a daughter of Ay, Tutankhamen's immediate successor, a member of the Yuya-Tjuyu family clique, and perhaps Tiye's brother. Supporters of this claimed association would interpret Ay's title, "Father of the God," as father-in-law to Akhenaten, on analogy with the "God's Father" Yuya's position as father-in-law to Amenhotep III. Perhaps significantly, it is a title that Ay continues to stress even after his accession, when it is enclosed within the cartouche of his nomen. It may or may not be relevant that Ay's Amarna tomb is one of the few places where reference is made to Nefertiti's shadowy sister and sole named blood relative, Mutbenret.[38] If Ay *was* Nefertiti's father, it is nonetheless clear that her natural mother was someone other than Ay's named wife, Tiy, who is described as merely wet-nurse to the queen.

Nefertiti's origins are intriguing, but her subsequent career is even more so. The intimacy of the royal family is depicted at every opportunity, and the development of the queen's status appropriately follows the elevation of Akhenaten himself. If there is any significance in her apparent absence from the earliest records of the reign, the queen's association with prince Amenhotep dates to the period after he became coregent. Her original name was simply "Nefertiti"; in year 5, however—around the same time the young king changed his nomen from Amenhotep to Akhenaten—the queen's appellation was elaborated by the addition of the prefix "Nefernefruaten."[39] The lady's active title throughout the early years of the reign was "Great Royal Wife" *(hemet nisu weret)*, but shortly after the disappearance of Kiya (see below) in or after regnal year 11, this title is found alternating with a slightly different designation, *hemet nisu aat*[40]—perhaps to distinguish the principal queen from her daughter Meretaten, who, like her aunt Sitamen before her, was now functioning in certain contexts with this principal queenly rank.

The gradual increase in status documented by these titular changes was, in fact, anticipated in Nefertiti's representations both in relief and in the round (fig. 59). From the very start, the queen's role as the female component of the Amarna triad (Aten–

Fig. 59 Relief of a royal barge with
Nefertiti smiting (cat. 110)

Images of a queen in the traditional
kingly pose of smiting an enemy are
unprecedented.

Akhenaten–Nefertiti) was emphasized to
an extraordinary degree: at Karnak, in
particular, where she could boast her
own shrine, the Hutbenben, and perhaps
other monuments besides, Nefertiti was
repeatedly shown of equal size to the
king in scenes of offering, while colossal
manifestations as the goddess Tefnut
(formerly and, it would seem, erroneous-
ly regarded as "sexless" representations
of Akhenaten), equipped with the kingly
crook and flail, were erected side by side
with similar statues of the king in the
guise of Shu.[41] Further and more obvious
increases in Nefertiti's status would follow the move to Amarna—these being
most tellingly displayed on the modest
private stela of the marine Pase, where
Akhenaten and his consort, though distinguished from each other by kingly
double and queenly single cartouches, are both shown wearing pharaonic headgear.[42]

Nefertiti had seemingly reached a pinnacle of power and influence, going so far as to
double her single, queenly cartouche in imitation of a kingly prenomen and nomen,[43]
when suddenly, after year 12 of Akhenaten's reign and following the burial of her second daughter, Meketaten (below), she dropped from view.[44] This disappearance was
not, as previously thought, the result of death or disgrace. On the contrary:[45] the
queen's gradual assumption of royal prerogatives can now be seen to have culminated
in a deliberate shedding of her previous style and the formal adoption of a new, kingly
titulary to match her iconographic affectations—confirming the tradition recorded by
the third-century B.C. historian Manetho of a ruling female ("Akenkheres") at the end
of the 18th Dynasty[46]: not only is the prenomen of Akhenaten's new coregent occasionally written with a feminine indicator, *t*, "Ankhe*t*kheprura" (with the epithet "Beloved
of Neferkheprura-Waenra"),[47] but the nomen, with equal force, perpetuates the first
element of Nefertiti's full name, "Nefernefruaten" (with the epithet "Beloved of
Waenra-Akhenaten").[48] Quite possibly Tiye's visit to Amarna represented in the tomb
of Huya,[49] and the reception of foreign tribute in year 12, as recorded in the tombs of
Huya and of Meryra II, superintendent of Nefertiti's household[50] (fig. 60), formed part
of the *sed*-festival celebrations during which this elevation took place. In the latter
scenes, the overlapping images of Akhenaten and Nefertiti are shown in such proximity
as to offer the viewer a virtually single outline, perhaps intended to echo the "oneness"
of their kingship. Ankhkheprura Nefernefruaten's only *named* image is that found in a

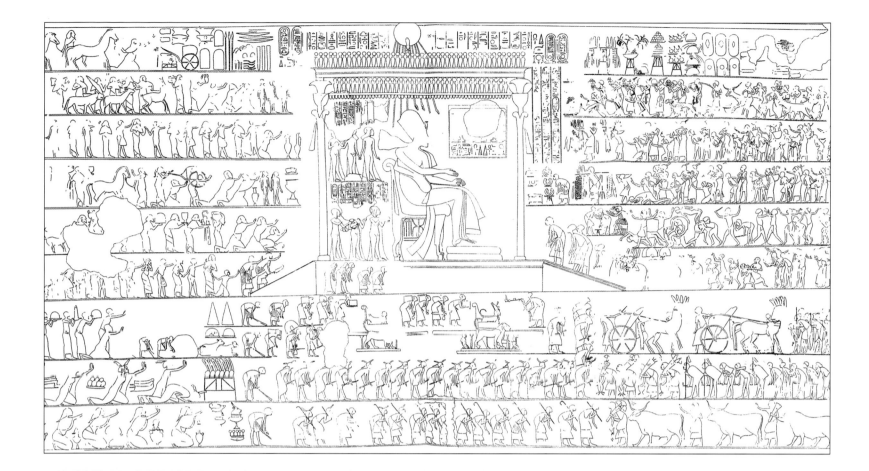

Fig. 60 The reception of foreign tribute, from the tomb of Meryra II

Akhenaten and Nefertiti, with their daughters behind them, sit in a kiosk receiving tribute. This was a major event in year 12 of Akhenaten's reign. (Line drawing from a relief.)

fragmentary document known as the "Coregency Stela"[51]; her highest attested regnal date is year 3, in a long graffito—a hymn to the god Amen written by the "*wab*-priest and scribe of divine offerings of Amen in the temple of Ankhkheprura, Pawah"—found in the Sheikh Abd el-Qurna tomb of the priestly official Pare at Thebes.[52]

Further changes in the epithets incorporated in Nefernefruaten's cartouched prenomen and nomen—"Beloved of Aten" and "Ruler" respectively[53]—hint at even greater power to come. Yet, upon his death, Akhenaten appears to have been succeeded not by Nefernefruaten but by a previously unattested individual by the name of Smenkhkara;[54] the new ruler is famously shown with his Great Royal Wife, Meretaten, in an outline scene in the tomb of Meryra II at Amarna.[55] The traditional view, which still has many adherents, is that this successor was male, and perhaps an elder brother of Tutankhamen.

The principal basis for the assumed youth, sex, and indeed independent existence of this male successor is the body from KV 55. Given the archaeological context of the deposit[56] and the latest, substantially increased estimate put forward for the corpse's age at death (thirty to thirty-five years),[57] however, the likelihood is that the KV 55 remains represent the body not of the much-vaunted "youth" Smenkhkara but of Akhenaten himself. This, combined with the fact that the mysterious successor not only bore the same prenomen as Akhenaten's coregent, "Ankhkheprura," but actually shared the ritualistic services of the same Great Royal Wife,[58] has led to the view that both coregent and successor were in fact different manifestations of one and the same person—Nefertiti. Certainly, it is an identification that accords well with Nefernefruaten's demonstrable

claims to supreme power at the height of her coregency with Akhenaten—and, as we shall see, with much else besides.[59]

The period of Nefertiti's independent rule as Smenkhkara was evidently short, and probably directed toward returning Egypt to normality following the traumas of the past—as witness the Pare graffito and the regular, Osirian form of the funerary equipment Nefernefruaten had prepared for herself at this time.[60] Historically, however, Nefertiti's role as restorer of the old regime was eclipsed by a single act. As we read in the annals of the Hittite kings discovered at their capital, Boghazkoy, negotiations were opened with Shuppiluliuma by a certain *dakhamunzu*, an appellation that is today recognized as a Hittite vocalization of the Egyptian *ta hemet nisu*—"*the* [particular] royal wife." Though other candidates have been mooted,[61] the queen in question (from seasonal and other considerations) can have been none other than Nefertiti.[62] The aim of the woman's parley with one of Egypt's great rivals in the Near East was to procure a prince to rule Egypt by her side.[63] It was, as the records suggest, an unprecedented act of sheer desperation, perhaps driven by Nefertiti's increasingly uncertain grip on power at home. The tactic would fail dismally and result in her fall; indeed, it was perhaps this one treasonable act—the inevitable outcome of defying *maat* (true order) by the elevation of a woman to supreme power—that would sound the final death-knell of the Atenist regime, and help ensure for it and its adherents the lasting enmity of successor kings. The anti-foreigner backlash that doubtless followed may well represent one of the strands making up the biblical tradition of Exodus.

Nefertiti clearly died a short time after the murder *en route* of her Hittite prince (who was possibly named Zannanza).[64] Despite her evident unpopularity, it may be guessed that she was interred, in kingly style,[65] in a subsidiary sequence of royal chambers prepared in the tomb of Akhenaten at Amarna. Supervising the interment (if, as a small child, only nominally) was her stepson and successor, the young Tutankhaten—whose own, legitimate succession Nefertiti had attempted to frustrate. Ironically, it would be this same boy, in death, who would appropriate much of Nefertiti's Amarna burial equipment, suitably reinscribed, for his own use (fig. 61); the queen herself his agents would presumably lay to rest a second time in a tomb yet to be identified, doubtless at Thebes and in the Valley of the Kings.

The three-dimensional portraits from the workshop of the sculptor Thutmose, findspot of the famous bust of Nefertiti, clearly represent several of the principal players in the Amarna episode, though aside from the more obvious images only a few individuals have so far been identified. Among them, recognizable from the characteristic circular ear-ornaments so frequently encountered in her depictions in relief, is the lady Kiya[66] (fig. 62). A secondary wife of Akhenaten,[67] Kiya bore a unique title—*hemet mererty aat*, "Greatly Beloved Wife"—that reflected her unique status at the Amarna court. Not only is she shown in the reliefs with a daughter[68] (fig. 63), but a good circumstantial case can be made for seeing Kiya as the mother of Akhenaten's only son, Tutankhaten.[69] It was perhaps the birth of the heir during the middle years of Akhen-

Fig. 61 Canopic coffinette from the tomb of Tutankhamen (Egyptian Museum, Cairo)

A container for embalmed viscera, the coffinette is covered in sheet gold inlaid with semiprecious stones and glass.

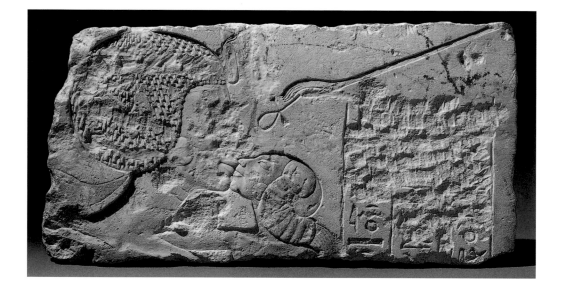

Fig. 62 Relief of Kiya, reworked for Meretaten (cat. 57)

Fig. 63 Relief of Kiya kissing her daughter (Brooklyn Museum of Art, New York)

Some images of Kiya, the Greatly Beloved Wife, were altered or erased after her death.

aten's reign that first brought Kiya to prominence, at a date prior to the change in the Aten's name—a prominence that was to culminate in her eventual depiction at the same scale as the king, most notably on a relief-decorated block found at el-Ashmunein (Hermopolis) and now in Copenhagen.[70] If such is the case, the suggestion that the woman died giving birth to Tutankhaten (based upon a relief in the Amarna Royal Tomb, Kiya's presumed place of original interment)[71] would appear to fall.

Further information on Kiya is sparse: she is sometimes identified as one of the Mitannian princesses—perhaps Tadukhepa, less likely (because of age considerations) Gilukhepa—while a folk memory of the lady and her charms seems to be preserved, in the guise of Bata's wife, in the "Tale of the Two Brothers."[72] Kiya's decline appears to have been as swift as her rise—and it is not beyond the realm of possibility that she fell from grace in a coup engineered by the jealous Nefertiti herself, whom, for a brief time (if perhaps in specific contexts only), she appears to have rivalled.

Kiya disappears from sight after year 11 of Akhenaten's reign, to be buried with a magnificent burial equipment furnished by the king. Her presumed initial interment in the communal Royal Tomb at Amarna,[73] to judge from the physical layout of the chambers, can have been made only after the burial of Meketaten (below); following the tomb's evacuation, Kiya's mummy will have been transferred to Thebes. Here, in the Southern City, her canopic jars and one of her coffins were clearly ready to hand to be appropriated for Akhenaten at the time of the reburial with his mother in Valley of the Kings tomb KV 55[74]—in which case Kiya's final resting place, though not yet recognized, will doubtless have been close by.

Following her death, a number of Kiya's representations in relief were defaced (fig. 63), or recarved as representations of Akhenaten and Nefertiti's eldest daughter,

Meretaten (fig. 62).[75] With Nefertiti's elevation to coregent status, the princess was promoted to the position of Great Royal Wife, presumably to fill the ritualistic void; born at an as yet undetermined date before year 5 of the reign,[76] the new queen was still little more than a child. Notwithstanding the daughter's tender age and the essentially functional character of the title "Great Royal Wife," scholars have long suspected the relationship between Akhenaten and Meretaten ultimately to have been a sexual one, resulting in the birth of Meretaten-tasherit ("Meretaten the Younger"). Since, unlike other forms of incest, no divine precedent could convincingly be cited, it was an arrangement that must have appeared abhorrent even to contemporaries. The elder Meretaten would continue to act as Great Royal Wife to Akhenaten's successor,

Fig. 64 Detail of a painting fragment showing two princesses
(Ashmolean Museum, Oxford)

The complete scene, from the King's House, showed Akhenaten and Nefertiti with all six daughters.

Fig. 65 Glass ring with the names of Ay and Ankhesenamen (Ägyptisches Museum, Berlin)

Smenkhkara, though her eventual fate (like that of her postulated child) is unknown.

The second daughter of Akhenaten and Nefertiti was Meketaten, who appears to have been born around year 5/6 of Akhenaten's reign (her image squeezed into the scene on one of the boundary stelae as an afterthought).[77] Meketaten's best-known act in life was her leaving of it: she was buried in the Amarna Royal Tomb (apparently before the interment of Kiya), in a room that includes a wall scene of the princesses's obsequies.[78] This scene appears to suggest that the young girl died in childbirth—which, given the likely fates of her sisters Meretaten and Ankhesenpaaten (below), should occasion little surprise.

Akhenaten's four remaining daughters by Nefertiti were Ankhesenpaaten, Nefernefruaten-tasherit, Nefernefrura, and Setepenra, all evidently born before year 10 but only the first and her two previously discussed elder sisters ever encountered in "official" texts or temple reliefs; representations of the three younger princesses are found only in palace decoration (fig. 64) and in the Amarna nobles' tombs.[79] As with Meretaten and Meketaten, an incestuous relationship may be postulated for the third of the progeny, Ankhesenpaaten, her union with her father probably resulting in the birth of the "King's Daughter" Ankhesenpaaten-tasherit ("Ankhesenpaaten the Younger"). The elder Ankhesenpaaten's subsequent marriage to the child-king Tutankhaten—her half-brother—may have been an attempt to heal wounds within a family that, by the time of Nefertiti's death, had become heavily factionalized. With the formal abandonment of the Aten cult—officially in regnal year 2 (the purported date of the royal proclamation known as the "Restoration Stela"), but perhaps as late as year 3 or 4[80]—the "-aten" element in each of the couple's names was replaced with "-amen." The new royal pair were now reconciled to the old religion as Tutankhamen and Ankhesenamen, with Ankhesenamen apparently forging the final link in the repair of the dynastic chain by a subsequent association—suggested by the couple's paired cartouches on a broken glass finger ring now in Berlin (fig. 65)[81]—with Tutankhamen's successor, the God's Father Ay (perhaps her maternal grandfather). This alliance followed Tutankhamen's untimely death—quite possibly murder[82]—after his ninth year of rule. The fate of Ankhesenamen—whose children by Tutankhamen died before or close to birth, denying the continuation of Akhenaten's line—is unknown.

1. Wildung 1997a; Dodson 1990, pp. 87–88; see Vandersleyen 1995, p. 398, n. 2.

2. See D. Redford 1967, pp. 88–169; Murnane 1977, pp. 123–69; W. R. Johnson 1990, pp. 42–46.

3. See J. R. Harris 1975, pp. 98–101.

4. Fritz 1991, pp. 207–14; Moran 1992, pp. xxxvii–xxxviii, n. 135, and p. 90, n. 20. The letter in question is EA 27, from the diplomatic correspondence in Akkadian cuneiform found at Amarna in 1887.

5. See van Siclen 1973.

6. Harris and Wente 1980, pp. 202, 208–9. The mummy was identified by the Dynasty 21 restorers' dockets on the wrappings and coffin.

7. Robins 1981a.

8. Reeves forthcoming.

9. *Pace* Loeben 1986; Krauss 1997b.

10. Letter EA 17.

11. Letters EA 22–24.

12. Legrain 1903; Legrain 1904—as observed by Millet 1988 and J. R. Harris 1993.

13. Davis et al. 1907; Quibell 1908; Reeves 1990b, pp. 148–53.

14. Aldred 1957, p. 32.

15. Epigraphic Survey 1980, pls. 8–9.

16. EA 26.

17. N. de G. Davies 1903–8, vol. 3, esp. pl. VIII.

18. Raven 1994. The principal burial chamber was E.

19. Davis et al. 1910, esp. pls. 28–29, 31–33 (=Davis et al. 1990, pls. 30–31, 33–35); M. Bell 1990, pp. 120–32.

20. See Reeves 1990b, p. 44.

21. Germer 1984.

22. Egyptian Museum, Cairo, CG 61070; see J. E. Harris et al. 1978.

23. See Hayes 1951, fig. 8, no. 95, and Leahy 1978, pl. 9, no. 107.

24. Helck 1969.

25. Hayes 1951, fig. 11, no. 137.

26. Block 831–VIIIC.

27. Gohary 1992, p. 30.

28. See Harris and Manniche 1976, p. 10. Other authorities, however, reject the idea of more than one *sed*-festival.

29. Reeves and Wilkinson 1996, pp. 113–15.

30. Murnane and van Siclen 1993.

31. Ibid., p. 213, n. 66.

32. Aten names: Baines and Málek 1980, p. 45.

33. Munro 1986 and Munro 1987 (summarizing Perepelkin 1967, 1984, vol. 1).

34. Reeves 1997.

35. Ägyptisches Museum, Berlin, 21300.

36. J. R. Harris 1976; J. R. Harris 1977b.

37. J. R. Harris, personal communication.

38. Despite much speculation to the contrary, Mutbenret seems to be no relation to Horemheb's wife, Mutnodjmet. *Pace* Hari 1976, et al.

39. See Vandersleyen 1995, p. 426.

40. Reeves 1978.

41. J. R. Harris 1977a.

42. J. R. Harris 1973b. The stela is Ägyptisches Museum, Berlin, 17813.

43. *Contra*: Krauss 1997b.

44. Samson 1976, pp. 34–35.

45. See J. R. Harris 1973a; J. R. Harris 1973b; J. R. Harris 1974b.

46. Other candidates have been proposed: Kiya (Perepelkin 1978, Helck 1984); and Meretaten (Krauss 1978, Gabolde 1993).

47. Samson 1976, pp. 36–37; Krauss 1978, pp. 30–36; Krauss 1990, pp. 210–12.

48. J. R. Harris 1992, p. 60.

49. N. de G. Davies 1903–8, vol. 3, pls. IV, VI, VIII–IX, XVIII.

50. N. de G. Davies 1903–8, vol. 3, pls. XIII–XV; vol. 2, pls. XXXVII–XL.

51. Petrie Museum, University College London, UC. 410 (+Egyptian Museum, Cairo, JE 64959): Martin 1974, p. 268; J. Allen 1988b, p. 118–19; Krauss 1989; Gabolde 1990.

52. Theban Tomb 139; see Gardiner 1928, pp. 10–11, with pls. 5–6.

53. J. R. Harris 1992, p. 60.

54. The name "Smenkhkara" may have been adopted before Akhenaten's death: see the jar inscriptions discussed by Loeben 1991 and Loeben 1994.

55. N. de G. Davies 1903–8, vol. 2, pl. XLI.

56. Reeves 1990b, pp. 42–49, but see J. Allen 1988b, pp. 121–26.

57. See J. Allen 1988b, p. 121, n. 31; J. Allen 1994, p. 8, n. 6; Hussein and Harris 1988, pp. 140–41.

58. See Robins 1981b.

59. J. R. Harris 1973a.

60. See J. R. Harris 1992.

61. Namely Tutankhamen's widow, Ankhesenamen (see Vergote 1961, and, most recently, Bryce 1990); for the possible claims of Meretaten, see Vandersleyen 1995, p. 460.

62. J. R. Harris 1993 and Krauss 1996.

63. Güterbock 1956.

64. See Vandersleyen 1995, p. 458, n. 1 and van den Hout 1994.

65. See the claimed occurrence of an erased "Smenkhkara" cartouche on one of Tutankhamen's miniature canopic coffinettes: Dodson 1994a, p. 62.

66. J. R. Harris 1974a; Krauss 1986a; Reeves 1988. For Kiya's portraits see J. R. Harris 1974a, pp. 28–29, n. 5 (Ägyptisches Museum, Berlin, 21239, 21341; Pushkin Museum, Moscow, 2141) and Krauss 1986a, p. 80 (suggesting further Ägyptisches Museum, Berlin, 21245).

67. Hanke 1978 believed "Kiya" was merely a pet-name of Nefertiti.

68. Cooney 1965, cat. 12 (Brooklyn Museum of Art, New York, 60.197.8). Meretaten-tasherit and Ankhesenpaaten-tasherit (see further below) have been mooted as possible candidates (J. R. Harris 1974a, p. 30, n. 6), as has Baketaten (Gabolde 1992a; van Dijk 1995).

69. J. R. Harris 1974a, p. 30, n. 6.

70. Jørgensen 1992, pp. 6–7 (Ny Carlsberg Glyptotek, Copenhagen, AEIN 1797).

71. Martin 1974, 1989, vol. 2, pl. 58. The relief is on wall F of room *alpha*.

72. Perepelkin 1978, pp. 117–20; Manniche 1975b; but see van Dijk 1995.

73. Martin 1974, 1989, vol. 2, pp. 27–41 (but see Vandersleyen 1993).

74. See Reeves 1990b, pp. 42–49.

75. J. R. Harris 1974b, pp. 29–30; Hanke 1978.

76. Murnane and van Siclen 1993, p. 178.

77. Ibid. Meketaten's added image is on Boundary Stela K.

78. Martin 1974, 1989, vol. 2, pp. 42–45. Room *gamma*, wall A.

79. Harris and Manniche 1976; Eaton-Krauss 1990, pp. 546–47.

80. J. R. Harris 1973b.

81. Krauss and Ullrich 1982.

82. Reeves 1990a.

The New Religion

John L. Foster

Although Atenism developed out of the worship of Egypt's traditional sun gods, Akhenaten designated the solar disk (Aten) as the only god, responsible for all creation.

The religion of ancient Egypt had many gods. They came with greater or lesser powers, from diverse places of origin, and ruled over different domains. Atum ("the Totality") was the god who created light and the cosmos out of the dark, windy, watery chaos that preceded creation. His children, Tefnut and Shu, the first couple, were moisture and air; and their children, Nut and Geb, were the heavens and the earth. Then there was Ra, the sun god from Heliopolis, the first center of Egyptian religious activity. And there was Ptah of Memphis, the divine craftsman. Both of these later also developed into creator gods. Thoth was the moon god and the god of justice, records, scribes, and the sacred writings. Osiris was the ruler of the afterworld (also called the underworld or otherworld), originally a good king slain by his jealous brother Seth, but regenerated by his sister/wife, the great goddess Isis, who later bore Horus, their son. There was Hathor, the goddess of love, pleasure, and merry-making; and Sakhmet, the lion goddess, of pestilence and punishment. Khnum was the potter god from Elephantine, who created humankind on his potter's wheel, and Hapi, the divine force that brought the Nile flood each year. And among many others, there was Amen, "the Hidden One," whose major development did not occur until the Middle Kingdom (about 1980 to 1630 B.C.), in Thebes, but who came to represent the chief and most powerful god in Egypt. Even the king was divine; he was the living Horus, given the land and people of Egypt to rule and care for during his time on earth. After "death" he simply returned to dwell eternally with his peers, the gods, while his eldest son became the new embodiment of Horus on earth.

Sun Hymns in Ancient Egypt

The Egyptians worshipped these gods in several ways: through rituals and other activities in the temples, festival days dedicated to each deity, and, in writing, through hymns and prayers. As early as the Pyramid Texts of Dynasties 5 and 6, about 2300 B.C., the deified king himself prays to the gods. He envisions himself as a star fading in the dawn light:

> I have come to you, O Nephthys,
> > I have come to you, Sun Bark of night;
> I have come to you, You who are Just in the Reddening;

Fig. 66 Detail of a colossal statue of Amenhotep IV/Akhenaten from Karnak (Egyptian Museum, Cairo; full view, fig. 4)

I have come to you, Stars of the Northern Sky—
  remember me.

Gone is Orion, caught by the underworld,
  yet cleansed and alive in the Beyond;
Gone is Sothis, caught by the underworld,
  yet cleansed and alive in the Beyond.
Gone am I, caught by the underworld,
  yet cleansed and alive in the Beyond.

It is well with me, with them,
  it is quiet for me, for them,
Within the arms of my father,
  within the arms of Atum.[1]

Unlike this expression of faith, serenity, and trust in Atum, a great many of the earlier hymns were directed to Ra, the sun god, who replaced Atum as chief god; Atum became an aspect of Ra. An entire tradition of hymns developed in praise of the sun god, either as Horakhty (god of the resurrected and rising sun of morning), as Ra himself (god of the sun in its course across the sky during the day), or as Atum (who became the fading sun at the end of day as the god goes to his rest in the otherworld, to undergo rejuvenation and be reborn the next day).

Ra, chief deity of the Old Kingdom and sharing that eminence with Amen through the Middle Kingdom and most of Dynasty 18 in the New, was worshipped as creator, maintainer, and guide of the universe. Part of one hymn specifically to Ra says,

Hail to you,
  Great One and son of a Great One!
The walls of the Shrine of the South are eager for you
  and the Shrine of the North attends you;
The doors to the windows of heaven open for you
  and the ways of the sunlight are loosened.[2]

A term that came to be associated with the solar hymns was *Itn* (Aten or Aton), which designated the physical disk of the sun where dwelt the divinity of the sun god, Ra himself. An early use of this term is seen in the opening lines of "The Tale of Sinuhe," where the deceased King Amenemhat I, founder of Dynasty 12, "rose to the sky, united with the aten, the royal body commingling with Him who made him."[3]

Well into the 18th Dynasty, during the reign of Amenhotep III, the Aten itself begins to display attributes of the divine and to be thought of as a deity. One of the most striking bits of such evidence is the "Hymn of Suty and Hor," who were overseers of the herds of Amen in the reign of Amenhotep III. The hymn is divided into three parts, the first of which is addressed to Amen as Ra-Horakhty ("The praise of Amen when he rises as Ra-Horakhty"). The third portion is a small-scale biography of the twin brothers. But it is the second section that is of most interest. Amen is here equated with

Aten, who is a god, no longer a physical sun-disk:

> Hail to you, Aten, Sundisk of day,
>   who have fashioned all things and made them to live;
> Great Falcon with many-hued plumes,
>   Scarab who raised himself up by himself,
> Who came into existence all by himself, not being born,
>   Elder Horus in the midst of the sky ...[4]

In this poem many of the Egyptian deities who figured in the more traditional sun hymns are pictured as outgrowths or forms of Aten, who is himself taking on the attributes of Ra. That these two deities should be equated with Amen is striking.

"The Great Hymn to Aten"

Then, about 1350 B.C., everything seemed to change. Amenhotep IV came to the throne. Perhaps trained by the priests of Heliopolis, the seat of Ra in an age of Amen, he brought with him his new awareness of the Egyptian sun god, Aten; changed his own name to Akhenaten ("One Who Serves Aten"); and introduced what we now call the Amarna Period in Egyptian history. A good deal of evidence survives from this period — from statuary and small objects, from buildings, from the history carved in picture and hieroglyph on the walls of these buildings and of the tombs cut into the Amarna hillsides. The evidence includes, of course, the ruins of the palace-city of Akhetaten, Akhenaten's hand-picked site for the worship of Aten.

One of the most precious of the survivals is a poem called "The Great Hymn to Aten." It is one of the most significant and splendid pieces of poetry to survive from the pre-Homeric world. The most complete version is carved on the wall of the tomb of Ay (fig. 67), the courtier who later became pharaoh for a few years, following the death of Tutankhamen. The poem is "spoken" by Akhenaten, though there is no proof that the king himself composed the hymn. The text was a popular one in the tombs behind Akhetaten, where no fewer than five copies are extant, and this popularity may point to a central document or body of doctrine promulgated by Akhenaten. In his tomb Ay says that he followed the king's "teaching" and that the king himself gave instruction in it. "The Great Hymn to Aten" may be a digest or the core of that teaching.

The poem is an expression of ecstatic joy in creation, the creatures, and the god who created it all. The world basks in divine light; the human creatures and the animals offer worship; and the world scene is one of plenitude and order. A sense of awe underlies the poem.

Fig. 67 The Great Hymn

Carved in its most complete version in the Amarna tomb of the official Ay, "The Great Hymn to Aten" remains one of the world's outstanding examples of religious literature.

The poem opens with sunrise, the dawn of a new day:[5]

> *Let your holy Light shine from the height of heaven,*
>   *O living Aten,*
>   *source of all life!*
> *From eastern horizon risen and streaming,*
>   *you have flooded the world with your beauty.*

With night—sunset—comes darkness, a darkness like death because of the absence of Aten, who lies low in his "tomb." Then, after this pause of darkness the new dawn comes, treated almost as a resurrection of light (a point present in the sun hymns since early times). The creatures rise, bathe, and give praise to Aten, and then turn to their tasks.

> *The herds are at peace in their pastures,*
>   *trees and the vegetation grow green;*
> *Birds start from their nests,*
>   *wings wide spread to worship your Person.*

Procreation also is the work of Aten, overseen by the god whether it concerns as small a creature as a chick breaking out of its shell or a person being born:

> *When the new one descends from the womb*
>   *to draw breath the day of his birth,*
> *You open his mouth, you shape his nature,*
>   *and you supply all his necessities.*

The plenitude and intricacy of the creation are praised:

> *How various is the world you have created,*
>   *each thing mysterious, sacred to sight,*
> *O sole God,*
>   *beside whom is no other!*
> *You fashioned earth to your heart's desire,*
>   *while you were still alone,*
> *Filled it with man and the family of creatures,*
>   *each kind on the ground, those who go upon feet,*
>   *he on high soaring on wings,*
> *The far lands of Khor and Kush,*
>   *and the rich Black Land of Egypt.*

Aten places each creature in its proper station, and he makes Hapi, the Nile River, nourish not only the land of Egypt but all the foreign countries as well. He is a universal god, working through the river, the sunlight, and the succession of the seasons:

> *How splendidly ordered are they,*
>   *your purposes for this world.*

As the poem rises toward its climax, the oneness of god is reiterated:

> You are the one God,
> > shining forth from your possible incarnations
> > > as Aten, the Living Sun,
> Revealed like a king in glory, risen in light,
> > now distant, now bending nearby.
> You create the numberless things of this world
> > > from yourself, who are One alone—
> > cities, towns, fields, the roadway, the River;
> And each eye looks back and beholds you
> > to learn from the day's light perfection.

In the final section Akhenaten portrays himself as having Aten in his heart—no one truly knows Aten except for his only son, Akhenaten. He asks Aten for wisdom and guidance in helping the creatures aspire to Aten's condition. Then, after another cycle of night and day, darkness followed by light, Akhenaten ends his "teaching":

> Lift up the creatures of earth for your Son
> > who came forth from your Body of Fire!

This sketch of the poem's contents has been made to convey its major assertions and to give a hint of its tone and flavor. Some scholars have maintained that the Great Hymn contains few original phrases or concepts, that almost every phrase and image has its parallels in other sun hymns. To an extent, this is true and, apart from its beauty as a poem, "The Great Hymn to Aten" can be characterized more by what has been left out than what has been put into it. More of this in a moment.

Atenism, the Religion of Akhenaten

Aten developed out of the tradition of the sun gods of Egypt, particularly Ra, once that god took the place of Atum as chief of the Ennead (the conclave of the Nine Great Gods ruling the universe). Aten is Akhenaten's understanding of the sun god in the mid-fourteenth century B.C., toward the end of Dynasty 18. He bears many of the characteristics of Ra, and in a way he is Ra. (Note that one of the names of Akhenaten is Waenra, "the One Belonging to Ra.")

What can be said about the characteristics of Aten?

First of all, Aten is one. He is a unity, the only deity, the lord of the universe. This status was not established immediately upon Akhenaten's ascension to the throne. As many have pointed out, Aten's name was written in cartouches, just as the earthly pharaohs' names had been for dynasties. An early inscription in these cartouches includes the names of Ra-Horakhty; Shu, the air god; and the goddess Maat (Truth), written with the goddess sign of a seated female figure with the feather of truth on her head. But on into the reign, Aten's cartouches were changed to omit the first two of these deities, and Maat was written phonetically, without the goddess sign. That is, Maat had become a concept—to be sure, the concept associated with Akhenaten, the one in harmony with which he ruled. For Maat, deified or not, was a central concept in ancient Egypt, a fusion of the modern ideas of not only truth, but justice and cosmic order. In the evidence we have, especially in the Great Hymn, Akhenaten's emphasis was primarily upon the cosmic order created by Aten.

Aten is alone. The hymn specifically states that he fashioned the world while he was alone, introducing the divine mystery of how the Many (the multifariousness of the cosmos) came out of the One. This oneness is contrasted later in the poem with the various visible forms that Aten might take while still remaining himself.

Aten is creator of the universe. This is apparent throughout the hymn and is nothing new in the tradition of the sun hymns. The supreme god in Egypt had always been the god of creation.

Aten is the span of time. Toward the end of the poem, in a passage difficult to interpret, Akhenaten seems to say that the universe will end sometime in the future:

> Once you rose into shining, they [the creatures] lived;
>   when you sink to rest, they shall die.
> For it is you who are Time itself,
>   the span of the world;
>   life is by means of you.

In the poem this passage is followed by sunset and evening rest. But the end of the creation is still far off; the poem closes with the triumphant return of Aten, his resurrection and rebirth, so that the creation revives once more.

Aten is universal. In earlier dynasties the supreme god tended to be the god of Egypt alone. The wider and farther-ranging experience of Egyptians with foreign countries and peoples provided an awareness of other ways and other gods. This in turn resulted in the Egyptian supreme deity, whether Ra, Amen, or Aten, becoming a universal god, ruling over and caring for all peoples and countries. In the Great Hymn, Aten cares for the mountain countries by giving them a celestial Nile to rain down on their fields and villages, and he is specifically the god of Khor (Syria-Palestine) and Kush (Nubia) as well as the Black Land (Egypt).

Aten is light. Light is pervasive in Akhenaten's hymn; images describe the divine light falling upon the objects of the world, bathing them in light, striking deep into the Great Green Sea, opening and securing the roadways. If there is a set of contrasting images— a fundamental motif—to the poem, it is the contrast between light and darkness, the rising and setting of the sun, life and death; between the darkness of chaos and the creation of light in the Beginning, when the creator god began to organize the universe, turning disorder into cosmos. Perhaps this is why Amarna temples and family shrines lacked roofs—the rays of Aten could directly penetrate the lives of the worshippers. Those same rays were depicted as ending in caressing or caring hands when bathing the royal family (figs. 68, 70).

Fig. 68 **Akhenaten as a sphinx (facing left)** (cat. 89)

Akhenaten was often shown as a sphinx, a powerful royal image linked to the sun god as it rises in the east. Here the loving rays of Aten reach out to the king, offering life, protection, and sustenance.

Aten is beauty. This follows from the previous characteristic: Aten's light gives the definition and contour to objects that make them beautiful. There is a perfection to the objects of the creation, and to the creation in general, that gives rise to the adoration so widely expressed, not only in the Great Hymn, but everywhere carved on the *talatat*, or blocks, of the Amarna Period buildings. In his hymn, in addition to cosmic order, Akhenaten stresses those aspects of Maat that we would see as beauty.

Aten is love. This may not seem so evident at first; yet it is certainly attested in the poem, and it is one of the characteristics that make Aten a bit different from Ra. Indeed, this attention to the created objects (persons, animals, plants—all of it), this compassion for his creation, has perhaps not been stressed enough in treatment of the hymn and of Akhenaten's conception of god, and thus in our understanding of the Amarna religion. This caring is obvious in the wall-carvings, but it is seconded by phrasing in the hymn. Aten bends low, near the earth, to watch over his creation; he takes his place in the sky for the same purpose; he wearies himself in the service of the creatures; he shines for them all; he gives them sun and sends them rain. The unborn child and the baby chick are cared for; and Akhenaten asks his divine father to "lift up" the creatures for his sake so that they might aspire to the condition or perfection of his father, Aten.

Aten is father. Aten has a caring, paternal attitude toward his creation; indeed, the creatures are a family. In a cosmic sense, of course, Aten is the father of all; but in this hymn he is specifically father to the divine king Akhenaten, his only son, who came forth from his own body. Indeed, Pharaoh had been the son of the sun as far back as Dynasty 6 in the Old Kingdom. But taken in conjunction with the ideas of the cosmos

Fig. 69 Fragment of a column drum featuring the royal family worshipping (cat. 69)

The many representations of the royal family worshipping Aten are evidence of the central role the family played in the spiritual life of the city.

as Aten's own creation, his care for the totality as well as the individual, and his paternity of the king, it is not too great a step for Aten to become God the Father.

Finally, Aten is within. He lives within the consciousness (heart) of Akhenaten, his son, the only one who truly comprehends his father. Akhenaten asks for wisdom and guidance from Aten, and asks him to nurture ("lift up") the creatures of earth for Akhenaten's sake. As with the concept of "God the Father," the concept of "the god within" is not widely applied; in this hymn it pertains only to the king himself. In this case, however, there is a bit of additional evidence, from the prayers in the tomb of Pahery of Esna, earlier in Dynasty 18:

> *I came and went*
> > *with my heart my sole companion.*
> *I did not speak falsely to another person,*
> > *knowing the god who dwells in humankind—*
> *I could perceive him*
> > *and thus distinguish one path from another.*[6]

How widespread this concept of "the god within" was is unknown, but it obviously extended beyond the person of Pharaoh.

Other divine attributes might be cited; Aten was order, plenitude, sovereign, and fate, in the sense of the god determining human destinies. But the foregoing are sufficient to indicate the character of Akhenaten's god. In the Great Hymn these attributes are presented as praises of Aten in a tone of happiness and joy that borders on ecstasy.

What does *not* appear in the hymn is reference to any of the other gods of traditional Egyptian religion, alone or together. Nor is there reference to the realm of the dead, the Osirian afterworld. It is these two characteristics that mark this hymn as so different from traditional sun hymns. For instance, only a hundred years after Akhenaten and the Amarna interlude, the Leiden Hymns (so called because the papyrus on which these hymns were written is housed in the Netherlands) to Amen, whose worship had been restored throughout Egypt, show the poet-theologian grappling once more with the problem of the One and the Many. His solution is to present the other Egyptian gods as manifestations or appearances *(kheperu)* of the one god, Amen. In Leiden Hymn 200, the poet says:

> *Rê himself joins to shine in God's visible form,*
> > *and God is that Craftsman [Ptah] praised in the city of Sun;*

> *What is said of the earth god in truth pictures him;*
> *and when Amen emerged from out the ur-waters,*
> *it was God's image strode over them.*
> *He flowed forth again as the eight of Hermopolis,*
> *procreated the primal deities, was midwife to Rê,*
> *Perfected himself in Atum—one flesh together;*
> *and he alone, Lord of all things at creation.*[7]

In the religion at Amarna there was no mention of Osiris or the elaborate preparations and rituals for the dead, those activities that took so much time and wealth to ensure eternal life for the deceased. (Indeed, in the Book of the Dead, the deceased was so much identified with Osiris that he or she was called "an Osiris.") At Amarna, the dead did continue to live on, worshipping Aten each day at sunrise; but what they did or where they were during the time Aten was below the horizon was not specified.

Akhenaten, the High Priest of Aten

The figure responsible for all the change at Amarna was a son of Amenhotep III, the Sun King. He came to the throne in about 1353 B.C. as Amenhotep IV, ruled for about seventeen years, and then disappeared from history. Almost every aspect of his actions, his character, and his beliefs is still controversial. His religion disappeared with him; it was later dismissed as heresy and he himself branded "the criminal of Akhetaten."

Akhenaten remains enigmatic still. He has been called "the first individual in history," a "god-intoxicated man," a visionary, the first monotheist—but also a freak, a virtual "atheist," and an "intellectual lightweight."[8] The religion he articulated has been called henotheism,[9] pantheism, or monotheism; the only name it has not been given is polytheism. Surviving portraits and statues show him as misshapen, with an elongated head and chin, female breasts and hips, spindly arms and legs, and a protruding belly—a person distorted and seemingly diseased.

How can such a picture of the grotesque be reconciled with the beauties and insights of the Great Hymn or the flowing and sinuous lines of Amarna art? Perhaps they cannot be reconciled on the basis of existing evidence; and as scholars attempt to interpret known facts, they come up with varying and often conflicting conclusions.

Akhenaten, like all his predecessors on the throne of Egypt, was a god on earth: they all were sons of Ra or, later, of Amen, the Hidden One. But, as the Great Hymn clearly states, Akhenaten is the only son of Aten, the sole God.

> *There is no other who truly knows you*
> *but for your son, Akhenaten.*
> *May you make him wise with your inmost counsels,*
> *wise with your power,*
> *that earth may aspire to your godhead,*
> *its creatures fine as the day you made them.*

Akhenaten alone knows the will of Aten; and he is its sole interpreter. Some have called Akhenaten a kind of prophet; but unlike other prophets, he is also a divine son.

Akhenaten began his career at Thebes, in apparent harmony with the priesthoods of the other Egyptian gods. He built there—witness his great temple at East Karnak (the Gempaaten). But the Aten cult was in direct competition with the cult of Amen, which had grown increasingly wealthy in the New Kingdom and especially under Amenhotep III. A break with the other priesthoods came in Akhenaten's fifth regnal year; and he moved his court to Amarna, the place in Middle Egypt that he dedicated to Aten and named Akhetaten ("the Horizon [or Holy Precinct] of Aten"). Here he built a new capital, and vowed never to leave Aten's holy territory. The believers—the Atenists—went with him and established the court. The temples back in Thebes and elsewhere in the land were presumably closed and the worship of the other Egyptian gods banned. However, it seems that only Amen and his priests were pursued with a particular fury. Amen's name was hacked from the temples in an attempt to efface his memory; and even plural signs (which intimated a plural number of gods) were destroyed. This essentially left only Aten. But the evidence becomes particularly sketchy here: it comes primarily from Akhetaten and the people loyal to Aten. We do not know much about how the people fared outside the royal city.

Akhenaten designated himself the high priest of Aten, but another high priest (or priestess) served alongside him—Nefertiti, his wife and queen. As the evidence becomes clearer, it seems that she was all but Akhenaten's equal—in divinity, in rank, in officiating at the offering to Aten, in her omnipresence at Akhenaten's side. Nefertiti is the goddess, the female principle, in the Amarna religion (fig. 69). The prologue and epilogue of the Great Hymn give her status equal to the king's. The implications of all this are not yet clear; but one might start with the idea that Aten was both mother and father to the creation. And as at least one scholar has said, Akhenaten and Nefertiti were equated with Shu and Tefnut, the first sexually differentiated offspring of the androgynous god of creation (fig. 71). Thus, they form a true divine pair, the beginning of the differentiation of the One into the Many. The king and queen, under Aten, symbolize this differentiation. The androgyny of the creator god and the differentiation in the second generation of gods may relate to the shape of the Amarna figures of the king and queen, as well as the nude but sexless colossal statues of Akhenaten.

The institution of the Holy Family also was present at Akhetaten. It had long been comfortable in the traditional religion of Egypt. At Memphis there was Ptah; his consort, Sakhmet; and their son, Nefertem. At Thebes we have Amen; his consort, Mut; and their son, Khonsu. The most famous of these triads, with its own myth, was that of Osiris, the dying and reviving god; his sister/wife Isis; and their child, Horus, who ascended the throne of Egypt after the death of his father. At Amarna, the Family consisted of Akhentaten, Nefertiti, and their six daughters. Not only are one or more of the children depicted in formal or ritual scenes with their parents; they also join them in informal family scenes, suggesting the value of family life, with the affection and intimacy natural to its activities (fig. 70).

Fig. 71 Sphere with mythological scene (cat. 97)

Akhenaten and Nefertiti were often worshipped as Shu and Tefnut, children of the androgynous god of creation.

Fig. 70 Painted limestone stela of the royal family (Egyptian Museum, Cairo)

Intimate domestic scenes of the royal family under the nurturing rays of Aten were featured on stelae installed in household shrines.

Fig. 72 The god Bes (cat. 181)

Although Aten may have been the sole god worshipped by Akhenaten, age-old household gods such as the leonine Bes remained popular among Amarna's inhabitants.

Effects of the New Religion

Akhenaten and Nefertiti worshipped Aten directly, and the nobles gathered at Amarna worshipped the king and queen as divinities. Remains of family shrines in the villas of the nobility, open to the air and Aten's rays, show the family worshipping the Holy Family of Akhetaten. It is more difficult to determine how the humbler people worshipped. Presumably at Akhetaten they worshipped both the Holy Family and Aten. But one wonders if, outside the sacred precinct of the royal city, people did not simply continue their traditional ways, worshipping not so much the great cosmic gods and Amen as lesser and more personal deities like Bes (fig. 72) and Taweret (fig. 15).

The fate of the other gods during the Amarna Period is sketchy at best. They were certainly demoted or de-emphasized, but, at least during the early years of Akhenaten's reign, they seem to have been tolerated. Only Amen was the object of animus, probably because he had become the most powerful god, and had the most powerful priesthood, in Egypt. Exactly what caused the break is speculation, but it could well have been a new and inexperienced pharaoh, with a new vision of God to give the world, insisting on his own way against a powerful, perhaps complacent, and highly traditional priesthood. That is, a combination of religious ideals and a political power struggle caused the break.

With the god Osiris, there was no pursuit or persecution; the entire Osirian religion simply disappeared. Aten was interested in life, fertility, abundance, joy, and light. The dead did live on; mummification of the body continued; tombs were cut into rock; and funeral ceremonies were held. But the whole rich mythology of the weighing of the deceased's heart against the feather of Maat—with the resulting judgment of vindicated or doomed—was ignored. The passage of the sun god through the underworld, the feasting of the redeemed with Osiris each day, life in the underworld and invisible passage back to the scenes of one's former life—all these ceased to exist in the Amarna religion. The dead had eternal life with Aten, but the process of resurrection is not mentioned.

The Fate of Atenism

It is probable that worship of Aten was essentially limited to the city of Akhetaten and its inhabitants—some were firm believers in the religion, some were probably hangers-on, some were opportunists who advanced their careers by following Akhenaten and Nefertiti. Atenism also was probably limited to court circles and, at most, many of the citizens of Akhetaten. The humble people of Egypt, whose views we cannot detect, probably toiled on as before the change in official religion, perhaps giving lip-service to Aten, but offering their private devotions to their local gods or the great cosmic deities of the traditional religion.

Akhenaten did not begin his royal career as a monotheist. Especially when he was still at Thebes, he tolerated the traditional Egyptian gods while developing his vision of

Aten. But once events drove him to build Akhetaten, and still at his death, in about 1336 B.C., Aten was sole god, creator of the cosmos, father and mother of all creatures, watchful, caring, nurturing, source of all light and joy, lover of beauty and order, ruling in harmony with Maat, and governing Egypt through the divine son of his body, King Akhenaten.

Atenism failed. Akhenaten's successor, King Nefernefruaten (quite possibly Nefertiti) began reverting to the worship of Amen, even at Akhetaten. Next came Smenkhkara, for a very short reign; then Tutankhaten, who soon became Tutankhamen, ruling for some ten years. At his death, the elderly Ay took the throne, only to be succeeded, after a reign of three years, by General Horemheb. Dynasty 18 ended in about 1292 B.C.

Twenty years after it began, and three years after Akhenaten's death, the worship of Aten was already on the wane. The clearest indication of this is the name-change of the boy-king who became Tutankhamen, shifting the royal allegiance from Aten to Amen. The old temples reopened, the traditional priesthoods were reactivated; and Egypt—probably with a sigh of relief—returned to the worship of its age-old gods, those who appeared in the Beginning out of the chaos of Nun, the primordial waters.

The Legacy

> But, one alone is the hidden God,
> being behind these appearances,
> veiled even from gods,
> his nature cannot be known;
> He is more distant far than heaven,
> deeper profound than the world below,
> not all gods in concert discern his true features.
> No likeness of him is sketched on papyri,
> no eyewitness tellings to picture him.[10]

This passage—again from Leiden Hymn 200, to Amen, a century after Amarna—shows that the idea of the one god persisted even in the return of polytheism to Egypt, and that the Ramesside poet-theologians were still at work tracing the Many back to the One.

---

1. From Pyramid Text 216. Foster 1995, pp. 30–31. All translations of texts in this essay are the author's.

2. Pyramid Text 456. Foster 1995, p. 38.

3. Foster 1992, p. 86.

4. Stela of Suty and Hor. Foster 1992, p. 57.

5. "The Great Hymn to Aten" can be found in Foster 1992, pp. 5–10. There is also a good translation by William Murnane: Murnane 1995b, pp. 112–16 (§58-B.4). A good translation in German is by Jan Assmann, one of the foremost students of Egyptian religion: Assmann 1975, #92.

6. From "The Prayers of Pahery," Foster 1995, p. 130.

7. Foster 1992, p. 75.

8. Breasted 1934, p. 292, and D. Redford 1984, p. 233.

9. Belief in one god without denying the existence of others.

10. Foster 1992, p. 75.

Art in the Service of Religion and the State

Rita E. Freed

By means of his art, Akhenaten promoted a new god and enhanced the
status of the royal family. In the
process, he elicited from his legion
of artists works of great beauty that
celebrate the natural world and the
details of daily life.

For fifteen hundred years Egyptian art remained largely static and unchanging. Aloof, youthful faces and perfectly sculpted bodies in a set repertoire of poses formed an ideal that was ageless and timeless. Then came Akhenaten.

The genius of Akhenaten's art was its ability to bend and stretch a fifteen-hundred-year-old framework so that it met the demands of a new religion and a new political order. Innovation within tradition had characterized the earlier years of the New Kingdom, especially during the reign of Amenhotep III, Akhenaten's father (see the essay "The Setting: History, Religion, and Art"). But it was Akhenaten who went further than any prior king to create a novel artistic vocabulary to serve his needs.

This new vocabulary permeated every aspect of society, affecting representations of the royal family, high officials, common workmen, and foreigners. While it presented constraints, particularly with regard to depictions of Egypt's myriad gods, it also allowed artists a new creative license, and they exploited this license to the utmost. As a result, in more than three thousand years of ancient Egyptian art, what was produced during Akhenaten's seventeen-year reign stands apart and is immediately recognizable. Moreover, it created shock waves whose ripples are still felt today.

The Early Years

Works from the beginning of the reign of Akhenaten—then still known as Amenhotep IV—betray no sign of the radical style and iconography that was to develop within a short time. A large-scale smiting scene from Karnak (fig. 74),[1] for example, is traditional in every way. But it was left unfinished.

Akhenaten's early years remain a mystery for scholars of art history as well as for general historians. Many scholars believe that, as Amenhotep IV, he at first ruled jointly with his father.[2] According to an intriguing theory proposed by W. Raymond Johnson,[3] Amenhotep IV functioned as high priest of his deified-but-still-living father, who had assimilated with a multitude of Egypt's gods, most notably the falcon-headed sun-god Ra-Horakhty. Some early works created under Amenhotep IV at Karnak show him in conjunction with that falcon-headed god (fig. 75).[4] The king's pudgy face and stocky build, executed in relatively flat and unadorned raised relief, are reminiscent of what has been called the youthful style of Amenhotep III's later years,[5] and were it not

Fig. 74 Reconstruction of an unfinished smiting scene of Amenhotep IV from Karnak

A king with upraised arm, preparing to smite Egypt's foes, is one of the most potent of pharaonic images. The subject dates back to the beginning of Egyptian history.

for the cartouche of Amenhotep IV, the image would be thought to represent his father.[6] On another large block in yet a different style (fig. 38), a fleshy, full-bellied Amenhotep IV twice offers incense to the sun god shown as a disk, called Aten, whose rays end in human hands presenting him with the hieroglyphic symbols for power and jubilee festivals. This form of Aten[7] became the most important element in Akhenaten's art and iconography for the remainder of his reign. Whether or not Amenhotep III was alive when these blocks were carved, his artisans must have been responsible for them, because stylistically they are similar to his late works.

The depiction of Amenhotep III (see fig. 28) and his son as portly represented a substantial departure from the age-old manner in which kings had been represented: trim, youthful, and idealized. But an even more dramatic break with the past may be found in the series of temples Amenhotep IV erected at Karnak's easternmost extreme. One temple, known as the Gempaaten ("Aten is Found"), consisted of a large court, about 600 meters long and 210 meters wide (2,000 feet by 700 feet), lined with a colonnade.[8] Resting against the piers of the south side of the colonnade and the southern half of the west wall were six-meter-tall (twenty-foot) sandstone images[9] of Akhenaten and possibly of his wife Nefertiti (figs. 4, 5), depicted in a manner that can only have been shocking to the ancient viewer accustomed to the traditional rendering of the human figure. As many as thirty such colossi, mostly fragmentary, have been found to date.[10]

In these colossi, the elongated head is made to appear taller with a high, often composite crown. The head and upper torso are an interplay of oblique lines, beginning with the diagonal folds of the *nemes* headcloth and continuing in the attenuated facial features. Slit eyes with sharply projecting upper lids angle inward toward the elongated nose, whose V-shaped tip matches the shape of the lips. A prominent pendant chin is given further emphasis by the long, narrow beard. The diagonals continue in the pronounced sinews of the neck and prominent collar bones, which parallel the lines of the king's crook and flail.

The narrow upper torso tapers further toward a high waist and then flares dramatically into voluptuous hips and a belly that pushes the belt of the kilt sharply downward into a U. The fullness of the legs continues only to the knees. The spindly calves would hardly have been able to bear the weight of the body had they not been anchored to a back pillar. Large plaques bearing Aten's name, placed like jewelry at the neck, upper and lower arms, and waist, further contribute to the eerie look of the colossus. Illuminated by the sun's raking light in the open-air courtyard, these statues, with their interplay of diagonals and plastic modeling, must have come alive to transport the viewer into a surreal world.

The distortions of each body part expressed a fundamental and deliberate change in the idea of how the body was constructed. According to standards of proportion from the Old Kingdom on, the standing figure was divided into eighteen equal units of height, with each line marking specific body parts. Under Amenhotep IV, two units were added above the knee, thereby increasing the height of the upper body relative to the lower.[11] Some of the king's ideas must have evolved as the colossi were carved, since many show corrections in the area of the eyes, the headgear, and the navel.

In other ways these statues are quite traditional. Their crossed arms holding the crook and flail suggest an association with Osiris, primeval king and god of the underworld and rebirth. Those with double crowns may represent Atum, the androgynous god, identified with the sun,[12] who created the world at the beginning of time. Those with feather crowns (at least four) evoke Shu,[13] his firtborn son, while those with tall crowns recall Tefnut, Shu's female twin. Thus the courtyard sculptures may have featured the triad of the sun god and his divine offspring—Atum, Shu, and Tefnut—representing Amenhotep III, Amenhotep IV, and Nefertiti respectively. One well-preserved colossus that appears to be nude seems especially suggestive of Nefertiti (fig. 5),[14] and others may have depicted her as well. Whether or not some of the colossi portrayed

Fig. 75 Amenhotep IV and Ra-Horakhty (cat. 20)

A pudgy-faced Amenhotep IV, from the early years of his reign, bears a great resemblance to late images of his father, Amenhotep III. The sun god, shown as the falcon-headed Ra-Horakhty, appears at left on this relief. Later in Akhenaten's reign the god would be represented solely as an abstract disk.

Fig. 76 The quarries at Gebel es-Silsileh.

Amenhotep IV's workers cut sandstone for his Karnak temples here.

Nefertiti, all of them have pronounced breasts and full hips, reflecting the fertility of nature or the dual masculine and feminine qualities embodied in the creator god and his son.[15] In any case, the decorative program of Amenhotep IV, at Karnak and later at Amarna, shows that Nefertiti enjoyed an exceedingly prominent role in religion, politics, and daily life. Changing gender roles seem to have gone hand-in-hand with a certain gender ambiguity.

Statuary was not the only decoration in Amenhotep IV's temples. The walls behind the colonnade in the Gempaaten, as well as the pillars and walls of his other Karnak temples, were covered with reliefs, which were later systematically dismantled and reused as ballast inside pylons at Karnak and elsewhere. They were distinctive not only because of their style of decoration, but also because of their material—sandstone[16] quarried from Gebel es-Silsileh (fig. 76)—and their small size (about 52 by 24 by 26 centimeters, or 20 by 10 by 10 inches), which made them light enough to be carried by a single person. The recovery, to date, of more than one hundred thousand[17] of these blocks known as *talatat* provides a unique opportunity to view the next stages in the evolution of Akhenaten's art, religion, and politics.

Construction of up to eight distinct temples or temple subdivisions[18] to the east and south of Karnak undoubtedly filled the precinct of the god Amen with a frenzy of activity. Building on such a grand scale[19] in a single location within a few years was unprecedented. This would never have been possible had Amenhotep III not employed a large contingent of artisans for his own extensive construction projects. And his son—to judge from the many different styles of sunk relief that decorated his temples—must have made use of every available one.

The Decoration of Amenhotep IV's Karnak Temples

Each temple or shrine appears to have had a distinct function within the king's theology, and its relief decoration was specific to that function.[20] Nevertheless, many themes developed for Karnak appear at Amarna as well. In fact, nearly all of the themes and vignettes generally associated with the art of Amarna actually originated in the creative environment of Karnak, where they were depicted on temple walls for the first time. Aten and the royal family were the primary subjects, replacing the traditional gods and the celebrations of their cults. Aten appeared, with repetition bordering on monotony, in nearly every scene with the royal family: its rays terminated in human hands caressing the king and Nefertiti, or offering them life. In return, the king offered Aten incense or food, or demonstrated his devotion by raising his hands in adoration or lying prostrate on the ground.[21] Tables were piled high with additional food for Aten. The royal family riding in chariots between temple and palace replaced the divine processions of former times, in which images of the gods in their shrines were conveyed by boat or on the shoulders of priests between Karnak and Luxor. Retinues of servants, bowing low, assisted the king, entertained him, or guarded him. A substantial number

Figs. 77, 78 Nefertiti in two styles
These *talatat* reliefs are both from Amenhotep IV's Karnak period. Nefertiti in the extreme style (cat. 27), at left, has an elongated face, pendant chin, and angular features. Nefertiti shaking a sistrum (cat. 26) is more characteristic of works from the time of the king's father, Amenhotep III.

of these attendants were Syrian or Nubian, a reflection of the extent of Egypt's empire, the internationalism of the time, and the all-encompassing nature of Akhenaten's god, as eloquently expressed in "The Great Hymn to Aten," versions of which were inscribed in a number of tombs, most completely in the tomb of Ay, a general under Akhenaten and later king (see "The New Religion").

Amenhotep IV's Karnak temple reliefs included some scenes that had never before appeared in temple contexts. They were used subsequently at Amarna, but seldom, if ever, again. They included vignettes of daily life—farm work, household activities, administration, and Nile scenes—that had previously been standard in private tombs. Among the new themes were also animals awakening at sunrise, as described in the Great Hymn, and workers transporting mortar to a building site. For the first time temple reliefs made major political statements about the queen's important role in affairs of state. The queen was depicted smiting enemies or in the presence of bound captives—iconography previously restricted to the king. (Ironically, when Nefertiti was portrayed alongside Amenhotep IV, she was shown at a smaller scale than he, although she possessed her own temple at Karnak, the Hutbenben, in which the king was not depicted at all.) The royal daughters, who numbered three by the time Amenhotep IV left Karnak, were also shown on a regular basis. The depiction of temple and palace interiors with accompanying details of the royal family's personal life was unique to this period.

Stylistically, the Karnak reliefs were striking. The eccentricities of form that characterized the colossi—the attenuated upper body and spindly limbs, the swollen belly and hips, and even tiny details such as the incised diagonal line connecting nostril to lip—were replicated in reliefs of the royal family particularly (fig. 81), and private individuals to a lesser extent. Key components, such as Aten's disk or the royal family, were carved deeply, while less important elements, such as the sun's rays, interior detailing of the figures, and minor vignettes, were much more shallowly carved. In strong sunlight, this differential treatment gave special prominence to divine and royal subjects, particularly on a crowded wall. Originally, everything was brightly painted.

Not all the reliefs feature the distortions described above. A few royal representations, primarily of the queen (fig. 78), as well as many depictions of attendants and laborers, bear a much greater resemblance to works of the previous reign. It seems clear that these less extreme reliefs were carved by artists who had served Amenhotep III.

Who was the inspiration for the new, extreme style? On a stela carved into the rock at Aswan, Amenhotep IV/Akhenaten relates that he personally instructed his Chief Sculptor, Bak.[22] Bak's diminutive image on this stela and the much larger one of the king, whom he worships, were carved in the new style. In a mirror image on the same monument, however, Bak's father, Men, who was Chief Sculptor under Amenhotep III, worships a statue of Amenhotep III (perhaps one of the Memnon colossi)[23] carved in the older, traditional style. The distinction between the two styles was thus very clear to the artists themselves.

Innovations at Amarna

The king brought the radical style and iconography to his new capital, Akhetaten (Amarna), sometime after year 5 of his reign, presumably at about the time he changed his name to Akhenaten. Fifteen boundary stelae carved into the cliffs on both sides of the river defined the city's limits and were among the earliest monuments erected.[24] They repeated the iconography of the sun-disk shining down upon the royal family, but this time Nefertiti was shown at the same scale as her husband. Carved from the cliffs at the foot of many of these stelae were statues of the royal couple worshipping and offering to Aten. As in reliefs, they were accompanied by their growing family of daughters.[25] Small but perfectly proportioned according to Akhenaten's ideal, the children stand with arms around one other, beside and behind their mother. In the true gesture of a child, the eldest extends an attenuated arm forward to touch her mother's leg, as if to reassure herself of her parent's presence and protection. Both the emotion expressed and the exploration of different planes to create a more three-dimensional effect appear here for the first time in the iconography of the royal family. These innovations would be more fully developed at Amarna in later years.

The demands on artisans multiplied as temples, palaces, private estates, and tombs were designed, built, and decorated on an unprecedented scale. Today, only tantalizing traces remain *in situ*. Thousands of reliefs that once decorated temple and palace walls were discovered across the river at Hermopolis, where they had been taken by the later kings Horemheb and (in Dynasty 19) Ramesses the Great, and reused as ballast inside pylons.[26] Additional thousands of statue fragments found in a cache outside the enclosure wall of the Great Temple, in the Small Temple, and in Amarna's palaces, shrines, and houses, bear testimony to rich sculptural decoration there as well. Over the last hundred years, archaeologists from England and Germany have found throughout the city architectural support elements, faience inlays, wall and floor paintings, statuary, and stelae that greatly contribute to our picture of how artisans animated a bleak and desolate landscape with vibrant color, life, and soul. But perhaps the most valuable documents for reconstructing and understanding art and life at Amarna are reliefs remaining on the walls of Akhenaten's tomb and the tombs of his highest officials.

Fig. 79 Head of a princess (cat. 45)

A series of heads of Akhenaten's daughters, intended for composite sculptures, was found in the Thutmose workshop at Amarna.

Themes and Composition in Amarna Art

Regardless of medium or venue, art at Amarna, like Amenhotep IV's art at Karnak, centered on the royal family and included others only as they related to it. Sculptures of the royal family were plentiful and varied in scale from a few centimeters to well over life-size. Fragments, complete sculptures, and representations of sculpture from tomb and temple walls show Akhenaten and Nefertiti seated, prostrate, in the traditional crossed-arm pose of Osiris, standing with their hands at their sides, or holding an offering. Materials varied, with some, such as black and red granite, brown sandstone, and red and yellow jasper, clearly chosen for their color. Statues of the royal family were also made in pieces, presumably with different stones used for different body parts.[27]

Fig. 80 Royal feet (cat. 59)

The rendering of individual toes on the right foot is an example of Amarna artisans' attention to naturalistic detail.

Private statuary was exceedingly rare and generally small in size, except for rock-cut images of the deceased in their tombs. Regardless of subject, all statuary incorporated Akhenaten's unmistakable style.

The repertoire of primary themes carved on palaces, temples, and the Royal Tomb was limited to the king and queen worshipping or offering to Aten in the company of their daughters or traveling in their chariots to or from such an event. Even in private tombs, the royal family enjoyed pride of place. Except for the entryway and the niche at the rear where a statue of the deceased received funerary offerings, the tomb owner was prominent only when depicted in conjunction with the royal family. In a single scene in most tombs, he was presented with the collar known as the Gold of Honor, or *shebyu*, a reward for loyal service to the king. In the tomb of the God's Father Ay, later king (regarding his title, see "The Royal Family"), both the tomb owner and his wife are rewarded.[28]

Although individual blocks surviving from Karnak clearly demonstrate that large scenes and minor vignettes found at Amarna had existed at the earlier location, many entire compositions may be seen and understood only in Amarna's tombs, where expanses of wall are preserved. The focal point of these often vast compositions is the royal family, which is not only centrally located, but also significantly larger than its attendants.[29] At times, rather than filling the registers of a wall with a sequence of subjects, Akhenaten's artists used one subject to fill an entire wall, the way a painting fills a canvas. When one wall proved insufficient, they simply continued on an adjacent wall.[30]

While artists may have had little choice in the primary subject of a composition, they probably enjoyed more freedom in the selection and execution of peripheral themes. Aside from activities in the fields or on the riverbank, these might have included men sleeping or eating, a casual conversation, or even an odd expression. These depictions demonstrate that the interest in nature and the immediacy of the moment expressed in the Great Hymn permeated visual art as well.

Despite the innovations, artisans at Amarna, as at Karnak, observed most of the traditional rules of Egyptian representation, such as the use of scale to signify importance, the combination of profile and frontal views in the same figure, the use of standard royal attributes, and the repetitive poses of subsidiary figures. Nevertheless, they were not constrained by the rules. Both at Karnak and at Amarna artists freely experimented with new and realistic ways of representing the human figure. Relaxation or tension in a figure, fully frontal torsos,[31] and the distinction between right and left feet through the depiction of toes (fig. 80)[32] are all variations that had been tried previously, but never before with the fluency and frequency of Akhenaten's time.

Fig. 81 Stela of the royal family (cat. 53)

The stela, probably from a shrine of a private house, shows the king and queen fondling their daughters under the life-giving rays of the sun.

Emotion and Immediacy

Yet another nuance conveyed by Akhenaten's art was the expression of affection between king and queen, between parents and royal children, and among the royal siblings. This was accomplished through a touch, a gesture, or a glance, and represents the first time members of a royal family had been depicted displaying emotion so overtly.[33] Reliefs showed, for example, Nefertiti tying a broadcollar around Akhenaten's neck as the two exchange an intimate glance (fig. 82, left). They portrayed Akhenaten and Nefertiti holding hands during state ceremonies[34] or lovingly playing with, and even kissing, their children, who—also for the first time in Egyptian art— assumed believable childlike poses and behaved in a suitably irascible manner.

For the populace at Amarna particularly, the royal family was not only the ideal family but also the holy family, which supplanted the traditional trinity of gods (see the essay "The New Religion") and served as the people's link to the light of the sun that was Aten. In this context it is noteworthy that the demonstrations of devotion most moving to the modern observer have been found not on public monuments but on small stelae that may have been objects of private worship in the chapels of wealthy estates.[35] As the Great Hymn related, worship of Aten through the royal family brought fertility and plenitude.

Grief was realistically expressed at Amarna as well, and for the first time by a royal family. The death of the beloved second daughter Meketaten sometime after year 12 was depicted in a suite of side chambers in the Royal Tomb (see "Preparing for Eternity"). Akhenaten is shown bending in sorrow as he places one hand on his forehead and reaches behind with the other to comfort Nefertiti, who is also overcome with grief.

Whether recording royal expressions of emotion or streamers on a flagpole flying in the breeze, the art of Akhenaten focused on the here-and-now, capturing the moment like a snapshot. Previous artists had recorded daily activities in an idealized, timeless form that would serve the deceased in the hereafter. But the hereafter had no place in Akhenaten's theology.

The Treatment of Space

The sun illuminated and vivified Akhenaten's world by extending its rays in all directions, and this may have inspired his artisans to treat space three-dimensionally even on a two-dimensional surface. Earlier, in a world that was viewed as two-dimensional, related elements on the same plane would have been shown above or beside one another. Aten, however, overlapped and embraced entire scenes like the spokes of a giant umbrella. A three-dimensional view of space permitted figures to move in new ways and assume new positions: Nefertiti relaxes on Akhenaten's lap as two of their daughters squirm over hers (fig. 82, bottom). Rather than approaching space as a void to be filled, artists came to understand the emotional potential of emptiness. On an otherwise crowded wall, a trumpeter stands alone in his register,[36] and the onlooker can almost hear the piercing blasts of his instrument.

The depiction of the sun's rays reaching into the inner courtyard of a temple[37] shows that buildings, too, were treated three-dimensionally. But this approach also presented challenges. To portray spaces in their totality, with all the essential elements, artists sometimes resorted to their old technique of rendering perspective by combining aerial and frontal views in the same image.[38] At Amarna, however, previously restricted interior spaces of temples and palaces, as well as the activities that took place within them, were open to the viewer for the first time.[39]

Fig. 82 Family intimacy

Royal emotions are on display in these fragments of reliefs: Akhenaten and Nefertiti, at left, exchange a glance as she secures a broadcollar around his neck (Ägyptisches Museum, Berlin). Two princesses (cat. 54) share a tender moment. Nefertiti perches on Akhenaten's lap with two of the daughters (Musée du Louvre, Paris).

Fig. 83 "Green Room" wall painting (facsimile)

Nowhere in the art of ancient Egypt is the exuberance of nature better expressed than in this mural from the North Palace at Amarna.

Fig. 84 Ground floor of the Thutmose workshop (computer reconstruction)

About two dozen pieces of sculpture, including the most famous bust of Nefertiti, were found at this site, which served as both living quarters and studio.

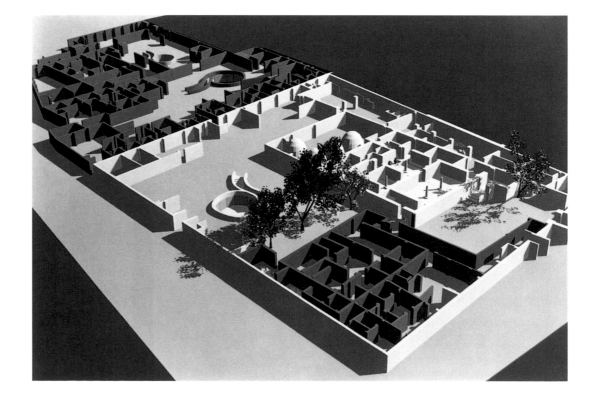

Painting and the Minor Arts

Akhenaten's distinctive style and choice of subjects is apparent not only in sculpture and relief, but also in painting and the minor arts. Painted walls, floors, and ceilings[40] adorned both palaces and private homes. The lush beauty of nature and its serendipity are nowhere better seen than in the wall paintings of the "Green Room" of the North Palace (fig. 83), where a variety of birds takes flight from a dense thicket on a river-bank. From a wall of the King's House comes an informal family "snapshot" showing Nefertiti slouching on a floor cushion beside Akhenaten and embracing her three eldest daughters as two younger ones, seated on their own cushions beside her, tickle each other. These paintings also testify to a love of bright colors and juxtaposed dense patterns: courtyard floors were transformed into dense carpets of favorite plants painted on plaster with the spontaneity of an experienced and confident artisan. The themes of nature and its bounty were repeated in faience and on ceramics (see "Crafts and Industries at Amarna"). Observations of how the human body moves are superbly rendered in a small wooden figure of a dwarf whose torso bends into a S-curve to accommodate a weighty jar on his shoulder (fig. 85). Tiny cartouches on the jar bear the names of Akhenaten and Nefertiti.

Artisans and Methods

Though the decorated material is often fragmentary and scattered, its profusion conveys the impression, probably accurate, that Amarna was a city with a vast number of artisans. Several sculptors' workshops have been identified from their archaeological remains,[41] and many more may await discovery. The unusually large number of sculptors' trial pieces found among the temples, palaces, and private houses suggests that additional artisans were being trained at a rapid pace. These trial pieces often consisted of one or more hieroglyphs carved repeatedly across the surface of a scrap of limestone until the trainee succeeded in copying the master or ran out of room. Another category of limestone reliefs can only have been sculptors' models. These were usually rectangular and often pierced at the top; many bore the profile heads of Akhenaten (fig. 87), Nefertiti, or both. Lightweight and portable, they could easily have been brought to a work site to serve as guides for the reproduction of the royal face. Yet other scraps of limestone display what may even be caricatures of the king, perhaps for the sole purpose of amusement (fig. 88).

To date, the most complete picture of a sculptor's workshop at Amarna comes from a villa in the South Suburb identified as belonging to Thutmose, who was Overseer of Works and Sculptor[42]; here he and his staff appear to have both lived and worked.[43] Given what remained in the studio when Amarna was abandoned, it is clear that its artisans created both sculpture and relief in a variety of stones.[44]

In 1912, some two dozen pieces—primarily heads, but also busts and complete statues—were discovered in a walled-off, closetlike space in the workshop, where they had

Fig. 85 Dwarf holding a jar (cat. 208)

Although just over two inches high, this statuette captures the salient characteristics of a dwarf and his struggle to accommodate the weight of the vessel he carries.

been either forgotten or deliberately abandoned because they had outlived their useful-ness. One of the pieces was the bust of Nefertiti (fig. 57) that has become arguably the most famous piece of Egyptian sculpture in the world and a contemporary icon for beauty.

An equally remarkable part of this discovery was a group of plaster heads of both the royal family and nonroyal subjects. The heads of the royal family,[45] which included Amenhotep III, Akhenaten (fig. 89), Nefertiti (fig. 86), and possibly Akhenaten's sec-ondary wife Kiya, varied in scale from life-size to one-quarter life-size, and for the most part were the standard, recognizable images. A number of the heads appear unfinished. In view of the tremendous production of statuary for Amarna and else-where,[46] it is conceivable that these pieces, like their counterparts in relief, served as models for sculptors working either in the studio or on site. In fact, a number of simi-lar plaster heads have been found elsewhere at Amarna.

Far more enigmatic are the nonroyal heads, which are all life-size. They represent both men and women, all of whom share unmistakable signs of advanced age (fig. 9), including sagging jowls, lined foreheads, "crow's-feet," and pouches under the eyes. It is unlikely that they served as sculptors' models in the same sense as the royal pieces, because there was very little demand for private sculpture at Amarna, apart from images of tomb owners cut directly into the rock of the tomb. If these tomb sculptures broke with tradition by showing their owners at an advanced age rather than as eter-

Fig. 87 Sculptor's model of Akhenaten (cat. 52)

The limestone plaque would have been copied to produce relief images.

Fig. 88 Sketches of Akhenaten's head and hand (cat. 136)

The head, with its peculiar propor-tions, suggests that this is either a caricature or the work of an unskilled apprentice.

Fig. 86 Unfinished Nefertiti (cat. 44)

Black lines mark the areas that need further attention on this unfinished head of Nefertiti from the workshop of the sculptor Thutmose.

Fig. 89 Face of Akhenaten (cat. 40)

Found in Amarna's South Suburb, in what was possibly a sculptor's studio, this plaster face may have served as a model for representations of the king in the mature style.

Fig. 90 Statue of an aging Nefertiti
(Ägyptisches Museum, Berlin)

The furrowed face and drooping breasts suggest that this is an image of Nefertiti in her later years. The attenuation of the upper body and the voluptuousness of the lower body are less pronounced than they would have been earlier in the reign.

nally youthful, the plaster heads may have been the models for them. Unfortunately, the faces of the tomb sculptures, without exception, are so damaged that it is impossible to tell.

Although it is tempting to see the private heads as true portraits—even life masks or death masks[47]—the presence of such superficially rendered features as very flat eyes or simple, slit mouths suggests they were not. In view of the fascination with realism and extremes in pose, body type, and facial configuration so apparent in reliefs, it is not out of the question that these heads were a vehicle for exploring different aspects of realism in sculpture in the round.

In a recent examination of the heads, the American sculptor Peter Rockwell confirmed how many were made. First, a head was fashioned out of wet clay, possibly with the sitter present. Then, before it could dry out and crack, the clay was covered with plaster. When the plaster dried, the clay was removed and discarded, leaving a negative mold in one or more parts. Wet plaster was then poured into the negative mold. When it dried, the mold was removed, revealing the plaster head inside. Finally, mold lines and other rough areas were trimmed away and incised details added.

The Mature Amarna Style

Of Akhenaten's seventeen-year reign, approximately twelve years were spent at the new capital.[48] Just as Akhenaten's art evolved during the Karnak years, so, too, did it evolve at Amarna. Although there are remarkably few monuments or events dated to a specific year during that time, the few that do exist,[49] others for which approximate dates are known,[50] and the archaeological record permit the development of a relative chronology. From this, it is apparent that within a few years of the move to Amarna, the eccentricities of style that had characterized Karnak art softened (fig. 18). The head and limbs became less attenuated.[51] Eyes lost their pronounced slit-like appearance and slant to become more horizontal, more almond shaped, and three dimensional.

The V-shape of the lips evolved into a curvilinear Cupid's bow with a fullness at the center of the lower lip, giving the mouth a particularly sensuous appearance. The skinny upper torso filled out slightly, the swollen hips and pendant belly were more restrained, and the imbalance less shocking. The new Amarna product exhibited an unsurpassed sensuality and an enduring classical beauty.

The new treatment of the face and figure in both sculpture in the round and relief represented a fundamental change in attitude toward the human body. The approach was much more organic and holistic, replacing the view of the body as a series of rigidly pre-structured elements.[52] In its fully developed form, it was a logical adjunct to Akhenaten's theology, which emphasized the beauty of the natural world down to its smallest details.

For Akhenaten's artists, there was not just one standard of beauty, but many. They explored various facial structures and played with the different ways flesh and bone

come together. The subtle and not-so-subtle changes in face and body that accompany advancing age became a focus for sculpture in the round, perhaps inspired by the maturing of the royal family (figs. 89, 90).

Most of the sculpture left or forgotten in Thutmose's workshop when the city was abandoned exhibited the later Amarna style. It has therefore been suggested that the sculptor Thutmose was the guiding force, and that the movement toward less extreme representation began when Thutmose replaced Akhenaten's earlier sculptor, Bak[53] (see above). For several reasons, however, the real catalyst may never be known. A number of styles existed contemporaneously during Akhenaten's last years (and in fact, the late-Amarna canon is apparent in Bak's own sculpture[54]: see fig. 91); more than one sculptor's workshop is known to have existed at Amarna; and the mechanisms of stylistic change in Egypt remain enigmatic. If, in fact, Bak's statement on his stela is true, and Akhenaten himself gave instructions for the new modes of representation at the beginning of his reign,[55] then it is not out of the question that in later years also, the king personally directed his sculptors both to explore realism further and to soften the extreme lines of the earlier works. Perhaps these changes accompanied Akhenaten's evolving religious beliefs and his changing image of himself. Regardless of the mechanism of change, it was this later ideal of beauty that persisted well after Akhenaten's death and influenced the art of succeeding dynasties. It became Akhenaten's lasting legacy.

Fig. 91 Naos of Chief Sculptor Bak and Taheri (cat. 131)

Akhenaten's first chief sculptor stands beside his wife on this stela. In the text, Bak claims to have been taught his craft by the king himself.

1. Sa'ad 1970, pp. 188–89, 191. More than one such smiting scene was made.

2. Aldred 1988, pp. 169ff. But see also D. Redford 1984, pp. 62–63.

3. W. R. Johnson 1996, pp. 62–72, 81. See also Johnson's essay in this book, "The Setting: History, Religion, and Art."

4. For additional blocks, see Chappaz 1983. These blocks came from a building Amenhotep IV erected in the vicinity of the Tenth Pylon.

5. W. R. Johnson 1996, pp. 69, 71.

6. In this, Akhenaten was no different from his ancestors. See W. R. Johnson 1990, p. 28, where Amenhotep III's early work is compared to his father's.

7. Akhenaten did not invent all aspects of this iconography. Aten with embracing arms occurs as early as the reign of Thutmose IV or Amenhotep II; see Tawfik 1973, p. 81.

8. See Donald Redford's essay in this book ("The Beginning of the Heresy") and also D. Redford 1984, pp. 102–4, and D. Redford 1994.

9. Chevrier 1926 and D. Redford 1994, pp. 485–87. Somewhat smaller statues in red quartzite, and yet smaller examples in black granite and red granite, may have adorned the north side of this court. Although many doubt Nefertiti's presence among the sandstone colossi, she is clearly represented in quartzite on the north side. (D. Redford 1983, p. 222; and D. Redford 1994, p. 487).

10. Noblecourt 1974, p. 11 and n. 4 and 6.

11. Robins 1994, pp. 123–33.

12. J. Allen 1988a, pp. 9–10.

13. J. R. Harris 1977a, p. 10, n. 39, and Aldred 1988, pp. 235–36.

14. It has, for example, the higher navel and other subtle attributes that distinguish her from her husband. See Eaton-Krauss 1981, pp. 258–64 and J. R. Harris 1977a, pp. 5–10. For an argument that this colossus does not represent Nefertiti but rather Amenhotep IV with both male and female attributes, see Robins 1993.

15. W. R. Johnson 1996, p. 81.

16. The few sandstone reliefs from Amarna appear to have come primarily from architectural support elements.

17. Many more await discovery inside Karnak's Tenth Pylon (D. Redford 1975, p. 22) and the east half of the Ninth. Of the extant examples, about thirty-five thousand were decorated (D. Redford 1979a, p. 54). It has been conjectured that as many as eighty-five thousand decorated blocks once existed (R. Smith 1970, p. 651).

18. D. Redford 1973, pp. 78ff.

19. Michael Mallinson, former member of the Egypt Exploration Society's Amarna excavation team, has estimated that the Karnak temples were larger than their equivalents at Amarna by a scale of 5:1. (Mallinson, oral communication.)

20. For example, the Gempaaten featured scenes of the jubilee festival. See D. Redford 1984, pp. 122ff.

21. Vergnieux and Gondran 1997, pp. 73–74. The prostrate royal family also appears on blocks from Akhenaten's temple at Heliopolis (Egyptian Museum, Cairo, JE 34175, for example, illustrated in Habachi 1971, p. 42, fig. a). Although this position is mentioned in literary sources as early as the Old Kingdom, the first representation of a prostrate king dates from the Middle Kingdom (Fischer 1980, col. 1126).

22. It has also been argued that these are simply stereotyped phrases that occur on earlier royal monuments as well. See Krauss 1986b, pp. 40–42.

23. Habachi 1965, pp. 87–88.

24. The existence of at least fifteen stelae is now definite. See Murnane and van Siclen 1993, p. 1.

25. Two daughters are shown in the sculptures. Three daughters, however, were incised in the negative space under the outstretched arms. The statues varied from less than life-size to colossal.

26. Spencer 1989, pp. 15–16, 26. Ironically, only some two thousand blocks are known to date (D. Redford 1979a, p. 54)—a strikingly small number in view of the more than one hundred thousand extant from Karnak.

27. Akhenaten made greater use of composite statuary than any prior or subsequent king, but he did not originate the technique. See J. Phillips 1994.

28. Such scenes occur first in the tomb of Khaemhat from the reign of Amenhotep III (Wreszinski 1923, pls. 203–5). Earlier in the dynasty, Gold of Honor collars appear on private statues such as those of Sennefer and Senai from the reign of Amenhotep II (Egyptian Museum, Cairo, CG 42126).

29. In this respect, Akhenaten did not differ at all from his predecessors.

30. Tomb of Meryra I, illustrated in N. de G. Davies 1903–8, vol. 1, p. 23 and pls. X-Xa.

31. Occasionally, from the Old Kingdom on, figures are shown with fully frontal torsos, as on the false door of Redines (Manuelian 1994), or with their backs to the viewer, as in the tomb of Rekhmira, illustrated in Mekhitarian 1978, p. 51.

32. Russmann 1980.

33. For a discussion of its significance, see Krauss 1991a, pp. 12–14.

34. Tomb of Meryra II, illustrated in N. de G. Davies 1903–8, vol. 2, pl. XXXVII.

35. For the circumstances of their discovery and reservations about this theory, see Krauss 1991a, pp. 34–36.

36. Tomb of Ahmes, illustrated in N. de G. Davies 1903–8, vol. 3, pl. XXXI.

37. Tomb of Mahu, illustrated in N. de G. Davies 1903–8, vol. 4, pl. XVIII.

38. The same technique had been used earlier to show such things as a pool and its contents, as seen in a fragment from the tomb of Nebamen, illustrated in James 1985, p. 30, fig. 28.

39. Previously interiors of private houses had been shown in private tombs such as Djehutynefer's, illustrated in Brovarski, Doll, and Freed 1982, p. 26, fig. 7.

40. Painted ceiling fragments were found in the shrine of a pavilion that may have been part of a house. (Pendlebury 1951, pp. 139–40 and pl. LV, 3. I am grateful to Barry Kemp for this reference.)

41. J. Phillips 1991, pp. 34–35.

42. A fragmentary horseblinker is the sole source of the identification; see Krauss 1983, pp. 119ff.

43. For a description of the different rooms and their function, see Arnold 1996, pp. 41ff.

44. J. Phillips 1991, pp. 32–33.

45. Specific iconography, such as the ear tabs or forehead band of a crown, leaves little doubt that these were representations of royalty.

46. Aten temples existed, at the very least in Memphis, Heliopolis, and Medinet el-Gurob. For a head of Nefertiti from Memphis, see cat. 41.

47. Both of these possibilities were explored and discarded by Roeder (Roeder 1941, pp. 160ff.). His conclusions were recently confirmed by the sculptor Peter Rockwell.

48. This represents the highest year date found on wine-jar seals; see the essay by Nicholas Reeves in this book, "The Royal Family."

49. The boundary stelae are dated to years 5 and 8. Foreign emissaries arrived for a celebration in year 12.

50. The form of Aten's name, or epithet, was altered between years 8 and 12. See J. Allen 1996, pp. 3–4.

51. This change is measurable in the grid of the canon of proportion, which shifted back slightly toward the norm (Robins 1994, pp. 131–32).

52. Arnold 1996, pp. 74ff.

53. Aldred 1973, p. 63.

54. Krauss 1986a, p. 24.

55. For advocates of this position, see Krauss 1986a, p. 41, nn. 114–15.

Crafts and Industries at Amarna

**Yvonne J. Markowitz
and Peter Lacovara**

Amarna offered artists and craftsmen an ideal opportunity. Within a relatively short period, an entire city was to be built—including palaces, temples, private residences, and tombs—and the need for skilled artisans was acute.

Fig. 92 Bullock in a thicket (cat. 78)

In such details as the overlapping papyrus plants, this polychrome faience tile shows the naturalism characteristic of the Amarna Period. The effect was achieved in part through the painterly application of color.

The city of Amarna, utopian brainchild of the iconoclast Akhenaten, was a hotbed of artistic activity from its inception. The new ideology, combined with the novelty of the site, the ambitious nature of the undertaking, and the urgency of construction, helped create an invigorating atmosphere that fostered experimentation and innovation.

Although the dramatic break with the artistic and religious conventions of the past began at Karnak, Akhenaten's unique world view found expression in an extensive building program at Amarna. It included palaces, temples, private residences, and tombs for the royal family and courtiers. The decoration and furnishing of these structures required scores of artisans skilled in design, ornamentation, and a range of crafts. Many, no doubt, were recruited from the temple and palace workshops of Akhenaten's father, Amenhotep III, in Thebes; others, employed in the residences of officials, would have welcomed the opportunity and adventure of a move to Amarna. The latter were most likely drawn to the cottage or domestic industries clustered in the suburbs north and south of the Central City, working to meet the consumer needs of a growing population.

To judge by the artisans' titles and the material resources afforded their various specialties, there was a clear division between the "fine" and "applied" arts in ancient Egypt. Sculptors were held in especially high regard. For example, Bak, Chief Sculptor in the Great and Mighty Monuments of the King in the House of Aten at Akhetaten, came from a family of illustrious artists. A master in his field, he supervised less accomplished sculptors and possibly a school for sculptors-in-training. We can assume that Bak and his wife were part of Akhenaten's immediate circle and received material rewards commensurate with the sculptor's ability and position. Of lesser influence were skilled painters, followed by outline draftsmen. Lowest in status were craftsmen who created the objects used in daily life. Although many items in this category show evidence of extraordinary craftsmanship and aesthetic sensibility, their makers failed to achieve the recognition reserved for creators of large-scale work.

Much of what we know about the organization and activities of Egyptian craftsmen comes from private-tomb decorations in which groups of artisans are portrayed busy at work. An informative vignette occurs in the Theban tomb of the Vizier Rekhmira, an early 18th-Dynasty official whose duties included inspection of the Amen temple

Fig. 93 Atelier of the sculptor Iuty, from the tomb of the Steward Huya

This line drawing, made from a painted relief, shows the variety of specialties Iuty's artisans engaged in.

Fig. 94 Amphora with gazelle and *ankh*s (cat. 103)

Blue-painted pottery was an 18th-Dynasty innovation popular at Amarna. This example features applied, hand-modeled decoration.

workshops. The crafts represented include stone-vessel carving, metal-smithing, jewelry-making, carpentry, and leatherwork. The detailed treatment of each specialty reflects the complex and elevated status afforded the temple ateliers.[1] In the Amarna tomb of Huya, who was Steward to Akhenaten's mother, Queen Tiye, a relief depicting the sculptor Iuty's workshop (fig. 93) demonstrates a division of labor, with the master sculptor adding the finishing touches to a statue of Baketaten,[2] one of Akhenaten's sisters. Iuty, shown seated with palette and brush in hand, dominates the scene, while an apprentice observes attentively nearby. Other artisans in this moderate-sized atelier fashion a head for a composite sculpture (which often incorporated different materials), a furniture leg, a stone vessel, and a wooden box—a range of activities typical of larger establishments.[3] Implements such as the palette, chisels, and adz are highlighted in this scene, perhaps reflecting a special interest on the part of the tomb carver.

Amarna artisans engaged in the same crafts depicted in the (pre-Amarna) tomb of Rekhmira—as well as the production of ceramics, faience and glass, and textiles. Our understanding of these activities comes not only from relief scenes, but also from excavated workshops where the remains of raw materials, tools, works in progress, finished goods, and waste materials have been recovered. Evidence shows that the craft industries at Amarna were as vigorous and extensive as the arts of architecture, sculpture, and painting (see the essay "Art in the Service of Religion and the State").

Pottery

Amarna artisans, working in specialized ateliers or in the compounds of the great estates, created remarkably fine wares out of Nile silt and desert clays, using a slow wheel that consisted of a pair of rough, round stones spun by hand on a pivot-and-socket joint. Recent excavations and replication experiments[4] have shown that a single workshop could produce a broad range of forms. Most vessels were undecorated, though they were finished with a fine, burnished red or white slip (a coating of thinned, creamy clay). Elaborately painted vessels may have been produced specifically for the royal court: the blue-painted pottery of Dynasty 18 has in fact been called "palace ware" because of its association with the court communities at Malqata (Thebes) and Medinet el-Gurob (Middle Egypt) as well as Amarna. It has also, how-

ever, been found in other contexts. There may have been royal workshops for ceramics, but none has yet been discovered.

Pottery in dynastic Egypt prior to the New Kingdom was rarely decorated with paint. Instead, artisans relied on symmetry of form and surface finish to convey elegance and beauty. As Egypt expanded its sphere of influence in the early 18th Dynasty, however, it absorbed foreign fashions in turn—including a taste for decorative products. By the Amarna Period, some vessels were lavishly embellished with paint and a variety of surface treatments, including handles and appliqué decorations (fig. 94). Though these elements suggest outside influence, the motifs, for the most part, were typically Egyptian. The blue-painted ware, thought to have been inspired by the garlands of blue lotus petals shown on plain pottery vessels in tomb paintings, most commonly had several floral registers circling the shoulder of the pot. These were usually outlined in black or red, using traditional iron pigments. The blue was a cobalt pigment derived from mineral deposits in the Eastern Desert as well as the Kakhleh and Kharga oases in the Western Desert. Other floral motifs used during this period were the white lotus, papyrus, mandrake, cornflower, and chrysanthemum. More elaborate scenes on ceramics, involving animals and people, appear to have been limited to the palaces of Amenhotep III and Akhenaten.

Vessels from the Aegean and the Levant have also been recovered from Amarna. Although these containers were imported for their contents—precious oils and wine—they were also valued as curiosities and were subsequently copied by Egyptian potters. Pots with pointed or rounded bottoms were set in sand or brick, or in stands of wicker, wood, or pottery. These allowed water to gradually seep out of the porous ceramic, keeping the contents cool through evaporation.

Metalworking

The Egyptians prized metal goods, particularly objects made of gold and silver, for their economic, artistic, and symbolic value. Gold, the most dazzling of nature's elements, held a unique position because of its sunlike brilliance, resistance to corrosion, and malleability. Regarded as "the flesh of the god," this immutable metal was seen as a means of attaining immortality. Silver, which the Egyptians called "white gold," was viewed as "the bones of the god" and associated symbolically with the moon. Gold was indigenous, found in both alluvial deposits and veins of quartz. Silver, on the other hand, entered Egypt through trade or as tribute from the Levant, Greece, and Turkey. Because the two metals were rare, objects crafted from them were usually small and therefore portable—which may account for the paucity of precious-metal finds in a city that was abandoned gradually. However, the fabulous riches from the tomb of Tutankhamen serve as a reference point for the quality and sheer quantity of materials set aside for burial during the 18th Dynasty.[5]

Although excavated examples of the goldsmith's art at Amarna are rare,[6] J. D. S.

Pendlebury, working in the 1930s near a public well in the North Suburb,[7] made a fortuitous find—possibly a jeweler's hoard or stolen goods. From a ceramic jar buried in the ground, he recovered twenty-three gold bars weighing a total of 3,376 grams (118 ounces) and several handworked silver ornaments totaling one-third the weight of the gold.[8] The silver included jewels of western Asian origin destined for recycling by Egyptian metalworkers.

A group of gold ornaments in Edinburgh, believed to be from the Royal Tomb at Amarna, are representative samples of Egyptian jewelry.[9] They include wirework finger rings with amuletic bezels (fig. 95), signet rings, various types of ear ornaments, and a selection of broadcollar elements. Several items incorporate semiprecious stones and glass elements in colors chosen for their symbolic value. All were fabricated using techniques well-established in Egypt by the New Kingdom: aside from wirework, there was sheet-metal assemblage, soldering, casting, and granulation. These jewels, which represented the high end of the market, were often imitated and mass-produced in less costly materials such as faience.

Prominently featured in the Amarna tombs is the gold *shebyu* collar, a neck ornament composed of multiple strands of gold-disk beads. The collar, a New Kingdom decoration, was a reward bestowed on male officials for valor or outstanding service.[10] One of the accouterments frequently worn by Amenhotep III after his first *sed*-festival,[11] it may have symbolized the king's identification with the sun god. Akhenaten, together with Nefertiti, continued the practice of awarding the collar to selected officials and courtiers at Amarna.

There are no known metalsmithing scenes or relief representations of metalcrafters from Amarna. There are, however, several limestone relief fragments in Cairo's

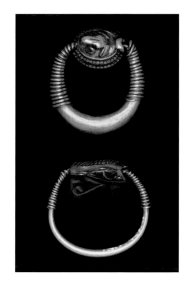

Fig. 95 Amuletic rings

The jewelry reported to have been found in the Royal Tomb at Amarna included these finger rings, with frog bezel (top, cat. 225) and *wedjat*-eye bezel (cat. 226).

Fig. 96 Ax blade (cat. 151)

This copper-alloy (bronze) ax was probably made in a simple open-face mold and hardened by hammering.

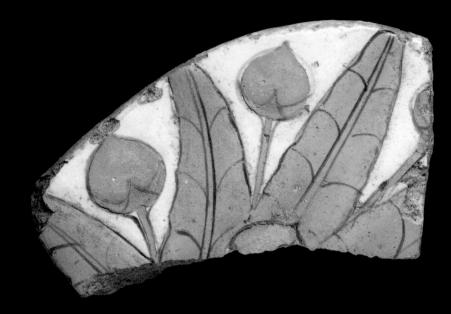

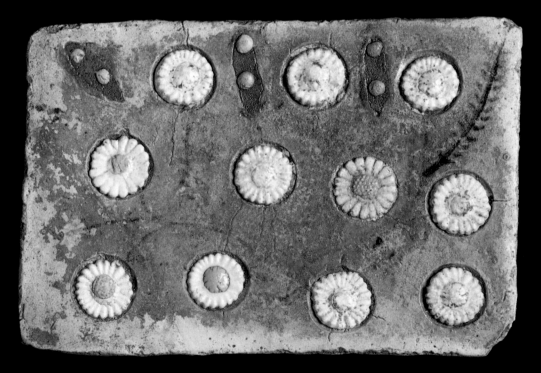

Egyptian Museum from the tomb of Ptahmay at Giza. The deceased, portrayed with the Amarna-style elongated head and protuberant belly, bears the title "Chief Worker in Fine Gold in the House of Aten." Metalworkers were named according to their specialty in smithing and it appears that Ptahmay was a gilder in the Memphite temple.[12]

Unlike precious-metal objects, those made of copper and copper-alloy (bronze) were widely used at all levels of society. Copper was imported in great quantities from the Sinai and the Mediterranean, usually in the form of flat ingots that could be cut or hammered into the desired shape. Artisans often mixed copper with tin to make bronze, which was both more durable and more easily worked. This alloy was typically used to make tools whose worn cutting edges could be hardened and sharpened through hammering (fig. 96). Metals could also be given a high polish, a treatment especially suitable for mirrors. Though commonplace, metal objects were valued, and few remained when the city was abandoned.

Faience and Glass

Excavating at Amarna in 1891–92, Sir Flinders Petrie discovered what he believed to be a number of "glass and glazing" workshops, rich in the tools and waste materials common to the faience and glass industries. The abundance of finely crafted, vibrantly colored, vitreous objects found at Amarna attests to their popularity during this period as well as to the high level of craftsmanship achieved through years of experimentation and practice. The technologies of production are complex, and ongoing research continues to offer new insights.

Faience, the most common of the vitreous materials, is a glazed, nonclay ceramic composed of materials common in the Egyptian landscape. The most important of these is silica, which occurs in nature in the form of sand, quartz crystal or pebbles, and flint. To the grains of ground quartz, the ancient craftsman added small amounts of lime and an alkali (soda or potash), which served the dual function of binding the quartz particles and reducing the temperature needed to melt the silica.

The next step was to add water to the silica mixture, creating a thick, malleable paste that could then be modeled by hand or pressed into a mold. To obtain the vibrant colors so fashionable at Amarna, oxides of copper (blue-green), cobalt (blue, violet), lead antimonate (yellow, light green), iron (red, black, green), manganese (black, purple), and titanium (white) were added to the batch. In the self-glazing method known as efflorescence—the most popular technique at Amarna—the paste was then air-dried, allowing the alkali salts to migrate to the surface, where they would "bloom," or form a crust. Fired in a kiln at 800° to 1000°C (1470° to 1800°F), the mixture hardened, creating a porous, pebbly core surrounded by a dense layer of fused glass that filled its interstices. On the surface would be a thin, glassy, gemlike coating. It is not surprising that the ancient Egyptians referred to faience as *tjehnet*, meaning "that which shines or dazzles."

In a second method used at Amarna, a water-based, silica-lime-alkali slurry was applied to an unfired quartz core, resulting in a softer-bodied faience that sometimes retained flow or drip marks as it dried after firing.[13] A third self-glazing technique, known as cementation, involved the immersion of dried faience paste in a glazing powder before firing. The final product was a thin, uniform surface recognizable by the absence of drying marks.

A multicolor effect, characteristic of New Kingdom faience, was achieved by painting with metallic-oxide paints or a faience slurry that incorporated the appropriate colorants. Another procedure, known as inlaying in faience, consisted of filling incised depressions with faience paste. Both methods, carried out on unfired, moderately dry faience, were used extensively at Amarna. Most dramatic are the polychrome decorative tiles in which the slurry was applied in a painterly fashion to create naturalistic impressions of plants and animals (fig. 97, top fragments).

Although colors were typically added in discrete applications, faience artisans at Amarna experimented with subtle color shading and blending—a technique also seen in wall and floor paintings of the period. They were also successful in producing a sparkling white body that was often used as a background, setting off the lively forms and bright colors.[14]

Inlaying in jewelry, vessels, and architectural tiles was a means of adding texture as well as color, since a fine channel separating the inlay from the base was formed after firing. A daisy tile from Amarna (fig. 97, bottom) shows the variations possible through a combination of techniques. Here the individually crafted yellow-and-white faience blossoms were cemented into hollows in a green faience background on which stems were then hand-painted. The daisies, modeled and set at irregular intervals, give a vivid impression of clustered wildflowers.

Another New Kingdom innovation exploited at Amarna was the use of a stronger faience body. This advance, which allowed the crafting of finer, more delicate objects, was a product of technical developments in the glass industry and may explain the large number of broadcollar elements and finger rings found scattered throughout the city.[15] While some of the rings may have served as votive offerings,[16] others were undoubtedly worn by ordinary inhabitants as amulets. Analyses of the distribution and manufac-

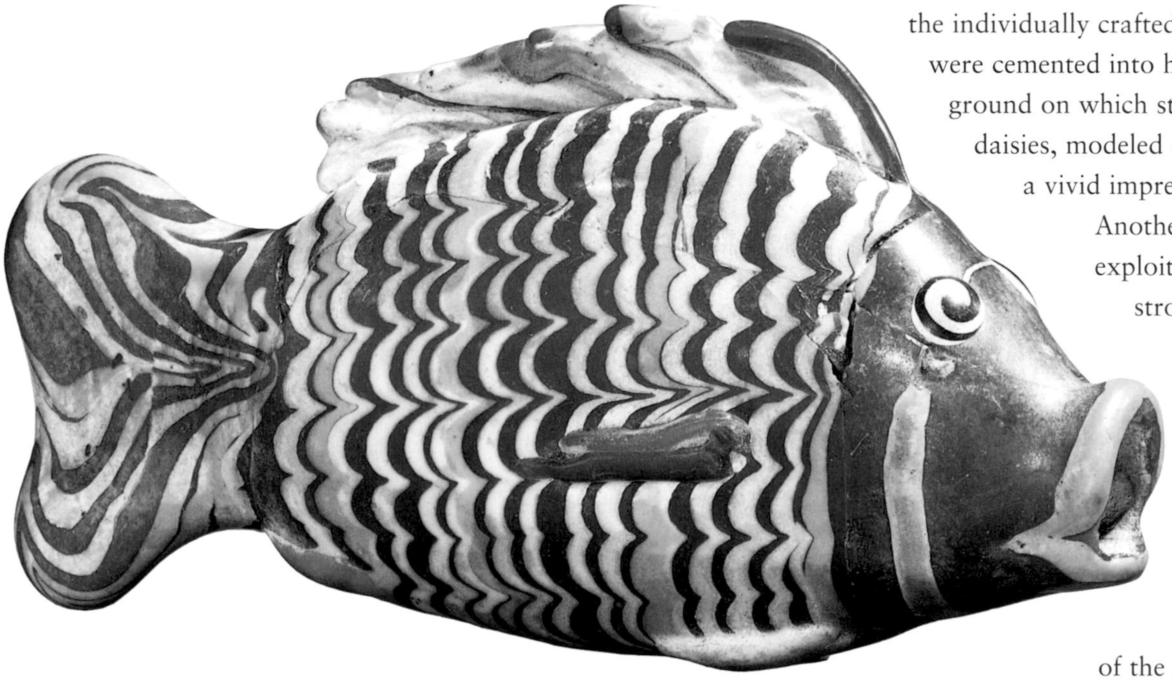

Fig. 98 Fish vessel (cat. 212)

ture of these small items and their open-face molds, recovered in great numbers by Petrie and by Barry Kemp, director of the current excavations, have provided insights into the technical and social aspects of the industry. Absent from known depictions of craft workshops at Karnak and Amarna, faience production at its most basic level appears to have been a cottage industry. Larger, complicated items requiring highly skilled artisans may have been produced at glassmaking workshops.

Although glassmaking and glassworking are closely related to faience manufacture, the basic composition of glass—silica, lime, soda, alumina, magnesia—is more complex,[17] and the temperatures required for melting are higher, somewhere between

1000° and 1150°C (1830° and 2100°F).[18] Unlike faience, which appeared in the Nile Valley during the fourth millennium B.C., glass was a relative newcomer—a result, perhaps, of extended contact with western Asia during the early 18th Dynasty, a period when foreign goods, new ideas, and craftsmen from abroad exerted a lasting influence on the decorative arts (see pottery, above).[19] Although raw glass in the form of ingots was imported, the archaeological record supports the idea that glass was also manufactured from its basic ingredients in Egypt during the Amarna Period.[20]

Historians of glass note that glassmaking in the ancient world was typically a two-step heating process. During the first phase (called "sintering"), the raw materials were crushed and mixed and then heated in clay crucibles. These were set in a brick furnace at temperatures around 800° to 850°C (1470° to 1560°F) until their contents turned into a viscous mass. Upon cooling, this solidified into "frit." Precipitated impurities were then chipped away, leaving a refined vitreous substance that was ground into a powder[21] artisans could also use as pigment.

The second phase entailed heating the pulverized material to around 1000°C (1830°F), until it fused or melted. As with faience, opacifiers and colorants could be added. For clear glass, decolorizing agents such as manganese were used, although the exact decolorizer employed at Amarna is unknown.[22] The viscous glass was then ready for working: it could be poured into molds, rolled into thin rods, or wrapped around a removable clay or dung core to form small ornamental vessels.

Although the two-step method was undoubtedly used in antiquity, recent research by Paul Nicholson and Caroline Jackson suggests that glassmaking at Amarna may have been a one-step process in which the raw materials were heated to around 1100°C

Fig. 100 Fragment of a blue-bodied vessel with "eyes" (cat. 216)

The stratified "eyes," made in a variety of colors, were pressed into the vessel while the glass was still hot.

(2000°F) for approximately eight hours. This discovery, made by members of the Egypt Exploration Society's Amarna Glass Project, was the result of replicating the brick furnace found by Petrie and using local ingredients and fuel to recreate ancient glass. The team found that they were able to eliminate the fritting phase, thereby simplifying manufacture.[23]

While glass had a variety of uses at Amarna—for small, personal ornaments, as inlays in sculpture and reliefs, and as architectural elements (fig. 99)—it was the exceptional quality of core-formed, polychrome glass vessels that established the city as one of the outstanding glassmaking centers of the period. Hundreds of fragments and several nearly complete vessels from the site attest to the wide range of shapes, colors, and decorative devices used in crafting these luxury items. A popular Amarna color scheme was a cobalt blue body with trails of yellow, white, and turquoise glass applied in bands or as trim. The technique required that the body be heated repeatedly and shaped by rolling ("marvering") on a flat, hard surface. Colored glass threads could then be wrapped around the body and pressed into the soft glass. On many vessels, festoons, chevrons, and swirls were created by combing these filaments with a metal tool. Finally, the friable core was removed after the vessel had cooled.

Possibly the finest example of an Egyptian core-formed glass container was found at Amarna. This flask, in the shape of a tilapia fish (fig. 98), was part of a cache discovered beneath the floor of a private house in the Central City.[24] The fish, whose dorsal fin gently curves and folds, appears to be swimming through mild resistance and about to gulp a mouthful of water. Considering the intractable medium and the Egyptian tendency toward symbolic representation, the artist's interpretation is amazingly lifelike—an outstanding example of naturalism in the applied arts.

Another ornamental device found on vessels and jewelry is the stratified "eye." It was fabricated in a multistep process that involved marvering into the body hot glass drops of decreasing size and contrasting colors. Only fragments of what must have been dramatic-looking vessels have survived (fig. 100). More common were "eyes" on beads and amuletic ornaments incorporating the Sacred Eye of Horus *(wedjat)*. So powerfully appealing were these trinkets that the technique and the motif spread throughout the ancient world.

Wood

Timber was scarce in Egypt, and the softwoods available locally, such as acacia *(Acacia nilotica)*, tamarisk *(Tamarix nilotica)*, and sycamore *(Ficus sycomorus)*, were difficult to work and of limited use. This was also the case with wood from the date- and dom-palm trees. The durable hardwoods—cedar from Lebanon, ash from western Asia and ebony from central Africa—were imported and therefore used sparingly. It is likely that beds, chairs, stools (fig. 101), pot stands, and chests crafted from wood were made only for royalty and the upper classes. Interior design even among the privileged, however, could be described as minimalist.

Woodworkers enhanced their products, including sculpture, with gold sheet and inlays of precious metal, ivory, faience, and glass. They sometimes disguised poor-quality wood with a veneer or a gessoed, painted surface. Palm logs were used for roofing and window grilles, but for security reasons, doors were more solidly constructed, and most of them appear to have been removed when the houses at Amarna were vacated.

Stone

Aside from its use in sculpture, stone at Amarna was turned into architectural elements, vessels, and utilitarian objects such as headrests and seats. Because of the scarcity of wood, much of the furniture found in the Workmen's Village was carved out of limestone. Stone was also used for mangers (fig. 102) and querns (grain mills). Although most Amarna buildings were constructed of mud brick and other perishable materials, stone was employed where strength and durability were required—for column bases; lintels, door jambs, and thresholds; and bathroom fixtures such as toilet seats.

Fine stones, such as creamy alabaster (calcite), red breccia, and blue-glazed steatite, were selected for making small vessels, cosmetic equipment, beads, amulets, and inlays. These refined items were worked with simple copper and/or bronze tools and sand abrasives.

Textiles

Materials commonly used for textiles in ancient Egypt were linen (from flax, *Linium usitatissimum*) and wool from domesticated sheep. Goat hair was used at Amarna, but less frequently; cotton did not appear in the Nile Valley until the Greco-Roman Period.

Fig. 101 Lattice stool (cat. 168)

Stools were the most common kind of furniture in the Egyptian household and workplace. They ranged in style from low, one-piece constructions of wood or stone to elegant figural items made of precious materials.

Fig. 102 Manger (cat. 84)

This limestone fragment, with an image of an ox, was one of more than a dozen feeding troughs found in an animal pen in the North Palace.

Fig. 103 Spinning bowl (cat. 156)

The limestone bowl held thread as it was spun from fibers.

Fig. 104 Basket (cat. 193)

Coil-made baskets of woven vegetable fiber were used to store items such as food and toiletries.

A wide range of finished goods—including clothing (for daily wear and for funerary use), household furnishings, sails, and awnings—demonstrates the central role of the textile industry in Egyptian culture.

Predynastic artifacts, such as whorls and tension pots for spinning and a ceramic dish with a depiction of a two-beam horizontal (floor) loom, attest to the antiquity of weaving. However, details of the processes involved in cloth manufacture first appeared in tomb representations and models in the Middle Kingdom. A fine example comes from the tomb of the Chancellor Meketra at Deir el-Bahari, in Thebes. It is a painted wooden model of an all-female weaving atelier[25] that includes three seated workers rolling flax fibers into loosely twisted strands on their knees ("roving"), three spinners drawing roves from tension buckets and guiding them onto spindles, two workers arranging spun thread into figure-eight warps on wall pegs, and several seated weavers working two floor looms. The beams of the looms are anchored by floor pegs, and tools such as weaver's swords, shed sticks, and shuttles are clearly delineated.

The use of the vertical loom during the 18th Dynasty was one of many innovations introduced by the Hyksos, who had ruled Egypt during the preceding Intermediate Period.[26] Its basic feature, a double-beam warp apparatus set in a rectangular wooden frame, is illustrated in the Theban tomb of the official Djehutynefer (fig. 105). Evidence for the use of this technical advance at Amarna—which allowed for complex constructions and tapestry weaving—turned up recently when Kemp recovered heavy limestone blocks with deeply carved sockets from the Workmen's Village. These were most likely placed in opposite corners of the room to secure the wooden loom to the floor.[27] Also recovered from this site were several thousand textile fragments, most of them made of spun vegetable fiber. A small percentage of the thread and cloth was colored with organic and mineral dyes—most frequently red (madder), blue (indigotin), and purple (the two combined).[28] The basic weaves of these textiles were of the tabby and basket varieties, and fringes were a primary decorative element. Textures ranged from very fine to coarse and uneven, depending upon use and the status of the owner.

Excavators at Amarna were surprised to find textile-related tools such as spindle whorls and spinning bowls (fig. 103) clustered in the North Suburb, the Central City, and the Workmen's Village rather than in palace and temple precincts. This distribution suggests that textile manufacture, like faience production, was decentralized and organized as a cottage industry. Workers presumably had more freedom under this arrangement—an ideal situation for artisans and craftsmen.

Closely related to weaving was basketry,[29] which used reed, dom-palm rib and leaf, halfa grass, and flax—all indigenous plants and readily available. A popular item during the New Kingdom was the lidded oval basket (fig. 104), made from a continuous spiral coil of reed or grass oversewn with palm leaf, and used to store fruits or toiletries. Sandals and rope were also woven from vegetable fiber.

Current Research

Whereas early investigators such as Petrie relied heavily on direct observation and classification in their study of material culture, the current generation of researchers has been applying the tools and methods of modern science in both the field and the laboratory. Further examination of plant and animal fibers used in textile production, chemical analysis of waste products recovered from manufacturing sites, replication of ancient kilns, and statistical evaluation of ring-bezel distribution patterns will help fill the gaps in our understanding of daily life at Amarna.

Fig. 105 Vertical loom as represented in the Theban tomb of Djehutynefer. (Line drawing from a relief.)

1. James 1984, pp. 182–83.

2. N. de G. Davies 1903–8, vol. 3, pp. 14–15, pl. XVIII.

3. J. Phillips 1991, p. 38.

4. Powell 1995, pp. 309–35.

5. Tutankhamen's tomb, which was plundered and resealed in antiquity, contained precious-metal objects of daily life adapted for funerary use as well as items made exclusively for burial. See el-Mallakh and Brackman 1978.

6. Pendlebury 1951, p. 65, no. 177.

7. Frankfort and Pendlebury 1933, pp. 59–61, pl. XLIII.

8. Kemp 1989, pp. 244–45.

9. For a description of this group, see Martin 1974, 1989, vol. 1, pp. 75–81. Though Martin notes that Aldred excluded several items of "Romano-Coptic" date, it is probable that several of the gold ear ornaments, especially the jewel with applied wirework and granulation (National Museums of Scotland, Edinburgh, A 1883.49.11, 12), are Ptolemaic. For comparable ornaments, see Williams and Ogden 1994, p. 98, nos. 51, 52.

10. The earliest preserved example, however, comes from the burial of a late Dynasty 17 woman at Qurna. See Aldred 1971, pl. 48, pp. 197–98.

11. W. R. Johnson 1990, pp. 36–38.

12. Gaballa 1977. See also C. Zivie 1975.

13. Nicholson 1998, pp. 53–54.

14. The white background found in many polychrome tiles was achieved by grinding clear or milky quartz into a fine powder. Desert sand contains impurities that can colorize the body.

15. Boyce 1989, pp. 160.

16. Ibid., p. 161.

17. Turner 1956, p. 171.

18. Turner 1954, p. 443.

19. Lilyquist and Brill 1993, p. 43.

20. This is based on the presence at Amarna of cylindrical vessels identified as ingot molds. See Nicholson, Jackson, and Trott 1997.

21. The continued importation of some forms of raw glass as ingots from Asia is supported by the archaeological evidence as well as the Amarna letters. See Nicholson 1993, pp. 49–51 and Moran 1992, pp. 347, 351–52, 354–55.

22. Nicholson 1993, pp. 42–44.

23. Kemp and Nicholson 1997, pp. 11–13.

24. It was found buried under the floor of a small room outside house N.49.20. The hoard included two other glass vessels and three silver containers. See Peet 1921, p. 175, pl. XXX.

25. Weaving, in contrast to other crafts, was a woman's profession.

26. R. Hall 1986, p. 15.

27. Kemp 1997, pp. 7–9.

28. Eastwood 1985.

29. Lucas and Harris 1962, pp. 128–33.

Administering Akhenaten's Egypt

Peter Der Manuelian

Akhenaten's administrators and military men seem to have spent much of their time keeping order at home, organizing temple activities, and erasing the names of proscribed gods from buildings and monuments.

Fig. 106 Before the revolution

Ramose, a Theban official, apparently did not follow Akhenaten to Amarna. In this image from his tomb at Thebes, the "revered one before Ra, Overseer of the City and Vizier, Ramose, justified" receives libations.

So fascinating is Akhenaten's character, so personal are his policies, that in any study of his reign he tends to draw all our attention. A brand-new capital city, a vastly reduced pantheon, a possible about-face on foreign policy, and his murky family succession all fix our interest on the king and court at this most unusual time in Egyptian history. But we are equally rewarded when we look beyond the palace at the administration of the country under the heretic pharaoh's regime. For no matter how personal Akhenaten's agenda was, its ultimate success or failure depended on its daily implementation and reception throughout the country—by the bureaucracy, the military, and the workforce.

Radical shifts in government policy always accentuate contrasts between the traditionalists and the reformers. There must have been a wide variety of reactions to Akhenaten's innovations, though we have no evidence of their expression. People supporting the pharaoh would have included faithful Aten-worshippers, political opportunists hoping to rise in the new bureaucracy, and, of course, those who accepted unconditionally the institution of pharaonic authority. Some scholars prefer to emphasize the political, rather than the religious, nature of the Amarna revolution, seeing it as Akhenaten's attempt to wrest power away from the ever-expanding priesthood of Amen and refocus it in the monarchy.

Among the Egyptians less likely to accept Akhenaten's new precepts were, as might be expected, those with something to lose. A priest of Amen at a typical Egyptian temple would have found himself suddenly deposed or reassigned, and his temple closed or its resources redirected to support the cult of the Aten. But we should bear in mind that the illiterate majority of the nation may have had little comprehension of the king's complex religious and philosophical reforms. A farmer in the Delta may hardly have cared what national god headed the Egyptian pantheon, as long as the local deities still watched over his harvest, family, and village; how long these traditional gods escaped the king's proscriptions remains a matter of debate.

Since the ancient written sources never represent the lower echelons of the Egyptian population, we will never know exactly how Akhenaten's program was first received; many tantalizing questions remain. Exactly who followed the king north from Thebes, after year 5, to Akhetaten? Only a few officials, such as the Cup-Bearer Parennefer, are attested (often by the presence of a tomb) at both cities, and their texts stress nothing

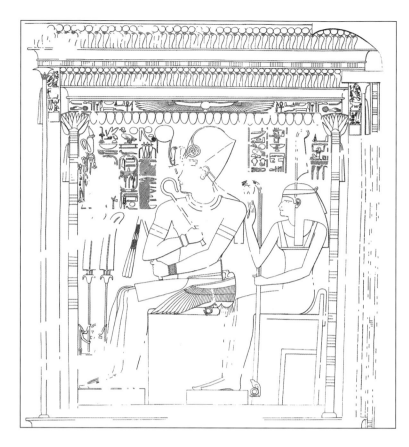

Fig. 107 Tradition and innovation

Akhenaten appears in both the traditional style (left, as Amenhotep IV) and his revolutionary style in the Theban tomb of Ramose. (Line drawings from tomb reliefs.)

but their undying allegiance to the new king. What happened, though, to those who chose not to relinquish their administrative stations at Memphis and Thebes, the northern and southern capitals? Were they left alone or were they purged? The tombs of some individuals, such as Kheruef, Steward of Queen Tiye at Thebes, certainly show marks of malevolence, including the erasure of texts and figures.[1]

The basic structure of the Egyptian administration during Akhenaten's reign probably continued unchanged from previous dynasties. In a land that knew no separation of religion and state, the latter was embodied in the divine person of the king, and the temples were state institutions that controlled all manner of public works, taxation, and economic redistribution. The land was still divided into nomes, or provinces, administered by local governors, priests, and *kenbet*s, or councils of judges, whose responsibilities included hearing petitions over land disputes after the Nile's annual inundation obscured boundaries. These officials reported in hierarchical sequence up to the king's northern and southern viziers, or prime ministers.[2]

At Thebes, the fate of several high officials who lived through the succession from Amenhotep III to Akhenaten remains unclear. Most interesting is perhaps the Vizier Ramose (fig. 106), in whose tomb Akhenaten appears twice on the same wall: in traditional style in one scene, and with all his physical eccentricities in another (fig. 107).[3] Ramose, like so many other Theban officials, is not attested at Amarna. Instead, a new cast of characters emerges there, known from two series of elaborate tombs cut into the cliffs east of the city (fig. 109; see also the essay "Preparing for Eternity"). Just how far afield Akhenaten may have had to go for new loyalty is suggested by the many foreigners who surfaced within the administration. One of the king's viziers, named

Aper-el, whose tomb was discovered at Saqqara, the Memphite necropolis, in 1989, may have been of Semitic origin.[4]

While estimates for the entire population at Amarna range from twenty thousand to as many as fifty thousand,[5] only a tiny number of these individuals are known to us by name. Most of the houses of the elite have long since lost the inscribed doorways and lintels that once bore their owners' names and titles. The tombs at Amarna provide us with an important cast of characters, but one that is limited to fewer than fifty individuals instead of the two hundred forty or so we would expect; many Amarna officials must have kept both their lands and their burial plans back in their towns of origin, or at Memphis or Thebes.

In addition to various private economic initiatives (crafts, trades and manufacture, and storage and distribution of grain, which was used as a form of currency as well as food), we must imagine an active bureaucracy at Amarna regulating temple wealth, facilitating communication with the rest of the country, organizing the visits of foreign emissaries, and even supervising construction of the unusually numerous wells throughout the city. Like Amarna tomb wall scenes, reliefs from temples and other structures dismantled after Akhenaten's death give us glimpses of administrative life.

The military played a large role in the formal aspects of life at Amarna, to judge from the representations of troops and escorts surrounding Akhenaten's sojourns along the Royal Road and his ritual appearances at the King's House in the Central City. The Chief of Police, Mahu, must have been quite preoccupied with the regulation of these events; a private stela depicts a Western Asiatic soldier who probably served in the king's bodyguard (fig. 121). Other military officials serving the king were May, General and Fanbearer at the King's Right Hand, and a scribe (what we might call a registrar)

Fig. 108 Stamped brick (Museum of Fine Arts, Boston)

This brick from the records office at Amarna identifies the building as the "House of the Correspondence of the Pharaoh."

Fig. 109 Mansions of eternity

General view of the North Tombs of Akhenaten's officials at Amarna.

Fig. 110 Private stela (cat. 175)

This stela of Menena and Yaya (the two men seated on stools) was found outside a house at Amarna. Their female companions are identified as Tashety and Mery.

of recruits named Ptahmose who, in the spirit of the times, changed his name to Ramose, emphasizing a solar deity over the traditional Memphite creator god, Ptah. The king's highest administrative official at Amarna was the Vizier Nakht, whose house lay nowhere near that of the king in the north, but far to the south of the Central City. Whether this distance bears any political significance remains unclear. Akhenaten's high priest, Meryra I, probably supervised the operations of at least some of the Aten temples, while the above-mentioned Parennefer was in charge of the distribution of grain to temples around the country. Foreigners of high rank at Amarna included Pentu, the Chief Physician, and the Chamberlain Tutu, who may have been in charge of the records office, where the foreign diplomatic correspondence now known as the "Amarna letters" was kept (see the essay "Foreign Relations" and cats. 119-121). A stamped brick from the records office (fig. 108) serves to identify this structure. These are just some of the highest officials at Amarna; there was, of course, a substantial corps of minor officials, as is suggested by the existence of a small votive stela, from a house near the Great Temple (fig. 110), showing two men whose specific contributions to the development of the new capital are not mentioned.

If the basic administration of the rest of the country continued as before, there was one activity pursued on a scale previously unknown in all of Egyptian history. Akhenaten gave orders nationwide to erase the names of Amen, several other deities he had rejected, and even the hieroglyphic word "god" wherever it occurred in the plural (*netjeru*, "gods").[6] Personal names that happened to include "Amen" or "Mut" (for example, Amenemhat or Mutemwia) were also erased (fig. 111). Temples were defaced, tomb chapels were opened and names hacked out; even small, portable objects were censored. One wonders if any single event in the king's reign could have polarized the populace quite so violently; no written accounts document the trauma. (For one possible explanation, see "The Setting: History, Religion, and Art.") How would a typical Egyptian have felt, watching an official of the new regime march into his parents' tomb with a crew of illiterate henchmen and efface so many carefully carved and painted inscriptions? To the Egyptians, erasing a name was tantamount to ritual murder.

That the iconoclasts were often illiterate, and perhaps given "cue cards" with lists of signs to obliterate, is shown by some of the errors they made. Hieroglyphs that resembled the hated signs but meant something completely different were often chiseled away, and an abbreviated spelling of the word for "gods" often escaped unscathed because it looked more like the singular "god" than the plural.

Textual evidence for Akhenaten's administrative policies is scarce. A fragmentary text from Karnak announces a tax throughout the land in support of the Aten cult.[7] Akhenaten's boundary stelae surrounding the site of Amarna (years 5, 6, and 8) obliquely refer to conditions not to his liking and outline his intentions for his new capital city.[8] Two other stelae, from Buhen and Amada, record a campaign to the south launched under his Nubian Viceroy Thutmose to quell a Nubian uprising.[9] And the famous international correspondence of cuneiform tablets from the records office at Amarna documents the king's foreign policy—or lack thereof—for the northeast, as the Hittite empire expanded at the expense of Egypt's sphere of influence.[10]

More detailed texts shed light on administration in the period immediately following the king's death. Successors Tutankhamen and Horemheb each inscribed stelae outlining governmental reforms and restorations that were in direct opposition to Akhenaten's short-lived policies. Tutankhamen—or, more likely, those wielding power for him—wrote of the ruinous state of the ancient temples and their subsequent re-establishment ("the temples and cities of the gods and goddesses ... were fallen into decay and their shrines were fallen into ruin, having become mere mounds overgrown with grass ...").[11] After taking the throne, Horemheb issued a series of decrees reorganizing *kenbet* councils; some of these reforms might have arisen in reaction to the Amarna age.[12] Akhenaten's buildings were dismantled, and the name of Amen was restored to many defaced monuments throughout Egypt and Nubia. It is thus hard to know who instituted more administrative activity and change—Akhenaten with his radical reforms, or his successors, reversing the ship of state to put it back on its original course.

Fig. 111 Sculpture of Amenhotep III (cat. 5)

The statue, from Gebel Barkal in Nubia, shows cartouches of Amenhotep III that were erased during his son's reign because they contained the name of the god Amen.

1. Epigraphic Survey 1980.

2. Pardey 1998. For inscriptions detailing the Vizier's responsibilities, see N. de G. Davies 1943, pls. CXVII-CXXII, and van den Boorn 1988. See also Munro 1987, cols. 137–43.

3. N. de G. Davies 1941, pls. XXIX and XXXIII.

4. A. Zivie 1990; Gessler-Löhr 1995, p. 151.

5. Kemp 1989, pp. 305–6.

6. Manuelian 1999.

7. Murnane 1995b, pp. 30–31 (§6).

8. Ibid., pp. 73–81 (§37).

9. Ibid., pp. 101–3 (§§55–56).

10. Murnane 1995a, pp. 705–6.

11. Murnane 1995b, p. 213 (§99); see also Murnane's essay in this book, "The Return to Orthodoxy."

12. Murnane 1995b, pp. 235–40 (§108); Kruchten 1981; Gnirs 1989.

The Spoken and Written Word

David P. Silverman

Among the changes Akhenaten brought about was the addition of vernacular to the Egyptian language.

Fig. 112 Statuette of Akhenaten holding a stela (cat. 36)

The painted hieroglyphic text that once covered the back pillar and the front of the stela is now missing.

Writing in ancient Egypt appears around 3300 B.C., and the first signs used to record the language take the form of concrete, recognizable images from the natural world. Today we call these signs hieroglyphs ("sacred writing"), based on a term used by the Greeks which may derive ultimately from the ancient Egyptian term *medu netjer,* "words of the gods." Indeed, the signs were thought to have magical properties and were associated with divinity. Because of the care and time needed to write these detailed characters, scribes quickly devised a less cumbersome method. When the situation did not demand the formal version, a more cursive writing script now known as hieratic was used. It became more of an "everyday" style, not associated with the gods. Though it, too, was derived from images, these were not immediately recognizable in the script. The two systems continued concurrently through most of pharaonic times, including the revolutionary Amarna Period. Each was specific to particular types of texts, although overlapping occasionally occurred.[1]

Early in the history of language in Egypt, a well-developed system of grammar came into being. Over time, the language evolved, and several distinct stages are now recognized, each with characteristic constructions, patterns, and forms.[2] For instance, the early synthetic verbal system, in which the stem of the verb itself can change to indicate semantic and syntactic distinctions, is replaced to large extent by a more analytic system marked by separate, more clearly distinguishable elements.[3] Other aspects of the language, some of them orthographic, change over time: the main negatives in the Old and Middle Kingdoms begin with *n*, which is replaced by *b* in Late Egyptian of the New Kingdom. This later stage of the language also sees the regular use of the definite articles, ⳣ *pa*, ⳣ *ta*, and ⳣ *na*, whereas these words hardly appear in the Old Egyptian and are infrequent in Middle Egyptian. Phraseology as well as paleography can be specific to a period of time, and language development is not limited to ancient cultures. The early stage of our language is called "Old English," and the recorded texts of several hundred years ago show many differences when compared with those of only one hundred years ago and those of more recent times.

As a rule, writing and speech can be expected to develop gradually over a long period; however, a more immediate modification (sometimes quite drastic) can result from a variety of factors, such as political, religious, or societal motivations. Egyptian

President Anwar Sadat made such a change during the early 1970s, when he introduced into his speeches a more informal pattern that had been limited mainly to radio and television broadcasts.[4] Often an invading nation will introduce its own language to the conquered people, and that can affect the indigenous language greatly. For example, when Alexander the Great conquered Egypt in 332 B.C., he brought with him the Greek language and its alphabet, which were quite distinct from the language and writing current in Egypt.

During the Amarna Period, Akhenaten made many changes in the traditional culture, which had existed for more than a millennium: the religion, the style of art and architecture, the content of hymns, and the iconography are only a few.[5] It would not be surprising, therefore, to see that he also modified the language, and, in fact, the texts of the Amarna Period contain several vernacular elements, such as the definite article and the possessive adjective. Although these "spoken" features had appeared sporadically in much earlier texts as well as in those of the late 17th and early 18th Dynasties,[6] the general practice had been to leave the definite article unexpressed and to indicate the possessive adjective by the suffix pronoun (like our possessive pronoun).[7] The king undoubtedly viewed his linguistic changes as a complement to his new doctrines, and some scholars have regarded the introduction of these vernacular features into the more formal style of Middle Egyptian as a "popularization" of the language.[8] Akhenaten's teaching apparently reflected oral components as well as suggesting oral transmission,[9] and it may well be tempting to see some correlation between the emphasis on natural philosophy in the writings of the monarch[10] and the use of less formal patterns of expression. However, the relationship, if any, is not founded on the desire of the king to make what he said more "understandable" or relevant to the common people.

The art of the Amarna Period, too, exhibited more naturalism than before, both in style and gesture. More than a programmatic attempt to portray the king as one of the people, however, the expressionistic rendering of Akhenaten's recognizable features may well have been an exaggerated example of the traditional practice of emphasizing certain pharaonic features during the reign of a particular ruler.[11] For example, during the 12th Dynasty (about 1836–1818 B.C.), images of deities, officials, the royal family, and ordinary people often exhibited the same careworn expression as images of their pharaoh, Sesostris III. Why, indeed, would Akhenaten wish consciously to have the language of his religious movement close to that of the people's speech and the art portraying him focus on his clearly human traits when no other aspect of his new religion was truly populist?[12] On the contrary, his religion was very restrictive and served to separate him from, and elevate him above, his subjects. It was he alone who worshipped the Aten, although sometimes Nefertiti did as well. Akhenaten was the sole priest of his deity, and the people worshipped through him. On temple blocks commemorating the jubilee, he appears as a deity with his own high priest.[13]

Fig. 114 Boundary stela

Carved into the cliffs on both sides of the Nile, the boundary stelae combine images with textual records of Akhenaten's intentions for his new city.

Fig. 113 Fragment of a decorated balustrade (cat. 72)

The king, the queen, and a princess are shown in Akhenaten's early, exaggerated style.

The motive for changes in language, as in other areas, was less a desire for popular appeal than part of an elaborate plan to emphasize the divinity of the living king.[14] An amalgam of classical literary forms with nonliterary and vernacular components, Akhenaten's language represented a distinct, almost artificial, literary style, one that differed from what preceded and what would succeed it. It focused on the king, demonstrating his uniqueness. Just as the physical traits that prevailed in visual art were his traits, the language that the people now spoke was Akhenaten's language, and this aided him in accomplishing his religious and sociopolitical reforms.

Close observation of all of the texts written at Amarna[15] reveals that the frequency and variation of spoken elements are quite limited in formal inscriptions relating to Akhenaten. That is not the case with contemporary nonliterary texts such as letters written in hieratic on papyri or ostraca (flakes of limestone) found at the capital and elsewhere. They document everyday activities and events, using an increasing number of vernacular features. This trend is also found in a Theban tomb scene, where the speech of the tomb owner, Parennefer, is recorded in hieroglyphs. It is precisely this genre, not Akhenaten's language, that represents the direct line of development to the new idiom of Late Egyptian.[16]

Akhenaten's amalgam does, however, bear some similarity to literary Late Egyptian, the language used in the composition of stories, and it may have served as an inspiration for this genre. For all its distinctiveness, the style in which Akhenaten chose to promote and document his new religion represents a visible link between royal monumental inscriptions of the earlier part of the 18th Dynasty, written in the classical idiom, and the later texts that would be composed under Ramesses II.[17] Akhenaten's language, like his other innovations, influenced Egyptian culture for many generations.

1 W. V. Davies 1987b, pp. 10–29; Silverman 1990, pp. 3–6; Forman and Quirke 1996, pp. 12–19; and Silverman 1997, pp. 233–35.

2. Stricker 1944, pp. 12ff.; Gardiner 1969, pp. 4–6; Junge 1984, cols. 1190–91; and Silverman 1990, pp. 8–12.

3. Groll 1975–76, pp. 237–46; J. Allen 1982, pp. 19–27; Junge 1996, p. 49.

4. Killean 1980.

5. See D. Redford 1984, pp. 142–80; Tobin 1986; Aldred 1988, pp. 66–90; O'Connor 1989; Assmann 1992, pp. 143–76; Assmann 1995; D. Redford 1995, pp. 178–81; J. Allen 1996; Arnold 1996, pp. 17–39; Baines 1996, pp. 165–66; and Baines 1998, 306–7.

6. Kroeber 1970, pp. I–XX; Smith and Smith 1976, pp. 48–76; Silverman 1981, pp. 64–65; Eyre 1990, pp. 145–48 and 160–65; and Junge 1996, pp. 1–22.

7. In dealing with "dead" languages, scholars often make analogies with living ones to determine in which types of texts the vernacular may appear. They investigate such material as letters and transcribed dialogues, quotations, recitations, and songs to note differences from other texts. In the case of Egyptian, beginning with the Old Kingdom, they can also examine the conversations among the figures appearing in scenes of daily life depicted on tomb walls. There grammar and phraseology are similar to those in letters and quotations but differ from the style of formal texts.

8. Aldred 1973, p. 15, and J. Allen 1996, p. 4. See also below, n. 10.

9. Tobin 1986 and D. Redford 1995, pp. 178–79.

10. Assmann 1992, pp. 143ff. and J. Allen 1989, pp. 89–101.

11. See, however, Nicolas Grimal, who regards the "naturalistic" elements in Amarna style, pose, and language as "giving a distinctly intimate impression." Such views of the royal family may reflect the triads of deities (male god + female consort + divine offspring) in the mythology of the by-then-discarded traditional pantheon (Grimal 1992, p. 233).

12. Silverman 1991a, pp. 76–81; Silverman 1995, pp. 77–78.

13. Silverman 1991a, p. 83; D. Redford 1995, pp. 175–78; J. Allen 1996, p. 4.

14. D. Redford 1995, pp. 175–78; Silverman 1995, pp. 80–87; and J. Allen 1996, p. 5. See also Baines 1998, pp. 298–99.

15. Sandman 1938.

16. Silverman 1991b, pp. 305–10; see, however, Junge 1984, cols. 1190–91; Junge 1996, pp. 15–22; and Baines 1998, pp. 306–7.

17. Silverman 1991b, p. 309 and Silverman 1995, p. 78.

Foreign Relations

Timothy Kendall

Fig. 115 Sculptor's model of a horse's head (cat. 124)

The horse, along with the chariot, was introduced into Egypt from the Near East early in the seventeenth century B.C. and immediately became the passion of Egyptian royalty and nobility. Only a few men of that time dared to ride the horse—which was done sitting back on the animal's rump, without saddle or stirrups!

When Akhenaten inherited his father's throne, Egypt's empire was unsurpassed—in wealth, military might, and sheer size. Just over a century earlier his dynastic forebears had pushed their frontier eight hundred miles up the Nile from Aswan, deep into Nubia (maps, page 14). This conquest not only gave them control of the gold mines of the Nubian deserts and the overland trade with central Africa, but also provided them with an inexhaustible supply of superb fighting men (fig. 116).[2] In the north, through equally energetic campaigning, they had fixed Egypt's imperial boundary at the great bend of the Euphrates, forcing into submission all the petty rulers of the Levantine coast and its hinterland. Thus, at the time of his accession, Akhenaten's empire extended two thousand miles from end to end, incorporated seemingly limitless lands and wealth, and included peoples of many races, cultures, and languages.[3] Small wonder that the Egyptian king could present himself as a veritable sun god on earth, giving the "breath of life" to all creation.

By Akhenaten's time, Nubia ("Kush") had long since been pacified and was being governed by an efficient Egyptian bureaucracy. Because it had become an almost exclusive preserve of the Amen religious establishment, the new king's interest in the province became primarily iconoclastic. At the beginning of his reign, when the king was still known as Amenhotep IV, he founded a town dedicated to Amen at Sesebi, north of the Third Cataract of the Nile, but quickly adapted it to the Aten cult.[4] Akhenaten was probably also the founder of a second Nubian town, south of the Third Cataract, at Kawa, which was named, like his new temple at Karnak, Gempaaten ("The Aten is Found").[5] As the ultimate blow to the Nubian Amen cult, he ordered his Viceroy of Kush to close and probably dismantle the "Nubian Karnak" at Gebel Barkal, near the Fourth Cataract, and to excise Amen's name wherever it occurred.[6]

We would know little of Akhenaten's Asian affairs were it not for a remarkable discovery made in 1887 by Egyptian peasants at Amarna. Digging among the ruins for limestone to be ground as fertilizer, they chanced upon nearly four hundred clay tablets inscribed in Assyro-Babylonian cuneiform. The documents were the nearly complete diplomatic correspondence between the Egyptian court and the various rulers of the Near East over nearly half a century, through the reigns of Amenhotep III, Akhenaten, Smenkhkara, Tutankhamen, and possibly even Ay.[7] Subsequent investigations deter-

Fig. 116 Nubian soldiers with
ostrich plumes (cat. 117)

mined that the tablets derived from a building called the "House of the Correspondence of the Pharaoh." It was, in effect, the site of Akhenaten's State Department.[8]

For the most part, the "Amarna letters," as they came to be called, were written in an artificial Babylonian (Akkadian) dialect, liberally infused with West Semitic and Egyptian words, that served as the international diplomatic language of the day. They reveal that at the capital Egyptian scribes studied and mastered the cuneiform script of the Near East and the several languages that employed it. Here the scribes also welcomed and conversed with messengers from abroad; they recorded and copied incoming documents and then probably translated them into hieratic script (cursive Egyptian) on papyrus scrolls, which have not survived. The letters were all written as if to be read aloud to Pharaoh.

More than three hundred of the letters came from Egypt's vassals in what is today Palestine, Israel, and Syria, who addressed Pharaoh in the most obsequious terms. Among them were the kings of such familiar cities as Jerusalem, Tyre, Sidon, Damascus, and Byblos, many of which bear the same names today. Approximately fifty letters in the archive came from independent foreign states, whose rulers spoke to Pharaoh as equals. These letters reveal that at this time there were six great kingdoms in the Near East whose rulers corresponded with Egypt: Kassite Babylonia (southern Iraq), Assyria (the upper Tigris River area), Mitanni (northern Syria and northern Iraq), Hatti—the Hittite empire (central Turkey), Arzawa (southwestern Turkey), and Alashiya (Cyprus).

It is evident from the letters that Amenhotep III managed his Asian empire with diligence and skill. He corresponded frequently with his fractious vassals, kept them under close scrutiny, appointed Egyptian governors, and quartered troops in the region. He also maintained good relations with the great powers beyond his borders—on one hand, to secure badly needed natural resources, such as copper, silver, and lapis lazuli, as well as exotic manufactured goods and beautiful women for his pleasure, and on the other, to prevent costly border disputes and open warfare. The kings of Arzawa, Babylonia, and Mitanni, for example, all gave him daughters in marriage, and he returned lavish gifts to the delighted "fathers-in-law." Since Mitanni lay immediately north of his Syrian territory, Amenhotep sought a particularly close relationship with its king, Tushratta, marrying a sister and a daughter of his and sending quantities of gold in return. His aim apparently was to cement and maintain a mutual defense pact

Fig. 118 Letter from the king of Alashiya (Cyprus) to Akhenaten (cat. 119)

The unnamed king was sending a personal gift to Pharaoh of one hundred talents of copper and congratulating him on his accession:

"An alliance should be made between the two of us, and my messengers should go to you, and your messengers should come to me.... I herewith send a jar of 'sweet oil' to be poured on your head, seeing that you have (now) sat down upon your royal throne."[10]

Fig. 117 Letter from Tushratta, king of Mitanni (northern Syria), to Queen Tiye (cat. 120)

Tushratta complains that Tiye's son Akhenaten fails to show him the same "love" that her late husband, Amenhotep III, did.

"I will not forget the love for Mimmureya [i.e. Nebmaatra = Amenhotep III], your husband. More than ever before, at this very moment, I show 10 times—much, much—more love to Napkhurreya [i.e. Neferkheprura = Akhenaten], your son. You are the one who knows the words of ... your husband, but you did not send all of my greeting gift that your husband ordered to be sent. I had asked your husband for statues of solid cast gold ... But now ... your son has (sent me) plated statues of wood. With gold being dirt in your son's country, why have they been a source of such distress to (him) that he has not given them to me? ... Is this love? ..."[9]

Fig. 119 Letter from Abi-Milki, king of Tyre, to Akhenaten (cat. 121)

In a long, poetic ramble, the Egyptian vassal king in the Canaanite port city praises Pharaoh obsequiously:

"I fall at the feet of the king, my lord, 7 and 7 times. I am the dirt beneath the sandals of the king, my lord. My lord is the Sun who comes forth over all lands day by day, according to the way of the Sun, his gracious father, who gives life with his sweet breath and returns with the north wind; who establishes the entire land in peace by the power of his arm ... who gives forth his cry in the sky like Baal, and all the land is frightened...."

The only important message is contained in the penultimate sentence: that his neighbor, Zimridda, king of Sidon, *"writes daily to the rebel Aziru ... (and tells him) every word he has heard from Egypt. I herewith write to my lord, and it is good that he knows (it)."*[11]

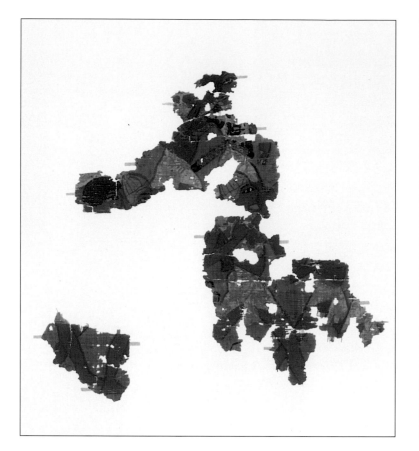

Fig. 120 Painted papyrus illustrating a battle scene (British Museum, London)

Fragments were found at Amarna in the "Chapel of the King's Statues" and the image was reconstructed in the line drawing at right. Although some of the soldiers wear Asiatic-style bronze helmets and short-sleeved corselets, all are beardless, which suggests that they are Egyptian troops. The armor was probably supplied as tribute to Egypt by dependent provinces in the Near East.

whereby Tushratta agreed to defend Egypt's Syrian interests and the Egyptian king agreed to help finance Tushratta's army to keep the menacing Hittites and their aggressive new king, Shuppiluliuma, in check beyond the Taurus mountains.

The letters suggest that after the death of Amenhotep III, the situation in Asia deteriorated rapidly. The crisis can only be attributed to Akhenaten's preoccupation with internal Egyptian affairs, the promulgation of his new cult, and the construction of his new capital. Though he received his father's foreign brides into his *harim*, he showed little other interest in matters international, and he was a poor correspondent. He sent little or no aid to loyal vassals when it was repeatedly requested, and he left many of them in desperate straits when the provinces surrounding them were ravaged by renegades; he even refused to punish these rebels when they were apprehended. The urgent pleas of Tushratta for a continuance of "familial" ties likewise fell on deaf ears (fig. 117). Akhenaten let the alliance lapse, while allowing himself to be flattered by friendly overtures from the Hittite court. Tushratta, now without moral and financial support from Pharaoh, was fatally compromised. His empire fell quickly to the Hittites; he was assassinated by a traitorous son; and many of Egypt's northern vassals, simply to save themselves, threw in their lot with Shuppiluliuma.[12]

By the time of Akhenaten's death, the Hittites had become a serious threat in the north, yet no military action seems to have been planned or taken. The suggestion has been made that Pharaoh required his troops in Egypt to maintain internal security.[13] When Tutankhamen assumed the throne, Egypt was in disarray. The crisis was attributed to the people's denial and neglect of the old gods. Now, with a pliant youth as their new king, military commanders Ay and Horemheb designed corrective action, both on the home front and abroad. Tutankhamen would restore the old gods and shore up the army, and he would be presented to the world as a warrior pharaoh.[14]

The last international crisis of the 18th Dynasty was precipitated by the sudden death of Tutankhamen and the irregular accession to the throne of the aging Ay. As indicated by cuneiform documents found at the Hittite capital, Hattusha (near present-day Ankara, Turkey), a widowed Egyptian queen, almost certainly Ankhesenamen, wife of Tutankhamen, faced the unpalatable prospect of marrying a commoner (presumably Ay) to retain her position; she thus secretly wrote to Shuppululiuma, begging him to send one of his sons to marry her and be king of Egypt.[15] Initially skeptical, the Hittite king finally sent the requested bridegroom. The plan was discovered, however: the prince and his retinue were intercepted and murdered, the queen disappeared, and power soon passed to Horemheb, the general who would end the 18th Dynasty, reinvigorate the empire, and pass it on to the Ramessides.

Fig. 121 **Stela of a Western Asiatic soldier, his wife, and his servant** (cat. 114)

1. Moran 1992, p. 39 (modified).

2. Vercoutter 1976; Adams 1977, pp. 217–34; Schulman 1964, p. 53.

3. Weinstein et al. 1998; D. Redford 1984, pp. 193–203.

4. Blackman 1937; Fairman 1938.

5. MacAdam 1955, pp. 12–14.

6. Reisner and Reisner 1933, p. 25, pl. 3; Dunham 1970, figs. 4, 5, 20, and ??

7. Giles 1997, pp. 41–147, and nn. 99–100; Moran 1992.

8. Giles 1997, pp. 17–40.

9. Moran 1992, pp. 84–86 (modified); for comment, see Giles 1997, pp. 101–19.

10. Moran 1992, pp. 105–6; for comment, see Giles 1997, pp. 120–23.

11. Moran 1992, 233–34 (modified); for comment, see Giles 1997, pp. 201–19.

12. Giles 1997, pp. 101–19.

13. D. Redford 1984, p. 199.

14. Martin 1989, p. 97; D. Redford 1984, p. 211.

15. On the Hittite texts describing this incident and the convincing identification of the deceased Egyptian king as Tutankhamen, see Giles 1997, pp. 311–18.

Fig. 122 Canopic jar with lid
(cats. 234, 235)

This jar, from a tomb in the Valley
of the Kings, had been inscribed
for Akhenaten's "greatly beloved"
Kiya —but her name was erased.

Preparing for Eternity

Sue H. D'Auria

Though the population of Amarna is
said to have been between twenty
thousand and fifty thousand, few
tombs have been found. The architecture and decoration of the Royal
Tomb and the tombs of the highest
officials contain an interesting mix
of the innovative and the traditional.

Belief in an afterlife was a fundamental component of religion in ancient Egypt.
For thousands of years, kings and wealthy commoners alike expended significant resources to prepare their tombs and supply them with all that was deemed
necessary for use in the next world. The physical preservation of their bodies through
mummification was integral to the survival of the spiritual aspects of each individual.
The *ka*, or life-force of the deceased, represented by a pair of upraised arms, was
believed to remain in the tomb and was given food and drink offerings in the chapel.
The *ba*, depicted as a human-headed bird, was free to travel to and from the tomb,
maintaining contact between the worlds of the living and the dead.

In the 18th Dynasty, the main body of funerary texts was the *Amduat* ("That Which
is in the Underworld") and, for nonroyals, the Book of the Dead. Recitations from
these collections, which invoked Ra, the sun god, and Osiris, god of the underworld,
helped the deceased enter the afterlife. While kings joined the sun god at death, traveling in the solar bark, nonroyal individuals were judged before Osiris, their hearts
weighed against the feather of Truth. If declared free of sin, the deceased were admit-
ted into the realm of the dead, but the monstrous figure of Ammit, a combination
of crocodile, lion, and hippo, lurked in the judgment hall to devour any who failed
the test.

This richly woven tapestry of beliefs and practices was severely rent during the
Amarna interlude. The disruption is reflected in the architecture, decoration, and furnishings of both royal and private tombs. To trace the development of these changes,
we begin with the years preceding Akhenaten's reign.

The Tomb of Amenhotep III

In a departure from tradition, most kings of the 18th Dynasty were buried not in pyramid complexes but in tombs tunneled deep into the limestone cliffs flanking a wadi in
Thebes known as the Valley of the Kings. Their mortuary temples, the venues for their
funerary cults, were separate from the tombs and located on the plain. Royal tombs
consisted of a series of passages leading via steps and ramps to a burial chamber housing the king's body in a stone sarcophagus. Tomb decoration focused on the journey of
the sun through the twelve hours of the night, each hour corresponding to a segment

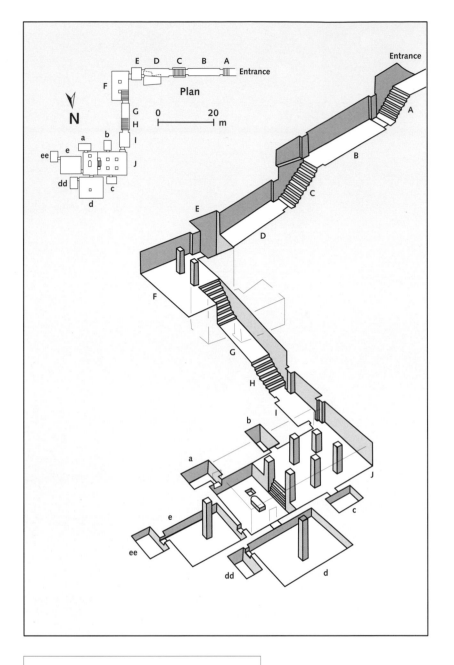

E D C B A
Entrance
Plan
N
0   20
m

F

G
H
I

a   b
e
ee
J

dd   c
d

Entrance

A

B

C

D

E

F

G

H

I

b

a

J

e

ee

dd   c

d

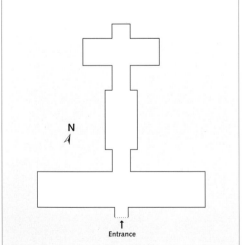

N

Entrance

of the underworld. The tombs were all rifled in antiquity, but even the scant remains of their furnishings show that the burials were opulent.

The burial place of Amenhotep III[1] (fig. 123) is one of these 18th-Dynasty rock-cut tombs. It is located in the more remote West Valley, though the king's mummy was transferred to the main valley during Dynasty 21. The tomb contains two long passages (B and D) connected by a flight of stairs. The second passage leads to a well shaft (E) whose wall decoration depicts the king standing before a variety of deities. Such shafts were a common feature of royal tombs of this era. They were probably intended to protect against floods (by diverting water from the burial chamber) and robbery (by making tunneling more complicated) and may have symbolically represented the tomb of Sokar, the Memphite god of the dead. Beyond the well in the tomb of Amenhotep III is an undecorated hall with two pillars (F). Here the tomb axis turns ninety degrees to the left. The bent axis is another feature common to royal tombs during this period. The turns may have reflected the journey to the netherworld, or, like the well, may have had the more practical role of deterring robbers. From this hall another passage descends to an antechamber (I) with decoration featuring the king offering to deities; from the antechamber there is another ninety-degree turn with the large, pillared burial chamber (J). The wall decoration here, as in other royal tombs of this dynasty, consists of scenes from the *Amduat*. Leading off the burial chamber are storerooms and two additional chambers (d and e) that may have been intended for Queen Tiye and the princess Sitamen.

The tomb of Tutankhamen is our most complete evidence for the sumptuousness of royal burials. From his and other tombs we know that the king's body was placed in a series of nested coffins within the stone sarcophagus and that furniture, clothing, and food, as well as baskets and boxes containing assorted personal items, were placed in the tomb for the king's use in the afterlife. Other necessities were the *shabti* figure—whose function was to work in the fields as a substitute for the deceased, perhaps providing sustenance in the afterlife—and a canopic chest to house the entrails removed from the mummified body.

Private Tombs in Thebes

The courtiers and high officials of the 18th Dynasty were buried in tombs cut into the cliffs between the Valley of the Kings and the Nile.[2] The size and plan of the tombs varied, but the "classic" 18th-Dynasty type was T-shaped (fig. 124) and consisted of an entrance forecourt, a hall that was transverse to the central axis, a long corridor, and an inner chamber with a niche at the rear for a statue of the deceased. A shaft led to a subterranean burial chamber that housed the body. This section of the tomb was blocked off after burial, but the upper rooms remained accessible for use in the funerary cult, including the deposit of offerings for the tomb

Fig. 125 The voyage to Abydos, from the tomb of Sennefer

Sennefer and his wife, Meryt, sit under a canopy before an offering table as an oarsman guides their papyrus-shaped boat down the Nile.

owner's *ka*. The halls and corridors of these Theban sepulchers were beautifully decorated with scenes painted on plastered walls or carved in delicate relief. Subjects included the profession of the deceased and lively vignettes of daily life, such as fishing, fowling, and agricultural work. More explicitly religious scenes featured figures of the deceased and his wife offering to the gods, depictions of the procession to the tomb, the ritual voyage to the holy city of Abydos (fig. 125), and the funeral banquet. The figure of the king seated under a canopy also appeared in many of these private tombs, occupying a prominent place. Though less elaborately furnished than royal burials of this era, private tombs also contained the requisite nested coffins, canopic jars, *shabti* figures, and personal belongings.

Several Theban tombs that belonged to officials whose careers spanned the reigns of Amenhotep III and Amenhotep IV provide a glimpse into the transition to the Amarna Period. The tombs of Kheruef and Ramose are among the largest in the necropolis. In each, the traditional decorated chamber of the T-shaped tomb is enlarged into a columned hall with delicate low relief and painting, and each has a curving subterranean passage leading to the burial chamber[3]: architectural features that continue in Amarna tombs. Kheruef[4] was Steward to Queen Tiye, who is shown several times in the tomb with Amenhotep III or her son Amenhotep IV. All of the depictions of the latter are in the traditional pre-Amarna style. Many gods are named in the texts, including Amen, Osiris, and the Aten. What is new here is the emphasis on depictions of the royal family in various roles, a trend we also see in the tomb of Ramose, Vizier and Mayor of Thebes (fig. 106).[5] His tomb is noteworthy because it incorporates both

Fig. 123 Plan and isometric rendering of the tomb of Amenhotep III

Fig. 124 Plan of an 18th-Dynasty T-shaped private tomb

Fig. 126 *Shabti* of Akhenaten with a bag wig (cat. 221)

a traditional depiction of Amenhotep IV seated under a canopy and one executed in the revolutionary new style (fig. 107), showing the king at the Window of Appearances from which he rewarded his subjects—a motif that was to become common in the tombs at Amarna. The Royal Butler Parennefer, called "Clean of Hands," is particularly interesting because he is the only official known from tombs both at Thebes and Amarna. His Theban tomb,[6] prepared during the early years of Amenhotep IV, features the king and the Aten prominently, but prayers are still addressed to Osiris and to Anubis, the god of embalming—indicating that the old funerary beliefs prevailed during the early years of the reign.

Amarna: The Missing Graves

The median age at death among Egyptians of the pharaonic period was about thirty years, which represents a 1.7 percent annual mortality rate.[7] In a city the size of Amarna, with a population of 20,000 to 50,000, between 340 and 850 people would have died each year, or a total of 5,780 to 14,450 by the time the city was abandoned.[8] We would expect a large cemetery to have been located in or near the city, but, surprisingly, this is not the case. The explanation may lie in the fact that the residents of Amarna were all transplanted from other towns: they may have buried their dead in their home cemeteries or removed the bodies of their loved ones from Amarna after the city's abandonment—though mass removals would themselves have left physical evidence. Or, perhaps Amarna residents were buried on the west bank of the Nile—the traditional realm of the dead—in a large cemetery that awaits discovery.

A few infant burials have been found—in large storage jars in or near houses in the Central City and North Suburb[9]—though house burial was not a standard Egyptian practice during this time. Other burials have also been found in domestic contexts,[10] but most of these were intrusive burials from a later period.

The Royal Tomb

Akhenaten intended his own burial place to be in the cliffs of Amarna, as he decreed on his early boundary stelae. He began cutting his tomb seven to eight miles east of the city, in a desolate side wadi off the main east-west wadi that opens in the cliffs. Though it was unfinished when he died, he was most likely buried there. The plan of the tomb (fig. 127) was innovative, featuring a passage leading to a well room (D), with a pillared burial chamber (E) beyond it—all placed on the central axis, without incorporating the ninety-degree turns found in his predecessors' tombs, though perhaps a turn was planned.[11] The two staircases in the tomb feature a central ramp flanked by steps, which would have made it easier to lower the sarcophagus. The tomb decoration was not the usual paint on plaster. Because the native rock was of poor quality, the walls were plastered and the decoration then chiseled into the plaster. Areas within the carving were modeled, sometimes when the plaster was still wet, and the reliefs were then painted. The well room features scenes of the royal family worshipping the Aten. The back wall of the burial chamber continues this theme, with the Aten depicted five times, increasing in size as it traverses the sky. Scenes of mourning, including one for a royal female, appear on the side walls. The tomb is also noteworthy in having two additional suites of rooms off the main axis, probably intended for family members. A series of six rooms opening off corridor B is unfinished and undecorated, and may have been intended for Nefertiti. The other suite accommodated the burial of princess Meketaten, Akhenaten and Nefertiti's second daughter. Room *alpha* was decorated with scenes of the worship of the rising and setting sun, with wonderful details that, some scholars have suggested,[12] are a visual rendering of "The Great Hymn to Aten" (see the essay "The New Religion"). The most famous scene in this room, however, shows the king and queen mourning a royal female while, outside the door, a nurse holds a baby: presumably the woman has died in childbirth. The identities of mother and child are debated, but a similar scene occurs in room *gamma*, where the figure lying on a bier is identified as Meketaten. An extended scene of mourning constitutes much of the decoration in this room (fig. 17), and includes a list of desired tomb equipment, such as jewelry and toilet articles.

During the backlash against Akhenaten, the Royal Tomb was desecrated: the reliefs in the burial chamber were severely damaged and tomb furnishings smashed. The granite sarcophagus of Akhenaten, now reconstructed, features figures of Nefertiti at its corners (the post-Amarna practice featured goddesses). Maarten Raven[13] and Edwin C. Brock[14] have identified fragments of a sarcophagus for Queen Tiye, suggesting that she was buried here as well. The presence of the king's canopic chest, which has also been reconstructed, indicates that mummification was still considered a necessity. Many *shabti* figures of the king[15] and one of Nefertiti,[16] presumably from this tomb, are now dispersed in museums and private collections. Geoffrey Martin has identified four main iconographic types in a variety of stones and faience (fig. 126). No *shabti*s, however,

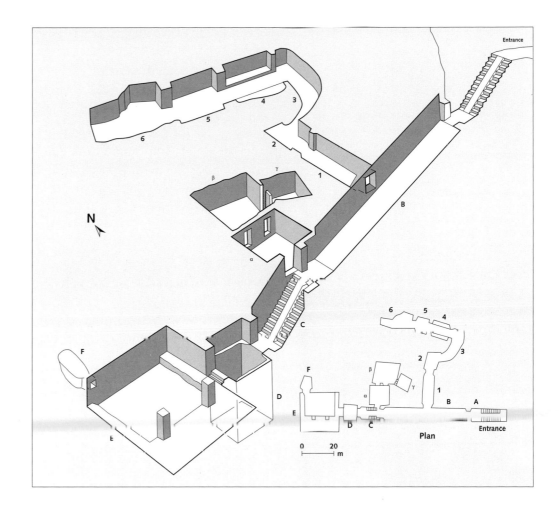

Fig. 127 Plan of the Royal Tomb at Amarna

Akhenaten was buried in the pillared hall (E), adapted to accommodate his sarcophagus when the unfinished tomb was needed. The two suites of rooms opening off the central axis were intended for family members.

appear to have been made for the princesses. Other items apparently deriving from the Royal Tomb include jewelry, a faience throw stick (see cat. 230), glass beads and rods, alabaster bowls and jars, and, interestingly enough, stone bowls bearing the names of kings Thutmose III, of the earlier 18th Dynasty, and Khafre, of Dynasty 4, who predated Akhenaten by about a thousand years.

The Royal Tomb is not the only tomb begun in the royal wadi.[17] Two additional tombs are located there, and two more in a side wadi nearby. One tomb has yielded a large number of potsherds, one of them bearing an inscription alluding to the "inner (burial) chamber of Neferneferure,"[18] which indicates that the fourth daughter of Akhenaten was probably buried here. Another tomb, though unfinished, was equipped with a central sarcophagus ramp, which suggests that it was intended to house the burial of a pharaoh, a successor of Akhenaten.[19]

Private Tombs at Amarna

High officials of Amarna had their tombs cut into the semicircle of cliffs at the eastern edge of the city.[20] There are forty-four rock-cut tombs in two groups, seventeen north of the royal wadi (fig. 129) and twenty-seven to the south. The plans of these tombs were variations on the traditional Theban T-shape, with an entrance façade, a transverse hall (fig. 130), and a shrine at the rear. Some tombs had a long corridor leading to the hall, while in others, the transverse hall was expanded to incorporate papyrus-shaped columns—up to twelve of them in the more elaborate tombs. An additional, undecorated chamber was occasionally added between the main hall and the shrine. A shaft or stairway in the floor of either the transverse hall or the second hall led to the burial chamber. Almost all of these tombs were unfinished, and there is little evidence that they were occupied during the Amarna Period, though they were used in later times as tombs, habitations, and in one case, a church.

It is in the decoration of the Amarna tombs—both the technical methods employed (similar to those in the Royal Tomb) and the selection of texts and scenes—that the break with tradition is most apparent (fig. 128). Gone are the "daily life" scenes of the deceased, the portrayals of family and guests at the banquet table, and the voyage to Abydos. In their stead are vignettes from the life of the royal family and the worship of the Aten. The god Osiris has been eliminated, and the way to life eternal now lies with the Aten and his intermediary, the king.[21] This is apparent right at the doorway to each tomb, where the lintel shows the deceased facing the cartouches of the god flanked by those of the king and queen, and texts on the jambs express adoration of the sun and the royal pair. The traditional funerary offering formula is addressed to the Aten and the king, and in the tomb of May, Fanbearer at the King's Right Hand, to Nefertiti as well.

Lining the passageway cut through the outer wall into the tomb interiors are some of the most interesting and beautiful texts of the period. These are variations of "The

Fig. 128 Tomb of Meryra I, outer hall

Large-scale representations of the royal family dominate the walls, with lesser figures occupying the lower registers. The high priest Meryra was the Greatest of Seers of the Aten.

Fig. 129 The North Tombs at Amarna

Fig. 130 Tomb of the Chamberlain Tutu

This is a view toward the south wall of the papyrus-columned hall, where the niches were intended to hold statues.

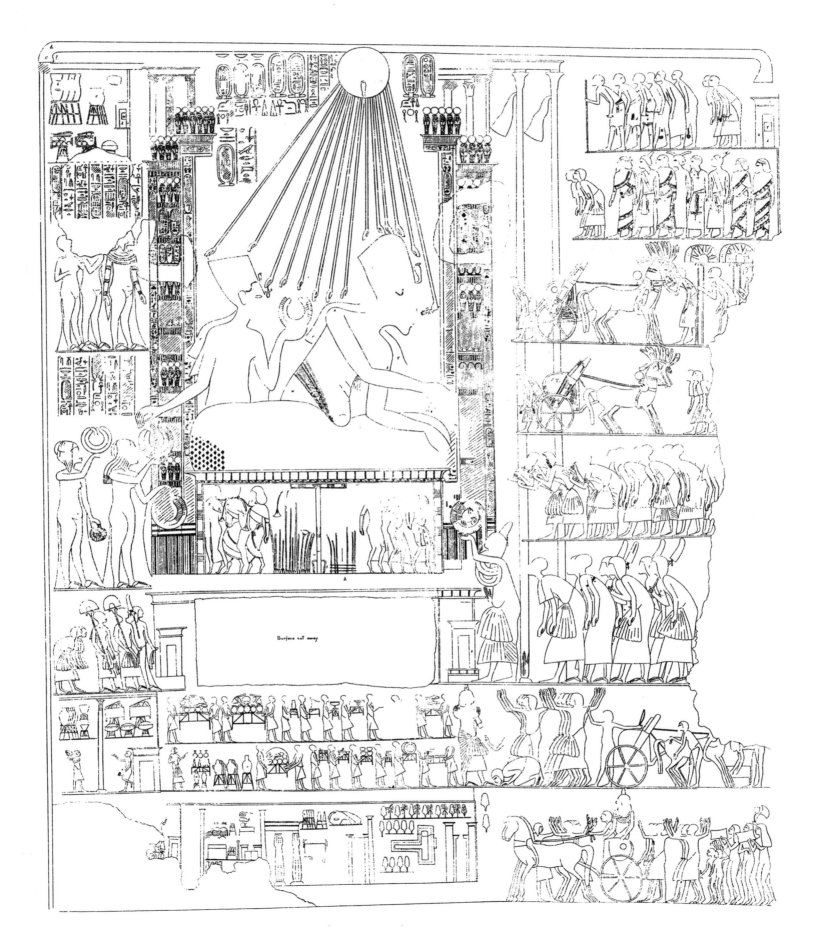

Surface cut away

Great Hymn to Aten."[22] A standing or kneeling figure of the tomb owner accompanies the text (fig. 132). In some cases a hymn to the rising sun appears on one wall, and on the opposite wall, a text addressed to the setting sun. Here also are funerary requests that give some hint of the beliefs that have replaced the traditional Osirian religion. From the tomb of Huya, Queen Tiye's Steward:

> *May you cause me to be continually in the place of favor, in my tomb of justifica-*
> *tion; (and as for) my Ba, may it come forth to see your rays and receive nourish-*
> *ment from its offerings.... May I partake of the things which issue [from the pres-*
> *ence, that I might eat shenes-loaves, bit-pastry, offering loaves, jugs <of beer,>]*
> *roasted meat, hot food, cool water, wine, milk, everything which issues [from the*
> *Mansion of the Aten in Akhet-Aten].*[23]

The Chief Physician, Pentu, prays:

> *May you grant that I rest in my place of continuity, that I be enclosed in the cavern*
> *of eternity; that I may go forth and enter into my tomb without my Ba's being*
> *restrained from what it wishes; that I might stride to the place of my heart's deter-*
> *mining, in the groves which I made on earth; that I might drink water at the edge of*
> *my pool every day without cease.*[24]

For the deceased, the perilous journey to the netherworld has thus been replaced by an earthly existence spent basking in the rays of the sun during the day, receiving offerings from the temple, and returning to the tomb at night.[25] There is very little in these texts to flesh out the personalities of the individuals. Only in rare cases do autobiographical details emerge, as in the tomb of May:

> *I was a poor man on both my father's and my mother's side—but the ruler built me*
> *up, he caused me to develop, he fed me by means of his Ka when I was without*
> *property.*[26]

This rags-to-riches story serves to emphasize the absolute dependence of the Amarna officials on the king's largesse in life and in death. Nowhere is this more manifest than in the decoration of the main chambers of the tombs. The king is no longer the passive recipient of homage, as in the earlier 18th-Dynasty tombs, but a participant in the action. The king and royal family loom large in these scenes, whereas we would be hard-pressed to locate the figure of the tomb owner among the throngs of courtiers, escorts, and servants. However, one scene emphasizing the deceased's relationship to the royal family is found almost universally in these halls, often on the front wall, to the left or the right of the entrance: the tomb owner being rewarded by the king and queen, who stand with the princesses in the Window of Appearances, distributing gold *shebyu* necklaces (fig. 131). The palace is often illustrated in minute detail, and the scene is witnessed by a crowd of officials, military men, and foreigners. A variety of other gifts is generally exhibited, including armbands, bracelets, rings, dishes, goblets, and items of dress. In the tomb of the God's Father Ay, later king, a gift that causes quite a sensation is a pair of gloves, rarely represented in ancient Egypt, which Ay dis-

Fig. 132 Ay and his wife, from the entrance passageway of his tomb

The text of "The Great Hymn to Aten" is inscribed above the figures.

Fig. 131 The rewarding of the deceased, tomb of Meryra II

The princesses (at left) hand *shebyu* collars up to Nefertiti, who passes them to Akhenaten. The king bestows the collars on Meryra, who was Overseer of the Royal Quarters. (Line drawing from a relief.)

Fig. 133 Shrine from the tomb of Ahmose, Amarna

This chamber, located on the central axis, was originally closed off with a wooden door.

plays to well-wishers outside the palace. Also notable is the presence of Ay's wife at the ceremony, apparently because of her role as the queen's nurse. In subsidiary registers, the king's retinue and chariots await the royal family. The deceased is shown returning home in triumph with a military escort, joyful friends, and a troupe of singers.

The royal family also appears in scenes related to the occupation of the deceased, often on the side walls of the larger columned halls. Huya's tomb, for example, has two banquet scenes in which the royal family sits at table with Queen Tiye (now queen mother) and her daughter Baketaten, as the tomb owner directs servants and serving dishes to Tiye, fulfilling part of his role as her Steward. In the tomb of the Police Chief, Mahu, the royal family undertakes a tour of inspection in its chariot, accompanied by Mahu and his men.[27] Two neighboring tombs of the north group depict what appears to be a single event, the "tribute of nations" that took place in year 12. One is in the tomb of Meryra II, Overseer of the Royal Quarters, where all six princesses appear with the king and queen, who sit in a kiosk holding hands; several subsidiary registers record the grand pageantry of foreigners presenting tribute to the king (fig. 60). Amid the whirl of activity, a figure that may represent the tomb owner, though he is not identified by name, approaches the king.

More common on the walls of the main hall are scenes of the royal family at worship, or in transit between the palace and temple. These abound in the North Tombs, whose owners, including the high priest Meryra I, tended to be affiliated with the temples. On a side wall of his tomb, the royal family departs from the palace (which is shown in great detail) in four decorated chariots, with a large escort. On the adjoining rear wall, we see the royals' arrival at the temple, where officials wait to receive them, accompanied by figures bearing offerings and serenaded by a band of female musicians. On the opposite side and adjoining rear wall, members of the royal family present offerings at the temple, while outside, their retinue waits.

At the rear of the tombs was the one area devoted entirely to the deceased. The shrine contained a standing or seated statue of the tomb owner (fig. 133), and was the focus of the funerary cult, where offerings were deposited to sustain the *ka*. Few shrines at Amarna were decorated, but one wall in the tomb of the First Servant of the Aten, Panehesy, contains a figure of the deceased and his family seated before the funerary meal, and there are rough sketches of similar scenes in the tomb of the king's scribe and steward, Any. The shrine of Huya is especially interesting because it incorporates the only depiction in the Amarna tombs of funerary rites. The mummy is shown standing upright before a pile of offerings. A priest wearing a leopard skin officiates, and mourners attend. This is a very traditional portrayal of a funeral, known from earlier 18th-Dynasty tombs, and indicates that, even in the absence of Osiris, many of the old rituals were carried on in the Amarna Period.

Most of the tombs had shafts that would have led to a burial chamber, but these were in various stages of completion. There is little evidence that any of these tombs were occupied (except for later, intrusive burials).[28] Only the tomb of Huya can be considered complete, with a finished burial chamber. Norman de Garis Davies[29] speculated that the tomb of the mayor of Akhetaten, Neferikheperu-her-sekheper, was in fact used for the owner's burial, since the burial chamber appeared to have been completed hastily, with little regard for the original plan of the tomb. Similarly, in the tomb of May, Fanbearer at the King's Right Hand, part of a column was removed to accommodate the stairway to the burial chamber, indicating a change in the original plan. It is the tomb of Any, however, that shows the surest signs of having been occupied: six votive stelae placed in three niches beneath the entrance portico. These were dedicated to Any by his brother and other members of his household, including the charioteer Tjay (fig. 134).

Though none of the usual funerary accouterments were discovered in the Amarna tombs, private *shabti*s of the Amarna Period are known, including some that may have been destined for these tombs.[30] Martin has identified five types in various materials, including limestone, calcite, faience, and wood. The text on many of them is not the customary spell from the Book of the Dead, but a formula incorporating the name of the Aten. From a *shabti* of Ipy, a woman with the title of "Royal Ornament":

> *Breathe the sweet breeze of the north wind which comes forth from the sky upon the hand of the living Aten. Your body is protected, your heart is glad. No harm shall happen to your body because you are sound. Your flesh will not decay. You will follow the Aten (from the moment) when he appears in the morning until he sets in life. There shall be water for your heart, bread for your stomach, and clothing to cover your body. O shabti, if you are counted off, if you are called, and if you are reckoned, "I shall do it, here I am," shall you say...*[31]

Surprisingly, there are many *shabti* spells that retain the traditional wording, even mentioning Osiris. These may derive from sites outside Amarna, where life, and funerary practices, must have continued relatively untouched by the new religion. That other traditional furnishings were provided is attested by the survival of a heart scarab addressed to the Aten.[32] Because of the small sampling of funerary artifacts from the Amarna Period, it is difficult to draw broad conclusions; it is apparent, however, from Amarna artifacts, as from funeral depictions in wall decoration, that the age-old practices were in no way eliminated, but modified to suit the new beliefs.

The Aftermath

With the abandonment of the city, any burials in the Royal Tomb, and perhaps those of nonroyal individuals, were removed and transferred. Thebes once again became the final resting place of the pharaohs. This leads us to perhaps the most hotly debated mystery in modern Egyptology: who was buried in KV 55?[33] The tomb was discovered

Fig. 134 Stela from the tomb of Any (Egyptian Museum, Cairo)

The stela, dedicated by the charioteer Tjay, shows him driving the tomb owner.

in the Valley of the Kings in 1907, and the clues are many—a wooden coffin (fig. 135), originally inscribed for Akhenaten's secondary wife Kiya, but altered for a king and housing an unidentified male mummy; four canopic jars with erased inscriptions of Kiya, placed in a niche; a dismantled shrine inscribed for Queen Tiye; and numerous small objects bearing several royal names, including that of Akhenaten himself. The mystery has yet to be solved, ninety years later, but the body has been variously identified by scholars over the years as Akhenaten or as Smenkhkara, who succeeded him (see the essay "The Royal Family"). It is likely that Queen Tiye was buried in KV 55 as well, but her body was later removed.

The tomb of Tutankhamen appears to have been a hastily altered private tomb,[34] and his successors Ay and Horemheb were interred in unfinished sepulchers in the West Valley and the main valley, respectively. Ay's tomb shares some similarities in plan with the Amarna Royal Tomb, and that of Horemheb has been viewed as transitional between 18th- and 19th-Dynasty types. The old gods reappear—along with many of the standard funerary texts, though these have some variations, additions, and deletions. Theban private tombs of the post-Amarna period[35] show continuing Amarna influence in the style of their decoration, but they, too, reflect the restoration of the old religion. There is an even greater emphasis on the god Osiris, and a new sense of personal piety is evident. In tomb decoration, scenes of Osiris enthroned replace those of the king.[36] This lessening of fealty toward the king is also apparent in the choice of many high officials, under Tutankhamen and later, to locate their tombs not in Thebes near that of their sovereign, but at Saqqara, near the northern administrative center of Memphis.[37] Many of the tombs at Saqqara are multichambered, free-standing structures arranged around a courtyard, and resemble temples. Included in this group are the tombs of Horemheb—a private tomb prepared before the owner became pharaoh—and of Maya, who was Overseer of the Treasury under Tutankhamen.[38]

Tombs at Amarna are still being documented,[39] and discoveries continue to be made in the Memphite necropolis. These include the recent, exciting find of the tomb of Tutankhamen's wet-nurse (also named Maya) by Alain Zivie.[40] Such discoveries illuminate our understanding of both life and death in the Amarna Period.

Fig. 135 The inlaid and gilded wooden coffin lid from tomb KV 55 (Egyptian Museum, Cairo)

1. The West Valley interment was in WV 22. For a recent discussion of this tomb, and further references, see Reeves and Wilkinson 1996, pp. 110–15.

2. For a good general discussion of these tombs, see Manniche 1987a, pp. 29–63. S. Smith 1992 is a study of intact private tombs and the standardization of funerary practices. An extensive recent study of the Theban necropolis may be found in Kampp 1996.

3. For a discussion of tombs with winding passages and their possible religious significance, see Assmann 1984. For analysis of subterranean tomb architecture, see Seyfried 1987 and Kampp 1995.

4. Theban Tomb 192; Epigraphic Survey 1980. Kheruef preceded Huya as Steward.

5. Theban Tomb 55; N. de G. Davies 1941.

6. Theban Tomb 188. See N. de G. Davies 1923, pp. 136 45; S. Redford 1995, S. Redford 1997.

7. Masali and Chiarelli 1972, p. 164.

8. This assumes an even distribution of ages. I would like to thank Mr. Ken Kreutziger for his help in determining this figure, and Dr. Brenda Baker for her valuable references. Discussion of a population estimate for Amarna may be found in Kemp 1989, pp. 269 and 305–6.

9. Peet and Woolley 1923, p. 17; Frankfort and Pendlebury 1933, p. 43.

10. Peet and Woolley 1923, pp. 75, 76, 85; see also p. 51; Frankfort and Pendlebury 1933, pp. 8, 18, 38, 43, 73. For remains in and near the desert chapels, see Peet and Woolley 1923, p. 94; Taylor and Boyce 1986; Hulin 1985. Roman Period cemetery, see Frankfort and Pendlebury 1933, pp. 66–67, also Kemp 1993, p. 13.

11. The unfinished state of the tomb leaves room for the possibility of additional chambers on a perpendicular axis. For detailed discussions of the Royal Tomb, see Martin 1974, 1989; reviewed in Krauss 1993.

12. Bouriant, Legrain, and Jéquier 1903, pp. 15ff.

13. Raven 1994.

14. In papers presented at the American Research Center in Egypt annual conference in 1990, and in 1994 at the symposium "In the Time of the Heretic of Akhetaten" in Toronto.

15. Martin 1974, 1989, vol. 1, pp. 38ff.

16. Loeben 1986; Krauss 1997b, p. 217.

17. The tombs are nos. 27–30. See el-Khouly and Martin 1987.

18. Ibid., p. 8.

19. Tomb no. 27: ibid., p. 16.

20. The original Egypt Exploration Society publication on the tombs is still invaluable; see N. de G. Davies 1903–8. For discussion of tomb decoration, see Meyers 1981 and Meyers 1985. For the sequence of work by craftsmen, see Owen and Kemp 1994. See also G. Johnson 1992.

21. See von der Way 1996 for a discussion of concepts of the afterlife in this period.

22. For recent translations, see Murnane 1995b.

23. Ibid., p. 131 (§66.1).

24. Ibid., p. 181 (§80.3).

25. Hornung 1992, pp. 43–49.

26. Murnane 1995b, p. 145 (§68.2).

27. For a discussion of this scene, see O'Connor 1987–88.

28. Davies (N. de G. Davies 1903–8, vol. 4, pp. 10–11) notes the presence of bones and mounds of sherds outside the larger southern tombs, and gives a tantalizing reference to "large numbers of coffins" found by Alexandre Barsanti and Urbain Bouriant, "many being burnt and others removed to Cairo." For model wooden objects that Flinders Petrie found in the southern tombs and that are now in University College London, see Petrie 1937, pp. 12–13.

29. N. de G. Davies 1903–8, vol. 4, p. 24.

30. Martin 1986; see also Webb 1995, p. 57.

31. Martin 1986, p. 115.

32. Ägyptisches Museum, Berlin, 15099, provenance unknown. A heart scarab was placed on the mummy to prevent the heart of the deceased from testifying against him on the Day of Judgment.

33. For recent discussions of KV 55, see M. Bell 1990; Davis et al. 1990, particularly the introduction and bibliography by Nicholas Reeves; Dodson 1994b; Brock 1995; Reeves and Wilkinson 1996, pp. 120–21; Brock 1997; and G. Johnson 1998.

34. Discussion of this, the only royal tomb found relatively intact, is beyond the scope of this essay. Details may be found in Reeves 1990a and the additional references listed there.

35. For a list and analysis of post-Amarna Theban tombs, see Strudwick 1994.

36. van Dijk 1988, p. 41.

37. See van Dijk 1988 for discussion of this necropolis.

38. Martin 1991 (Maya and Horemheb); Martin 1989 and Schneider 1996 (Horemheb).

39. Kemp and Nicholson 1997, p. 11.

40. A. Zivie 1998.

The Return to Orthodoxy

William J. Murnane

The period following Akhenaten's death was one of great political uncertainty. The "heretic's" most notable successor, Tutankhamen, restored the old cults and addressed mounting pressures from abroad. By the end of the 18th Dynasty, the break with Atenism was nearly complete.

Fig. 136 General Horemheb receiving an award (cat. 253)

The general, whose myriad titles under Tutankhamen included "King's Two Eyes Throughout the Two Banks (Egypt)," is decorated with the Gold of Honor in this relief from his Saqqara tomb.

The sun set quickly on the Amarna age, even before all of the prime movers had died. So little is known about the period surrounding Akhenaten's death, which occurred sometime after the grape harvest in his seventeenth year on the throne,[1] that we cannot even be sure of the number or identity of his immediate successor(s): a young man named Smenkhkara, the husband of his eldest daughter Meretaten, appears to have been one of them; but within the last quarter century the presence of a female pharaoh, "Nefernefruaten," has also been detected—either Meretaten herself or (more likely) her mother, the chief queen Nefertiti.[2] In any case the regime was clearly distancing itself from the heresy: by the third year of King Nefernefruaten we find the god Amen, proscribed under Akhenaten, back in royal favor, since a "temple of Amen in the mansion of (King) Ankhkheprura" (the throne-name shared by Akhenaten's two presumed successors) was in existence by this time.[3] This trend would intensify with the accession of the period's most famous figure, Tutankhamen, but paradoxes remain in plenty. Although Tutankhamen did restore the orthodox cults, and compensate them for the injuries sustained under Akhenaten, elements of the Amarna legacy would survive more tenaciously than these externals might indicate. And as well-documented as this reign is, by comparison with the preceding one, much of what happened—and why—is so obscure that the political legacy of Akhenaten's reign is less clear than we might wish.

Nothing highlights these uncertainties more than the controversy over the identity of Tutankhamen (fig. 137). We first know him as "King's Bodily Son, his beloved, Tutankhuaten"— from the chance survival of a single block transferred from Amarna to Hermopolis across the river when later pharaohs turned Akhenaten's abandoned city into a quarry for their own building projects.[4] Although this short text must have been a label that identified Prince Tutankhaten—almost surely in a scene from a wall of an official building at the heretic capital, where he was shown with other members of his family—neither this image of the young man nor any other, whether in relief or statuary, has survived from this time in his life. Still, we could be content with this meager evidence for Tutankhaten's royal origins were it not for some crippling ambiguities. First, whose "bodily son" was he? Both Akhenaten and his father, Amenhotep III, have been proposed,[5] with the latter seeming to have the stronger claim: indeed, in additions he made to the temples at Luxor and Soleb, Tutankhamen describes himself as "renewing the monument of his father" Amenhotep III, which must be balanced against the total silence that hangs over his relations with Akhenaten. In renewal texts, however, "father" can also mean "ancestor," and there are chronological difficulties as well: although King Tutankhamen may have been older at death than is usually supposed, perhaps dying in his mid-twenties,[6] it remains unclear that he would have been old enough to be a son of Amenhotep III unless the latter had had a long coregency with his son, Akhenaten—which is possible, but, given the controversy among scholars, hardly certain or even probable. Besides, must a King's Bodily Son have been born to a king? A number of individuals during the Old Kingdom seem to have held this title by virtue of their high office, and the same is true for some titular "king's sons" early in the 18th Dynasty.[7] Prince Tutankhaten was not one of these, since (with the exception of the King's Son of Kush, who served as the Viceroy of Nubia) this honorific usage had been curtailed by the middle of the dynasty. The title was sometimes applied to a more distant blood relationship, however, as in the case of the royal grandchildren who occasionally appear during the New Kingdom as "King's Son/Daughter;"[8] Tutankhaten could have been related to the dynasty through a collateral line of the family.[9] Even so, many scholars think it more likely that he was Akhenaten's son by a secondary wife, perhaps the mysterious Kiya.

Although Tutankhaten's parentage remains obscure, his other connections could only have strengthened his claim to the throne. His queen, Ankhesenpaaten, was by now Akhenaten's eldest surviving daughter, born to his chief queen, Nefertiti. She would have brought Tutankhaten the support of the royal family's main line—and if Nefertiti herself had reigned briefly as pharaoh before Tutankhaten ascended the throne (see note 2) her daughter's status would be all the higher, outranking even her young husband's, assuming his royal connections were less direct than hers. Scarcely less important, though, were supporters from Egypt's administration and its armed forces. One of these men, the Commander of Chariotry and Fanbearer at the King's Right Hand Ay[10] (cat. 232) had been a favorite courtier under Akhenaten: his most distinctive title of "God's Father" might refer to his being Queen Nefertiti's kinsman, even her father. For all of his old ties to Amarna, though, Ay seems not to have resisted the tide that already had begun to turn against the Atenists. Indeed, coming from the most prominent "holdover" from Akhenaten's circle, Ay's repudiation of the heresy would have undermined whatever respectability it still possessed. It must have galled Ay, then, to have to defer to a still more powerful man, the Great General of the Army, Horemheb.[11] Since this man's career, unlike Ay's, cannot be traced before he appears under Tutankhamen as commander of Egypt's armed forces, the circumstances of his rise to power remain hidden from view. Clearly, though, he was the young king's mightiest subject: not only did he bear what normally were the highest titles in military and diplomatic circles; he dominated other branches

Fig. 137 Granite sculpture of
Tutankhamen (Egyptian Museum,
Cairo)

Fig. 139 Back panel of Tutankhamen's throne (Egyptian Museum, Cairo)

Represented in the Amarna style, the young King Tutankhaten and his wife Ankhesenpaaten (before their name changes) face each other in an intimate moment.

of the government as well (cat. 253), even outranking the two viziers who traditionally served as prime ministers directly under the pharaoh.[12] A collection of highly unusual titles shows the range of his power—"King's Two Eyes Throughout the Two Banks (Egypt)," "King's Deputy in Every Place," "Foremost of the King's Courtiers," "Overseer of Generals of the Lord of the Two Lands," "Overseer of Every Office of the King," "Overseer of Overseers of the Two Banks," "Overseer of all Divine Offices": little in his country's business seems to have lain outside Horemheb's purview (see fig. 136). Still more striking is his standing as Hereditary Prince of Southern and Northern Egypt—a title that marked Horemheb as nothing less than his master's designated successor! Even if this was a concession negotiated between Ay and Horemheb, to take effect only in the unlikely event that Tutankhaten and his wife produced no heirs, nothing reveals more forcefully how dependent the young king and queen were on their "servants"!

These "overmighty subjects" must have been behind the accelerated return to orthodoxy that is this reign's defining event. Scarcely more than a year after mounting the throne, Tutankhaten changed his name to Tutankhamen, while his wife became Ankhesenamen (fig. 139). The court moved away from Amarna shortly thereafter, although the heretic's city continued to be occupied for some time after it had ceased being a royal residence.[13] All that remained, now that the king had distanced himself so publicly from Akhenaten's baleful influence, was to supplement symbolic gestures with legally effective acts. The public face Tutankhamen put on these measures is revealed by a decree issued in Memphis, at the palace Thutmose I had built almost two hundred years earlier—a venue chosen, perhaps, to underscore the traditional values implicit in the regime's new policy. This "restoration inscription,"[14] as it is known, opens with the usual proclamation of royal names and titles—but these pointedly associate the king with the orthodox divinities that had been pushed aside during the Amarna Period, emphasizing how he "performs benefactions for his (divine) father and all the gods ... having repaired what was ruined ... and having repelled disorder throughout the Two Lands" (fig. 140). There follows a bleak description of conditions in Egypt before Tutankhamen's accession. Akhenaten is never mentioned by name, but surely it is he whom readers would blame for what is described as the ruinous condition of the temples and the gods' consequent abandonment of the country: "if an army [was] sent to Djahy (in western Asia), to broaden the boundaries of Egypt, no success of theirs came to pass. If one prayed to a god, to ask something from him, he did not come at all...." Once the present king "appeared on the throne of his father and began to rule over the Shores of Horus," however, everything changed for the better. Both Amen-Ra and his northern counterpart, Ptah of Memphis, were singled out for special honor (although the Theban god's supremacy was also made clear: when Tutankhamen increased the number of carrying poles used to bear each god's processional shrine in public, Amen remained "two poles ahead" of Ptah). All the gods were recipients of the king's largesse: new statues were made to be their "bodies" on earth, their temples were refurbished and divine offerings flowed into them once more. Local priesthoods, which would have been dispossessed by Akhenaten to the extent they were not absorbed into the Aten cult, were now also restored as the king "installed lay priests and higher clergy from among the children of the officials of their cities, each one being the 'son-of-a-man' whose name was known." It is no wonder that Tutankhamen would claim the title "Repeater of Births" –initiator of a new age—on the strength of this comprehensive reversal, in which the royal treasury compensated the gods for what they had suffered at the hands of an earlier king (tactfully not mentioned) from the same dynasty.

The path of least resistance, so convenient to follow at home, was not open to Tutankhamen in the Near East. Over the two generations before the Amarna Period, peace in that region had depended on cooperation between the region's main superpowers—Egypt, Babylon, and the Hurrian kingdom of Mitanni—and the containment of states that might challenge the status quo (fig. 142). Under Amenhotep III and Akhenaten, though, the Hittites had emerged as contenders for Mitanni's position among the great powers: not only had Shuppiluliuma I of Hatti taken over Mitanni's possessions in Syria, and even raided its capital; he had, in the process, absorbed into the Hittite sphere of influence some vassals of Egypt.[15] In particular, the loss of the city-state of Kadesh, on the Orontes, was a sore point, for though its king continued to protest loyalty to the pharaoh, his actions, as reported by anxious neighbors, seemed those of a Hittite recruiter. When an Egyptian army had finally been sent, late in Akhenaten's reign or shortly thereafter, it had failed to retake the city—and worse, the enraged king of Kadesh had led Hittite troops in a retaliatory

Fig. 140 Restoration Stela of Tutankhamen (Egyptian Museum, Cairo)

Shortly after the move from Amarna, Tutankhamen announced his intention to restore the traditional god Amen. The midline perforations on the stela are evidence of a later attempt to reuse the stone.

raid on Egyptian territory nearby. Both sides had tacitly agreed not to expand these hostilities into a general war, but the issue lay unresolved and continued to rankle. Thus it is not surprising that, probably during Tutankhamen's ninth regnal year, the Egyptians launched a second attack on Kadesh. Once again, it failed, but this time the results were to be more decisive and far more serious for Egypt—for it was now that Shuppululiuma, taking advantage of conditions more favorable than before, swept to final victory over the Hurrians and consolidated his hold on northern Syria. The proximity of Hittite power confirmed Egypt's loss, not only of Kadesh but also of Amurru, its western neighbor: not until about 1259 B.C., when Ramesses II concluded his treaty with Hatti, would Egypt be able to accept the fact that its two northern-most border territories had been swallowed up by the Hittite empire.

Failure in western Asia aggravated the situation at home. According to the Hittite "Deeds of King Shuppiluliuma I," the Egyptians, already demoralized by recent defeats, were further discon-certed when "in addition, their lord Nipkhururiya (in Egyptian, "Neb-kheprura," Tutankhamen's throne name) died."[16] This event, in about 1322 B.C., precipitated one of the most extraordinary episodes in the diplomacy of any age: in a move so unexpected that Shuppiluliuma blurted out, "Nothing like this ever happened to me in my entire life!," the widowed queen of Egypt wrote, pleading with the Hittite king to send one of his many

Fig. 142 **Three foreigners** (cat. 262)
Shown in this relief block are two Western Asiatics bound as prisoners and led by a Libyan—possibly a mercenary in the service of the Egyptian king.

sons to marry her and become king in Egypt. Although that union would have settled differences between Egypt and Hatti, a less elevated reason for this approach suggests itself—for, as the queen tells Shuppiluliuma, "Never shall I take a servant of mine and make him my husband!" This unwelcome servant can only have been General Horemheb, whose rank as Tutankhamen's heir apparent would become effective now that the king had died childless. Fortunately for Horemheb's enemies at court (no doubt led by Ay, his chief rival) the general was in no position to prevent these negotiations—probably because he was fully engaged with Egyptian forces in Syria at the time—and, despite Shuppiluliuma's misgivings, the Hittite Prince Zannanza finally set off for Egypt. As it happened, though, neither side won or lost everything. When the prince died on his way to Egypt (if not murdered, as his father thought, then perhaps victim to a plague ravaging Egypt at the time) it was left to Ay, now king as Tutankhamen's "heir of burial," to deal with the war launched by the stricken Shuppiluliuma. But, though Horemheb had been effectively sidetracked, he was too formidable to eliminate altogether. After spending Ay's short reign (about 1322-1319 B.C.) in honorable obscurity, he would re-emerge at his old antagonist's death to claim the crown that had lain just beyond his grasp for so long.[17]

With King Horemheb (about 1319-1292 B.C.) the retreat from Amarna, begun so quickly after the heretic died, seems to have been completed. After all, it was Horemheb who dismantled the Aten's temples at Thebes, packing the blocks into his new buildings inside Amen's precinct at Karnak; and from the same period comes a legal document that refers to "the time of the enemy belonging to Akhet-Aten."[18] And yet, despite such gestures (made, one suspects, in deference to the gods whom the

Fig. 141 **Amen-Ra with features of Tutankhamen, Karnak**

Fig. 143 Present-day Amarna, from the eastern cliffs

This view shows the desert cliffs in the foreground, the ancient remains of the city, the cultivated plain, and the Nile.

Amarna episode had offended), Horemheb unleashed no general destruction of Akhenaten's legacy. Though virtually a ghost town by now, and even beginning to lose some of its buildings to recycling across the river, the heretic's capital still stood and was even, to some degree, functional: otherwise it is hard to explain how no fewer than two pieces of temple furniture dedicated by King Horemheb found their way into the Great Temple of the Aten.[19] The final repudiation of Amarna came only two generations later, when Ramesses II began the wholesale plunder that eventually reduced the site to its foundations. And yet, long after Akhenaten and his associates had become nonpersons, the monotheistic tendencies already present in Egyptian religion before the Amarna age continued to flourish and develop.[20] Perhaps it was the heretic's confrontational methods, and less the content of his thought, that earned him the defamatory oblivion from which he has had to be rescued in modern times (fig. 143).

1. For the most recent discussion of the temporal parameters of the period from Akhenaten's death to the early reign of Tutankhamen, see Krauss 1997a.

2. For Akhenaten's son-in-law, see Newberry 1928. Subsequently, with the identification of a number of feminine forms for one of the names associated with this individual (previously thought to have changed his personal name from Smenkhkara to Nefernefruaten, or vice-versa), Akhenaten's successor was believed to be one female (J. R. Harris 1974b; Samson 1978). More recent opinion has veered in favor of two rulers: a woman (Nefernefruaten, reigning into her third year) and a man (Smenkhkara, for whom only the first year is attested), with their sequence still in dispute (J. Allen 1991). The identity of the woman is still contested, proponents being divided between Akhenaten's chief queen, Nefertiti (in all but the earliest references above), and his eldest daughter Meretaten (Krauss 1978).

3. Murnane 1995b, pp. 207–8 (§ 94), with references. This temple, like the official who served in it, was presumably located at Thebes and may have been the foundation designated for the king's mortuary cult.

4. The block is published by Roeder 1969, pl. 106 (831-VIIIC) and translated in Murnane 1995b, p. 211 (§98-A). A. J. Spencer (Spencer 1989, pp. 15–16) shows how Horemheb reused blocks from Amarna at Hermopolis long before Ramesses II's similar operations at the site.

5. For Amenhotep III, e.g. Fairman 1972; Connolly, Harrison, and Ahmed 1976; L. Bell 1986. For Akhenaten, see, among others, Krauss 1978, pp. 79–80; Eaton-Krauss 1985, with references.

6. Wente and Harris 1992, especially pp. 10–11, 13–16 with references.

7. Schmitz 1976, pp. 65–79, 273–87.

8. Gomaà 1973, pp. 12–13.

9. Among others, D. Redford 1979b and Murnane 1990, pp. 132–33; see Wente and Harris 1992, pp. 14–15.

10. Schaden 1977, Gabolde 1992b.

11. Hari 1965; Martin 1989, pp. 161–65.

12. Schulman 1965.

13. Eaton-Krauss 1985, col. 812 with references; Kemp 1987.

14. Murnane 1995b, pp. 212–15 (§99), with references.

15. For all this see Murnane 1990, pp. 1–58, 115–44; but see also Giles 1997, who would like to push Shuppiluliuma's raid on the Mitannian capital back into Amenhotep III's time (assuming a long coregency with Akhenaten).

16. Güterbock 1956, pp. 93–94; see Bryce 1990. On the much discussed problem of the identity of "Nipkhururiya" see, for convenience, Schulman 1978, who persuasively rebuts the case for identifying the deceased pharaoh as Akhenaten (whose throne name was Neferkheprura, generally rendered as Napkhururiya in Akkadian, the international language of the day).

17. Murnane 1990, pp. 22–31; van Dijk 1993, pp. 11–64.

18. D. Redford 1984, pp. 222–31; Murnane 1995b, pp. 240–41 (§109).

19. Murnane 1995b, p. 234 (§107-B).

20. Assmann 1995.

Akhenaten's Artistic Legacy

Rita E. Freed

Although his successors did their best to eliminate Akhenaten from the official record, his legacy endures to this day.

The death of Akhenaten sometime during his seventeenth year of rule heralded the end of the supremacy of Aten and life in Amarna. Nevertheless, many of the king's innovative ways of reproducing the world around him in sculpture, relief, painting, and architecture endured well beyond his lifetime. Passed along, consciously or unconsciously, through the hands of his artisans to succeeding generations, they became Akhenaten's legacy.

Tutankhamen

Although the immediate succession to Akhenaten continues to baffle historians, the first king after him to leave a substantial number of monuments was Tutankhamen, who began his life and rule as Tutankhaten at Amarna. Within a few tumultuous years of inheriting the throne, this young king, no more than an adolescent, had abandoned Amarna in favor of Egypt's traditional capitals, Thebes and Memphis; reinstated the worship of Amen; embarked on a full-scale, nationwide program to restore Amen's monuments; and begun the demolition of Akhenaten's works[1]—all undoubtedly under the heavy hand of Amen's generations-old priesthood, which was eager to regain its hegemony. That the restoration of Amen occurred early in his reign and even at Amarna is shown by a stela featuring Tutankhaten worshipping Amen and his consort Mut, the venerable gods of Thebes.[2] Although stylistically it displays clear traces of Amarna's influence, its iconography recalls the years before Aten's supremacy and demonstrates the adaptability of Amarna's artisans.

When Amarna was abandoned, many of its artisans must have gone to Thebes, where a particularly massive building program was instituted. Their work with artisans who may never have been at Amarna, their unlearning of both the style and iconography in which they had been working for approximately twenty years, their attempt to adapt or readapt to Egypt's traditional and formal artistic philosophies, and their transmission of selective elements of Akhenaten's artistic philosophy to succeeding generations of artisans is the story of the rest of ancient Egyptian art. The story developed rapidly during the next few reigns.

At Thebes, a great many images of Amen were erected by Tutankhamen and his successors, Ay and Horemheb. Establishing a precise date for many of them is difficult because the royal name now associated with a particular statue may not necessarily

Fig. 144 Maya and Meryt (cat. 256) Ageless and emotionless, the couple gaze into the beyond in a manner reminiscent of Old Kingdom art. The statue is from the tomb of Maya, who was treasurer under Tutankhamen and Horemheb. (Full view, fig. 153.)

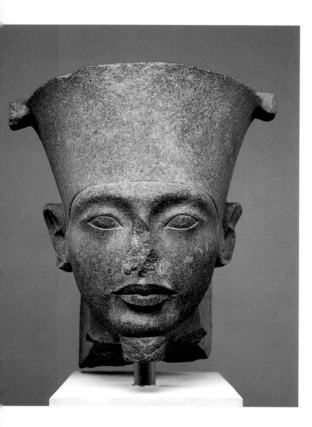

Fig. 145 Head of Amen (cat. 245)

The crown and plaited beard indicate that the god Amen was the subject of this statue, although the round face, naturalistically modeled eyes, and full lips are reminiscent of the later Amarna Period and recall the face of Tutankhamen.

Fig. 146 Amen and Tutankhamen (cat. 243)

Amen embraces Tutankhamen, who restored the god to prominence. Both are depicted in a conservative, idealizing manner that harks back to pre-Amarna years.

identify the king who originally commissioned it. In a campaign to obliterate all traces not only of Akhenaten but also of anyone connected with him or with Amarna, Horemheb frequently usurped the monuments of both his predecessors, substituting his name for theirs.[3]

It is ironic that some of the Amen statues, likely to have been made during the reign of Tutankhamen, exhibit the very traits most closely identified with Amarna works. These include a soft, fleshy face with high cheekbones, naturalistic eyes, and the full lips particularly reminiscent of Akhenaten's family in the later Amarna years (fig. 145 and cat. 246)—as well as pierced ears, a fullness at the breast, a flaccid torso, and a full, drooping abdomen. Some images of Tutankhamen (figs. 11, 12) have very similar features.

Another group of Amen statues displays a leaner, less modulated, and more formal treatment of the face and body (fig. 146 and cat. 247). Although these may be identical to the first group in size, pose, and accouterments, they are closer to the traditional, pre-Amarna style. In this second group the face exhibits fewer subtleties of modeling, the eyes are flatter and may be outlined by raised-relief cosmetic lines and brows, and the lips are thinner. Restraint replaces fleshiness in the torso. Breasts are treated as muscles, the mid-torso is bisected by a clear median line that terminates in a navel just above the belt, and the abdomen is less protruding. Statues of Tutankhamen were also executed in this style (fig. 137).

In all likelihood, the two groups represent the work of two ateliers.[4] The first may have comprised some of Akhenaten's skilled and experienced artisans, now relocated. The second perhaps consisted of recent recruits who began their service after Akhenaten's death, or more senior sculptors who had served under Amenhotep III, Akhenaten's father and predecessor. They were better able to distance themselves from Amarna and its ideas, conceivably at the urging of Amen's priesthood.

Tutankhamen ruled for nine years. Wall paintings in his tomb, preserved by chance in the Valley of the Kings, must have been done by Amarna-trained artisans. Not only do they show the distinctive protruding belly and lunate navel of Akhenaten's years, but they also make use of the Amarna canon of proportion, which, in the division of the vertical figure into equal units, added an extra two above the knee to make twenty.[5] A few objects in Tutankhamen's tomb—particularly a few statues of the king himself,[6] his small shrine, and his gilded throne—also exhibit strong Amarna influence, and may even have been made at Amarna.[7] Other royal statuary in the tomb and elsewhere, and the many anthropomorphic figures of gods, recall the conservative style of the pre-Amarna years.

While Thebes was home to many artistic interests after the Amarna Period, Memphis, which had regained its status as the center of political and administrative life, seems to have harbored primarily one trend. Because artistic activity had continued in the area without interruption from Amenhotep III through the Amarna years,[8] it is hardly surprising that Memphite artisans of the post-Amarna period continued

Fig. 147 Aged man (cat. 261)

The subtle gesture of the wrinkled arm and hand shows the influence of Amarna style.

to work in the elegant and detailed manner of Amenhotep III, though they infused it with decided Amarna influence.

Some of the finest examples of post-Amarna work[9] belong to Horemheb,[10] the Commander-in-Chief of the Army under Tutankhamen who later became king. The life-size statue of Horemheb shown in the cross-legged pose of a scribe (fig. 148)[11] exhibits not only selected details of the late Amarna style, but also an overall emotional sensitivity that would not have been possible without Amarna.[12] Horemheb's carefully curled hair, parted in the middle at a widow's peak, frames an oval face with high cheekbones. His naturalistically rendered eyes, also an Amarna hallmark, gaze slightly downward at his work, and his mouth displays the Cupid's-bow upper lip and full, protruding lower lip. Particularly telling is his splendid belly, whose abundance pushes the upper border of his garment to well below his navel, in true Amarna fashion. In contrast, his upper torso, with its carefully incised parallel wavy lines separating folds of flesh, is much more classical and recalls the scribes of pre-Amarna years.[13]

Reliefs from the tomb Horemheb built for himself at Saqqara[14] exhibit additional aspects of Akhenaten's legacy. One is the subtle technique of carving to various depths in the same relief so that it appears three dimensional[15]—an effect borrowed at Saqqara particularly for key scenes.[16] The Amarna heritage included not only the interest in depicting emotion, but also the ability to convey it by means of a hand gesture alone (fig. 147). In Horemheb's tomb the upraised arms of a mourner succeed in conveying his extreme anguish,[17] just as the splayed fingers of a scribe indicate concentration.[18] Emotion or emphasis is also expressed through the use of empty space or deliberate crowding, as at Amarna. Major themes such as the presentation of the Gold of Honor[19] (fig. 136), as well as vignettes depicting activity inside buildings,[20] different body types and unusual poses,[21] long processions of foreigners,[22] and manacled prisoners of war[23] also reflect the Amarna influence.

Another clear legacy of the Amarna years, found in both sculpture and relief, is the interest in old age, and the ability to render it naturalistically (figs. 147, 150). This is particularly true with nonroyal subjects. Like the Amarna examples cited above, with their emphasis on furrows, wrinkles, and sagging flesh, the later 18th-Dynasty pieces are superb studies of the aging process more than true portraits. This interest in the wizened visage continues into Dynasty 19 and appears again much later, particularly in Dynasties 25 and 30.

Ay

After Tutankhamen's death from unknown causes,[24] a commoner named Ay assumed the throne. Before becoming king, he built a tomb at Amarna, where he had served Akhenaten as Commander of Chariotry. As king, he buried Tutankhamen, in whose tomb he is shown performing the Opening of the Mouth Ceremony, a ritual of revivification generally executed by the heir. He also commissioned sculpture, relief, and his own royal tomb at Thebes. At each stage of his career, his image changed, but not in relation to how he actually looked. Rather, it varied with the artisans who executed the work and their relationship to the Amarna style, as well as his office at the time. In his private tomb at Amarna (cat. 232), he is shown, as most officials were, with Amarna-like features and gestures that are pronounced, though not as extreme as those of the royal family. In contrast, in the wall paintings from Tutankhamen's tomb in Thebes, Ay is shown with a decidedly more elongated face and pendant belly than at Amarna. Those features, hallmarks of Akhenaten, are in fact even more pronounced on Ay than on Tutankhamen, showing that even though the religious iconography had changed, the art style persisted. In this instance, at least, it was connected with royalty. In his own Theban tomb, Ay's abdomen, while still low, is more moderate in size,[25] even though the twenty-unit Amarna canon of proportion has been used.[26] A private tomb from Ay's reign belonging to the scribe Neferenpet also exhibits a distinct Amarna influence, clearly retaining the characteristic gestures and poses, as well as realistic landscape and a rich density of color.[27]

Other sculpture, relief, and painting from Ay's reign, both royal and private, seems more clearly to revert to the traditionalism of the past. Even in its fragmentary state, sculpture from the king's mortuary temple at Thebes[28] shows the more muscular torso, restrained abdomen, and eternally youthful appearance of the pre-Amarna years. Facial features no longer display the careful attention to naturalistic detail that they did under Akhenaten. This is particularly true for the eyes, which, although still three-dimensional, are now outlined, as are the eyebrows, by raised-relief bands. Overall, these pieces present a colder, more aloof image than those with the softer modeling of the Amarna style.

The tendency to return to a more conservative past, particularly for representations of gods, may also be seen in a relief from the throne of one of Ay's statues, which shows the rotund figure of a Nile god (fig. 149). His corpulence, however, recalls models from as far back as the Old Kingdom[29] rather than the Amarna years, and his facial features are noteworthy for their restraint and clarity. Ultimately, it was this restrained style that was favored in succeeding dynasties.

Fig. 148 General Horemheb as a scribe (cat. 251)

Horemheb was Tutankhamen's general before he became king. This statue, which shows him in the cross-legged pose of a scribe, is possibly from Memphis. It is similar to another statue of him that was found at Karnak.

Fig. 149 Relief of the god Hapi from a throne base (cat. 249)

The Nile god is shown tying together the heraldic plants of Upper and Lower Egypt, symbolizing the unification of the country. This classic representation, from the base of a statue of Ay, bears little trace of Amarna's legacy.

Fig. 150 Head of Ay (?) (cat. 248)

This head of an aging man was altered to accommodate the uraeus at the brow.

Although he ruled for only four years,[30] Ay must have been quite old at the time of his death, given his long pre-royal career. However, only one sculpture, tentatively identified as Ay, shows him with both a royal uraeus and the deep furrows of advanced age (fig. 150). Found at Asfun, it is nevertheless clearly a product of Akhenaten's style. If it is indeed Ay,[31] it was originally made for him before he became king and later adapted to accommodate the symbol of royalty.

Horemheb

Horemheb, another aging military man (the Commander-in-Chief of Tutankhamen's army; see above) became king after Ay. Later records give him an unbelievable reign of fifty-nine years[32] and make him the successor of Amenhotep III, thereby eliminating from history anybody who had anything to do with the Amarna interlude.[33] Inscriptions from his reign speak of his restoration of temples that had fallen into ruin and his reorganization of the entire administration.[34] Horemheb continued the dismantling of Akhenaten's temples at Karnak,[35] began the reuse of Amarna blocks in his construction at Hermopolis, across the river,[36] and possibly rededicated Amarna to Amen.[37]

Material from Horemheb's reign is further evidence that style was a product of the background of the artisans, even though subject matter may have been dictated by court or temple. By the time Horemheb came to the throne, Akhenaten had been dead for approximately fifteen years, and many of his artisans must have ceased work. Those who were still active were far removed, both temporally and spatially, from the Amarna works they had created. It is hardly surprising that the newer generation of artisans, surrounded in Thebes and Memphis by fifteen hundred years of tradition, would return to the canon and iconography of the pre-Amarna past. Moreover, Akhenaten's infamy, especially in view of his desecration of Amen and disenfranchisement of the god's all-powerful priesthood, must already have been widespread, although the epithet of "heretic" is known only from slightly later documents.

Ambition, religious zeal, or simple greed must have led Horemheb to aggressively usurp the monuments of Tutankhamen and Ay,[38] eliminating all traces of predecessors related to Amarna. It is noteworthy that those statues of King Horemheb that bear no obvious trace of recarving uniformly show a return to classical body forms, poses, iconography, and demeanor (fig. 151). Expressionless faces appear frozen in eternal youth. Although some have the almond-shaped, three-dimensional eyes of Akhenaten in his later years and others have flatter, more stylized, rimmed eyes, they all exhibit a mechanical precision that renders them lifeless (fig. 152). Horemheb's smaller, straighter lips are reminiscent of those of the early 18th Dynasty. His body is leaner than Tutankhamen's and his torso is bisected by the median line (see Amen statues, above) reminiscent of 18th-Dynasty style prior to Amenhotep III.

Horemheb built or completed the Second, Ninth, and Tenth pylons at Karnak, using *talatat* blocks from Akhenaten's temples as ballast. Reliefs on the pylon façades[39] must have been a product of Karnak's new generation of artisans, since they feature flat, formal renderings of king and god that bear little relationship to the Amarna material, except for the more rounded treatment of the eye area and lines at the neck, aspects of Akhenaten's style that became part of the standard repertoire.

Elsewhere at Thebes, however, artisans trained in the Amarna style were still active. A wall Horemheb had built between the Ninth and Tenth pylons at Karnak shows him with Amarna-like features and attributes.[40] Horemheb's relief-decorated tomb in the Valley of the Kings,[41] like the tombs of his two royal predecessors, featured the shorter lower leg of the Amarna standard of proportion, although other aspects of style and iconography, including the svelte, narrow-waisted figures of king and deities, followed the pre-Amarna norm.[42] The tomb of Horemheb's successor, Ramesses I, is the last one in which the Amarna proportions were employed.[43]

In at least one other place in Egypt, Amarna artisans were still active during Horemheb's reign. The quarry at Gebel es-Silsileh, north of Aswan—source of the

Fig. 151 Amen and Horemheb
(cat. 254)

Amen protects King Horemheb in one of two very similar statues found in the Luxor temple. The body proportions and rigid poses of both king and god, and the god's emotionless gaze, reflect pre-Amarna traditions.

sandstone for Akhenaten's *talatat* blocks—has a shrine that includes the Amarna body type, free-form poses typical of Amarna Period tombs, and even a sun-disk with multiple pendant *ankh* signs,[44] probably inspired by Amarna imagery. Left unfinished, the shrine was completed later in a mechanical style characteristic of much of Ramesside art, in marked contrast to the earlier, more painstaking work.

Private sculpture from Horemheb's reign exhibits the same trend away from the nuances of Amarna. On the seated statue of Maya (Overseer of the Treasury under Tutankhamen and Horemheb) and Meryt[45] from their tomb at Saqqara (fig. 153), youthful, unmodeled faces nearly identical in shape gaze directly forward without expression, in the timeless manner characteristic of Egyptian art beginning with the Old Kingdom. Both faces and bodies appear aloof compared to the statue of Horemheb as scribe, which was made during Tutankhamen's reign.[46] Still, their naturalistic eyes and full lips, and Maya's pierced ears, betray the influence of Akhenaten's artisans. Like their pre-Amarna forebears, they sit erect on their chairs, and although Meryt places her arm around Maya's shoulder, there is no emotional interaction between the couple. Her tall, slender body exhibits none of the voluptuousness of the Amarna years, although he still bears a trace of the Amarna paunch on his flaccid body. Their long, pleated garments and elegantly curled hair follow the trend begun in the mid-18th Dynasty, popularized by Amenhotep III, and elaborated upon at Amarna.[47]

Lasting Influence

Horemheb's death marked the end of the 18th Dynasty, a period that had seen the high point of Egypt's wealth and empire as well as religious controversy. By the time of his death, nearly thirty years after the Amarna interlude, advanced age had undoubtedly curtailed the productivity of those few Amarna artisans who were still alive. In all but isolated instances,[48] the stamp of Akhenaten's art vanished with the people who had created it. Indirectly, however, Akhenaten's influence continued for many more years.

The art of the next two (Ramesside) dynasties exhibited a number of different trends. Although fashions for hair and clothing continued along the same elaborate lines as before, stiff and formal figural renderings were favored over precise attention to naturalistic detail. In general, detail was limited to essentials and the delightful variations of pose and gesture reduced to fewer and more stereotyped versions. Yet attenuation and exaggeration at times exceeded even Amarna practice. The shaven skulls of priests were more elongated, garments longer and more flowing; the angle of the belt from back to abdomen was even more acute, giving the impression of a distended "Amarna" belly, particularly in relief. Aside from this illusion of a belly, however, Ramesside figures tended to be overly thin. In sculpture in the round, naturalism ultimately gave way to simpler, flatter planes and stylizations similar to those in relief.

Other, perhaps more subtle, aspects of Amarna art took hold. Ramesside artisans covered entire temple walls with a single narrative theme, ignoring the register system just as the artisans of Amarna's tombs had often done. The official Amarna prohibition

Fig. 153 Maya and Meryt (cat. 256)

This splendid statue comes from Maya's tomb at Saqqara, which was recently rediscovered by a joint mission of the Egypt Exploration Society, London, and the Rijksmuseum van Oudheden, Leiden.

Fig. 152 King Horemheb (?) as a Standard Bearer of Amen (Egyptian Museum, Cairo)

Despite its naturalistic treatment of the eyes, this head of a king has a cold, aloof gaze. The falcon-headed standard demonstrates the king's devotion to either Ra-Horakhty or Horus.

against the worship and representation of gods other than Aten may have fostered the overt personal piety of the Ramesside era, which manifested itself not only in the proliferation of votive objects and of religious themes in private tombs, but in literature as well.[49] Children continued to be depicted frequently, two or more at a time, in both the royal and private spheres, although usually in the formal manner of the pre-Amarna years. Images of women still occasionally exhibited full hips and rounded bellies.

Ramesses III, of the 20th Dynasty, had himself depicted in the style of earlier pharaohs,[50] including the fleshy-faced Amarna-like Tutankhamen,[51] apparently intending through this association with Egypt's noble past to legitimize his claim to the throne. When Kushite kings conquered Egypt in Dynasty 25, their artisans exhibited a renewed interest in the voluptuous female figure, representations of old age, and aspects of portraiture, all leitmotifs of Akhenaten's art. These characteristics reappear in the art of the last days of pharaonic Egypt, around 330 B.C.

Akhenaten's architectural legacy was also significant. Ramesside architects continued to erect lush composite floral columns,[52] made extensive use of faience inlays,[53] and included the Window of Appearances as an important component of temples.[54] Balustrades and broken-lintel gateways (with a gap at the center of the lintel, above the entrance) reappear in temples of the Ptolemaic Period (305–30 B.C.).

Akhenaten himself lived on in the Egyptian memory as well, but in a very different way. An inscription in a private tomb from the time of Ramesses II identified him as "the enemy of Akhet-Aten" (Amarna) and called his rule a time of rebellion[55]—even though officially he did not exist, since his name had been eliminated from the public record, including king lists of the 19th Dynasty.[56] Writing a thousand years or more after Akhenaten's death, Greek historians such as Herodotus, Diodorus Siculus, and Strabo likewise avoided mentioning him by name.[57] Nevertheless, Akhenaten's memory lived on in ancient writings as the heretic despoiler of temples, the source of plague, and the cause of evil.[58] He was conflated with historical figures as varied as King Khufu of the 4th Dynasty, the cruel builder of the Great Pyramid,[59] and Moses, who was blamed for plague and religious unrest.[60]

Two millennia later, the father of psychoanalysis, Sigmund Freud, offered his own association between Akhenaten and Moses: he viewed the pharaoh as the philosophical inspiration for the monotheism of Moses, and hence an ancestor to the Judeo-Christian tradition.[61] To the American historian James Henry Breasted, Akhenaten was "a prophet, an idealist, and the world's first individual."[62] Breasted also noted the similarities between "The Great Hymn to Aten" and Psalm 104 of the Old Testament.[63] Akhenaten's first biographer, Arthur Weigall, compared him to Christ, his sun-disk to the cross, and his sun hymn to the teachings of St. Francis of Assisi.[64] Akhenaten has been the subject of novels, operas, and plays, as well as recent erudite histories that sometimes revere, sometimes revile him.[65] For most of us, Akhenaten, his wife Nefertiti, and his successor Tutankhamen have come to symbolize the romance, mystery, and beauty that are synonymous with ancient Egypt in the modern mind.

1. Murnane 1995b, pp. 212–14 (§99), and Eaton–Krauss and Murnane 1991, pp. 31–35.

2. Ägyptisches Museum, Berlin, 14197. See Erman 1900, p. 113.

3. W. R. Johnson 1995, p. 1 and Hari 1984, pp. 96–97.

4. The contemporaneity of the two groups of Amen statues was suggested to me by Dr. Marianne Eaton-Krauss, oral communication.

5. Robins 1994, pp. 155–57.

6. For example, the head of Tutankhamen emerging from the lotus, found in his tomb. Egyptian Museum, Cairo, JE 60723, the frontispiece in Noblecourt 1963.

7. On a number of the objects from his tomb, the king is still called Tutankhaten. See Noblecourt 1963, pp. 86, 93–95; and Eaton-Krauss 1992, pp. 334–35.

8. Löhr 1975, A. Zivie 1988.

9. For others, see particularly Berlandini 1982 and Löhr 1970.

10. Martin 1989.

11. Depiction as a scribe signified importance; Horemheb's scribal status was pre-royal. Although this statue is said to have a Memphite provenance, it is not absolutely certain that it comes from the tomb Horemheb built at Saqqara before he became king. See Martin 1989, p. 23, n. 1.

12. For a scribal statuette found at Amarna, see cat. 185.

13. For example, Amenhotep, Son of Hapu (Egyptian Museum, Cairo, JE 44861), illustrated in Kozloff and Bryan 1992, p. 251.

14. A number of different artists' hands are apparent. Although most of the relief carving appears to have been done under the reign of Tutankhamen, some of it may date to Ay's reign (Martin 1989, pp. 23, 25, and van Dijk 1993, pp. 28, 32, 34–36.).

15. Arnold 1996, pp. 91, 103–104. This may be seen on blocks not only from Amarna, but from Karnak and Medinet el-Gurob as well.

16. Martin 1989, pls. 110A–111, for example.

17. Ibid., pl. 121.

18. Ibid., pl. 88.

19. This scene first appears in relief in the tomb of Khaemhat at Thebes, from the reign of Amenhotep III (Wreszinski 1923, pls. 203–5).

20. Martin 1989, pl. 125. Compare at Amarna in the tomb of Ahmes, illustrated in N. de G. Davies 1903–8, vol. 3, pl. XXXIII.

21. Martin 1989, pls. 31–32, for example.

22. Ibid., pls. 78ff., found at Amarna in the tomb of Huya, for example (N de G. Davies 1903–8, vol. 3, pl. XIV).

23. Ibid., pls. XCIX–C, found at Amarna in the tomb of Huya, for example (N. de G. Davies 1903–8, vol. 3, pl. XIV).

24. Several scholars have advanced the theory that Ay murdered Tutankhamen (Reeves 1990a, p. 33, and Brier 1998), although the idea remains highly controversial (Eaton-Krauss 1994, p. 254, and Hart 1998, p. 11).

25. Piankoff 1958, pl. 24.

26. Robins 1994, p. 157.

27. Strudwick 1994, pp. 331–32.

28. Ägyptisches Museum, Berlin, 1479; Oriental Institute, Chicago, 14088; and Egyptian Museum, Cairo, JE 59869/60134 and CG 632. Although these are often labeled as Tutankhamen, W. Raymond Johnson, following a suggestion made by Marc Gabolde, presents a convincing argument that they were made for Ay and later usurped by Horemheb. (W. R. Johnson 1994, pp. 142–44, including n. 48, p. 143.)

29. Baines 1985, pp. 83ff.

30. Murnane 1995b, p. 226 (§103-D).

31. Ay was the only older official definitely attested at Amarna who later became king. For a discussion of the similarities between this head and a representation of Queen Tiye (cat. 39), see Russmann 1989, pp. 121–23.

32. Thirteen years is more likely; see Murnane 1995b, pp. 234–35 (§107-C).

33. Ibid., pp. 240–42 (§109–11).

34. Murnane 1995b, pp. 235–40 (§108), and Gnirs 1989.

35. D. Redford 1986, p. 190, n. 184.

36. Spencer 1989, pp. 15ff.

37. Hari 1984–85, pp. 115–16.

38. Eaton-Krauss 1988, p. 11.

39. For two illustrations, see Page-Gasser and Wiese 1997, cat. 108.

40. Mysliwiec 1976, pp. 90–91. I am grateful to Dr. Marianne Eaton-Krauss for this reference.

41. Hornung 1971.

42. Robins 1994, pp. 157–59.

43. Ibid., p. 179.

44. To date, the best publication of the Horemheb shrine is Wreszinski 1935, pls. 161–62. A number of the details, particularly the treatment of the Nubian captives, appear also in Horemheb's Saqqara tomb (Martin 1989, pl. 90, for example).

45. Recent evidence has shown that Maya began his career under Akhenaten and continued in royal service until his death around the eighth year of Horemheb's reign (van Dijk 1993, pp. 74–77). His Saqqara tomb was certainly begun under Tutankhamen (van Dijk 1993, pp. 18–19, 76),

although the style of the statues suggests a slightly later date (Schneider 1974, p. 46).

46. Life-size seated statues of the tomb owner, with or without his wife, are found at Amarna in the private tombs, although unfortunately their damaged state makes comparison difficult (for example, N. de G. Davies 1903–8, vol. 4, pl. XLV showing Ramose and his wife). Maya's tomb, however, featured a greater-than-life-size statue of his wife alone as well as one of Maya alone (Schneider and Raven 1981, p. 89).

47. Robins 1997b, p. 254ff.

48. As in the tomb of Ramesses I (see text above) which must have been decorated just a few years later, since Ramesses I ruled for only about two years.

49. Assmann 1995, pp. 190ff.; Gaballa 1976, p. 91.

50. For example, Museum of Fine Arts, Boston, 29.733 copies the style of Thutmose IV.

51. For example, Museum of Fine Arts, Boston, 75.10. By then, enough years had passed and Akhenaten's existence had been so completely expunged from historical records that Ramesses III was probably unaware of any association of this style with the heretic Akhenaten.

52. For example, Egyptian Museum, Cairo, S.R. 13015, from Medinet Habu.

53. For example, Egyptian Museum, Cairo, JE 36261 from Medinet Habu.

54. In Medinet Habu, for example.

55. Murnane 1995b, p. 241 (§110).

56. D. Redford 1986, p. 19.

57. Hornung 1992, p. 44.

58. D. Redford 1986, pp. 293–94. Akhenaten may even have been the inspiration for a myth known as "The Destruction of Mankind" (Lorton 1983, pp. 614–15).

59. Meltzer 1989, p. 51. Here it is noteworthy that the Great Pyramid predates Akhenaten by more than a millennium.

60. Assmann 1997, pp. 29ff.

61. Freud 1939.

62. Hornung 1992, p. 46 and n. 8.

63. Ibid. For a detailed analysis, see Assmann 1997, pp. 180ff.

64. Hornung 1992, p. 46 and n. 10.

65. See Eaton-Krauss 1990.

Prelude to Amarna

2. Stelophorous statue of Amenwahsu

Probably from Thebes
Dynasty 18, reign of Thutmose III,
1479–1425 B.C.
Quartzite
H. 56 cm, w. 19 cm, d. 34 cm
The Trustees of the British Museum, London,
EA 480

2

Amenwahsu, who served as high priest of the Theban war-god Montu at Thebes and at Tod, another of the god's cult sites, kneels with hands raised, palms up, in the attitude of worship. His hands are supported by a stela bearing a prayer to the sun-god Ra-Horakhty. The same deity, now combined with the great state god Amen, is depicted in the lunette at the top as a man with a ram's head, crossing heaven in a bark.

The stela-shaped back pillar of the statue is inscribed in mirror image with two offering formulae, one addressed to the composite sun-god Ra-Horakhty-Atum, and the other to Osiris, god of the dead. The deities are asked to grant the deceased free movement in the necropolis and through the portals of the underworld and to ensure the provision of bread, air, water, wine, and milk, the requisites for the afterlife.

This form of statue first appears in Dynasty 18, and Amenwahsu's features are in the style of the Thutmoside period (1493–1390 B.C.). However, a man with the same name who held identical offices was the owner of Theban Tomb 274, which is dated to the Ramesside period (1292–1075 B.C.). Either the owner of this statue is an ancestor of the owner of that tomb or the statue itself comes from tomb 274, as one scholar has suggested,[1] and the later Amenwahsu had his likeness carved in a consciously archaized style. Considering the hardness of the stone, the carving is particularly fine.
CA

1. Habachi 1956, p. 61 and n. 5.

3

1. Sculpture of King Thutmose III

Karnak (Amen temple cachette)
Dynasty 18, reign of Thutmose III,
1479–1425 B.C.
Granite
H. 107 cm, w. 33 cm, d. 56 cm
Egyptian Museum, Cairo, JE 39260

This magnificent statue,[1] a traditional portrayal of kingship, shows a trim, youthful King Thutmose III seated upon the throne, wearing the standard royal costume: a *shendyt* pleated kilt, a *nemes* headdress, and a ceremonial royal beard. In his right hand he holds a folded kerchief.[2]

A bull's tail, symbol of physical power, hangs between his legs. The king treads on hieroglyphs representing nine bows, ensuring that he will subjugate and defeat the traditional enemies of Egypt. The hieroglyph *sema*, symbolizing the unification of Upper and Lower Egypt, is represented on the side panels of the throne.

The subtle modeling of facial features occurs in many other sculptures in the round, but here we easily recognize the soft, sensitive, idealized features of this sovereign—the long, arched eyebrows, the feline eyes with long cosmetic lines, the pronounced arch of the aquiline nose, the full cheeks, and the delicate mouth with accentuated philtrum (the hollow in the upper lip). MS

1. Griffith 1906–7, p. 21.

2. Hornemann 1957, pl. 270. For a discussion of this sculpture, see Matthias Seidel in Müller and Settgast 1976, cat. 1.

3. Stela of Amenhotep worshipping the sun

Provenance not known
Dynasty 18, reigns of Thutmose III and
Amenhotep II, 1479–1400 B.C.
Sandstone
H. 70.5 cm, w. 45.5 cm
Rogers Fund, 1917, The Metropolitan
Museum of Art, New York, 17.2.6

On this round-topped stela, the priest
Amenhotep is shown twice, in back-to-
back representations, worshipping the
rising sun (at right) and the setting sun
(at left).[1] According to the inscription,
he was a mortuary priest of three 18th-
Dynasty kings—Amenhotep I, Thutmose I, and Thutmose III. The inscription also lists his other numerous titles
and the names of his parents and grand-
parents.[2] The decoration of the lunette
at the top is separated from the rest of
the stela and contains, besides the protective *wedjat*-eyes and *shen*-sign, hieroglyphs for *hatet net tjehenu* (sacred oil
and incense). The name of Amen was
erased throughout the inscription during the reign of Akhenaten. EP

---

1. Hayes 1959, p. 172, fig. 94; Dewachter 1984,
p. 84.

2. For a translation, see Kees 1960.

4. Osiris with the features of Amenhotep III

Provenance not known
Dynasty 18, reign of Amenhotep III,
1390–1353 B.C.
Quartzite
H. 52.5 cm, w. 21.2 cm, d. 26.2 cm
Gift of Miss Anna D. Slocum, Museum of
Fine Arts, Boston, 09.288

Although this head bears no inscription,
the relatively flat, narrow eyes with
their thick cosmetic lines, and the
mouth with its overbite and pronounced central dip, leave little doubt
that the face is that of King Amenhotep
III. However, the remains of a plaited
beard (an indication of divinity) and the
Upper Egyptian crown indicate that the
king was depicted as Osiris, god of the
netherworld.[1] Such statues were often
found in mortuary temples.[2]

Another head, virtually identical to
this one in style, iconography, size, and
material, was recently confiscated from
thieves by the Egyptian authorities and
is now in the Egyptian Museum, Cairo.[3]
It is likely the two once stood as a pair
in Amenhotep III's mortuary temple at
Kom el-Hetan in western Thebes. REF

---

1. Betsy M. Bryan in Kozloff and Bryan 1992, p.
158.

2. Ibid., p. 159.

3. Egyptian Museum, Cairo, JE 98832. I am
grateful to Mr. Adel Mahmoud, Curator, New
Kingdom Section, for this information.

5

4

5. Sculpture of Amenhotep III

Gebel Barkal, sanctuary of Temple B 700
Dynasty 18, reign of Amenhotep III,
1390–1353 B.C.
Peridotite
H. 108, w. 20.1, d. 42.8 cm
Harvard University–MFA Expedition,
Museum of Fine Arts, Boston, 23.734

This statue was found at Gebel Barkal,
the "Holy Mountain," near modern
Karima, Sudan, 580 miles up the Nile
from Aswan.[1] Under Thutmose III,
Gebel Barkal was identified not only
as the southern limit of the Egyptian
empire but also as the primary Nubian
residence of Amen.[2] Akhenaten obviously carried his campaign against the
Theban god even to this remote outpost
of his cult, since every instance on this
statue of the old king's given name,
Amenhotep (meaning "Amen is at
Peace"), has been carefully erased.[3]

Many centuries later, Amenhotep III
was still venerated at Gebel Barkal. The
faceless statue was found in a temple of
the seventh century B.C., where it had
been re-erected by later Nubian kings
and, in the second century A.D., buried
in a landslide. TK

---

1. Reisner 1918, p. 102.

2. Kendall 1994.

3. Dunham 1970, p. 17, fig. 5, pl. 5.

6

7. *Sah* statue of Tjenura

Saqqara
Dynasty 18, reign of Amenhotep III,
1390–1353 B.C.
Limestone
H. 112 cm, w. 35 cm, d. 24 cm
Purchase 1828 (ex Anastasi Collection),
Rijksmuseum van Oudheden, Leiden,
AST 15

The inscription on this statue mentions
Tjenura, a mayor of Memphis. With its
mummiform body and tripartite wig,
the object looks like a *shabti*, yet it is
perhaps more appropriate to speak of a
sah-statue: a depiction of the deceased
as a privileged being, revivified by the
rays of the sun.[1] Therefore, it has been
assumed that the statue once adorned
the courtyard of Tjenura's tomb, where
it would have been exposed to the sunlight. The physiognomy, with its banded
eyebrows, folds in the upper eyelids,
and full lips, is very characteristic of the
reign of Amenhotep III. There is a similar figure of Tjenura's wife, Ipay, in
Leiden. Five *shabti*s of either husband
or wife have been spotted in the Vatican
museums and in private collections.[2]
MJR

1. Schneider 1977, vol. I, pp. 65–67.

2. Gessler-Löhr 1997, pp. 38–51.

7

6. Ptah-Sokar-Osiris with the fea-
tures of Amenhotep III

Probably from western Thebes, the mortu-
ary temple of Amenhotep III
Dynasty 18, reign of Amenhotep III,
1390–1353 B.C.
Granite
H. 67.3 cm, w. 34.3 cm, d. 28.4 cm
The Thalassic Collection, Ltd., Courtesy
of Theodore and Aristea Halkedis

The elegant elongation of the eyes,
the arched brows, and the distinctive
Cupid's-bow shape of the mouth identify the face as that of Amenhotep III,
even though the titulary of King Merneptah of Dynasty 19 was later carved on
the back pillar. The long lappet wig,
plaited beard, and composite headdress
consisting of horizontal ram's horns,
sun-disk, and tall feathers indicate that
not the king but a deity is represented,
specifically Ptah-Sokar-Osiris. The god
also wears an enveloping garment and

holds a scepter that combines symbols
of stability, life, and power. Although
this composite deity is first mentioned
in texts of the Middle Kingdom, it is
not until the New Kingdom that he is
represented in the form shown here.[1]
    In the tomb of Kheruef, from the
reign of Amenhotep III, Ptah-Sokar-
Osiris is identified with the rising sun,
and this solar association endeared him
to Amenhotep IV during his early years
of rule.[2] Amenhotep III included in his
funerary temple a chapel, since destroyed, to Ptah-Sokar-Osiris,[3] and much of
this material was later reused by Merneptah in his own funerary temple
nearby.[4] REF

1. Brovarski 1983, cols. 1060–61.

2. Ibid., col. 1061.

3. Brunner 1979, pp. 61–62; Ricke 1981, pp.
31ff.

4. Bickel 1997.

8

8. Head of Amenhotep III wearing a solar diadem

Provenance not known
Dynasty 18, reign of Amenhotep III,
1390–1353 B.C.
Quartzite
H. 17.3 cm, w. 17 cm, d. 25.3 cm
Purchase from the Leonard C. Hanna, Jr.
Fund, The Cleveland Museum of Art,
Cleveland, 1961.417

9. Queen Tiye wearing an elaborate wig

Probably from Sedeinga
Dynasty 18, reign of Amenhotep III,
1390–1353 B.C.
Magnesite marble
H. 20.3 cm, w. 11.5 cm, d. 12 cm
Gift of George A. Reisner, Museum of
Fine Arts, Boston, 21.2802

Thanks to recent scholarship, it is now
understood that, despite their childlike
appearance, the fussy cherubic images
of Amenhotep III and his court, as
exemplified by these heads of the king
and Queen Tiye, belong to the latter
years of his reign.[1] Both pieces have
characteristic round faces framed by
elaborately detailed wigs, and eyes
whose large size and almond shape are
emphasized by heavy rims and brows.
The king's fillet, with its pendant uraei
wearing solar disks, refers to his interest
in solar deities, and may associate him
with the god Neferhotep, son of the
goddess Hathor, daughter of Ra. The
top of the back pillar contains the
beginning of the king's titulary, "King
of Upper and Lower Egypt, Ruler of
J<oy>."[2]

The head of the queen, identified as
Tiye on the basis of its distinctive style,
wears not only the royal uraeus at the
brow, but also the sun-disk and horns
that liken the queen to Hathor, the goddess with whom she was associated at
her temple in Sedeinga.[3] The nature of
the break in the back pillar indicates
that the image of the queen was originally from a group statue, and that at
least one figure was at its left.[4] REF

9

---

1. W. R. Johnson 1990, pp. 34ff.; Bothmer 1990,
p. 87.

2. Betsy M. Bryan in Kozloff and Bryan 1992, p.
160.

3. Morkot 1986.

4. Bryan in Kozloff and Bryan 1992, p. 176.

10

10. Amenhotep III offering

Provenance not known
Dynasty 18, reign of Amenhotep III,
1390–1353 B.C.
Glazed steatite
H. 13 cm, w. 3.8 cm, d. 5.3 cm
Gift of Mrs. Horace L. Mayer, Museum of
Fine Arts, Boston, 1970.636

A kneeling image of King Amenhotep
III, so identified by the cartouche on the
back pillar, presents a now-destroyed
offering to a god. Prior to Amenhotep
III, kings had always been depicted with
athletically trim bodies. This king's
round face and ample torso, despite
their youthful appearance, were characteristic of the latter years of his rule.[1]
The decided plumpness, together with
the *shebyu*-collar, arm bands, and multiple uraei wearing sun disks (visible on
the apron) are elements that appear
after the king's first jubilee festival, in

his thirtieth year of rule, and associate
him with the sun.[2]

Traces of pigment indicate that this
votive statuette was once covered with
a glaze of blue-green, a color symbolic
of vegetation and rebirth.[3] The Egyptian
word for glazed objects was *tjehenut*,
which may also be translated as "dazzling," a common epithet for Amenhotep III.[4] REF

---

1. W. R. Johnson 1990, pp. 34ff.

2. Ibid., p. 35.

3. Brunner-Traut 1975, cols. 124–25.

4. Betsy M. Bryan in Kozloff and Bryan 1992, p.
198.

11

12

11. Head of Amenhotep III wearing the crown of Upper Egypt

Thebes, Medinet Habu
Dynasty 18, reign of Amenhotep III,
1390–1353 B.C.
Granodiorite
H. 44 cm, w. 13 cm, d. 30 cm
Egyptian Museum, Cairo, JE 59880

12. Torso of a corpulent Amenhotep III

Thebes, Kom el-Hetan
Dynasty 18, reign of Amenhotep III,
1390–1353 B.C.
Granodiorite
H. 115 cm, w. 56 cm, d. 59 cm
Egyptian Museum, Cairo, JE 33900

The torso, one of a pair, depicts Amenhotep III in a tight sleeveless cloak on
the occasion of his third *heb-sed* (jubilee
festival), a ceremony of rejuvenation,
two years before his death. His health
had so deteriorated by then that the
Babylonian king sent him a statue of
the goddess Ishtar, famous for her heal-
ing powers. The weakening Amenhotep
needed a drastic remedy to re-create
himself.

Viewed in profile, his clasped hands
create a protuberance in the pubic area:
he is Min, god of fertility. With his
abdomen distended like that of a
pregnant woman, he is also Taweret,
patroness of fecundity and birth, a
counterpart necessary for all creation.
Embodying both figures, the king can
create himself by himself: he has certainly anticipated the vision of his son
Akhenaten.

The head shows the same disappoint-
ed, bitter expression seen on images of
his wife: two heads of Tiye, one from
Sinai and one from the Fayum, are
thought to date from the third *heb-sed*
or later. We are far from the satisfied,
mysterious smile of Amenhotep III's
early reign, evidenced in cat. 4. MT

13. Amenhotep III with *nemes* headdress

Deir el-Bahari, forecourt of the Hatshepsut
temple
Dynasty 18, reign of Amenhotep III,
1390–1353 B.C.
Granite
H. 26. 5 cm, w. 21.5 cm, d. 21 cm
Rogers Fund, 1923, The Metropolitan
Museum of Art, New York, 23.3.170

Until ten or fifteen years ago, conventional wisdom would have identified
this life-size royal head as that of a
post-Amarna king. Recent research by
W. Raymond Johnson, however, has
demonstrated that the subject is
Amenhotep III.[1] His chubby face,
almond-shaped eyes, and protruding,
sensuous lips resemble those of a small
group of heads, including cat. 11, of
that king and his queen, Tiye, which
can be dated to the end of his reign and
forecast the style of the next. Further,
Johnson has shown that the vertical tra-
gus of the ear found on this sculpture is
a trait specific to Amenhotep III.[2]

Although the head was reportedly
found at Deir el-Bahari, it may have
come originally from Amenhotep III's
vast mortuary-temple precinct nearby.
REF

13

1. W. Raymond Johnson, unpublished correspondence with Mohamed Saleh, 2 September 1995;
provided by the author. See also Bothmer 1978,
pl. x.

2. Ibid.

14

14. Relief of Amenhotep III

Memphis, temple of Ptah
Dynasty 18, reign of Amenhotep III,
1390–1353 B.C.
Quartzite
H. 41 cm, w. 65 cm
Gift of the British School of Archaeology
in Egypt, Museum of Fine Arts, Boston,
10.650

One of the finest examples of the artistic style immediately preceding the Amarna revolution, this fragment displays Amenhotep III in a gesture of offering to the goddess Sakhmet, whose lioness face is just visible at right. The Memphite sunk-relief carving reveals similarities to royal images from the king's temples at Thebes, several hundred miles to the south. Both regions portray Amenhotep with characteristically sloping, almond-shaped eyes; slightly rounded nose; and straight, prominent lips. He wears the *nemes* headdress and the uraeus, or cobra, diadem, both features of his royal status. The goddess holds her emblematic papyrus staff. The text to the left of the cartouche (which bears the prenomen of Amenhotep, Nebmaatra) declares that he is "given life, prosperity, and dominion, like Ra." There is an elegance to the relief carving, especially visible in the king's facial features, that will be exaggerated later under the reign of Amenhotep's successor, Akhenaten.[1] PDM

1. For previous publications of the relief, see Petrie 1910, pl. XXIX, 2, p. 39; Simpson 1977, cat. 38 and p. 68.

15. Prince Thutmose ("Thutmose V") on a bier

Probably from Memphis
Dynasty 18, reign of Amenhotep III,
1390–1353 B.C.
Schist
H. 4.9 cm, w. 10.5 cm, d. 4.2 cm
Verein zur Förderung des Ägyptischen
Museums e.V. Berlin, Ägyptisches Museum
und Papyrussammlung, Berlin,
VAGM-112-97

16. Relief of Prince Thutmose ("Thutmose V")

Probably from Saqqara
Dynasty 18, reign of Amenhotep III,
1390–1353 B.C.
Limestone
H. 37 cm, w. 53 cm
Purchase from Bissing Collection,
Staatliche Sammlung Ägyptischer Kunst,
Munich, GL 93

The mummified person on the lion-headed bier[1] is identified by the hieroglyphic inscriptions on the body and on the sides of the bier as "The King's Son, the *sem*-priest Thutmose, the justified." This epithet and the iconography of the mummy-shaped body are sufficient criteria for determining that this is a representation of Thutmose in death. As the firstborn son of King Amenhotep III, he was supposed to succeed his father on the throne. His premature death made his younger brother Amenhotep's accession possible and gave Amenhotep the opportunity to make his vision of god the new theology of Egypt.

The iconographic form of the mummified figure with the human-headed soul-bird (the *ba*)—an illustration of Chapter 89 of the Book of the Dead—seems to be an invention of the time of Amenhotep III.

In the relief,[2] Thutmose, identified by the inscription, is depicted with a youthful face and a priest's side lock, presiding over the burial of a sacred bull, a ritual of the traditional religion. The style is typical for the reign of Amenhotep III, whose shoulder and head are partly preserved in front of the prince. DW

1. Wildung 1998, with references to Thutmose.
2. Wildung 1997a.

15

16

17. Stela of Wesi

Memphis
Dynasty 18, reign of Amenhotep III, 1390–1353 B.C.
Limestone
H. 92.5 cm, w. 64 cm
Ex Michel Collection, Staatliche Sammlung Ägyptischer Kunst, Munich, AS 11

Wesi, who was Commander of the Navy and Chief of Archers under Amenhotep III, and his wife Ipuy are represented in the upper register of this large stela,[1] offering to the god Osiris. Ipuy, Chantress of Amen-Ra, holds a sistrum and a *menat*, a ritual ornament (see cat. 99). In the lower register, the couple, seated at right, receive floral offerings from their four daughters.

Within the very rigid structure of these reliefs, which recalls the traditional style of the earlier 18th Dynasty, the figures already show clear signs of the coming stylistic evolution toward Amarna art: Wesi's proportions, his belly protruding over the belt, and Ipuy's and her daughters' knees, bent backward, are indications.

Akhenaten's religious revolution eventually left its traces on this stela: the name of Amen-Ra in Ipuy's title has been hacked out. SS

1. Wildung 1976, pp. 87–88; Schoske 1990, cat. 35.

17

18. Statuette of a woman

Probably from Medinet el-Gurob
Dynasty 18, late Amenhotep III–early Amenhotep IV, 1360–1350 B.C.
Wood, gold
H. 35.5 cm
Private collection

19. Statuette of Tiya, Chief of the Household

Medinet el-Gurob
Dynasty 18, late Amenhotep III–early Amenhotep IV, 1360–1350 B.C.
Wood, gold, semiprecious stones
H. 24 cm
Rogers Fund, 1941, The Metropolitan Museum of Art, New York, 41.2.10

The aging Queen Tiye lived for a period of time in a palace at Medinet el-Gurob, a town in Middle Egypt near the entrance to the Fayum oasis.[1] A number of wooden statuettes depicting upper-class women are believed to derive from tombs in that area that date from the final years of Amenhotep III's reign or the early rule of his radical son.[2] These figures, sensuous and superbly carved, bridge the two reigns stylistically in that the facial features often bear a resemblance to Amenhotep III while the bodies, with their elongated arms and abdominal bulges, reflect Amarna practice.[3]

The elegant ladies are typically attired in fringed linen tunics with pleated shawls. Their wigs, surmounted by cones representing scented fat, are elaborate, and jewelry is indicated by gilding or miniature replicas. Similar figures, clearly funerary in nature, have been found at Saqqara.[4] YJM

1. For a description of the palace, see Lacovara 1997, pp. 36–37. Dorothea Arnold, however, points out the lack of palace remains, particularly decorative tile fragments, at the site and suggests that, rather than a royal residence, the area was a cult center dedicated to Tiye's late husband, Amenhotep III. See Arnold 1996, p. 28.

2. Betsy M. Bryan in Kozloff and Bryan 1992, pp. 258–59.

3. Russmann 1989, cat. 52.

4. A fine example is that of Lady Henutnakhtu from Saqqara tomb 1859. See Saleh and Sourouzian 1987, cat. 155.

18

19

20

21

20. Amenhotep IV and Ra-Horakhty

Karnak, vicinity of the Tenth Pylon
Dynasty 18, reign of Amenhotep IV/
Akhenaten, 1353–1336 B.C. (years 1–2)
Sandstone
H. 70 cm, w. 150 cm, d. 28 cm
Ex Lepsius Collection, 1845, Ägyptisches
Museum und Papyrussammlung, Berlin,
2072

Reused by King Horemheb in the Tenth
Pylon of the Amen temple at Karnak,
this block[1] is one of the few extant
examples of relief decoration depicting
Amenhotep IV at Karnak immediately
after his accession. The temple where it
originated was dedicated to the sun-god
Ra-Horakhty, represented here in his
traditional shape, as a falcon-headed
man with the sun-disk on his head. The
epithets after his name in the accompanying text are identical with the early
form of the name of the sun-god Aten.
Thus the iconography still follows the
traditional patterns, whereas the termi-
nology has already made the step to the
new theology. Another harbinger of
future developments can be seen in the
sun-disk above the head of King
Amenhotep IV. The *ankh*-signs fixed on
the disk would soon be transformed
into the rays of the Aten, holding these
signs of life in their human hands. DW

1. Porter and Moss 1972, p. 190; Chappaz 1983;
Vergnieux and Gondran 1997, p. 84 (illustration
reversed!).

21. Amenhotep IV censing an altar

Karnak, vicinity of the Tenth Pylon
Dynasty 18, reign of Amenhotep IV/
Akhenaten, 1353–1336 B.C.
Sandstone
H. 60 cm, w. 130 cm
Ex Bibliothèque Nationale, Cabinet des
Médailles, 1843, Musée du Louvre, Paris,
E 13482 ter

This fragmentary relief belongs to one
of the structures built by Amenhotep IV
at the very beginning of his reign, in the
vicinity of the Amen temple at Karnak.
The king, wearing the *afnet (khat)*
headdress, is represented twice, censing
an altar laden with offerings under the
rays of the solar disk. Several peculiar
features make this relief one of the most
interesting examples of the iconographic
changes that occurred early in the reign.
The sun god no longer appears in the
traditional form of a falcon-headed
man, but as a radiant disk granting the
king *was* scepters— symbols of well-
being and dominion—and the hieroglyph of the jubilee festival (*heb-sed*).
Both symbols ceased to appear after the
move to Amarna, when the sun-disk
was shown offering the *ankh*, the symbol of life.

The depiction of the king is interesting in that the "mirror" images differ
slightly, showing the evolution from
Amenhotep III's "baby-face" style
(right) toward the style that would be
used in the reliefs of the Gempaaten at
Karnak (left). The figure of Nefertiti
added on the left and the overwriting
of the king's cartouches show that the
carving was made in several stages. The
rarity of mirror-image symmetry in representations of the king has led scholars
to believe that a matching block, found
in the courtyard between the Ninth and
Tenth pylons of the Amen temple,
belongs to the same temple built by
Amenhotep IV.[1] ME

1. Vergnieux and Gondran 1997, pp. 88–93. For
more information on this relief, see Müller 1988,
p. 84 and pl. 38a; Chappaz 1983, pp. 38–39;
Asselbergs 1923.

22

23

24

22. Colossal statue of Amenhotep IV with *nemes* and Shu feathers

Karnak, Gempaaten
Dynasty 18, reign of Amenhotep IV/
Akhenaten, 1353–1336 B.C. (years 2–5)
Sandstone
H. 154 cm, w. 85 cm, d. 60 cm
Egyptian Museum, Cairo, JE 98894

23. Colossal statue of Amenhotep IV with *nemes* and double crown

Karnak, Gempaaten
Dynasty 18, reign of Amenhotep IV/
Akhenaten, 1353–1336 B.C. (years 2–5)
Sandstone
H. 205 cm, w. 111 cm, d. 60 cm
Egyptian Museum, Cairo, JE 98915

24. Fragment of a face from a colossal statue

Karnak, Gempaaten
Dynasty 18, reign of Amenhotep IV/
Akhenaten, 1353–1336 B.C. (years 2–5)
Sandstone
H. 32.2 cm, w. 18.8 cm, d. 23 cm
Staatliche Sammlung Ägyptischer Kunst,
Munich, ÄS 6290

Elongated faces with pendant chins, narrow eyes with upper lids projecting sharply outward, and noses and mouths extended into V-shapes make these images instantly recognizable as Amenhotep IV. Ethereal, if not haunting, they are the earliest positively identified sculpture in the round of that king[1] and derive from colossal statues that originally stood at intervals of about six feet in front of the rectangular pillars of a colonnade in his Gempaaten temple at Karnak.[2]

In examples here, the king wears the *nemes* and tall feathers of the god Shu, god of air and son of the creator-god Atum (cat. 22) and the *nemes* with the combined crown of Upper and Lower Egypt (cat. 23). The complete statues would have shown the king in the crossed-arm pose of Osiris, god of rebirth, and carrying the crook and flail (see fig. 4). Most wore a wrapped, pleated kilt whose belt was pushed into a U-shape by a pendant belly. At least one colossus, which shows no trace of such a garment, may represent Nefertiti (fig. 5).[3]

These statues, with their varied crowns and garments, may have represented the royal family as the primeval triad of Atum, Shu, and Tefnut. REF

1. For a suggestion of an earlier piece, see Reeves 1996.
2. D. Redford 1984, p. 102.
3. J. R. Harris 1977a.

25. *Heb-sed* (jubilee) representation

Provenance not known
Dynasty 18, reign of Akhenaten,
1353–1336 B.C.
Limestone
H. 23 cm, w. 53 cm, d. 6.5 cm
Lent by the Syndics of the Fitzwilliam
Museum, Cambridge, England,
EGA.2300.1943

Akhenaten is shown twice in a narrative on this limestone sunk relief: once within a structure identified as "Jubiliation in the Horizon of the Aten,"[1] worshipping the sun before an offering table laden with foodstuffs and vessels, and once in procession, dressed in a festival *(heb-sed)* cloak with flail—under sun rays bearing *ankh* and *was* signs (representing life and dominion,[2] respectively)—and flanked by his bowing chief priest bearing sandals and his lector priest holding a papyrus roll. The block was thought so improbable for the Amarna Period that it was believed to pre-date the name change from Amenhotep IV (and frequently published as such), but re-examination of the cartouche suggests that it was not recarved.[3] EV

1. Aldred 1973, cat. 11.

2. Griffith 1918, pp. 61–63, pl. 8.

3. Vassilika 1995, cat. 26.

26. Nefertiti shaking a sistrum

Karnak
Dynasty 18, reign of Amenhotep IV/
Akhenaten, 1353–1336 B.C. (years 2–5)
Sandstone
H. 21.5 cm, W. 47.5 cm
Luxor Museum, Luxor, 267

Traces of the uraeus at her brow and the modius on her wig identify this figure as a queen who shakes a Hathor-headed sistrum behind a much larger figure of the king. A matching block below, discovered by the Akhenaten Temple Project, not only provides more of the king's figure, but also identifies the queen as his Great Royal Wife[1] (Nefertiti). Complete, Nefertiti's headdress would have included a sun-disk, horns, and feathers above her modius (crown base),[2] which, like her sistrum, are attributes of Hathor, goddess of fertility, femininity, and music,[3] and daughter of the sun-god Ra.

Representations of Nefertiti shaking a sistrum and situated behind a larger figure of Amenhotep IV offering to Aten are found a number of times on *talatat* blocks from Karnak,[4] and allude to her role as priestess. This function is directly referenced in a tomb inscription at Amarna, which says that Nefertiti "propitiates the Aten with her pleasant voice and with her beautiful hands holding the sistra"[5]—despite the fact that at Amarna, Nefertiti assumed a role in the cult equal to that of Amenhotep IV (then called Akhenaten), and sistrum-shaking was left to the royal daughters.[6]

In this example Nefertiti's face exhibits none of the attenuations and exaggerations of the extreme style seen on other *talatat* (cat. 27) from the same site. Amenhotep IV's extensive building activity at Karnak must have employed every available artisan, and some craftsmen continued to work in an earlier, more restrained relief style of Amenhotep III. REF

1. Smith and Redford 1976, pl. 10.

2. Ibid.

3. Daumas 1977.

4. Smith and Redford 1976, pp. 80–81, especially n. 35.

5. N. de G. Davies 1903–8, vol. 6, p. 29.

6. Arnold 1996, pp. 85–86.

27. Nefertiti in the extreme style

Karnak
Dynasty 18, reign of Amenhotep IV/
Akhenaten, 1353–1336 B.C. (years 2–5)
Sandstone
H. 20 cm, W. 45 cm
Collection of Jack A. Josephson, New York, 118.89

This block from a wall in one of the several Aten temples at Karnak dates to the early years of King Akhenaten's reign.[1] It portrays his queen, Nefertiti; the presence of their daughter, Meretaten, is evidenced only by the inscription "... of his body, his beloved Meretaten." Although the queen was then very young, her representation is that of an older woman. She wears a long, echeloned wig with a fillet, or headband, holding a double uraeus in place. On her head is a modius encircled by cobras, the base of a high crown. Near her face are an *ankh* sign, signifying life, and an open hand offering the life-giving power of the sun's rays—the embodiment of the Aten.

The Karnak reliefs are the genesis of later representations at Amarna. Those exaggerated images, contrasting with the idealized beauty of the royal family traditionally depicted in New Kingdom portraits, were developed during this early period.

The Aten temples in Karnak and other structures built by Akhenaten were destroyed after his death, but their masonry was salvaged and utilized as fill and foundation for later buildings. The preservation of this block is excellent, with traces of paint on its surface, and the soft stone retaining a crisp image of the queen. JJ

1. Arnold 1996, p. 18, fig. 11.

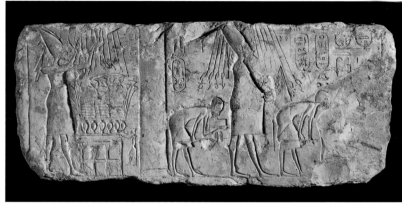

25

26

27

28

28. Amenhotep IV and a jackal-headed god (Soul of Nekhen)

Karnak, Ninth Pylon
Dynasty 18, reign of Amenhotep IV/
Akhenaten, 1353–1336 B.C. (years 2–5)
Sandstone
Abu'l Good storeroom, Luxor, AG 2420

This block illustrates some of the revolutionary innovations in Amarna art. It presents a traditional scene of Pharaoh kneeling with the "Souls of Pe and Nekhen," hawk- and jackal-headed ancestral beings, who beat their chests to acclaim the rising sun.[1] Amarna novelties are the distended belly of the jackal-headed figure, which imitates Akhenaten's, and the king's figure surmounted by the Aten, bathing him in life-giving rays.[2] TK

1. Walker 1991, pp. 22–29.

2. Smith and Redford 1976, pl. 80, 2.

29. Musicians with giant lyre

Karnak
Dynasty 18, reign of Amenhotep IV/
Akhenaten, 1353–1336 B.C. (years 2–5)
Sandstone
H. 23 cm, w. 53 cm, d. 26.5 cm
Luxor Museum, Luxor, 210

30. Dancing women

Karnak
Dynasty 18, reign of Amenhotep IV/
Akhenaten, 1353–1336 B.C. (years 2–5)
Sandstone
H. 22.5 cm, w. 52.5 cm, d. 25 cm
Luxor Museum, Luxor, 803

31. Musicians with various instruments

Karnak
Dynasty 18, reign of Amenhotep IV/
Akhenaten, 1353–1336 B.C. (years 2–5)
Sandstone
H. 22 cm, w. 53 cm, d. 25.5 cm
Luxor Museum, Luxor, 266

Choral and instrumental music had always been a part of Egyptian life, both secular and sacred. Eighteenth-Dynasty reliefs show small bands of musicians playing harps, lutes, lyres, and double oboes.

Akhenaten's innovations extended to the realm of music and dance. The *talatat* reliefs from Karnak depict groups performing in the palace, including musicians playing the traditional instruments (cat. 31)[1] and acrobatic dancers with long, unbound hair (cat. 30).[2] Also pictured are new types of instruments and new groups of musicians. Cat. 29[3] depicts two groups. On the left is a band of Egyptian women, wearing sheath dresses and unguent cones with flowers, playing two lyres, a lute, and a double oboe while one of the women claps her hands. On the right is a band of foreign, probably Near Eastern, performers, dressed in long, flounced garments and tall, peaked caps. Two of them play the giant lyre,[4] the only instrument requiring two players. This instrument disappears after the Amarna Period and does not occur again until Ptolemaic times. Interestingly, the foreign musicians, who are thought to be male,[5] are blindfolded, as are other male musicians of the period. The blindfolds are believed to represent symbolic blindness,[6] possibly for religious purposes. SD'A

1. Manniche 1975a, fig. 25, pl. XIV; Chevrier 1938, pl. CX.

2. Karl-Theodor Zauzich in Müller and Settgast 1976, cat. 29; Chevrier 1938, pl. CX. See Epigraphic Survey 1980, pls. 33–38. For dance in ancient Egypt, see Brunner-Traut 1986 and references found there.

3. Manniche 1991a, fig. 54, Manniche 1975a, fig. 23, pl. XIV; Luxor Museum 1979, cat. 174; Karl-Theodor Zauzich in Müller and Settgast 1976, cat. 30; Chevrier 1938, pl. CX.

4. See Green 1993 for this instrument and its players.

5. Manniche 1991a and 1991b; but see Green 1993, p. 57.

6. Manniche 1978; see also Vergnieux and Gondran 1997, pp. 152–53.

29

30

31

32

33

34. Workers carrying heavy loads

Karnak
Dynasty 18, reign of Amenhotep IV/
Akhenaten, 1353–1336 B.C. (years 2–5)
Sandstone
H. 23.5 cm, W. 53 cm, D. 24 cm
Luxor Museum, Luxor, 211

The basic building material used in Amenhotep IV's temples at Karnak was the *talatat*—a sandstone block that was about twenty inches long, half as wide, and half as deep. The structures were dismantled by later kings, who used the stones as fill for pylons. The blocks, retrieved in modern times, have been the subject of considerable study by scholars such as Donald Redford (Akhenaten Temple Project), who have attempted to match scenes on tens of thousands of blocks, much as one would assemble a giant jigsaw puzzle.[1]

Many of the Karnak *talatat* are decorated with painted relief carvings depicting the royal family and scenes of daily life. Redford notes that domestic activities, such as maintaining livestock, baking bread, and construction, were associated with the Tenimenu, one of four major religious structures Amenhotep IV erected at Karnak.[2] YJM

1. For an overview of this enormous undertaking, involving photographic documentation, statistical analysis, and computerization of data, see D. Redford 1973.

2. The blocks from this structure were found in the Ninth Pylon of the Karnak enclosure, and it has been suggested that the temple was located nearby. See D. Redford 1973, pp. 84–85. The specific function of the Tenimenu ("Exalted are the Monuments [of the Sun-Disk Forever]") is unknown. See D. Redford 1984, pp. 63, 71. For domestic scenes from this temple, see Daniel 1971, pp. 151–54.

34

32. Bowing man offering

Karnak
Dynasty 18, reign of Amenhotep IV/
Akhenaten, 1353–1336 B.C. (years 2–5)
Sandstone
Abu'l Good storeroom, Luxor, AG 1791

33. Two men in conversation

Karnak
Dynasty 18, reign of Amenhotep IV/
Akhenaten, 1353–1336 B.C. (years 2–5)
Sandstone
Abu'l Good storeroom, Luxor, AG 2642

Among the temple activities prescribed for the daily ritual were censing and libating. Here (cat. 32) a man with slender limbs but a hefty middle bends over to pour a libation with one hand while holding a brazier high in the other. In front of him is a table with tall vessels and behind him, additional braziers. In the second relief, two men slouch about in the shade of a corniced structure, while other individuals toil nearby. Such intimate vignettes are typical of Amenhotep IV's new relief style and subject matter at Karnak. PDM

35. Chalice

Provenance not known
Dynasty 18, reign of Amenhotep IV/
Akhenaten, 1353–1336 B.C. (years 1–4)
Calcite
H. 14 cm
Gift of Edward S. Harkness, 1922, The Metropolitan Museum of Art, New York, 22.9.1

This graceful chalice is shaped like a white lotus flower.[1] The inscription includes a number of cartouches. Two of them name the god Aten, two contain the prenomen and nomen of Amenhotep IV, and a fifth contains the name of the principal queen, Nefertiti. As the king changed his name to Akhenaten in the fifth year of his reign, the chalice can be dated to the first four regnal years. The lotiform shape is a popular one for vessels in Amarna.[2] Surviving representations of Akhenaten and Tutankhamen with chalices of this shape show that they were used by royalty for drinking.[3] This chalice is said to come from a private tomb in Upper Egypt,[4] which suggests that it was given by the king to a worthy official, possibly to serve as grave goods. EP

1. Hayes 1959, pp. 293–94, fig. 181.

2. Winlock 1922, p. 171; for a list of known Amarna lotiform chalices, see Tait 1963, pp. 95–97.

3. N. de G. Davies 1903–8, vol. 4, pp. 4–7, pl. VI; Tait 1963, p. 97.

4. Winlock 1922, p. 171.

35

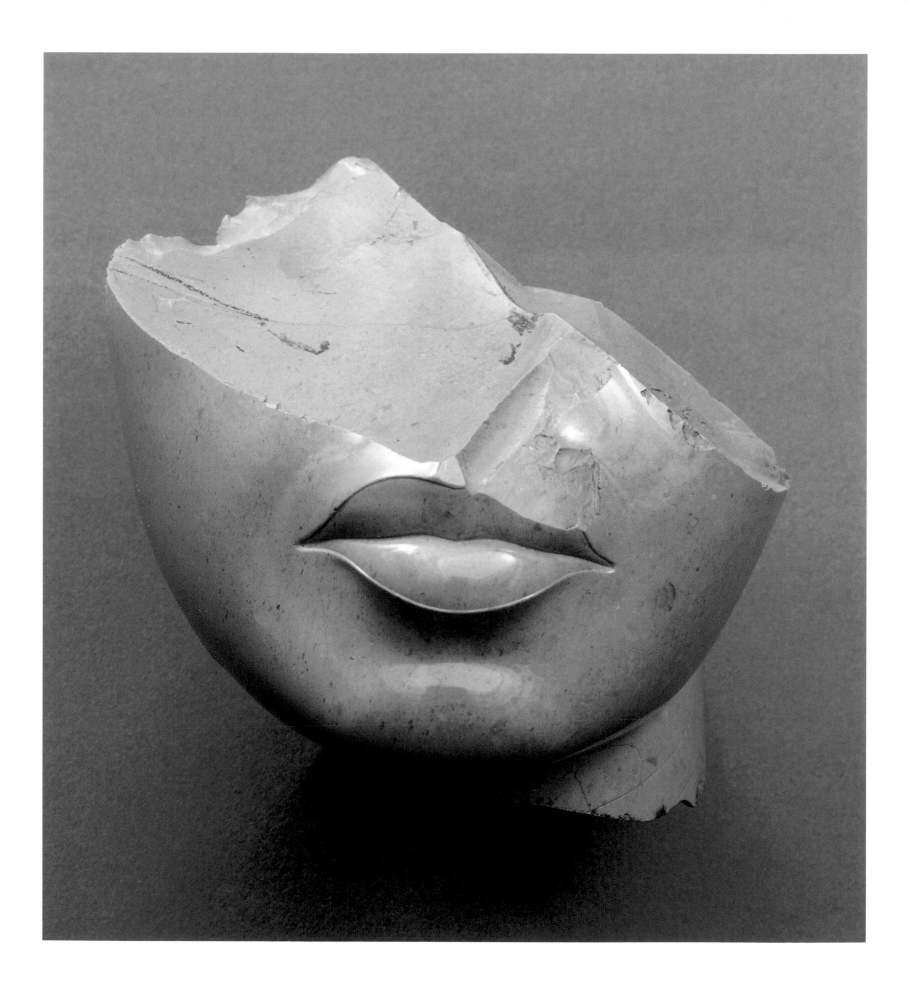

Amarna

36

36. Statuette of Akhenaten with stela

Amarna, house N.48.15
Dynasty 18, reign of Akhenaten,
1353–1336 B.C.
Calcite
H. 12.2 cm, w. 3 cm, d. 5.8 cm
Excavations of the Deutsche Orient-
Gesellschaft, 1912, Ägyptisches Museum
und Papyrussammlung, Berlin, 21835

Out of the geometric frame created by
the deep back pillar and the low rectangular base, the king leans forward, holding in his outstretched arms a stela presumably bearing the names of the sun-
god Aten. In all likelihood the statuette
was painted (traces of blue pigment
remain) and the hieroglyphs have long
since disappeared. The statuette[1] embod-
ies "The Great Hymn to Aten" (see John
L. Foster's essay, "The New Religion");
the text on the stela functioned as a
record of the king's speech. As an offering to Aten, it replaces the material
offerings of earlier times.

Found in one of the houses at Amarna,
the statuette was part of a private
chapel. DW

---

1. Porter and Moss 1934, p. 205; Aldred 1973,
cat. 1; Grimm, Schoske, and Wildung 1997, cat.
98.

37. Fragment of a boundary stela with Nefertiti and Princess Meketaten

Amarna, Boundary Stela N
Dynasty 18, reign of Akhenaten,
1353–1336 B.C. (year 6)
Limestone
H. 48.6 cm, w. 65.1 cm, d. 3.5 cm
Purchase: Nelson Trust, The Nelson-
Atkins Museum of Art, Kansas City,
Missouri, 44-65

38. Fragment of a boundary stela with Nefertiti and two princesses

Amarna, Boundary Stela S
Dynasty 18, reign of Akhenaten,
1353–1336 B.C.
Limestone
H. 51 cm, w. 30.4 cm, d. 7.4 cm
Ex Brummer Collection, Marilyn M.
Simpson Fund, Museum of Fine Arts,
Boston, 1992.18

The site of Amarna was ringed by stelae
cut into the rock to mark the perimeter
of Akhenaten's new city. Some of the
massive stelae were accompanied by
rock-cut statues of the royal family.
These impressive monuments had
antecedents in Middle Kingdom stelae[1]
and in the great stela of Amenhotep III,
which recounts the disposition of monuments in Thebes. However, none of
these compares in scale to the Amarna
stelae. Unfortunately, because of their
exposure, many have suffered from ero-
sion and vandalism. The surviving fragments demonstrate that these propagan-
distic works were statements not only
of territorial control but also of the new
art style.

On the fragment of Stela N (cat. 37),
the queen is shown in the exaggerated
style typical of the early years of
Akhenaten's reign. She would have been
standing behind her husband as both
worshipped the Aten. Behind the queen
is the figure of a princess—undoubtedly
Meketaten—holding a sistrum.[2] The
fragment of Stela S shows the back of
the queen and her two eldest daughters,
Meretaten and Meketaten, holding sistra.[3] All worship the Aten. PL

---

1. Wainwright 1925, pp. 144–45.

2. For a more detailed discussion of the fragment, see Aldred 1973, cat. 28.

3. This fragment, once in the Brummer
Collection, was incorrectly identified as part of a
balustrade, owing to the fine quality of the stone.
However, Dr. William J. Murnane has correctly
identified it as coming from Boundary Stela S
(personal communication).

37

38

41

39. Queen Tiye wearing a Hathor headdress

Medinet el-Gurob
Dynasty 18, reign of Akhenaten,
1353–1336 B.C.
Yew and acacia woods, silver, gold, linen, glass
H. 22.5 cm, w. 7.6 cm, d. 7.9 cm
Purchased 1904, Ägyptisches Museum und Papyrussammlung, Berlin, 21834 (head), 17852 (headdress)

Recent research has afforded new insights into this most famous portrait of Akhenaten's mother. The results of scanner tomography show that the small head,[1] originally part of a statue made of a different material, was altered in antiquity. The rounded linen wig, covered by (partly preserved) tiny blue glass beads, hides a silver headdress, which can still be glimpsed above the forehead, at the neck, and through a hole on the head. The original headdress had four golden uraei: two on the forehead and two behind the ears. The head was also adorned with ear ornaments and a broad gold band at the temples. The tall feather crown, part of the alteration of the statue, is the type worn by Isis and Hathor, and therefore an iconographic expression of the divinization of the queen. Either toward the end of the reign of Amenhotep III or on the occasion of his death, Queen Tiye was assigned the status of a goddess.

The highly individualized features of the elderly queen underline her active role during the reign of her husband and in the first ten years of the reign of her son Amenhotep IV/Akhenaten. DW

1. Arnold 1996, pp. 27–35, figs. 23, 26; Wildung 1992; Wildung 1995b.

39

40. Face of Akhenaten

Amarna
Dynasty 18, reign of Akhenaten,
1353–1336 B.C.
Plaster
H. 17.4 cm, w. 12.5 cm, d. 8.5 cm
Egyptian Museum, Cairo, JE 59289

Although most of the plaster masks and faces found at Amarna were in the studio of the sculptor Thutmose, excavated by the Deutsche Orient-Gesellschaft (cats. 139, 140), a few additional examples appeared in other contexts. This plaster face was found in 1933 by the Egypt Exploration Society (London) in another sculptor's workshop, south of the Central City.[1]

The lack of exaggerated signs of age suggests that the face is royal, though a face in any case would bear no royal iconography. Cast from a clay original, the face has full lips and a square chin, similar to such representations in stone as British Museum 1336, presumably also an image of the king. AAM

1. Pendlebury 1933a, p. 630.

40

41. Nefertiti with eyes prepared for inlays

Memphis, Palace of Merneptah
Dynasty 18, reign of Akhenaten,
1353–1336 B.C.
Quartzite
H. 18 cm, w. 15.5 cm, d. 21 cm
Egyptian Museum, Cairo, JE 45547

This exquisite head,[1] probably sculpted in the royal Memphite workshop, shows Nefertiti's softened and sensitive female features. Its style is moderate, something between the deformation and exaggeration of early Amarna style and the nearly traditional later phase. The head was once part of a composite statue, carved from different elements and then assembled—a practice, common in Amarna art, that had its roots in Old Kingdom wooden statuary. This head was prepared for connection with a tall cap or crown, which would have been fitted to the tenon protruding at the top. The eyes and eyebrows were hollowed out to receive inlays that would have enhanced the contrast with the warm, reddish quartzite. The eyebrows are slightly arched; the lids are heavy and have double folds. The feminine lips are accentuated and the earlobes are pierced. The excellent modeling of the face and the perfect polish of the hard stone show a high degree of refinement. MS

1. Aldred 1973, fig. 37; Vandier 1958, p. 345, pl. CXIV, 2; Noblecourt 1967, p. 68;. Saleh and Sourouzian 1986, cat. 162.

42. Youthful Nefertiti

Amarna, house P.47.2
Dynasty 18, reign of Akhenaten,
1353–1336 B.C.
Quartzite
H. 30 cm, w. 14.8 cm, d. 18 cm
Excavations of the Deutsche Orient-
Gesellschaft, Ägyptisches Museum und
Papyrussammlung, Berlin, 21220

43. Older Nefertiti

Amarna, House P.47.3
Dynasty 18, reign of Akhenaten,
1353–1336 B.C.
Granodiorite
H. 25 cm, w. 16.5 cm, d. 16 cm
Excavations of the Deutsche Orient-
Gesellschaft, 1912–13, Ägyptisches
Museum und Papyrussammlung, Berlin,
21358

These heads, found by Ludwig Borchardt in the studio of the sculptor
Thutmose, are unfinished. The surface
has not had its final polish, and stylistic
details such as the folds on the neck,
the eyelids, and the ears are indicated
only with guide lines in black. On both
heads, the lips have been enhanced with
red.

Though the styles of the heads differ—cat. 42¹ has a sweet youthfulness
about it, whereas cat. 43,² with its
slightly sunken cheeks and its marked
cheekbones, has a more serious expression—they both seem to represent
Queen Nefertiti, whose characteristic
tall crown would have been fixed on the
high tenons. The quartzite head was
part of a composite statue; the granodiorite head, supported by a back pillar,
has broken off a statue. DW

1. Arnold 1996, pp. 74–77, figs. 66, 67.

2. Arnold 1996, pp. 79–83, figs. 41, 72, 74;
Grimm, Schoske, and Wildung 1997, cat. 66.

42

43

44. Unfinished Nefertiti

Amarna, house P.47.1–3
Dynasty 18, reign of Akhenaten,
1353–1336 B.C.
Limestone, black pigment
H. 29.8 cm, w. 18.2 cm, d. 22 cm
Excavations of the Deutsche Orient-
Gesellschaft, Ägyptisches Museum und
Papyrussammlung, Berlin, 21352

This unfinished head¹ is in a less
advanced state of elaboration than the
heads in quartzite and granodiorite
(cats. 42 and 43). Parts of the surface to
be removed are indicated by black lines
on the left and right cheeks, on the left
jaw, and beside the bridge of the nose.
Details intended for the eyes are indicated with thick black lines. A median line
can be seen below the nose and on the
lower lip. The cutouts over the ears and
the socket for a tenon are typical for a
queen's head. The extremely long neck
recalls the painted bust of Nefertiti in
Berlin. Probably at a later stage the
large mouth would have been shaped to
exhibit the characteristic features of the
queen. DW

1. Aldred 1973, cat. 100; Arnold 1996, pp.
69–70, fig. 61.

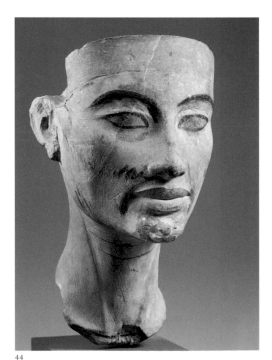

44

45

45. Head of a princess

Amarna, house P.47.2
Dynasty 18, reign of Akhenaten,
1353–1336 B.C.
Quartzite
H. 25 cm incl. tenon, w. 13 cm, d. 13 cm
across skull
Egyptian Museum, Cairo, JE 44870

The workshop of the sculptor Thutmose contained, in addition to many heads in plaster, a number of heads in quartzite whose broad and elongated skulls identify them as Akhenaten's daughters.[1] The heads are in various stages of completion, but each has a tenon at the base of the neck, indicating it was designed to be part of a composite sculpture. It is possible that the bodies were made of a different material, especially in view of the fondness for contrasting color at Amarna.

On this beautifully modeled head, the sculptor has outlined the eyes and eyebrows in black, perhaps intending to carve them out for inlays.[2] Additional black lines on the left cheek, philtrum, earlobe, and neck designate those as areas for further work. When such a piece was completely finished, the superb high polish of the face would extend to the neck as well. REF

1. For illustrations of some of the others, see Arnold 1996, figs. 46–48, 51.

2. Arnold 1996, fig. 48.

46. Princess with a side lock

Provenance not known
Dynasty 18, reign of Akhenaten,
1353–1336 B.C.
Limestone
H. 15.4 cm, w. 10.1 cm, d. 35 cm
Musée du Louvre, Paris, E 14715

This head of a statuette[1] depicts a daughter of the royal family wearing a pleated garment adorned with a broad-collar. Her youth is indicated by the heavy side lock, here attached to a cap wig. This kind of representation is well known in statuettes forming part of a group sculpture in which the young princess holds her mother's hand. However, reliefs in Amarna tombs show that there were individual statues of princesses as well. In some of them, composed of red quartzite and found in private houses, the princess is bald and nude.

A comparison with reliefs shows that the side lock is usually cut on a slant at the bottom, and that it is the youngest princess in the scene who wears the lock cut straight. Since this practice seems not to apply to the various known statues, the cut of this young woman's side lock cannot be used to identify her—nor can her precise identification be established from her facial features. ME

1. Arnold 1996, pp. 121–22, figs. 117–19; Aldred 1973, p. 118, fig. 50.

47. Statuette of a princess

Amarna
Dynasty 18, reign of Akhenaten,
1353–1336 B.C.
Calcite
H. 7.4 cm, w. 2.4 cm, d. 2.5 cm
Purchased by Borchardt, 1907, Ägyptisches Museum und Papyrussammlung,
Berlin, 17951

Despite its small dimensions, the statuette[1] has a monumentality all its own, with a back pillar supporting the extremely elongated skull. The proportionally small body and the nakedness of the figure indicate that this is the representation of a child. The left arm was cut separately and attached to the body with a mortise at the left hip. The right hand, lifted to the breast, would probably have held a fruit or a small animal. The body is delicately modeled and the creases at the top of the left leg are a detail that reflects close observation of children. DW

1. Ägyptisches Museum 1967, cat. 750 (which lists the wrong accession no.); Möller 1965, figs. 53–54.

47

46

48

49. Royal torso

Provenance not known
Dynasty 18, reign of Akhenaten,
1353–1336 B.C.
Quartzite
H. 29.4 cm, w. 13 cm, d. 12.6 cm
Musée du Louvre, Paris, E 25409

This fragment[1] is one of the masterpieces of Amarna Period sculpture, and
one of the most beautiful examples of
sheer fabric translated into stone. The
body is rendered through a tight-fitting
garment made of very fine linen. A
bronze peg is evidence of an ancient
repair.

As the back pillar is not inscribed,
the identity of the subject remains
unknown. The figure may represent one
of the princesses, or Queen Nefertiti,
dating to the beginning of the reign. It
could be an isolated image or belong to
a group sculpture. The smaller-than-life-
size statues recently excavated at East
Karnak, also made of red quartzite and
dating from the same period, are worth
comparing. ME

1. Arnold 1996, pp. 24–25, figs. 21–22; M.
Müller 1988, Teil 4, p. 142–43; Aldred 1973,
cat. 22.

49

48. Fragment of a royal woman's face

Provenance not known
Dynasty 18, reign of Akhenaten,
1353–1336 B.C.
Jasper
H. 13 cm, w. 12.5 cm, d. 11.5 cm
Purchase, Edward S. Harkness Gift, 1926,
The Metropolitan Museum of Art, New
York, 26.7.1396

This extraordinary fragment is part of a
composite statue—one made of different materials. A deep groove in the center of the back functioned as a mortise
for a tenon that connected the head
with a body probably made of alabaster.[1] Treatment of the neck limits the
possible headgear to either a *khat* (see
cat. 221) or a Nubian wig (cat. 235).

The yellow semiprecious stone and the
quality of the work suggest that the
subject was a woman of royal rank.
The sensuous, well-defined lips; the gen-
tle modeling of the face; and an incredi-
bly high polish, which makes the lips
look moist, create the image of youth
and beauty. This rules out the fragment's traditional identification as a
"lady of wisdom"—Queen Tiye. The
subject is presumably one of the king's
wives, Nefertiti or Kiya. The style of the
statue can be linked to the late, idealizing period of Amarna art. EP

1. Hayes 1959, p. 260, fig. 156; Aldred 1973,
cat. 21; Spanel 1988, p. 91; Arielle P. Kozloff in
Kozloff and Bryan 1992, p. 177, pl. 15; Arnold
1996, pp. 34–38, figs. 27, 29.

50

50. Sculpture of a princess

Probably from Amarna
Dynasty 18, reign of Akhenaten,
1353–1336 B.C.
Limestone
H. 31.1 cm, w. 13 cm, d. 10 cm
Loaned by the University of Pennsylvania
Museum of Archaeology and
Anthropology, Philadelphia, E 14349

The title "Bodily Daughter of Akhenaten" was held by nine princesses who
lived at Amarna, and six of them were
born to Queen Nefertiti. Depictions of
these individuals in both two and three
dimensions were not uncommon, and,
despite the missing head on this limestone statue of a female figure, its delicately pleated garment, its posture, and
its style of carving indicate clearly that
it is another representation of an
Amarna princess.[1]

It also bears a resemblance to a late
statue of Nefertiti (fig. 90); however,
most of its stylistic features, such as
body proportions, suggest that it was
carved late in the Amarna Period, probably after Akhenaten had died.[2] The
gesture of the figure's upraised left arm
and the nature of the break on the left
side of the figure indicate that it was
originally part of a group sculpture.
Although the absence of facial features
precludes a precise identification, it is
likely that this princess originally
accompanied either her father, Akhenaten, or one of his successors, Smenkhkara or Tutankhamen. DPS

---

1. Compare, for example, cats. 46, 47, 49, 88,
and 133, as well as Petrie Museum, University
College London, UC. 002.

2. For a full discussion of cat. 50, see Arnold
1996, pp. 122–24 and 134, and fig. 121.

51. Profile of Akhenaten

Probably from Amarna
Dynasty 18, reign of Akhenaten,
1353–1336 B.C.
Limestone
H. 15.3 cm, w. 11.2 cm, d. 3.3 cm
Ägyptisches Museum und
Papyrussammlung, Berlin 14512

52. Sculptor's model of Akhenaten

Probably from Amarna
Dynasty 18, reign of Akhenaten,
1353–1336 B.C.
Limestone
H. 26.3 cm, w. 21.3 cm, d. 4.3 cm
Courtesy of the Trustees of the National
Museums of Scotland, Edinburgh,
A 1969.377

The employment of different sculptors
and the general tendency to soften the
most extreme aspects of Akhenaten's
iconography during the latter part of
his reign explain the variation in the
king's physiognomy. In cat. 51, the pronounced elongation of his eye and nose;
the fleshy lips; the exaggerated droop of
his chin; and the narrow concave neck
denote the early Amarna style. Though
superficially the relief resembles a sculptor's model because of its size and
shape, modern saw marks indicate it
came from a larger relief, perhaps even
from a boundary stela.[1]

Cat. 52[2] offers an example of
Akhenaten's later, more moderate style.
The eye is larger; the nose, lips and chin
more restrained; and the neck thicker,
shorter, and straighter. Its superb quality, size and shape; the fact that all edges
appear to have been worked in antiquity; and the drill hole for suspension
make it likely that this piece functioned
as a model of royal iconography. It
would have been made by a master
sculptor for use by apprentices in the
studio or perhaps to be taken to a work
site and copied. The king's blue crown
is decorated with concentric circles, two
of which are carved separately on the
bottom right, providing a "how-to" for
the copier. RFF

---

1. Aldred 1973, cat. 6.

2. Ibid., cat. 12.

51

52

53

53. Stela of the royal family

Probably from Amarna
Dynasty 18, reign of Akhenaten,
1353–1336 B.C.
Limestone
H. 33 cm, w. 39 cm, d. 3.8 cm
Ägyptisches Museum und
Papyrussammlung, Berlin, 14145

This stela depicting an intimate family
scene is among the most delightful
examples of Amarna art.[1] Akhenaten,
Nefertiti, and three daughters are rendered in sunk relief in the extreme style
characteristic of the early part of the
reign. The royal family is seated beneath
the protective rays of the Aten in what
has been variously identified as an open-
air kiosk, a room in the palace, and a
birth bower.[2] The focus is on the activity
of the children. At left, Akhenaten lifts
Meretaten to bestow a kiss upon her,
while she gestures toward her mother.
Ankhesenpaaten rests against Nefertiti's
shoulder, cupping her hand under a
uraeus pendant from Nefertiti's crown,
while Meketaten, dandled on her mother's knee, turns her face toward her
mother and gestures toward her father.
   Stelae like this one are dedicatory in
nature, and are thought to have been

placed in shrines to the royal family in
the larger private houses.[3] SD'A

1. For recent discussions of the piece, see Arnold
1996, pp. 97–100, figs. 88, 91, 97; Krauss 1991a.

2. Arnold, pp. 97–100.

3. See Griffith 1926 and Ikram 1989.

54. Two princesses

Amarna, found at Hermopolis
Dynasty 18, reign of Akhenaten,
1353–1336 B.C.
Limestone
H. 23.2 cm, w. 29.2 cm, d. 2.2 cm
Gift of Norbert Schimmel, 1985, The
Metropolitan Museum of Art, New York,
1985.328.6

Innovative poses, the expression of intimacy, and the use of space to convey
emotion are three areas in which the art
of the Amarna Period expanded the traditional boundaries of Egyptian representation. All three are in evidence in
this relief of two of Akhenaten's daughters. The older one, so designated not
only by her larger size, but also by the
fact that she is clothed and wears a
short, curled wig in addition to the side
lock of youth, rests her hand casually
on the shoulder of her younger sister
and turns back to look at her. In turning, her torso shifts so that both breasts
are shown frontally, a pose that is seldom found in Egyptian art.[1] At the
same time the younger child gazes rev-
erently up at her older sibling as her
splayed fingers clasp her sister's upper
arm. In its use of gesture and of empty
space, the scene conveys a tenderness
that finds frequent expression at
Amarna. REF

1. Arnold 1996, p. 114, fig. 111.

55. Relief of the nurse Tia

Amarna, found at Hermopolis
Dynasty 18, reign of Akhenaten
1353–1336 B.C.
Limestone
H. 23.1 cm, w. 54.3 cm, d. 3.7 cm
Gift of Norbert Schimmel, 1985, The
Metropolitan Museum of Art, New York,
1985.328.5

In this relief a woman holds two loaf-
shaped objects, possibly bread, on plat-
ters.[1] Behind her a large stand, or group
of stands, with flaring sides is draped
with a garland. The female has been
identified by some as a princess.[2]
However, although a similar hairstyle,
with a large side lock, is seen in depictions of princesses, it was also worn by
female members of the royal retinue.[3]
The scarf or sash the figure holds is held
by the royal attendants as well.[4] The figure's pose, bent forward at the waist,
also suggests the subject is not royal.
The Amarna princesses are shown
standing upright, and in the tomb of
Parennefer and May, where they are
accompanied by their nurses, only the
nurses bend forward.[5] This suggests that
the female is the nurse Tia, as identified
in the text behind her. She is likely facing one or more members of the royal
family, perhaps Ankhesenpaaten, who
would be facing left, like the larger figure seen here to the left.[6] This would
explain why the larger figure is standing
with her back to the nurse. JLH

1. Aldred 1973, cat. 129.

2. John Cooney suggested that this was the image
of the princess and that the text refers to a tiny
image, now lost, of Ankhesenpaaten's nurse.
Cooney 1965, p.19.

3. N. de G. Davies 1903–8, vol. 1, pls. XXIV
and XXX.

4. For attendants of the princesses carrying this
sash see Davies 1903–8, vol. 1, pl. XXVI.

5. Davies 1903–8, vol. 6, pls. III and IV; vol. 5,
pl. III.

6. Compare the named individuals serving in the
scene in Davies 1903–8, vol. 2, pls. IV and VI.

54

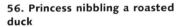

57. Relief of Kiya, reworked for Meretaten

Amarna, found at Hermopolis
Dynasty 18, reign of Akhenaten,
1353–1336 B.C.
Limestone
H. 24 cm, w. 52 cm, d. 2 cm
Ny Carlsberg Glyptotek, Copenhagen,
AEIN 1776

In its original form, this palimpsest depicted Akenaten's secondary wife Kiya, but in its reworked version it is a portrait of Meretaten, eldest daughter of Akhenaten and Nefertiti. The reworking occurred during a period of Akhenaten's reign when Kiya was removed from the official picture-repertoire and replaced by Meretaten and her younger sister Ankhesenpaaten.[1] The reworking entailed enlarging the back of Kiya's head and reducing her wig to a side lock, but the face itself was never altered.

Traces of the original, now-erased inscription disclose part of Kiya's titulary, "The Wife and Great Beloved of the King of Upper and Lower Egypt,"[2] while the superimposed characters read: "The Daughter of the King, of his Flesh, his Beloved ... Meretaten." MJ

1. Hanke 1978, pp. 133–204.

2. J. R. Harris 1974a, p. 28, n. 3, fig. B; Hanke 1978, p. 140, Abb. 43. For further information on this relief, see Cooney 1965, cat. 186; Jørgensen 1988, pp. 7–26; Arnold 1996, pp. 106, 132–33, fig. 100; Jørgensen 1998, cat. 46.

56. Princess nibbling a roasted duck

Amarna, North Palace
Dynasty 18, reign of Akhenaten,
1353–1336 B.C.
Limestone
H. 23.5 cm, w. 22.3 cm, d. 3 cm
Egyptian Museum, Cairo, JE 48035

This charming little sculptor's model[1] was excavated in 1924[2] just outside the entrance pylons of an open-air temple belonging to the North Palace, a queen's residence that appears to have been utilized in the later years of Akhenaten's reign by his daughter Meretaten. The drawing shows a figure whose wide side lock identifies her as a princess, seated languorously upon a cushion. Her pose is reminiscent of that of the princesses in a painting from the King's House (fig. 64). She holds a whole roasted duck to her mouth with one hand while stretching the other toward a table bearing other delicacies. Though she appears to be nude, a thin garment is suggested by lines at her neck and over her arm. The piece is unfinished, and only the lower part has been carved, leaving us a glimpse into the creative process of the Egyptian artist. SD'A

1. Vergnieux and Gondran 1997, p. 157; Arnold 1996, pp. 112–13, fig. 108; Saleh and Sourouzian 1987, cat. 169; Peck 1978, cat. 12; Terrace and Fischer 1970, cat. 27.

2. Newton 1924, p. 295, pl. XXIII, fig. 1.

56

58. Royal hand

Amarna, found at Hermopolis
Dynasty 18, reign of Akhenaten,
1353–1336 B.C.
Limestone
H. 23.8 cm, w. 27.9 cm, d. 3.6 cm
Gift of Norbert Schimmel, 1985, The
Metropolitan Museum of Art, New York,
1985.328.1

This is presumably a representation of
a hand of the king.[1] Elegant, elongated
fingers are shown in profile, while a
thumb is shown frontally. The index
finger is separated from others and outstretched. The position of the hand suggests that the arm was bent at the
elbow. Interpretation of this gesture is
difficult because of the fragmentary
condition of the scene and because the
bottom part was recarved in antiquity.[2]
The usual explanation, that the king
was dropping a piece of incense on an
altar, seems doubtful. Such an action
was not a part of official offering ceremonies. Furthermore, the gesture of
dropping was represented differently in
Amarna art.[3] This gesture might have
been pointing, with the intention of
averting evil forces.[4] Turned ninety
degrees counterclockwise, the relief
could have been a representation of
Akhenaten's hand hanging down from
the arm of his chair and pointing at one
of his daughters sitting below.[5] EP

1. Aldred 1973, cat. 147; Cooney 1965, cat. 2;
Roeder 1969, p. 404, pl. 173; John D. Cooney in
Muscarella 1974, cat. 241; Catharine Roehrig in
Metropolitan Museum of Art 1992, pp. 25–32,
57–58.

2. Observation of Ann Heywood, associate con-
servator, The Metropolitan Museum of Art.

3. Arnold 1996, figs. 83, 94.

4. Arnold 1996, p. 100 and figs. 88, 91, 92.

5. For parallels, see Arnold 1996, p. 113, fig.
110; Aldred 1973, p. 39.

58

59. Royal feet

Amarna, found at Hermopolis
Dynasty 18, reign of Akhenaten,
1353–1336 B.C.
Limestone
H. 23.4 cm, w. 55.6 cm, d. 3.3 cm
Charles Edwin Wilbour Fund, Brooklyn
Museum of Art, New York, 60.197.7

The sandaled feet of a large-scale figure
are carved with the plasticity characteristic of the finest Amarna sunk relief.[1]
The floor-length gown identifies the
subject as a royal woman, probably
Nefertiti.

Her royalty is confirmed by an odd
detail: the depiction of all five toes on
the foot nearer the viewer. On earlier
Egyptian reliefs, the feet always appear
identical, each showing only the big toe.
This more naturalistic rendering is one
of several innovations that Amarna
artists borrowed from slightly earlier
tomb paintings at Thebes. But whereas
the painters had limited innovative
anatomical details to figures of lesser

59

importance, the Amarna sculptors reserved them exclusively for representations of Akhenaten and his family.[2] In this way, certain naturalistic features of Amarna art actually served to differentiate royalty from their subjects. ERR

1. Cooney 1965, cat. 13, pp. 25–26; Aldred 1973, cat. 58; Russmann 1980, pp. 69 70, fig. 5.

2. Russmann 1980; another example is the frontal rendering of the female bosom. See cat. 54 and Catharine Roehrig in Metropolitan Museum of Art 1992, pp. 26–27.

60

60. Royal face with missing inlays

Amarna, Great Temple
Dynasty 18, reign of Akhenaten,
1353–1336 B.C.
Quartzite
H. 12.1 cm, w. 11.8 cm, d. 4.3 cm
Gift of the Egypt Exploration Society,
Brooklyn Museum of Art, New York,
33.685

61. Inlay of a royal face

Probably from Amarna
Dynasty 18, reign of Akhenaten,
1353–1336 B.C.
Quartzite
H. 10.8 cm, w. 10.1 cm, d. 2.5 cm
Purchased in Cairo, 1905, Ägyptisches
Museum und Papyrussammlung, Berlin,
17800

62. Inlays of a royal arm and hand

Probably from Amarna
Dynasty 18, reign of Akhenaten,
1353–1336 B.C.
Quartzite
Arm: l. 16.7 cm, w. 5.4 cm, d. 1.3 cm
Hand: l. 9.7 cm, w. 3.7 cm, d. 2.5 cm
Purchased in Cairo, 1905, Ägyptisches
Museum und Papyrussammlung, Berlin,
17540

From the denuded remains of the site of Amarna today, one would never guess that the city's buildings were alive with color. The few traces found *in situ* indicate that the walls of temples and palaces were decorated with scenes and inscriptions inlaid with a variety of colored stones and faience, in both high and low relief. Smaller inlays in glass were used for the embellishment of wooden boxes and furniture.

Cat. 60,[2] found near a wall of the Great Temple at Amarna, represents the profile of a king or queen. The eyes and eyebrows were once inlaid in glass, and a crown, possibly of faience, would have been provided. Cat. 61 has more subtly modeled features, including an eye that might have been painted rather than inlaid. The profile is shown here with an arm and hand although the three were not originally part of the same composition. Each would have joined a body made of a different material. SD'A

1. Pendlebury 1951, p. 226 and pl. CV, 8; Pendlebury 1933b, pp. 116–18, pl. XVI; Peet and Woolley 1923, pp. 120–22 and pl. XXXV, 1–2. See also Boyce 1995, pp. 84–87; Samson 1978, pp. 66–76; Müller and Settgast 1976, cat. 52; Samson 1973 and Lucas 1939.

2. Aldred 1973, cat. 91; Pendlebury 1933b, p. 116, pl. XVI, 2; Pendlebury 1951, pl. LVII, 4.

61, 62

63. Blue crown from a composite sculpture

Provenance not known
Dynasty 18, reign of Akhenaten,
1353–1336 B.C.
Faience
H. 9.6 cm, w. 10.9 cm, d. 9.6 cm
The Thalassic Collection, Ltd., Courtesy of
Theodore and Aristea Halkedis

63

64. Queen's wig with fillet

Provenance not known
Dynasty 18, reign of Akhenaten,
1353–1336 B.C.
Faience
H. 12.7 cm, w. 14 cm, d. 5.8 cm
The Thalassic Collection, Ltd., Courtesy of
Theodore and Aristea Halkedis

65. Echeloned wig for a composite sculpture

Amarna
Dynasty 18, reign of Akhenaten,
1353–1336 B.C.
Granodiorite
H. 25 cm, w. 14 cm, d. 6.5 cm
Courtesy of Petrie Museum of Egyptian
Archaeology, University College London,
UC. 076

64

The heads of the beautiful composite statuary of the Amarna Period were often provided with wigs or crowns in a variety of materials. Although none has been found intact, the method of attachment can be observed on both the heads and the headdresses. The "Nubian" wig (cat. 65),[1] a type worn by both men and women in the Amarna Period, belonged to a life-size statue. Though broken, nearly half of the wig is preserved. Its concave interior would have been affixed to the head with an adhesive, for it shows no other means of joining.

The faience wig (cat. 64)[2] was most likely crafted for a figure in high relief rather than a sculpture. It represents a queen's wig in the blue color that was preferred during this period, with a fillet encircling the top. A large rectangular hole in the top indicates that a crown may have once been added.

The blue *khepresh* crown (cat. 63)[3] was favored by Akhenaten. It originated in the Second Intermediate Period, evolving from the cap crown.[4] This example from a statuette has a slot in front for a uraeus.   SD'A

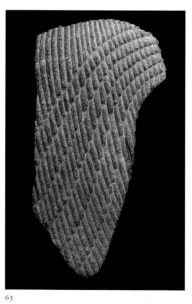
65

1. Arnold 1996, p. 62, fig. 56; J. Phillips 1994, pp. 66 and 69; Samson 1973, pl. XXVIII, p. 56.

2. Compare Florence D. Friedman in Friedman 1998, cat. 26; pp. 83, 184, and n. 49, p. 201.

3. Compare Geneviève Pierrat-Bonnefois in Friedman 1998, cat. 29; pp. 82, 186; Müller and Settgast 1976, cat. 43; Samson 1973, pl. XXVI n, o, and p. 54.

4. W. V. Davies 1982, pp. 71, 74–75.

66

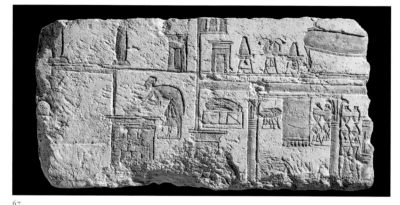
67

66. Palace scene featuring the Window of Appearances

Amarna, found at Hermopolis
Dynasty 18, reign of Akhenaten,
1353–1336 B.C.
Limestone
H. 23.8 cm, w. 52.9 cm, d. 3.3 cm
Helen and Alice Colburn Fund, Museum
of Fine Arts, Boston, 63.427

67. Palace interior

Amarna, found at Hermopolis
Dynasty 18, reign of Akhenaten,
1353–1336 B.C.
Limestone
H. 23 cm, w. 43 cm, d. 3.5 cm
Marilyn M. Simpson Fund, Museum of
Fine Arts, Boston, 1997.98

One of these reliefs depicts the façade and the other, the innermost rooms of the royal palace. The first shows the Window of Appearances behind (to the left of) a pillared portico. Here the king would greet his subjects and reward some of them bountifully for their service. As the site of the royal family's interaction with residents, the Window of Appearances is the feature of the palace most often rendered in Amarna art. The balcony is shown on a second story, with two entrances below, at ground level. An elaborate broken-lintel balustrade flanks the window and a series of columns is set behind it. Courtiers are shown at the margins of the scene conversing and sweeping, while another carries a jug of water. A guard with a stick stands by the entrance gate, where the shields and weapons of the palace guard are stacked.[1]

The private apartments at the rear of the palace are shown on the other block. In the top right corner are a bed with a thick mattress and tables on which a broadcollar and unguent cones sit. In the neighboring room, probably a bath, a man leans over a wash basin; beyond him are a table, a portico with draped cloth and stands of food and drink.

These images represent typical features of a palace; it would be difficult to identify in them a particular structure at Amarna, if one was intended at all. They do, however, evoke a clear picture of the bustle that was part of everyday life in the royal residence.   PL

1. For additional information and references on this relief scene, see Aldred 1973, cat. 63.

68

69

71

70

68. Depiction of a column with ducks

Amarna, found at Hermopolis
Dynasty 18, reign of Akhenaten,
1353–1336 B.C.
Limestone
H. 22.5 cm, w. 53 cm, d. 3.5 cm
Arthur Tracy Cabot Fund, Museum of
Fine Arts, Boston, 62.320

69. Fragment of a column drum featuring the royal family worshipping

Amarna, found at Hermopolis
Dynasty 18, reign of Akhenaten,
1353–1336 B.C.
Limestone
H. 22.4 cm, w. 52.5 cm, d. 6.1 cm
Mary S. and Edward J. Holmes Fund,
Museum of Fine Arts, Boston, 67.637

70. Model of a papyrus column

Amarna
Dynasty 18, reign of Akhenaten,
1353–1336 B.C.
Limestone
H. 21.4 cm, diam. 7 cm
Gift of the Egypt Exploration Society, San
Diego Museum of Man, San Diego, 11869

71. Column drum with duck heads

Amarna, Maruaten
Dynasty 18, reign of Akhenaten,
1353–1336 B.C.
Limestone
H. 35 cm, diam. 50 cm
Egyptian Museum, Cairo JE 47199

The kiosks represented at Amarna were festooned not only with fruits and flowers, but also with animals such as the cluster of ducks featured in cat. 68. Tied at their tails, they are suspended from the top of a column supporting a kiosk. The figure of a woman, only partially preserved, stands in front of the structure. Ducks were associated with the apartments of the royal women, so it is possible that the structure depicted here is dedicated to one of the court ladies.[1]

The fragment featuring the royal family (cat. 69) was apparently part of a column drum of considerable size. The complete image would have shown Akhenaten, Nefertiti, and Meretaten worshipping, facing right, and the reverse of the image, with the family facing left.[2] The image at far left, of Meketaten back-to-back with her own image, is all that remains of the segment in reverse. This scene, which is ubiqui-

tous at Amarna, underscores the central role the royal family played in the city's spiritual life.

Ostraca with sketches of columns,[3] and models such as cat. 70, must have served as guides for Akhenaten's architects as they hurriedly executed commissions. This type of papyrus-bud column—squat, with highly articulated parts—was a particular favorite in the Amarna Period. However, it is an ungainly descendant of far more elegant papyrus pillars from earlier dynasties. Examples of these papyriform supports can be found in tomb architecture, such as the sepulcher designed for Ay at Amarna,[4] and in temple architecture.[5] Since they required so much space, they were apparently not used in domestic architecture, where the slender palm column was favored.

An actual column drum from the Maruaten at Amarna (cat. 71) has a series of duck swags as well as friezes of petals and grape clusters.[6] PL

1. Aldred 1973, cat. 142.

2. Aldred 1973, cat. 17.

3. For an ancient sketch of a column, see Musée du Louvre, Paris, E 25334 (unpublished).

4. N. de G. Davies 1903–8, vol. 6, pl. XXXVII.

5. It was used in the Kom el-Nana temple; see Michael Mallinson's essay in this book, "The Sacred Landscape."

6. For a similar column fragment, see Peet and Woolley 1923, pl. XXXI.

72

72. Decorated balustrade fragment

Amarna, Great Palace
Dynasty 18, reign of Akhenaten,
1353–1336 B.C.
Crystalline limestone
H. 102 cm, w. 51 cm, d. 15 cm
Egyptian Museum, Cairo, JT 30/10/26/12

On this balustrade fragment from the
right side of the ramp of the Great
Palace at Amarna,[1] Akhenaten and
Nefertiti pray under the rays of the sun,
offering a libation to the god. Their
eldest daughter, Meretaten, shakes a
cultic rattle (sistrum) behind them. The
Amarna artist, working in the early
period, was still influenced by the
extreme style, so that the figures look
severely deformed. The king has an
elongated skull, protruding chin, narrow neck, half-closed eyes, thin arms
and legs, rounded breast, and heavy
buttocks and thighs. Behind his white
crown flares a scarf and on his chest
are the names of Aten inscribed in royal
cartouches. The king wears a knee-
length pleated kilt and Nefertiti wears
the *khat* headdress and a long, pleated,
transparent dress open in the front so
that her body is visible. Princess Meretaten wears a similar dress, but has her
hair in a side lock. MS

1. Aldred 1973, p. 56, fig. 33; Müller and
Settgast 1976, cat. 46; Pendlebury 1951, p. 77,
pl. LXIX, 5; Saleh and Sourouzian 1986, cat.
164.

73

73. Architectural frieze of uraei

Amarna, Maruaten
Dynasty 18, reign of Akhenaten,
1353–1336 B.C.
Quartzite and granite
H. 31 cm, w. 24 cm, d. 7 cm (restored)
The Visitors of the Ashmolean Museum,
Oxford, 1922.92

This elaborate cornice in the form of
rearing cobras has antecedents that go
back to the Step Pyramid of Djoser
(Dynasty 3). However, this type of
frieze was particularly fashionable at
Amarna, perhaps because it added a
flourish to the rather odd invention of
the broken lintel. Depictions of this lintel with a gap in the middle often show
it capped by the uraeus frieze. The
uraeus with sun-disk was a traditional
motif retained by the new religion since
it emphasized not only the solar cult
but kingship as well.[1]

The Maruaten appears to have been a
large, open structure with lavish ornamentation. This carefully executed
frieze, composed of a block of reddish-
brown quartzite inlaid with gray granite serpent heads projecting outward,
could have decorated one of the gateways to the Maruaten's great lake.
Additional inlays, now lost, would have
been set into depressions carved in the
serpents' bodies, adding color and texture. PL

1. For additional information on this object, see
Peet and Woolley 1923, p. 122, pl. XXXIII, 5.
See also Aldred 1973, cat. 155.

74

75

76

77

74. Polychrome grape cluster

Amarna, possibly North Palace
Dynasty 18, reign of Akhenaten,
1353–1336 B.C.
Glass, bronze
H. 18 cm (as strung), diam. 7.5 cm
The Visitors of the Ashmolean Museum,
Oxford, 1924.69

75. Grape cluster

Provenance not known
Dynasty 18, reign of Akhenaten,
1353–1336 B.C.
Faience
H. 12.7 cm, diam. 6.3 cm
The Thalassic Collection, Ltd., Courtesy of
Theodore and Aristea Halkedis

76. Lotus blossom

Amarna, private house
Dynasty 18, reign of Akhenaten,
1353–1336 B.C.
Polychrome faience
H. 4 cm, diam. 5 cm
Excavations of the Deutsche Orient-
Gesellschaft, 1913, Ägyptisches Museum
und Papyrussammlung, Berlin, 21878

77. Lotus bud

Possibly from Amarna
Dynasty 18, reign of Akhenaten,
1353–1336 B.C.
Faience
H. 5.5 cm, diam. 1.5 cm
Gift in Memory of Dows Dunham,
Museum of Fine Arts, Boston, 1988.339

Grape clusters and floral elements are
depicted as hanging from kiosks shading
the royal throne, and these imitations
may well have served as more perma-
nent architectural embellishments. The
examples found demonstrate a variety
of manufacturing techniques and methods of attachment. The grapes on the
faience example (cat. 75) appear to have
been formed separately by hand and
then pressed together before firing. A
means of attachment would have been
fitted through the hole in the top.

The Amarna grape cluster (cat. 74)
illustrates the lavish use of glass at the
site. Here spherical glass beads are
strung together with bronze wire
around a wooden central core. A bronze
wire ending in a loop for suspension
runs through the core. Such free-hanging elements may also have been suspended from the beaks of ducks, as
found in the palace of Amenhotep III at
Malqata.[1] These magnificent ornaments
would not only have been decorative,

but would have served to underscore
the abundance at Pharaoh's command.

The floral elements of polychrome
faience (cats. 76, 77) represent a blue
lotus[2] and a lotus bud.[3] Although three-
dimensional ornaments could have been
used on furniture, they were more likely
to have been architectural embellishments. Andrew Boyce has suggested
that they would have been part of an
elaborate artificial bouquet on a door
frame, as occasionally represented on
reliefs.[4]

The lotus, which had powerful associations with rejuvenation and rebirth,
was another peculiar feature of domestic architecture at Amarna.[5] Whatever
their function, these exquisite faience
pieces are indicative of the quality of
craftsmanship found in the city. PL

1. Tytus 1903, p. 14, fig. 4.

2. Schoske, Kreissl, and Germer 1992, cat. 23.

3. Brigit Crowell in Friedman 1998, cat. 41.

4. Andrew Boyce, personal communication.

5. Stephen Harvey, "The Decoration of Amarna
Houses," unpublished.

78

Fabricated as individual units, they served as architectural enhancements that were often assembled to form larger compositions on walls, floors, and columns.

Many of the polychrome patterned tiles from Amarna have a painterly appearance, an effect achieved by applying a slurry of pigmented glaze to the moist, prefired faience. Others have clearly demarcated designs created by inlaying colored faience paste into spaces carved into the faience body—a technique akin to champlevé enameling on metal.[1] Shaped tiles were typically used as inlays: for example, fish plaques were set in pond scenes amid papyrus plants, lotus flowers, and water fowl.[2] They could also be used as lids for decorative containers.[3]   YJM

80

1. For a discussion of the various techniques, see Nicholson 1998.

2. Samson 1972, pp. 90–91.

3. Brigit Crowell in Friedman 1998, cat. 110.

78. Bullock in a thicket

Possibly from Amarna
Dynasty 18, reign of Akhenaten,
1353–1336 B.C.
Faience
H. 10.8 cm, w. 11.4 cm
Alphonse Kahn Bequest, Musée du
Louvre, Paris, E 17357

This fragment of a polychrome faience tile[1] exemplifies the skill of the faience workers of the Amarna Period. A spotted male calf is represented browsing among marsh plants. The rear of another calf is visible at left. This decorative pattern was used frequently in wall and floor paintings and inlays in the palaces and private houses of Amarna. This representation of nature is exceptional for the minor arts in the way it realistically evokes movement. Here, the undulating curve formed by the back of the calf and the lifted tail counterbalances the stems of the plants bending in the breeze.   ME

1. Aldred 1973, cat. 86; Brigit Crowell in Friedman 1998, cat. 33.

79. Tile fragment with mandrakes

Amarna, reportedly acquired at Hermopolis
Dynasty 18, reign of Akhenaten,
1353–1336 B.C.
Faience
H. 10 cm, w. 14 cm, d. 1.6 cm
Charles Edwin Wilbour Fund, Brooklyn Museum of Art, New York, 52.148.2

80. Tile fragment with cornflowers and leaves

Amarna
Dynasty 18, reign of Akhenaten,
1353–1336 B.C.
Faience
H. 9.4 cm, w. 9.3 cm, d. 1.3 cm
Rijksmuseum van Oudheden, Leiden,
F 1958/4.2

81. Fish

Possibly from Amarna
Dynasty 18, reign of Akhenaten,
1353–1336 B.C.
Faience
H. 3.4 cm, w. 9.1 cm
Kestner-Museum, Hannover, 1951.181

Brightly colored faience tiles decorated with naturalistically rendered plant and animal motifs on a white ground were a specialty of Amarna craftsmen.

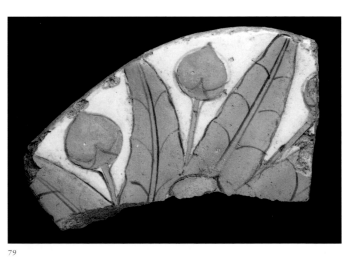

79

81

82

82. Floor painting with marsh plants

Amarna, water court of the Maruaten
Dynasty 18, reign of Akhenaten,
1353–1336 B.C.
Painted plaster
H. 103.5 cm, w. 69.5 cm (top), 45 cm
(bottom)
Gift of the Egypt Exploration Society, San
Diego Museum of Man, San Diego, 14912

83. Floor painting with bird and marsh plants

Amarna, palace in the Maruaten
Dynasty 18, reign of Akhenaten,
1353–1336 B.C.
Painted plaster
H. 120, w. 103, d. 7 cm
Loaned by the University of Pennsylvania
Museum of Archaeology and
Anthropology, Philadelphia, E15726

Among the features of royal buildings
at Amarna were gorgeously painted
pavements, walls, and pillars.[1] Although
most walls and columns have disappeared, many splendid floors have survived. In the Great Palace, the king
walked through halls painted with
repeating images of prostrate foreign
foes, thus magically ensuring his daily
dominance of them.[2] In the *harim*,
columned courts were painted with
cooling *faux* ponds featuring fish,
ducks, and lotuses amid ripples of
water. Similar pavements, like both of
these examples, were discovered surrounding a series of raised stone water
tanks in the Maruaten, a huge temple
complex in the southern part of the city
with a lake, gardens, and several small
shrines dedicated to Meretaten,
Akhenaten's eldest daughter.[3] TK

1. Badawy 1968, pp. 82–84, 209–14, pl. 5; Peet
and Woolley 1923, pp. 118–89; Pendlebury
1951, pp. 40–41; A. Thomas 1994, pp. 76–77.

2. Petrie 1894, pp. 12–14, pls. 2–4.

3. Kemp 1995.

84. Manger

Amarna, North Palace
Dynasty 18, reign of Akhenaten,
1353–1336 B.C.
Limestone
H. 26.6 cm, w. 76.2 cm, w. 12.7 cm
Gift of the Egypt Exploration Society, San
Diego Museum of Man, San Diego, 14848

Fourteen limestone feeding troughs
were found ranged about the walls of a
large animal pen in the North Palace at
Amarna.[1] Each was carved in relief with
figures of animals preparing to eat from
a similar trough. It was as if the carved
images secured eternal existence for
each real trough and all the animals
around it. Judging by the animals represented on these troughs, the pen contained both wild and domesticated
species and probably functioned as both
a zoological exhibit and a ready reserve
of animals needed for sacrifice.[2]

This fragmentary manger preserves
the image of an ox with his head poised
over a similar trough. The legs, tail, and
body of the animal still bear traces of
red pigment. TK

1. Newton 1924, pp. 295–96, pl. 30; Aldred
1973, cat. 151.

2. Doll 1982a.

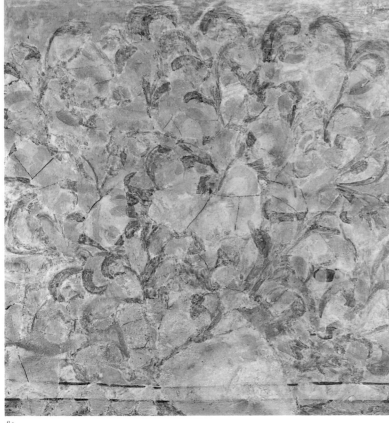

83

84

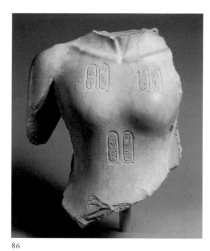

86

87

86. Torso of Akhenaten with cartouches

Amarna, Great Temple, southeast side
Dynasty 18, reign of Akhenaten,
1353–1336 B.C.
Indurated limestone
H. 35.5 cm, w. 25.5 cm, d. 23.3 cm
Gift of Edward S. Harkness, 1921, and
Purchase Harris Brisbane Dick Fund,
1957, The Metropolitan Museum of Art,
New York, 21.9.3

87. Torso of Nefertiti with cartouches

Amarna, Great Temple, southeast side
Dynasty 18, reign of Akhenaten,
1353–1336 B.C.
Indurated limestone
H. 28 cm, w. 29.5 cm, d. 21.5 cm
Gift of Edward S. Harkness, 1921, The
Metropolitan Museum of Art, New York,
21.9.4

During his 1891–92 excavation season,
Sir Flinders Petrie found identifiable
parts of seventeen statues of the king
and queen, as well as "about a ton of
fragments," in a huge pit outside the
southern wall of the Great Temple.[1]
These two torsos belong to that group.
Originally they must have formed part
of a colonnade or portico of the half-
mile-long temple, depicted in a number
of Amarna's private tombs.[2]

Nefertiti's torso is distinguished by the
delicately incised lines of her garment,
draped over her left arm and shoulder,
and the presence of her cartouche on
the side of the back pillar. The upper
border of a male kilt leaves little doubt
that Akhenaten is represented in the
other statue, despite the fact that the
full breasts and narrow waists are strikingly similar in both, in keeping with
the gender ambiguity of Amarna art.
Both torsos are festooned with cartouches inscribed with the early form
of Aten's name.

Although the pieces were deliberately
smashed in antiquity, enough remains of
both to show that they came from
standing statues. Akhenaten stood with
his hands at his sides,[3] whereas Nefertiti
clasped an object, perhaps a stela, in
front of her.[4] Her figure may have formed part of a dyad, with Akhenaten to
her right.[5] REF

1. Petrie 1894, p. 18 and pl. I, 13.

2. For example, N. de G. Davies 1903–8, vol. 1,
pls. XXV and XXXIII, or Davies, vol. 3, pls.
VIII, X–XI.

3. Aldred 1973, p. 93, but compare Williams
1930, pp. 86–88.

4. Williams, p. 88.

5. Ibid., pp. 88–89.

85

85. Sculpture of Akhenaten

Provenance not known
Dynasty 18, reign of Akhenaten,
1353–1336 B.C.
Yellow stone
H. 64 cm, w. 17.2 cm, d. 35 cm
Musée du Louvre, Paris, N 831

This figure[1] belonged to a seated pair
depicting the king with his wife or
mother. The woman's left arm and the
fringe of her garment are visible. The
king is sitting on a cushion, wearing the
royal *nemes* headdress and holding the
crook and flail in one hand. A bull's tail
is attached to the kilt. Those features,
as well as the pierced ears, the pot belly,
and the lunate "Amarna navel" are
found on representations of royalty
from the time of Amenhotep IV until
the beginning of Horemheb's reign.
Since the buckle of the kilt is not

inscribed, the king's identity is not
absolutely certain, despite the facial
features suggesting Akhenaten. Still,
although seated pair statues of the royal
couple are rare, this figure is usually
identified as Akhenaten. ME

1. Berman and Letellier 1996, cat. 13; Christiane
Ziegler in Humbert, Pantazzi, and Ziegler 1994,
pp. 378–79; Aldred 1973, pp. 48, 66, fig. 29.

89

90

and top of the back pillar were originally made from a separate piece of sandstone, but the head must have been replaced at least once, since the site of the break has been smoothed over and covered with plaster.

The inscription on the back pillar gives the titles and name of Nefertiti and the later form of the Aten's name, which does not occur before year 9.[1] The queen's physique, too—although she has prominent breasts, a well-rounded stomach, large buttocks, and over-developed thighs—exhibits the less exaggerated style of the later years of the reign. CA

1. D. Redford 1984, p. 186.

88

88. Nefertiti offering

Amarna, House I.50.12
Dynasty 18, reign of Akhenaten,
1353–1336 B.C.
Sandstone
H. 71 cm, w. 22.5 cm, d. 22 cm
The Trustees of the British Museum,
London, EA 935

This headless and footless figure of Queen Nefertiti depicts her standing, wearing a full-length diaphanous pleated gown colored white, with one sleeve fashionably shorter than the other. The ends of her sash fall down the front of each leg as far as the shin. On the left side of the figure the plain edge of her garment runs from elbow to ankle. Traces of red and blue indicate the figure was wearing a bead collar; the flesh is colored red. Although one forearm and both hands are lost, it is clear the queen once held something before her. It was not an altar, however, which would have been supported from beneath; whatever it was, she held it by the sides. The head, back of the neck

89. Akhenaten as a sphinx (facing left)

Probably from Amarna
Dynasty 18, reign of Akhenaten,
1353–1336 B.C.
Limestone
H. 51 cm, w. 105.5 cm, d. 5.2 cm
Egyptian Curator's Fund, Museum of Fine
Arts, Boston, 64.1944

90. Akhenaten as a sphinx (facing right)

Probably from Amarna
Dynasty 18, reign of Akhenaten,
1353–1336 B.C.
Limestone
H. 56.7 cm, w. 93.2 cm, d. 6 cm
Kestner-Museum, Hannover, 1964.3

These two relief slabs depict Akhenaten as a sphinx worshipping the Aten. They are inscribed with the early forms of the names of the god as well as Akhenaten's names and titles.[1] The Aten is described as being "within the Sunshade of the Fashioner of the Horizon of the Aten," presumably an unknown temple at Amarna. The sunshades were usually temples at the periphery of the site, dedicated to the royal women.[2]

Although the images on these two slabs have similar inscriptions and could have faced one another, they do not seem to be an exact pair. On one slab Akhenaten reclines before three offering stands and offers up the cartouches of Akhenaten, Nefertiti, and the Aten, whereas on the other only two stands are shown and Akhenaten holds up a ritual vessel. The sphinx, an incar-

nation of the sun-god Ra-Horakhty, would have been an appropriate image for use in the new religion. Its ancient association with "Horus of the Horizon" and the concept of liminality would have made it particularly fitting for use in doorways. Such images can indeed be found flanking doorways and on transom grilles and door lintels.[3]

These slabs were probably used as orthostats, placed on either side of a door or gateway in a series that would have mimicked the avenues of sphinxes in the great temples at Thebes. A similar example was found *in situ*, set into a wall off the central corridor in the Great Palace at Amarna.[4] PL

1. Aldred 1973, p. 99.
2. Kemp 1995, p. 461.
3. See Musée du Louvre, Paris, E 15589.
4. Pendlebury 1951, p. 70, no. 313b, pl. LXVIII.

91

91. Princess offering unguent

Amarna, found at Hermopolis
Dynasty 18, reign of Akhenaten,
1353–1336 B.C.
Limestone
H. 23 cm, w. 27 cm, d. 3.7 cm
Charles Amos Cummings Fund, Museum
of Fine Arts, Boston, 1971.294

The Amarna princesses are commonly
included in the royal family's adoration
of the Aten. A jar of unguent, flowers,
and the sistrum are the items most frequently held.

With arms bent gracefully forward
and delicate fingers surrounding the vessel, this princess offers a jar piled high
with unguent.[1] Her unusual hairstyle,
with partly shaved head and short curls,
can be found on other royal women at
Amarna.[2] JLH

1. For a princess offering ointment, see N. de G.
Davies 1903–8, vol. 2, pl. XXXII.

2. For a similar princess hairstyle, with partly
shaved head and headband, see cat. 92.

92. Purification of Kiya, reworked for Meretaten

Amarna, found at Hermopolis
Dynasty 18, reign of Akhenaten,
1353–1336 B.C.
Limestone
H. 22.8 cm, w. 47 cm
Gift of Norbert Schimmel, 1985, The
Metropolitan Museum of Art, New York,
1985.328.8

This relief fragment shows a royal
woman undergoing a ritual of purification.[1] The zigzag lines represent the
water being poured over her head from
a jar held by the small hand at the
upper left corner of the fragment. It
has been suggested that the hand of
the Aten itself was represented.[2] The
woman originally wore a Nubian wig
that was transformed into the broad
side lock worn by Akhenaten's daughters. Presumably the representation is
Queen Kiya changed into Princess
Meretaten. Although the relief is uninscribed, the facial features of the
woman—the long chin, slightly smiling
mouth, and almond-shaped, slanted
eyes—are those of Kiya.[3] During the
king's last years, her name and figure
were changed on almost all monuments
to those of one of the elder princesses.
EP

1. John D. Cooney in Muscarella 1974, cat. 249;
Roeder 1969, p. 404, pl. 172.

2. Cooney 1965, p. 30.

3. Arnold 1996, pp. 105–8.

93. Plaque with the early car-touches of Aten

Possibly from Amarna
Dynasty 18, reign of Akhenaten,
1353–1336 B.C. (years 6–9)
Calcite
H. 9 cm, w. 4.2 cm, d. 1.3 cm
Ägyptisches Museum und
Papyrussammlung, Berlin, 2045

94. Adoration of the king

Probably from Amarna
Dynasty 18, reign of Akhenaten
1353–1336 B.C.
Limestone
H. 26.3 cm, w 24.6 cm, d. 3.2 cm
Seth K. Sweetser Fund, Museum of Fine
Arts, Boston, 62.1168

93

92

94

"Offer praises to the living Disc and you shall have a prosperous life."[1] This sage advice from the God's Father Ay reflects how the citizens of Amarna worshipped the royal family as gods. Their cult is evidenced in numerous relief scenes, stelae, and statues of Akhenaten, Nefertiti, and the princesses found in private houses and domestic shrines.[2] The adoration scene (cat. 94)[3] and the cartouche plaque (cat. 93)[4] both likely reflect such worship.

The adoration scene shows the Overseer of Works User-Seth with arms raised before Akhenaten's prenomen.[5] The hieroglyphs above him state that he is "praising the living Aten." This piece is probably part of a lintel from a house at Amarna, as similar scenes of worship are found on other lintels.

The unusual calcite cartouche plaque is possibly a votive object.[6] It shows Akhenaten kneeling in the pose of the god Heh, who personified infinity, and holding two large cartouches of the Aten above him.[7] The king is flanked by his own cartouches and one of Nefertiti's, which is the second one behind him.[8] JLH

1. D. Redford 1984, p. 180, and p. 181, n. 6.

2. Ikram 1989, pp. 90–92.

3. Aldred 1973, cat. 62, dates this piece to Akhenaten's "Middle Period."

4. Ägyptisches Museum 1985, p. 85. The tablet has been dated between the sixth and ninth years of Akhenaten's reign, as the king adopted the name Akhenaten in his sixth regnal year and these cartouches of the Aten are documented as having been written before year 9.

5. Aldred 1973, cat. 62. "The Lord of the Two Lands Nefer-kheperure-waenre, Given Life."

6. Aldred 1973, cat. 47, also suggests it may be a foundation deposit—an assemblage of model tools and offerings deposited during foundation ceremonies—for a building dedicated to the Aten.

7. "Re-Horakhty, rejoicing in the horizon, in his aspect of the sunlight which is in the Aten." Ägyptisches Museum 1985, p. 85.

8. "Chief wife of the king, Perfect is the goodness of the Aten." Nefertiti ("The Beautiful One Is Come"). Ägyptisches Museum 1985, p. 85. An additional epithet of Akhenaten is written cryptographically by the king holding the two large cartouches of the Aten: "He who elevates the name of the Aten." Ägyptisches Museum 1985, p. 85.

95. Running quadruped

Amarna, found at Hermopolis
Dynasty 18, reign of Akhenaten,
1353–1336 B.C.
Limestone
H. 26.5 cm, w. 22.3 cm
Musée du Louvre, Paris, E 32559

This running animal[1] was carved on a *talatat* block, one of the standard-sized building blocks (about 20 inches by 10 by 10) specific to the Amarna Period. It belongs to a series of well-known scenes depicting life in the desert under the light of the solar disk. Several others in the series depict a herd of antelopes. Here the young animal is running next to an adult whose body is only partly visible. The vividness of the stance and the attention to detail (the tail is raised in warning) are good examples of the interest and skill Amarna artists exhibited in rendering nature. The pale red-brown color is difficult to account for. It may have been a later, even modern, addition, but it can also be the result of a change in the original color caused by the block's reuse in the foundation of the pylon built by Ramesses II in the main temple of Hermopolis, across the Nile from Amarna. ME

1. Roeder 1969, p. 239 and pl. 215, PC 299B.

96. Sanctuary of the Great Temple

Amarna, found at Hermopolis
Dynasty 18, reign of Akhenaten,
1353–1336 B.C.
Limestone
H. 22.7 cm, w. 26.9 cm, d. 3.8 cm
Charles Amos Cummings Bequest Fund, Museum of Fine Arts, Boston, 63.961

This relief has been identified as a representation of the sanctuary of the Great Aten Temple at Amarna.[1] At the center of the composition is the main altar, heaped high with offerings and flanked by two statues of the king holding trays piled with more offerings. At the bottom of the relief are representations of stone altars, ceramic offering stands, and a wooden or wickerwork cradle for jars. Through the open temple doors on the left, one capped by a broken lintel, are more offering stands and altars. On the right is a high, thin wall representing the exterior of the temple; along the damaged right edge are the remains of a columned portico.

Although this not a strictly accurate depiction of the temple, the profusion of offerings is an indication of the ostentatious display of food that must have characterized the Amarna cult. PL

1. Cooney 1965, cat. 61; Aldred 1973, cat. 81.

96

95

97

97. Sphere with mythological scene

Provenance not known
Dynasty 18, reign of Akhenaten,
1353–1336 B.C.
Faience
H. 3.5 cm, diam. 4.2 cm
Ny Carlsberg Glyptotek, Copenhagen,
AEIN 1791

This sphere is decorated with figures of
Akhenaten and Nefertiti, who are identified by cartouches above their heads
(see fig. 71). Each is seated in a boat
and raises his or her arms in salutation
to a solar disk in the prow.

The arrangement of the figures suggests an identification of the king and
queen with Shu and Tefnut, children of
the creator-god Atum, who was also the
sun god of Heliopolis.[1] In addition, the
composition may allude to the next
world, where the dead are granted
places in the solar bark.[2]

A cylindrical hole through the vertical
axis probably served to fasten the
sphere to a shaft, perhaps a staff or
other item of regalia in the equipment
of a royal tomb. MJ

---

1. J. R. Harris 1976, p. 81; Friedman 1986, p.
102.

2. J. R. Harris 1976, p. 81.

98. Stirrup ring featuring Akhenaten and Nefertiti as Shu and Tefnut

Possibly from Amarna
Dynasty 18, reign of Akhenaten,
1353–1336 B.C.
Gold
H. 2.5 cm (bezel length), diam. 2.5 cm
Purchase, Edward S. Harkness Gift, 1926,
The Metropolitan Museum of Art, New
York, 26.7.767

Few gold signet rings have survived
from the Amarna Period.[1] The image on
the bezel of this cast example can be
interpreted as an ideogram. Although a
direct parallel for this scene is not
known, the iconography is typical for
Amarna art. A sun-disk with two uraei
at the top of the scene is the sun god,
whose children, Akhenaten and Nefertiti, are represented below. Akhenaten is
shown with a Maat feather (emblem of
the goddess of Truth) in his hands.
Nefertiti wears a headdress surmounted
by double plumes, a crown that is usual
for her early iconography, and holds a
"fly-whisk" scepter in her hand.[2]
Represented between the sun and the
earth, which is shown below by the
hieroglyph *ta*, the royal couple appears
as the primeval "first pair" of the genesis myth.[3] EP

---

1. Hayes 1959, p. 293, fig. 180; Petrie 1894, p.
28, pl. XIV, 31; Lansing 1940, pl. 12.

2. Aldred 1973, cats. 28–30.

3. Arnold 1996, p. 99.

98

99

99

99. *Menat*

Amarna
Dynasty 18, reign of Amenhotep III,
1390–1353 B.C.
Bronze, electrum
H. 11.1 cm, w. 3.8 cm, d. 0.3 cm
Excavations of the Deutsche Orient-
Gesellschaft, 1911–14, Ägyptisches
Museum und Papyrussammlung, Berlin,
21838

Though excavated at Amarna, this
counterweight for a *menat* (a ritual
necklace)[1] was made during the reign of
Amenhotep III. Represented in relief at
the top of the handle-shaped ornament
is a profile image of the goddess Isis,
who is identified as "Isis, Mother of the
God, Mistress of Heaven," in a band of
text that surmounts a full profile view of
the same goddess holding a *was* scepter.
In an oval at the bottom is a cow standing in a boat amid a papyrus thicket—
a symbol of the goddess Hathor as sky
goddess. The reverse of the counterweight is detailed in a similar fashion.

In all likelihood, this jewel was
brought to Amarna by someone who
moved with the king to the new capital.
DW

---

1. Betsy M. Bryan in Kozloff and Bryan 1992, pp.
363–64.

100

100. Staff finial

Amarna, house N.50.28
Dynasty 18, reign of Akhenaten,
1353–1336 B.C.
Calcite, bronze
H. 2.9 cm, w. 2.6 cm, d. 2.2 cm
Excavations of the Deutsche Orient-
Gesellschaft, 1911–12, Ägyptisches
Museum und Papyrussammlung, Berlin,
20721

A socket behind the neck of this tiny
royal head[1] defines its function as part
of a small standard or finial on an item
of furniture or a ritual implement. The
head is supported by a broadcollar
whose shoulders are adorned with separately cut uraei (the one on the left
shoulder is missing) fixed by bronze
plugs. Despite its scale—it seems to
be the smallest portrait of Akhenaten
known so far—the head shows a high
degree of realistic detail, typical of the
early phase of Amarna art. DW

1. Ägyptisches Museum 1967, cat. 748.

101. Miniature *hes* vase with a princess on a lotus

Provenance not known
Dynasty 18, reign of Akhenaten,
1353–1336 B.C.
Calcite, carnelian, obsidian, glass
H. 10.8 cm
Rogers Fund, 1940, The Metropolitan
Museum of Art, New York, 40.2.4

This calcite model vase in the shape of
a ritual *hes* jar (for water libations) was
made of two vertical sections glued
together. Each section was carved as a
single unit with half of the conical stopper. The smaller, front section is almost
flat on the inner surface, while the corresponding part of the back section is
hollowed out. The back part of the
stopper is broken, but the configuration
of the break indicates that there was no
opening in the top.[1] There is no evidence of residual material inside the jar;
only the adhesive used to glue the two
sections together is visible. This shows
that the vase was a model.

The imagery of the colorful appliqué
on the exterior suggests the vessel had a
funerary purpose. A nude girl, carved
of carnelian, with an obsidian side lock,
stands in a pose of greeting atop a blue
lotus flower made of gold, carnelian,
and colored glass. Although a blue
lotus alone is a flower of the afterlife, a
child in a lotus is a traditional symbol
of rebirth and rejuvenation.[2] The vase
could have been a part of the funerary
equipment of princess Meketaten, who
died in childhood. EP

1. Observation of Ann Heywood, associate con-
servator, Metropolitan Museum of Art.

2. Hayes 1959, pp. 314–15, fig. 199; Arnold
1996, pp. 115–16.

102. Clappers

Amarna, King's House
Dynasty 18, reign of Akhenaten,
1353–1336 B.C.
Ivory
H. 21.5 cm
Gift of Mrs. John Hubbard and Egypt
Exploration Society, 1932, The
Metropolitan Museum of Art, New York,
32.5.2a,b

Pairs of ivory clappers in the form of
human arms wearing bracelets were a
popular ancient-Egyptian musical
instrument.[1] These clappers were carved
out of a single hippopotamus tusk split
in half. The assembly holes at the upper
end show that the clappers were tied
together and held in one hand. Sound
was produced by shaking them. This
pair was found on the premises of the
King's House at Amarna in a pit south
of the pond; along with another pair,
they were in a small wooden anthropoid coffin.[2] Since clappers of this type
were not in use during the Amarna
Period, these seem have been made as
funerary objects.[3] Their ritual character
could have been reinforced by the interpretation of the traditional hand shape
as a manifestation of Aten.[4] EP

1. Hayes 1959, p. 316.

2. Pendlebury 1951, pp. 89–92 and pl. LXXIV,
10.

3. Manniche 1971, p. 162, fig. 10.

4. Manniche 1976, pp. 3–4.

101

102

103. Amphora with gazelle and *ankh*s

Provenance not known
Dynasty 18, reign of Akhenaten,
1353–1336 B.C.
Ceramic
H. 27.4 cm
Ex collection of George Halpern, lent by
Pamela and Benson Harer, The Harer
Family Trust

During the mid-18th Dynasty a new
type of decorated ceramic appeared in
Egypt. It incorporated a rare powdered
blue pigment derived either from cobalt
deposits in the desert oases[1] or from
imported glass ingots that were ground
down. The blue was ideal for rendering
the petals of the blue lotus, which was
depicted in garlands decorating plain-
pottery amphorae at feasts. The lotus
decoration was not only attractive but
also evoked rebirth, as the lotus opens
anew each day with the sunrise.

Elaborate vessels decorated with
human, animal, and plant forms are
depicted in tomb scenes as presentation
pieces, often carried by foreign dignitaries.[2] Although these prized gifts may
have been made of metal, they appear to
have inspired new pottery versions. The
calf, the young gazelle, and the *ankh*—
like the lotus—were associated with
rebirth and rejuvenation, a theme that
continued to be popular during the
Amarna Period. Fragments of vessels
bearing these motifs have been found in
temple contexts at Elephantine and in the
palace complex at Malqata in Thebes. PL

1. Arnold and Bourriau 1993, pp. 100–101.
2. For vessels with applied animal decorations, see
N. de G. Davies 1903–8, vol. 3, pl. XIV.

106

105

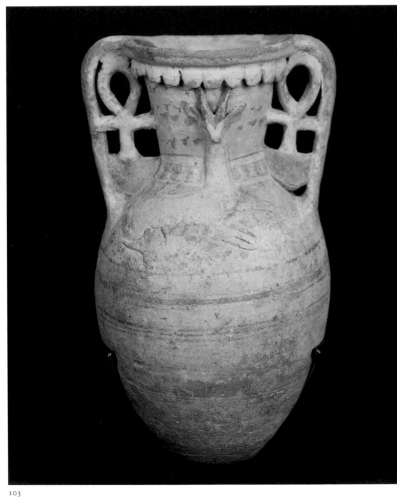

103

106. Squat jar with handles

Amarna, house U.36.33
Dynasty 18, reign of Akhenaten,
1353–1336 B.C.
Ceramic
H. 24 cm, diam. 32 cm
The Visitors of the Ashmolean Museum,
Oxford, 1929.418

The petal decoration on painted ceramic vessels could be combined with other
floral motifs, such as the marguerite on
the squat vessel, or with images of animals, such as the tilapia fish—another
symbol of rejuvenation and rebirth.
Even more elaborate decoration is seen
on a very large amphora (cat. 105) decorated with bands of lotus petals, mandrake fruits, and large *ankh*s, combined
with geese and lotuses.[1]

Although occasionally called "palace
ware," blue-painted pottery had many
uses and a broad geographical spread.
Nevertheless, it is found in the greatest
quantities at the Malqata palace in
Thebes and at Amarna, and disappears
soon after the end of the 18th Dynasty.
PL

1. Hope 1991, p. 46, fig. 13a, pls. 9–11a.

104. Vessel with a fish motif

Amarna, house O.50.2
Dynasty 18, reign of Akhenaten,
1353–1336 B.C.
Ceramic
H. 60 cm, diam. 43 cm
Ägyptisches Museum und
Papyrussammlung, Berlin, 22355

105. Vessel with a marsh scene

Amarna
Dynasty 18, reign of Akhenaten,
1353–1336 B.C.
Ceramic
H. 93 cm, diam. 70 cm
The Visitors of the Ashmolean Museum,
Oxford, 1926.109

107. Armed soldiers

Provenance not known
Dynasty 18, reign of Akhenaten,
1353–1336 B.C.
Limestone
H. 17.5 cm, w. 25 cm, d. 6 cm
Gift of R. G. Gayer-Anderson, lent by the
Syndics of the Fitzwilliam Museum,
Cambridge, EGA.4514.1943

This relief, depicting a pair of soldiers running to the right, was probably part of a composition showing troops mustering for a royal parade.[1] The man on the right grasps a sling and holds an oval shield awkwardly under his right arm, as if not quite prepared for inspection. The other man, with receding hairline and protruberant belly, lofts an ax in his left hand, clutches a spear in his right, slings his shield over his right shoulder, and seems to be rushing to his place in line. It is characteristic of Amarna art that the sculptor eschews the artificial formality of traditional style and attempts to capture a real moment frozen in time—with all its fleeting, incidental detail of human activity and natural life. TK

1. N. de G. Davies 1903–8, vol. 1, pls. X, XV; vol. 3, pls. XXXI, XXXIX; vol. 4, pls. XX–XXII, XXVI; Aldred 1973, cat. 39; T. Phillips 1995, cat. 1.49.

108. Bowing woman

Amarna, found at Hermopolis
Dynasty 18, reign of Akhenaten,
1353–1336 B.C.
Limestone
H. 23 cm, w. 53 cm, d. 3.5 cm
Gift of Schimmel Foundation, in honor of
William Stevenson Smith, Museum of Fine
Arts, Boston, 62.501

"Kissing the ground" (in Egyptian, *sen ta*) is the theme of this relief fragment. To the left of the large-scale, sandaled toes, probably belonging to Akhenaten, a woman kneels in prostration (in the wake of the king). Her image appears less competently carved than that of the royal foot; her costume consists of a striated wig with simple fillet and perhaps a full-length garment, although it is not indicated.[1] From earliest times, Egyptian artists preferred to portray the inner edges of both feet, showing two big toes and two arches. The "transition" to the outside of the foot first occurs on a few minor painted figures in early New Kingdom Theban tombs,

and then with regularity only on royalty during the Amarna Period.[2] The detailed example preserved here represents one of many Amarna innovations, although we can only guess at the true artistic or ideological motivation behind it. PDM

1. For previous publications, see Cooney 1965, cat. 11; Roeder 1969, pl. 182, PC 45; Terrace 1962.

2. See Russmann 1980, especially pp. 64–76.

109. Faces from a procession

Probably from Amarna
Dynasty 18, reign of Akhenaten,
1353–1336 B.C.
Limestone
H. 22 cm, w. 52 cm
Kestner-Museum, Hannover, 1926.207

This fragment, worked in high relief, shows four male faces in a group of people facing left.[1] They are set off in pairs by formation and by hairstyle. The two men on the left wear wigs of straight, short hair; the wigs of the two men on the right have twisted or braided hair elaborated by three tiers at the front. All four men wear large, disk-shaped earrings. The faces, with their full lips, slightly slanted eyes, and prominent nose, mouth, and chin, are expressive and carefully rendered.

Between the two pairs is the upper part of a fan handle in the form of a papyrus umbel, to which a feather is fastened. This fan is carried by the third person in line. Above the heads more feathers can be seen, from the fans of the other three men.

Groups of fanbearers like these can often be found in the vicinity of the king in representations from the Amarna Period and after.[2] They were courtiers and high officials accompanying the king on official occasions. RD

1. Drenkhahn 1989, cat. 32.

2. Martin 1987, cat. 34, pls. 12 and 45.

107

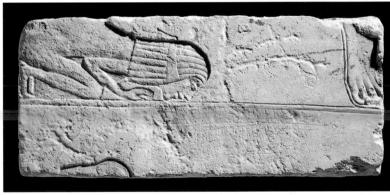

108

109

110, 111

112

113

110. Relief of a royal barge with Nefertiti smiting

Amarna, found at Hermopolis
Dynasty 18, reign of Akhenaten,
1353–1336 B.C.
Limestone
H. 23.9 cm, w. 54 cm, d. 3.5 cm
Egyptian Curator's Fund, Museum of Fine Arts, Boston, 64.521

111. River scene with royal barges

Amarna, found at Hermopolis
Dynasty 18, reign of Akhenaten,
1353–1336 B.C.
Limestone
H. 23.4 cm, w. 53.1 cm, d. 3.6
Helen and Alice Colburn Fund, Museum of Fine Arts, Boston, 63.260

112. Royal barge with Akhenaten smiting

Amarna, found at Hermopolis
Dynasty 18, reign of Akhenaten,
1353–1336 B.C.
Limestone
H. 24 cm, w. 54.2 cm, d. 3.5 cm
Gift of Norbert Schimmel, 1985, The Metropolitan Museum of Art, New York, 1985.328.15

113. Relief of tow boats

Amarna, found at Hermopolis
Dynasty 18, reign of Akhenaten,
1353–1336 B.C.
Limestone
H. 22.5 cm, w. 51.5 cm, d. 5.3 cm
Horace and Florence Mayer Fund, Museum of Fine Arts, Boston, 1989.104

These four reliefs most likely form part of the same scene, though only two join directly. The royal barges are shown docked at the bank of the river or a canal. On the two adjoining blocks (cats. 110 and 111),[1] Nefertiti's barge is represented, identifiable by the two large steering oars at the stern, with finials in the form of the queen's head with its characteristic crown surmounted by plumes and sun-disk. Two helmsmen man the tiller, while rowers pull at their oars. On the roof of a central cabin two servants bow obsequiously. It is the scene in the kiosk at the stern, however, that commands our attention, for here Nefertiti appears, under the benevolent rays of the Aten, slaying a female enemy. Though depictions of the king as triumphant conqueror appear on warships of the earlier 18th Dynasty,[2] the queen in this role is highly unusual, and is further evidence of the

elevated role of the royal women in this period.[3] A complementary scene probably depicting the king in the same pose is found on the prow of the boat directly behind the queen's. The relief from the Metropolitan Museum (cat. 112)[4] has yet another portrayal of a smiting Akhenaten, accompanied by the queen and a princess, this time at the forecastle of a barge with a large central cabin. The fourth block[5] shows two towboats[6] upon which are kiosks embellished with royal sphinxes trampling enemies. The decoration of the hulls of the barges continues this theme of domination, with figures of foreigners offering tribute. SD'A

1. Anne K. Capel in Capel and Markoe 1996, p. 112, fig. 3; Werner 1986, fig. 18; Aldred 1973, cat. 57; Cooney 1965, cats. 51–51a; Terrace 1964, p. 53.

2. Werner 1986.

3. Nefertiti also appears in this attitude at Karnak; see Smith and Redford 1976, p. 81; pl. 23:2. For other examples of Nefertiti smiting, see E. Hall 1986, pp. 25–26 and Tawfik 1975, pp. 162–63. See also the female sphinx trampling enemies on the side of Queen Tiye's throne in the tomb of Kheruef: Epigraphic Survey 1980, pls. 48–49, and further discussion in Troy 1986, pp. 65–66.

4. Werner 1986, fig. 19; Aldred 1973, cat. 55; Cooney 1965, cat. 50; Terrace 1964, p. 53.

5. Münzen und Medaillen 1974, cat. 24.

6. Recognized as such by W. Raymond Johnson in personal correspondence with the Egyptian Department, Museum of Fine Arts, Boston, in 1989; see N. de G. Davies 1903–8, vol. 6, pl. V.

114

116

117

114. Stela of a Western Asiatic soldier, his wife, and his servant

Probably from Amarna
Dynasty 18, reign of Akhenaten,
1353–1336 B.C.
Limestone
H. 29.5, w. 23.5 cm, d. 3.3 cm
Ägyptisches Museum und
Papyrussammlung, Berlin, 14122

115. Drinking tube and strainer

Amarna
Dynasty 18, reign of Akhenaten,
1353–1336 B.C.
Lead
Tube fragment: h. 10.2 cm, w. 10.2 cm
Strainer: h. 7.3 cm, w. 2.4 cm
The Trustees of the British Museum,
London, 55148 (tube), 55149 (strainer)

The subject of the stela is extraordinary.
A man, coiffed and dressed in Western
Asiatic style, sits on a stool drinking
beer through a bent tube while his wife
sits languidly on a chair.[1] The spear
behind him identifies him as a soldier—
probably a recruit from Egypt's vassal
provinces in Canaan. Inserted into the
beer jar is a long, angled "straw,"

which a servant puts into the man's
mouth, enabling him to drink.
Surprisingly, fragments of an identical
drinking tube have also survived from
Amarna. From the original we see that
its bottom was a perforated bulb that
strained the dregs from the liquid as
one drank. The object is made of lead,
which means that its frequent use
would eventually have poisoned the
user. TK

1. Karl-Heinz Priese in Priese 1991, cat. 80.

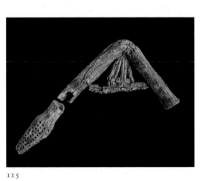

115

116. Sculptor's model of a Nubian

Probably from Amarna
Dynasty 18, reign of Akhenaten,
1353–1336 B.C.
Limestone
H. 10.2 cm, w. 9.2, d. 2 cm
Rogers Fund, 1922, The Metropolitan
Museum of Art, New York, 22.2.10

117. Nubians with ostrich plumes

Probably from Amarna
Dynasty 18, reign of Akhenaten,
1353–1336 B.C.
Limestone
H. 10 cm, w. 21 cm, d. 4 cm
Musées Royaux d'Art et d'Histoire,
Brussels, E. 8194

Amarna renderings of Nubians
("Kushites") are among the earliest,
most vivid pictorial records of black
Africans in art.[1] If some of these people
were depicted as war prisoners, others,
wearing Egyptian dress and jewelry,
clearly had high status.[2] Some served in
Egypt as palace servants or fanbearers;
others, in the Egyptian army. Typically
armed with bows and wearing ostrich
plumes in their hair, they even appear

dancing to drums or wrestling in com-
petitions before Pharaoh.[3] "Bowmen of
Kush" must have been crack troops,
since Akhenaten's Canaanite vassals, in
the Amarna letters, frequently requested
units of them for their defense.[4] They
were depicted with black or dark-
brown skin and yellow or red hair, the
latter probably indicating ochre hair
pomades of the type still used in parts
of central Africa.[5] TK

1. Vercoutter 1976; Wildung 1997b, cat. 157.

2. Martin 1974, 1989, vol. 2, pls. 81–93; L. Bell
1997, fig. 1; Simpson 1963.

3. N. de G. Davies 1903–8, vol. 1, pls. 8, 14, 26;
vol. 4, pl. 5; Aldred 1973, cat. 138; Davies
1903–8, vol. 2, p. 38, pl. 37; Kendall 1989, p.
628; Kendall 1997.

4. Moran 1992, pp. 207, 212, 215, 328–29.

5. Kendall 1989, pp. 683–84; Beckwith and
Saitoti 1980, pp. 126–27.

118. Foreigners with a harp

Amarna, found at Hermopolis
Dynasty 18, reign of Akhenaten,
1353–1336 B.C.
Limestone
H. 23 cm, w. 54 cm, d. 4 cm
Kestner-Museum, Hannover, 1963.2

The two figures on the left whose upper bodies are preserved probably form the end of a group of musicians. The man in front is holding a harp, recognizable by its frame and four strings.[1] His sleek hair, which leaves the ear exposed, parts at the back of the head. It covers his chest and back, ending in a curl similar to that found on the wig of the goddess Hathor. The musician is wearing a sleeveless dress that has a V-shaped overlap on the chest. The garment and the hairstyle are probably the reason for identifying these men as Libyans. The identification is problematic, however, since Libyans were always depicted— even during the Amarna period—wearing a side plait, a decorative plume on the head, and a pointed goatee. Also, there are no known representations of Libyans as musicians.

Near the center of the fragment, in a higher register, stands an Egyptian official or courtier, bending. He wears a long pleated tunic and a kilt with a sash.

The vertical furrow near the right edge of the block indicates that this slab formed the end of a wall. RD

---

1. Roeder 1969, pp. 187, 199, 314, pl. 177, PC 80.

119. Letter from the king of Alashiya (Cyprus) to Akhenaten

Amarna
Dynasty 18, reign of Akhenaten,
1353–1336 B.C.
Clay
H. 8.9 cm, w. 6.4 cm, d. 3.8 cm
The Trustees of the British Museum,
London, 29789

120. Letter from Tushratta, king of Mitanni (northern Syria) to Queen Tiye

Amarna
Dynasty 18, reign of Akhenaten,
1353–1336 B.C.
Clay
H. 14 cm, w. 6.4 cm, d. 2.5 cm
The Trustees of the British Museum,
London, 29794

121. Letter from Abi-milki, king of Tyre, to Akhenaten

Amarna
Dynasty 18, reign of Akhenaten,
1353–1336 B.C.
Clay
H. 8.9 cm, w. 5.1 cm, d. 3.2 cm
The Trustees of the British Museum,
London, 29812

These cuneiform documents[1] are typical of the letters received by Akhenaten at Amarna, from independent potentates of the Near East and from his vassal rulers in Canaan and Syria.[2] Nearly four hundred such documents were found in a building called the "House of the Correspondence of the Pharaoh," where

Egyptian scribes learned to read and write Babylonian (Akkadian), the international language of the day. See the essay "Foreign Relations" for a discussion of the archive, including details on these tablets. TK

---

1. Reference numbers: BM 29789 is EA 34; BM 29794 is EA 26; and BM 29812 is EA 147.

2. For translations, see Moran 1992, pp. 84–86, 105–6, 233–34. For background, see Giles 1997, pp. 101–19, 120.

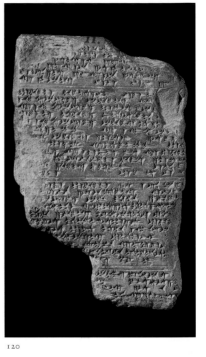

120

119

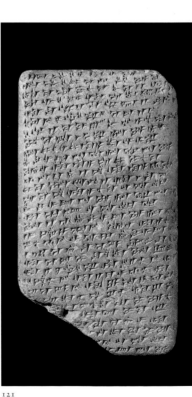

121

118

122

122. Commemorative scarab of Akhenaten and Nefertiti

Provenance not known
Dynasty 18, reign of Akhenaten,
1353–1336 B.C.
Glazed steatite
H. 6 cm, w. 4.4 cm, d. 3.2 cm
Helen and Alice Colburn Fund, Museum
of Fine Arts, Boston, 1973.108

The Egyptians drew parallels between the scarab beetle *(Scarabaeus sacer)*, rolling its ball of dung across the ground, and the sun god's daily passage across the heavens. As a hieroglyphic sign (read *kheper*), the scarab meant "to come into being," and its generative power was worshipped in the form of the god Khepri. Often mass-produced, faience or steatite scarabs were inscribed on the bottom and distributed to mark particular events under the reigning king. Akhenaten's father, Amenhotep III, commissioned large scarabs recording a wide range of events.[1] This scarab lists epithets and portions of the titulary of Akhenaten, and bears the inscription "Great Royal Wife Nefertiti, may she live, prosper, and be healthy forever." The early form of the king's name (Amenhotep IV) has been erased in a cartouche on the bottom, although the agent(s) who erased it apparently missed an identical cartouche, visible here, on the side of the scarab. The beetle shows a single line between the wing cases and the prothorax, and is pierced longitudinally.[2] PDM

1. See Blankenberg-van Delden 1969.

2. For previous publications, see Simpson 1974, pp. 140–41, pl. 33 [1–3]; Meggs 1992, p. 19, figs. 2-17, 2-18.

123. Chariot and horses

Amarna, found at Hermopolis
Dynasty 18, reign of Akhenaten,
1353–1336 B.C.
Limestone
H. 23.3 cm, w. 53.5 cm, d. 3.2 cm
Gift of the New Hermes Foundation,
Brooklyn Museum of Art, New York,
60.28

124. Sculptor's model of a horse's head, with a princess on reverse

Amarna, found at Hermopolis
Dynasty 18, reign of Akhenaten,
1353–1336 B.C.
Limestone
H. 10.5 cm, w. 12.3 cm, d. 2.3 cm
Ägyptisches Museum und
Papyrussammlung, Berlin, 23717

At no time since its introduction into Egypt from the Near East in the seventeenth century B.C.[1] had the horse been represented in art so naturalistically or the chariot so frequently as in the Amarna Period. The royal family's daily "commute" by chariot from palace to palace, followed by a cavalcade of other chariots and footmen, was a common subject for artists.[2] Cat. 123 is extraordinary, not only in depicting one of the horses' heads frontally, but also in revealing that the driver carries a pair of sandals—doubtless for his master, the royal functionary who was required, for ceremonial purposes, to run on foot beside the royal chariot.[3] The driver of this vehicle would eventually have picked up his weary master and returned him home.

The horse depicted in cat. 124[4] is rendered quite naturalistically, with its wrinkles about the mouth and veining below the eyes. TK

1. Emery, Smith, and Millard 1979, pp. 191–95 and references.

2. Kemp 1989, pp. 275–79.

3. Aldred 1973, cat. 51, and see pp. 148, 151, 153, 154, 207–8, 210–11.

4. Ägyptisches Museum 1967, cat. 774.

123

124

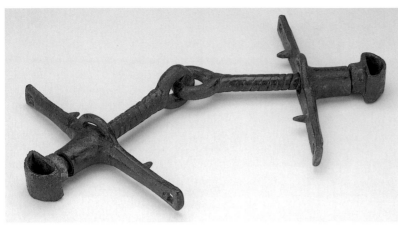

125

126

125. Snaffle bit

Amarna, house O.47.16 (surface find)
Dynasty 18, reign of Akhenaten,
1353–1336 B.C.
Bronze
H. 11 cm, w. 20.2 cm
The Visitors of the Ashmolean Museum,
Oxford, 1933.1209

126. Yoke finial from a chariot

Amarna
Dynasty 18, reign of Akhenaten,
1353–1336 B.C.
Barite
H. 4 cm, diam. 3 cm
Courtesy of Petrie Museum of Egyptian
Archaeology, University College London,
UC. 132

Elements of harness were recovered
from the debris of several private houses at Amarna. Since the horse at this
time was used almost exclusively to
draw a chariot,[1] these objects, like the
numerous reliefs depicting chariots,
attest to the popularity of the vehicle
among the wealthy there. This is hardly
surprising, given the great expanse of
the city and the need for swift trans-
portation.

The snaffle bit was clearly designed to
control a temperamental horse. It has a
mouthpiece formed of two interlinked
bars, which, when pulled back by the
reins, caused the barbed sidepieces to
prick the corners of the horse's mouth.[2]
The other object is a finial from a chariot yoke,[3] identical to those visible, for
example, on the chariots excavated
from Tutankhamen's tomb.[4] TK

–––––––––

1. Martin 1989, p. 43, pl. 323; Aldred 1973, cat.
157.

2. Emery, Smith, and Millard 1979, p. 192;
Littauer 1969.

3. Several comparable yoke finials were found in
the police and military barracks. See Pendlebury
1951, pp. 131–36.

4. Littauer and Crouwel 1985, p. 81 and n. 1,
pls. 14, 23, 24, 57.

127. Cypriot base-ring juglet

Amarna, Central City, no. 21/231
Dynasty 18, reign of Akhenaten,
1353–1336 B.C.
Ceramic
H.12 cm, diam. 7 cm
Gift of the Egypt Exploration Society, The
Visitors of the Ashmolean Museum,
Oxford, 1922.102

128. Mycenaean pilgrim flask

Amarna, "Mycenaean" house, T.36.39,
no. 30/24
Dynasty 18, reign of Akhenaten,
1353–1336 B.C.
Ceramic
H. 16 cm, w. 10.2 cm
Gift of the Egypt Exploration Society, The
Visitors of the Ashmolean Museum,
Oxford, 1931.490

129. Mycenaean stirrup jar

Probably from Amarna
Dynasty 18, reign of Akhenaten,
1353–1336 B.C.
Ceramic
H. 7.2 cm, diam. 7.4 cm
Gift of R. G. Gayer-Anderson, lent by the
Syndics of the Fitzwilliam Museum,
Cambridge, EGA. 5008.1943

127

128

129

3. This vessel was found by the Egypt Exploration Society excavators in the Central City in 1921. See Peet and Woolley 1923, pl. LIV, no. LXXVII/231. For a discussion of the juglet, see Merrillees 1968, p. 81, no. 87.

4. See Peter Lacovara in Brovarski, Doll, and Freed 1982, cat. 65.

5. Bourriau 1981, pp. 124–26.

130. Egyptian pilgrim flask

Amarna
Dynasty 18, reign of Akhenaten,
1353–1336 B.C.
Ceramic
H. 14 cm, w. 10.2 cm, d. 6.4 cm
Gift of the Egypt Exploration Society,
Cincinnati Art Museum, Cincinnati,
1924.273

Foreign vessels are the clearest evidence of the New Kingdom's far-flung trading network. Precious commodities such as perfume oils and unguents were stored in small, finely crafted jars and pots, which were apparently prized as exotic objects and sometimes reused. The Egyptians also copied their distinctive shapes in pottery, faience, and glass.

The large quantity of Mycenaean pottery associated with one structure at Amarna, house T. 36.39, caused J. D. S. Pendlebury to speculate, rather fancifully, that it had been the residence of a Mycenaean merchant.[1] Flinders Petrie, however, found more than a thousand Aegean sherds in waste heaps in the Central City. Recent analyses of these fragments indicate that much of the imported pottery was made in the Argolid of Greece.[2]

Foreign pottery finds at Amarna reveal there was also trade with Cyprus. It has been suggested that the distinctive shape of the Cypriot base-ring juglet[3] came from a poppy pod, and that these vessels contained opium, but that theory remains unproven.[4]

The stirrup jar was another ceramic form that derived from the Aegean world. The shape was practical, with a vertical side spout that made accidental dripping of the precious contents impossible. Both this vessel and the more popular pilgrim flask would probably have held precious oils.[5] PL

Foreign pottery and its decoration inspired local imitations. The pilgrim flask was a practical and attractive form that originated in the Aegean[1] and was popular for centuries throughout the Mediterranean world. This type of flask, which first appears in Egypt during Dynasty 18, is double-handled and lenticular in form. The earliest imitations, decorated with concentric circles, eventually gave way to plain, curved surfaces of clay covered with a heavy slip and burnished. Surface colors range from greenish-white through pinkish-cream. Pilgrim flasks were also made in other materials, including metal, faience, and glass.[2] PL and YJM

130

1. Pendlebury 1935, pp. 120–23. On the find-spot of the Mycenaean pilgrim flask, see Frankfort and Pendlebury 1933, pp. 46, 85, pl. LX, no. 5.

2. Hankey 1997, p. 194.

1. Janine Bourriau has suggested that the source of this form is Mycenae or Syria-Palestine. See Bourriau 1981, cat. 143.

2. For a comparable though larger vessel, see Frankfort and Pendlebury 1933, pp. 67–68.

3. Bourriau in Brovarski, Doll, and Freed 1982, cat. 63.

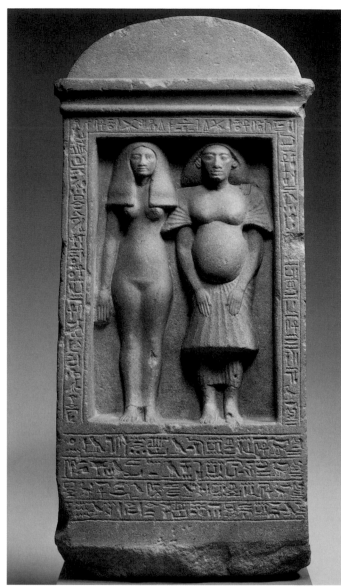

131

132. Unfinished statuette of Akhenaten kneeling

Amarna, house P.47.1
Dynasty 18, reign of Akhenaten,
1353–1336 B.C.
Limestone
H. 13.7 cm, w. 4.8 cm, d. 16.2 cm
Excavations of the Deutsche Orient-Gesellschaft, 1912–13, Ägyptisches Museum und Papyrussammlung, Berlin, 21238

133. Unfinished sculpture of a princess

Amarna, house P.47.1 and .2
Dynasty 18, reign of Akhenaten,
1353–1336 B.C.
Limestone
H. 34 cm, w. 12.5 cm, d. 10.7 cm
Excavations of the Deutsche Orient-Gesellschaft, Ägyptisches Museum und Papyrussammlung, Berlin, 21254

Amarna's remains have yielded numerous unfinished representations of the royal family in sculpture and relief.[1] These two pieces come from a private house in the South Suburb.[2] The rough-cut kneeling figure shows the king in the attitude of the bearer of an offering, almost prostrate. Black guide lines designate areas for future work[3] and show an incense burner in his left hand. From his right hand emerges a row of black dots indicating grains of incense. The sculptor worked on both sides of the figure at once, with a median line running from the king's crown to the back of his feet, to ensure symmetry.

The female statuette, with its smooth-

133

er, more articulated surface, is more nearly finished. The absence of clothing indicates that a pre-adolescent princess, rather than an older female, is the subject. DW and REF

1. For example, Pendlebury 1951, pls. LIX, 1–4 or LXIV, 1–2.

2. Unpublished excavation notes supplied by the Ägyptisches Museum.

3. Schäfer 1931, pl. 50; Grimm, Schoske, and Wildung 1997, cat. 99.

131. Naos of Chief Sculptor Bak and Taheri

Provenance not known
Dynasty 18, reign of Akhenaten,
1353–1336 B.C.
Quartzite
H. 63.5 cm, w. 29.4 cm, d. 15.6 cm
Ägyptisches Museum und Papyrussammlung, Berlin, 31009

This stela represents the chief sculptor Bak and his wife, the mistress of the house, Taheri.[1] Bak's figure, its corpulence emphasized by the placement of his arms, is clothed in an elaborate pleated garment. His wife wears a simple sheath dress, and one arm is placed around her husband's shoulder. The inscription is a request for offerings for the *ka*s of the couple.[2]

Bak, whose official title was "Chief of Works and Chief Sculptor" during the early years of Akhenaten's reign, emphasizes in his inscription that he was instructed by the king himself. Bak is also known from an inscription[3] carved on a large rock in Aswan, where he is shown worshipping the figure of Akhenaten (now erased). His father, who held a post similar to Bak's under Amenhotep III, is represented before a colossal sculpture of that king. SD'A

1. Ägyptisches Museum 1967, cat. 766; Aldred 1988, pp. 93–94; Müller and Settgast 1976, cat. 83; Krauss 1986b.

2. For a translation of the text, see Murnane 1995b, pp. 129–30 (§63-C).

3. Habachi 1965, pp. 85–92; Murnane 1995b, p. 129.

132

134. Sculptor's model of Nefertiti, with a worshipper on reverse

Amarna, near the Great Temple
Dynasty 18, reign of Akhenaten,
1353–1336 B.C.
Limestone
H. 27 cm, w. 16.5 cm, d. 4 cm
Excavations of the Egypt Exploration
Society, 1932–33, Egyptian Museum,
Cairo, JE 59296

Artists' ateliers in the ruins of Amarna contained many interesting trial pieces—figures of the royal family, commoners, and animals, as well as hieroglyphic signs. Artists used them to experiment with the new style before applying it to royal monuments.

This small piece of stone has a relief of Nefertiti's head on one side and a kneeling figure on the other.[1] The head shows the queen's characteristic features and her usual flat-topped crown—ornamented with two cobras, one at the top and the other suspended on a wire near the ear. She has a long, thin neck, almond-shaped eye, thick lips, and a protruding chin. The relief on the reverse side shows a kneeling foreigner, praying. He has Nubian facial features and short, curly hair. MS

1. Pendlebury 1935, p. 134 and pl. V, 3.

134

135

135. Akhenaten and Nefertiti (the "Wilbour plaque")

Purchased near Amarna in 1881 by
Charles Edwin Wilbour
Dynasty 18, reign of Akhenaten,
1353–1336 B.C.
Limestone
H. 15.7 cm, w. 22.1 cm, d. 4.2 cm
Gift of the Estate of Charles Edwin
Wilbour, Brooklyn Museum of Art, New
York, 16.48

The royal figures represented in sunk relief on this sculptor's model have most often been identified as Akhenaten (left), wearing a *khat* headdress with uraeus, and Nefertiti, wearing a cap-crown and uraeus.[1] Although the relief has sometimes been viewed as a forgery,[2] there are compelling reasons to see it as the work of an accomplished artist of the Amarna Period.[3] In fact, some scholars see the plaque's heads, especially the head of the queen, as closely related to works from the Amarna workshop of the master sculptor Thutmose.[4]

Carved in the curvilinear, organic, and sensuous late Amarna style, the queen appears mature and—admittedly a subjective view—forceful. Indeed, as has recently been suggested, this relief may represent Nefertiti as an "active and energetic" coregent with Akhenaten.[5]
RAF

1. For other identifications, see, for example, Bothmer and Keith 1970, p. 52: Smenkhkara and Meretaten, which the authors later revised (Bothmer and Keith 1974, p. 52) to Akhenaten and Nefertiti; James Romano in N. Thomas 1995, cat. 10, for the suggestion that the king with Nefertiti might be Tutankhamen; and Brooklyn Museum of Art 1999, cat. 53: Akhenaten, Smenkhkara, or the young Tutankhaten.

2. Twenty-five years ago Cyril Aldred (Aldred 1973, cat. 121) argued against some unspecified individuals who doubted the plaque's antiquity. For recent skepticism about the plaque, see Hoving 1996, pp. 330–31.

3. Arnold 1996, pp. 89–90 and 146–47, and Fazzini 1997. In both the identification of the king and queen as Akhenaten and Nefertiti is accepted.

4. For example, Aldred 1973, cat. 121; Fay 1986.

5. Arnold 1996, p. 90.

136

137

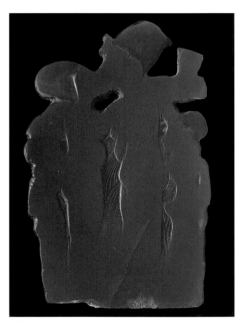

138

137. Unfinished stela of the royal family

Amarna, house O.49.12
Dynasty 18, reign of Akhenaten,
1353–1336 B.C.
Limestone
H. 17.2 cm, w. 13.3 cm, d. 2.8 cm
Ägyptisches Museum und
Papyrussammlung, Berlin, 20716

Despite this stela's unfinished state, its subject seems clear. Beneath Aten's disk, a standing figure pours a libation into a cup held by a larger, seated figure. The standing figure wears a blue crown, a headdress of kings. Yet the distinct outlines of a breast and large hips leave little doubt that a female is represented—specifically Nefertiti, who is shown elsewhere at Amarna assuming other nontraditional roles, such as smiting enemies (cat. 110) or officiating in affairs of state.[1] The seated figure is most certainly Akhenaten, given the *khat* headdress with uraeus, the three-quarter-length kilt, and the lack of a pronounced breast. The stela was probably made late in the reign of Akhenaten, when gender ambiguities expressed by body shape had lessened[2] and attenuated profiles were softer, as they are here. A similar scene of Nefertiti filling Akhenaten's cup occurs in the tomb of Meryra II at Amarna,[3] and it is later repeated with Ankhesenamen and Tutankhamen on material from that king's tomb.[4]

Judging from its size and the fact that it was carved in raised relief, this stela probably would have been installed in a domestic shrine. Raised relief was rare at Amarna (for other examples, see cats. 124 and 169). It is possible that the crack in the stone to Nefertiti's right developed during carving and rendered this relief unusable. REF

---

1. N. de G. Davies 1903–8, vol. 3, pl. XXXVI, for example.

2. Robins 1994, p. 131.

3. N. de G. Davies 1903–8, vol. 2, pl. XXXII.

4. Noblecourt 1963, pl. VII, upper right.

136. Sketches of Akhenaten's head and hand

Amarna, Great Palace (south section)
Dynasty 18, reign of Akhenaten,
1353–1336 B.C.
Limestone
H. 11.6 cm, w. 13.8 cm, d. 2.3 cm
Gift of the Egypt Exploration Society,
Brooklyn Museum of Art, New York,
36.876

These are two sketches, evidently by the same hand, from a figure of Akhenaten in a blue crown.[1] Since a horse's reins hang from the closed hand,[2] the full scene must have shown Akhenaten driving his chariot.[3] The reins have been left off the hand itself, a common type of omission. The lack of fingernails and the unorthodox cuff design are harder to understand[4]; one may hypothesize that they are intended to indicate a protective glove.[5]

The king's face, too large for the crown and much too large for his neck, suggests caricature. Since this is clearly the work of a trained draftsman,[6] the effect may be intentional. However, numerous Amarna sketches of heads of commoners and royals show comparable distortions, indicating that even some trained artists had trouble mastering the Amarna style.[7] ERR

---

1. Pendlebury 1951, p. 69 and pl. LXX, 2.

2. Originally ending in a loop; see N. de G. Davies 1903–8, vol. 2, pl. XVI; N. de G. Davies 1903–8, vol. 4, pl. XXI–XXII.

3. For the context of the frequently represented chariot scenes, see Aldred 1973, p. 70.

4. Though shaped like a bracelet, the cuff is decorated differently: see Arnold 1996, p. 57, fig. 49, (painting fragment, right).

5. E. Eggebrecht 1976, cols. 948-49; Martin et al. 1988, p. 12, n. 21; N. de G. Davies 1903–8, vol. 6, pl. XXIX (wrongly cited in both the preceding); Carter and Mace 1923, pl. 79; compare Reeves 1990a, pp. 156–57.

6. He was familiar with such conventions as the convex curve at the back of Akhenaten's neck; for example, Catharine Roehrig in Metropolitan Museum of Art 1992, cat. 34, (MMA 1985.328.3); Aldred 1973, cat. 12; see Müller 1988, pp. 11, 77–78.

7. For example, Pendlebury 1951, pls. LXII, 1, LXV, 16, LXX, 1-6, LXXI, 9, LXXIV, 5; for differing views on whether the last example is caricature, see p. 107.

138. Royal family kissing

Provenance not known
Dynasty 18, reign of Akhenaten,
1353–1336 B.C.
Carnelian
H. 5.7 cm, w. 3.8 cm, d. 0.6 cm
Given by R. G. Gayer-Anderson, lent by
the Syndics of the Fitzwilliam Museum,
Cambridge, EGA.4606.1943

This unfinished open-work plaque
shows the rough contours of Akhenaten
embracing and kissing his wife
Nefertiti. The intimate couple is flanked
by young daughters, each embraced by
a free parental arm. The royal crowns
and one daughter's wig were deeply
abraded, apparently to be detailed in
another material, perhaps sheet gold.
One of the largest known Egyptian
semiprecious worked stones, this was
perhaps meant to be mounted in a gold
pectoral jewel. The crack from the bottom of the stone may have forced the
craftsman to abandon his work. In a
theocratic society where the pharaoh
was divine, royal scenes of intimate
contact and kissing were rare before the
time of Akhenaten.[1] EV

---

1. For further information on this plaque, see
Aldred 1973, cat. 123; Vassilika 1995, cat. 27.

139. Plaster head of an older woman

Amarna, house P.47.2
Dynasty 18, reign of Akhenaten,
1353–1336 B.C.
Plaster
H. 26.7 cm
Excavations of the Deutsche Orient-
Gesellschaft, 1912–13, Ägyptisches
Museum und Papyrussammlung, Berlin,
21261

140. Plaster head of a youthful woman

Amarna, house P.47.2
Dynasty 18, reign of Akhenaten,
1353–1336 B.C.
Plaster
H. 27.5 cm, w. 16.5 cm, d. 13 cm
Excavations of the Deutsche Orient-
Gesellschaft, 1912–13, Ägyptisches
Museum und Papyrussammlung, Berlin
21341

The extraordinary late-Amarna plaster
heads from the workshop of Thutmose
can be divided into two groups—one
extremely realistic, the other more idealizing. The face of an old woman,[1]
with drooping cheeks, deep furrows
between nose and mouth, and circles
under the eyes, gives a highly individual
impression of a woman living in Amarna. The head of the young woman,[2] on
the other hand, conforms to the traditional ideal of beauty. Whereas the realistic group is confined to nonroyal persons, both male and female, the second
group seems to be limited to members
of the royal family. The young woman,
therefore, is probably one of the
princesses or one of Akhenaten's consorts. DW

---

1. Aldred 1973, p. 46, fig. 27; Arnold 1996, pp.
47–48, fig. 36.

2. Aldred 1973, cat. 111; Arnold 1996, pp.
47–48, fig. 38.

139

140

141

142

143

144

141. Ostracon with practice hieroglyphs

Amarna, house J.53.1
Dynasty 18, reign of Akhenaten,
1353–1336 B.C.
Limestone
H. 19.3 cm, w. 38.2 cm, d. 5.8 cm
Excavations of the Deutsche Orient-
Gesellschaft, 1911, Ägyptisches Museum
und Papyrussammlung, Berlin, 24994

Akhenaten's building program at
Amarna surely demanded a significant
number of artisans as more and larger
structures were erected. Training of new
recruits must have been constant, judging from the many scraps of limestone,
known as ostraca, that were found primarily in temples[1] and palaces,[2] but also
in houses[3] throughout the site. They
were covered with beginners' often
imperfect attempts to reproduce a master's example of a royal profile (possibly
cat. 136), another body part, or a hieroglyph. In the present example, two
rather competent depictions of hands
(perhaps carved by the teacher) and several wobbly circles are partly overlaid
by the results of at least thirty attempts
to render a basket, the Egyptian word
for "all," which is read *neb*. For an
example of a master sculptor's model,
see cat. 52. REF

1. Pendlebury 1951, pl. LIX, 1–4, for example.

2. Ibid., pl. LXV, 6–8, 11–12, for example.

3. Peet and Woolley 1923, p. 36, for example.

142. Paintbrushes

Amarna
Dynasty 18, reign of Akhenaten,
1353–1336 B.C.
Vegetable fiber
H. 8.5 cm, w. 2.5 cm
H. 7 cm, w. 2 cm
Excavations of the Deutsche Orient-
Gesellschaft, Ägyptisches Museum und
Papyrussammlung, Berlin, 26510

143. Pigments

Amarna
Dynasty 18, reign of Akhenaten,
1353–1336 B.C.
Frit
H. 3.7–6.6 cm, w. 3.5–4.3 cm,
d. 2.5–3.2 cm
San Diego Museum of Man, San Diego,
14717, 14719–20, 14723

144. Metalworking mold

Amarna
Dynasty 18, reign of Akhenaten,
1353–1336 B.C.
Limestone
H. 3.7 cm, w. 15.5 cm, d. 11 cm
Excavations of the Deutsche Orient-
Gesellschaft, Ägyptisches Museum und
Papyrussammlung, Berlin, 21867

Amarna was a rich and invigorating
environment for artisans, as evidenced
by the abundance of raw materials and
tools found there. Excavators have
recovered metalworking molds, brushes
made of bound vegetable fiber,[1] and
clumps of pigment in the form of frit, a
solid silica-lime-ash mixture with miner-
al-oxide colorants, formed by heating.

Brushes at Amarna were used for
cleaning as well as for the application
of gypsum (whitewashing) and ground
frit. The pigments, found in the Central
City and the Workmen's Village, included blue, turquoise, green, yellow, red,
and black.[2] An analysis of their distribution revealed a close relationship
between raw materials and decorated
wall surfaces in chapels, houses, and
tombs.[3] Preparing the frit for painting
involved grinding it and adding a medium such as egg white or gelatin.
Paintings in ancient Egypt were of the
tempera (water-based) variety. YJM

1. For a description of brushes from the Workmen's Village, see Wendrich 1989, pp. 194–97.

2. Weatherhead and Buckley 1989, p. 202.

3. The analysis was conducted on distribution
patterns in the Workmen's Village and the indus-
trial area in the Central City. See Weatherhead
1995, pp. 384–98.

145. Relief of female musicians

Amarna, found at Hermopolis
Dynasty 18, reign of Akhenaten,
1353–1336 B.C.
Limestone
H. 22.6 cm, w. 53.1 cm, d. 3.2 cm
Gift of Norbert Schimmel, 1985, The
Metropolitan Museum of Art, New York,
1985.328.12

This group of five female musicians
shown in raised relief is part of a larger
scene in sunk relief that could have represented the royal family. The musicians
are playing a harp, lutes (shown with
their plectrums), and a lyre. A woman
without an instrument, fourth from the
right, is usually described as a singer or
a pipe player.[1] The elegant, elongated
bodies with heavy hips and slightly
bulging bellies are softly, sensuously
modeled in the late Amarna manner.
The uneven intervals between the figures and the expressionistic rendering of
long, curved fingers seem to correspond
to a musical rhythm. The musicians
look nude, but they wore light, pleated
dresses, which were painted over the
bodies. It has been suggested that palace
music, besides giving pleasure, was considered a form of offering to the Aten.[2]
EP

1. Aldred 1973, cat. 74; Catharine Roehrig in
Metropolitan Museum of Art 1992, p. 28;
Cooney 1965, cat. 42; John D. Cooney in
Muscarella 1974, cat. 253; Roeder 1969, p. 404,
pl. 171.

2. Manniche 1991b, pp. 62–65.

145

148. Food preparation

Amarna, the Great Palace
Dynasty 18, reign of Akhenaten,
1353–1336 B.C.
Sandstone (?)
H. 22 cm, w. 36 cm, d. 11 cm
The Visitors of the Ashmolean Museum,
Oxford, 1893.1–41 (169)

Among the glimpses of daily life recorded on Akhenaten's relief blocks are a
wide range of pastoral and household
scenes. In cat. 146, two men—or does
the earring on the right-hand figure
indicate a female?—attend to cows;
note especially the expressive bovine
face, and the mouth tether, presumably
to aid in force-feeding.[1] Cat. 147 shows
a grazing long-horned goat and a bald-
ing, bearded herdsman with protruding
belly, carrying a staff and a stick with a
jar appended. Background trees, placed
far above the ground line, liberate the
scene from any canonical rigidity. The
raised groove at the far right identifies
the relief as a corner block.[2] Cat. 148
preserves two individuals, one seated,
the other crouched over a wide bowl,
engaged in the preparation of foods that
are possibly destined for Pharaoh's
table.[3] PDM

1. For previous publication of the relief, see
Cooney 1965, cat. 39.

2. For previous publication of the relief, see
Aldred 1973, cat. 72.

3. For previous publication of the relief, see
Petrie 1894, p. 11, pl. XI, 9

146. Force-feeding a cow

Amarna, probably found at Hermopolis
Dynasty 18, reign of Akhenaten,
1353–1336 B.C.
Limestone
H. 22.8 cm, w. 52 cm, d. 35 cm
Charles Amos Cummings Bequest Fund,
Museum of Fine Arts, Boston, 63.960

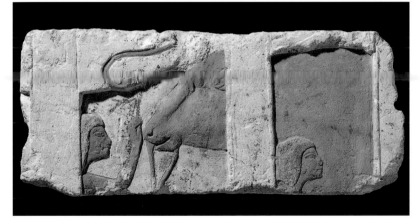

147. Herdsman with a goat

Probably from Amarna
Dynasty 18, reign of Akhenaten,
1353–1336 B.C.
Limestone
H. 22.4 cm, 45.1 cm, d. 6.1 (without
raised ridge)
Gift of the Ernest Erickson Foundation,
Brooklyn Museum of Art, New York,
86.226.30

146

147

148

149

150

to make it brittle. Reheating the bronze—annealing— would allow it to be hammered again.

The trapeziform ax appeared in the Second Intermediate Period and was popular throughout the New Kingdom.[1] It consisted of a tapering, rectangular blade with two tangs to attach it to a wooden handle. The tanged edge would be set in a groove in a wooden handle and lashed with wet leather thongs. The thongs were woven together, and when dry they would hold the blade fast. This type of ax appears to have had a variety of uses, from woodworking to warfare.

The adz was another important woodworking tool. With leather lashings, the blade was tied to the wooden handle at an acute angle. Adz blades have been recovered in a range of sizes, indicating that the ancient carpenter would have had a wide selection to work with for planing, shaping, or joining wood. PL.

149. Seated man eating

Possibly from Amarna
Dynasty 18, reign of Akhenaten,
1353–1336 B.C.
Limestone
H. 16.4 cm, w. 10.5 cm, d. 4.4 cm
Given by R. A. Gayer-Anderson, lent by the Syndics of the Fitzwilliam Museum, Cambridge, EGA.2302.1943

150. Houses on a canal

Amarna, found at Hermopolis
Dynasty 18, reign of Akhenaten,
1353–1336 B.C.
Limestone
H. 23.4 cm, w. 52.8 cm, d. about 4 cm
Charles Amos Cummings Bequest Fund,
Museum of Fine Arts, Boston, 63.962

The relief fragment of houses shows a flurry of activity, at a number of scales.[1] Below the zigzagging water lines at the top, three women rejoice at the far left; perhaps the king's flotilla is passing by. Most of the relief is taken up by two houses, each with a central courtyard. The man in the left house is probably tending a brazier; the room "above" him contains beer vessels and foodstuffs on low latticework tables. To the right, a staircase leads up to the roof, where the mysterious object at the upper left may represent a pigeon trap. The house on the right shows a bedroom, with bed, mattress, headrest, and even a pair of sandals on the wall. More storage vessels appear in the other rooms, and the woman at the lower left grinds

grain with a mortar and pestle. The activity of the woman bending over in the courtyard is lost.

The smaller relief fragment depicts a meal scene; the folds of the man's pleated kilt are particularly well carved. PDM

1. For previous publications of the relief, see Aldred 1973, cat. 64; Cooney 1965, pp. 74–75, cat. 47.

151. Ax blade

Amarna, house U.35.1
Dynasty 18, reign of Akhenaten,
1353–1336 B.C.
Bronze
H. 10.7 cm, w. 13.9 cm
Gift of the Egypt Exploration Society, San Diego Museum of Man, San Diego, 14985

152. Adz blade

Amarna, house U.35.24
Dynasty 18, reign of Akhenaten,
1353–1336 B.C.
Bronze
H. 5 cm, w. 19.5 cm d. 5 cm
Gift of the Egypt Exploration Society, Bolton Museum and Art Gallery, Bolton, England, 28.29.2

Metal tools were of great value in Egypt and, as the records from Deir el-Medina (Thebes) show, workmen were required to keep track of their whereabouts and condition. Tools like these were hammered or made in simple open-face molds. Hammering the bronze hardened the edge, but care had to be taken not

1. W. V. Davies 1987a, pp. 45ff.

2. For similar adzes found in the North Suburb, see Frankfort and Pendlebury 1933, pl. XXXIII, 4.

3. Three adzes were recovered from house U. 35.16 and .24. See Frankfort and Pendlebury 1933, pp. 36–37.

151

152

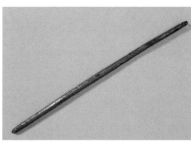

153

154

155

156

153. Double-eyed needle

Amarna
Dynasty 18, reign of Akhenaten,
1353–1336 B.C.
Bronze
Length 9.5 cm
Courtesy of Petrie Museum of Egyptian
Archaeology, University College London,
UC. 24277

154. Loom weights

Amarna
Dynasty 18, reign of Akhenaten,
1353–1336 B.C.
Limestone, modern stringing
H. 9 cm, w. 6 cm, d. 5 cm
Gift of the Egypt Exploration Society,
Bolton Museum and Art Gallery, Bolton,
England, 30.24.35

155. Spindle whorl

Amarna, Workmen's Village
Dynasty 18, reign of Akhenaten,
1353–1336 B.C.
Wood, modern thread
Length 21 cm
Gift of the Egypt Exploration Society,
Bolton Museum and Art Gallery, Bolton,
England, 15.22.7/1

156. Spinning bowl

Amarna
Dynasty 18, reign of Akhenaten,
1353–1336 B.C.
Limestone
H. 20.3 cm, diam. 35.3 cm
Gift of the Egypt Exploration Society, San
Diego Museum of Man, San Diego, 14879

The manufacture of textiles was widespread in the houses of Amarna.[1]
Objects used in various stages of production have been excavated throughout the domestic areas.[2] Spinning bowls
were used to feed out thread under tension during the process of spinning
fibers into thread. Most bowls were
made of pottery, either silt or marl, but
stone bowls were also used, perhaps
when more tension was required.[3] The
fibers were spun onto a spindle with a
whorl at the top. At Amarna, whorls of
limestone, alabaster, wood, clay, and
mud have been excavated.[4] The vertical
looms (fig. 105) on which the spun
threads were woven had loom weights[5]
attached to the warp threads. Needles
of bronze were also found to be widely
distributed at the site; cat. 153 is of particular interest because it has two eyes
at right angles to each other, possibly
for use in elaborate embroidery.[6]   SD'A

157

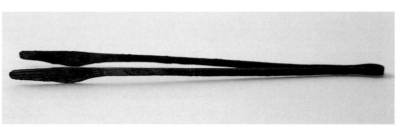

158

1. See the essay "Crafts and Industries at
Amarna."

2. Kemp 1997.

3. S. Allen 1997, p. 28.

4. Kemp 1997.

5. See Mace 1922; Barber 1991, pp. 91–113; but
see Vogelsang-Eastwood 1992, p. 35.

6. See Petrie 1917, pl. LXV, no. 87. For needles,
see also Vogelsang-Eastwood 1995, pp. 35–36.

157. Knife

Amarna
Dynasty 18, reign of Akhenaten,
1353–1336 B.C.
Bronze
H. 12 cm, w. 2.3 cm
Courtesy of Petrie Museum of Egyptian
Archaeology, University College London,
UC. 24384

158. Tongs with hands

Amarna, house T.36.2
Dynasty 18, reign of Akhenaten,
1353–1336 B.C.
Bronze
H. 3 cm, w. 19.5 cm, d. 1 cm
Bolton Museum and Art Gallery, Bolton,
England, 23.27.10

Knives of all sorts were used at
Amarna—for food preparation, leather-
working, textile production, medicine,
and defense. The broad-bladed knife

shown here is not unlike a modern spat-
ula, and was probably employed in
crafts. Its wide, flat tang was in all likelihood set into a wooden handle. A
number of similar knives were found at
Amarna with painting materials, which
suggests that they served as a type of
palette knife.[1]

Although tongs were used in metalworking, glass production, and faience
manufacture, the elaborate instrument
shown here most likely had a more specialized use. A similar pair of tongs
with human hands was found in the
"House of the King's Statue" (R.43.2)
at Amarna.[2] The cultic association and
the presence of the hieroglyphic *ka* sign
suggest these tongs were for ritual use.
They could have been employed to
place burning pellets of incense in a
brazier, perhaps in the private worship
of the Aten and the royal family by the
residents of the fine house in the North
Suburb where the tongs were found. PL

1. Pendlebury 1951, pl. LXXVI.

2. Kemp 1989, pp. 284–85.

159

159. Bull's-head weight

Amarna, house Q.46.33
Dynasty 18, reign of Akhenaten,
1353–1336 B.C.
Bronze
H. 2.5 cm, w. 3.7 cm
The Visitors of the Ashmolean Museum,
Oxford, 1924.70

160. Scales

Amarna, house U.36.41
Dynasty 18, reign of Akhenaten,
1353–1336 B.C.
Copper, wood
Length of balance arm 30 cm
Gift of the Egypt Exploration Society, The
National Museum of Science and Industry,
London, 1929-657

In an era without coinage, the standard
means of valuing commodities was by
weight. During the 18th Dynasty this
was measured in a unit called the *deben*
(approximately 91 grams, or a little
more than three ounces), which was
subdivided into tenths, called *qedet*, or
twelfths, called *shat*. Commodities were
traded according to a system of weight
and value equivalencies, and rations
were issued by weight. Naturally, sets
of scales and weights were essential articles for the palace, home, and market-
place. It is hardly surprising, therefore,
that scale pans and weights were recovered from a number of houses at
Amarna.[1] The weights were sometimes
made of stone or glass; others were cast
hollow in bronze and brought to precise
measure by means of lead fills. The hollow weights often took the form of animal heads or recumbent animals.[2] TK

1. Frankfort and Pendlebury 1933, p. 122 and
pl. 33.

2. Doll 1982b; Bailey 1997.

160

161. Branding iron

Probably from Amarna
Dynasty 18, reign of Akhenaten,
1353–1336 B.C.
Copper
Length 11 cm, w. 9 cm
Staatliche Sammlung Ägyptischer Kunst,
Munich, ÄS 5520

Judging by the frequency with which
branding irons were represented in the
tombs of Dynasty 18, their use must
have been widespread on large private
and institutional estates with sizable
cattle herds. The irons consisted of
twisted handles terminating in splayed
prongs that supported the brand marks.
This example (an "iron" made of copper) is one of two surviving from
Amarna. It consists of a pair of joined
metal rings, each containing a hieroglyphic sign, *ankh* ("life") or *nefer*
("good, beautiful"). These signs may
have signified "living and perfect" or,
as has been suggested, "perfect small
cattle"—or they may have been merely
good-luck symbols employed for easy
recognition.[1]

The other extant branding iron, in the
British Museum (58817), takes the form
of a pair of ox horns. TK

1. Susan K. Doll in Brovarski, Doll, and Freed
1982, cat. 19.

161

162. Yoke

Amarna
Dynasty 18, reign of Akhenaten,
1353–1336 B.C.
Wood, plant fiber
H. 19.5 cm, w. 19.5 cm, d. 4 cm
Gift of the Egypt Exploration Society, San
Diego Museum of Man, San Diego, 14814

This wooden yoke would have been
strapped to the back of a donkey by
passing the rope behind the front legs.
It appears to have been made from the
crook of a tree for added strength.
Green staining at one of the notched
ends may have been from a bronze handle or ring. The yoke could have been
used to help control the animal when it
was ridden or to help load it with bur-
dens. The donkey is extremely adapt-
able and was used by the Egyptians
(who had no camels at the time) for
crossing the desert.[1] Donkeys would
have been the principal means of overland transport for bringing goods into
the city and moving around town.
Horses were reserved for military functions and official pageantry. PL

1. Borowski 1998, pp. 90–99.

162

163

164

163. Window grille

Amarna, Central City
Dynasty 18, reign of Akhenaten,
1353–1336 B.C.
Limestone
H. 81 cm, w. 88 cm, d. 15 cm
The Visitors of the Ashmolean Museum,
Oxford, 1893.1-41 (102)

164. Oil lamp

Amarna, house Q.47.4
Dynasty 18, reign of Akhenaten,
1353–1336 B.C.
Ceramic
H. 6 cm, w. 13 cm, d. 11 cm
Ägyptisches Museum und
Papyrussammlung, Berlin, 22110

Window grilles were made of stone,[1]
wood, or even mud-plastered reeds.
They served to keep out birds, bats, and
perhaps unwanted visitors, as well as
the full glare of the sun. At the same
time they allowed some light to filter in
and hot air to escape (windows were
usually set high in the wall so that heat

would exit easily). This stone grille was
finished only on the outside, where it
could be seen by passersby. The faceting
would have let in more light while still
offering the protection of narrowed
openings. The lintel was apparently
arched to relieve some of the weight of
the wall and roof on the grille.

Lamps used in New Kingdom Egypt
tended to be shallow pottery bowls
largely indistinguishable from the bowls
used for food.[2] The wick was floated in
the center or draped over the side, and
the pool of oil in the vessel would have
done double duty as fuel and reflector.
This deep, thick-walled vessel differs
from most lamps, but shows traces of
burning on the rim and may have
served less as a light than as a source of
flame for a craftsman. PL

1. In Amarna house P.46.11, excavators found
fragments of four stone grilles. See Peet and
Woolley 1923, p. 32, pl. VI.

2. Petrie 1894, p. 137, pl. XLVI (type IV).

165. Latrine seat

Amarna, house T.35.22
Dynasty 18, reign of Akhenaten,
1353–1336 B.C.
Limestone
H. 53 cm, w. 40 cm, d. 10 cm
Egyptian Museum, Cairo, JE 55520

Many of the houses at Amarna had a
bathroom, which was generally part of
the "master bedroom" suite.[1] There was
an area for bathing, where jars of water
would be poured over an individual
who stood on a stone slab or basin. An
adjoining space contained a latrine consisting of a seat, sometimes supported
by a brick structure, and a jar filled
with sand, placed below. Several types
of latrine seat were found at Amarna,
manufactured of stone, wood, or plastered brick. This limestone example,[2]
with contoured surface and keyhole-
shaped opening, was found in a house
in the North Suburb. SD'A

1. For a general discussion of these rooms and
their furnishings, see Honigsberg 1940.

2. Kendall 1982; Frankfort and Pendlebury
1933, p. 47, pl. XLII, 3; Pendlebury 1931, pl.
LXXI, 2.

165

166. Three-legged stool

Amarna
Dynasty 18, reign of Akhenaten,
1353–1336 B.C.
Limestone
H. 16 cm, w. 39.5 cm, d. 27 cm
Gift of the Egypt Exploration Society, San
Diego Museum of Man, San Diego, 14866

167. Headrest

Amarna, house U.36.46
Dynasty 18, reign of Akhenaten,
1353–1336 B.C.
Limestone
H. 14.7 cm, w. 24.1 cm, d. 6.9 cm
Gift of the Egypt Exploration Society, San
Diego Museum of Man, San Diego, 14878

168. Lattice stool

Amarna
Dynasty 18, reign of Akhenaten,
1353–1336 B.C.
Wood
H. 30.5 cm, w. 29 cm, d. 27.5 cm
Gift of the Egypt Exploration Society, San
Diego Museum of Man, San Diego, 14858

The dry Egyptian climate has preserved
a wealth of ancient furniture, from the
simplest stone and wooden stools to the
most ornately gilded and inlaid thrones
from the tomb of Tutankhamen. The
assemblage here clearly derives from the
homes of the less affluent at Amarna.
Both the simple headrest and the three-
legged stool are carved from single
blocks of limestone; the minimal height
of the stool posed no problem for the
Egyptians, who were comfortable with
crouching on or near the ground. The
more elaborate wooden stool shows a
common latticework pattern and holes
pierced through the concave seat to take
some sort of woven "upholstery."
Mortise and tenon joints hold the pieces
together, accompanied by a number of
pegs. PDM

167

166

168

169

170. Statuette of a king

Amarna, house Q.44.1, room 8
Dynasty 18, reign of Akhenaten,
1353–1336 B.C.
Limestone
H. 21.9 cm, w. 4.8 cm, d. 4.4 cm
Gift of the Egypt Exploration Society,
Brooklyn Museum of Art, New York,
29.34

The king wears the blue crown with a
uraeus, a broadcollar necklace, and a
pleated kilt. The back pillar is uninscribed. In a pose relatively unusual for
sculptures of kings, he is shown with
his feet together and his arms at his
sides. The feet and base are modern
restorations. The head was broken off
and seems to have been reattached in
antiquity.[1]

The king has sensuous, drooping lips,
a heavy jaw, breasts, a protruding stomach, heavy hips and buttocks, thick
thighs, and thin calves. Carved in late
Amarna style, these features could indicate that the sculpture depicts
Akhenaten,[2] although it is possible that
it was an image of Smenkhkara or
Tutankhamen.[3] Whoever the king, the
figure was probably venerated in a
household shrine, where it could act as
an intermediary with the Aten. RAF

170

1. Aldred 1973, cats. 52 and 96; Bojana Mosjov
in N. Thomas 1995, cat. 11.

2. For instance, Aldred 1973, cat. 96; Fazzini
1975, cat. 64; Mosjov in N. Thomas 1995, cat.
11; and Robins 1997a, p. 156.

3. For instance, Jürgen Settgast in Karig and
Zauzich 1976, cat. 37; Roland Tefnin in De
Meulenaere 1976, cat. 37; and Brooklyn
Museum of Art 1993, fig. 3.

169. Stela featuring Amenhotep III and Queen Tiye

Amarna, house R.44.2 (house of
Panehesy)
Dynasty 18, reign of Akhenaten,
1353–1336 B.C.
Limestone
H. 32.5 cm; w. 30 cm, d. 5 cm
Gift of the Egypt Exploration Society,
1924, Trustees of the British Museum,
London, EA 57399

This stela from a domestic shrine,
capped by a cavetto cornice and frieze
of uraei, depicts Amenhotep III and
Tiye seated on draped thrones before
offering tables heaped with food and
floral decorations. The scene is framed
by elaborate bouquets and a frieze of
grapes, all beneath the beneficent rays
of the Aten.

The king slumps in his chair, his stomach distended, his breast like that of a
woman; he wears a long pleated and
fringed gown and the blue crown. A
three-dimensional representation identical in physique and dress has been identified as Amenhotep III as fertility god.[1]
The king has his hand on his wife's
shoulder.

In the inscription, the king's prenomen, Nebmaatra, has been written
twice to avoid mention of Amen, proscribed since year 5 of the reign of
Akhenaten.[2] The Aten's name appears in
its later form, which does not occur
before year 9.[3] For some scholars these
facts have provided further evidence of
a coregency of Amenhotep III and
Akhen-aten.[4] For others, however, they
suggest only that there was a posthu-
mous cult of Amenhotep III at Amarna.[5]
CA

1. Betsy M. Bryan in Kozloff and Bryan 1992, p.
204.

2. D. Redford 1984, pp. 175–76.

3. Ibid., p. 186.

4. D. Redford 1967, pp. 99-102.

5. Bryan in Kozloff and Bryan 1992, p. 214.

171. Clasped hands from a composite sculpture

Amarna, house P.49.6
Dynasty 18, reign of Akhenaten,
1353–1336 B.C.
Quartzite
Right hand: length 9.2 cm, w. 3.4 cm
Left hand: length 8.4 cm, w. 3.6 cm
Depth 3.2 cm
Ägyptisches Museum und
Papyrussammlung, Berlin, 20494

In family-group sculptures, the holding
of hands is a means of defining the relationship. These finely carved light-
brown quartzite hands from two figures
derive from a half-life-size, possibly
composite, sculpture.[1] The smaller left
hand gently holds the right, whose nail
beds are detailed and cut away to provide space for inlays. The left hand may
have come from a princess or a royal
woman,[2] and the right from the king,
the queen, or an elder daughter. YJM

1. The hands are from the Ipu studio, South
Suburb. Borchardt and Ricke 1980, pp. 266–67.

2. Aldred 1973, cat. 87.

171

172. Seated man in the Amarna style

Amarna, house T.35.4
Dynasty 18, reign of Akhenaten,
1353–1336 B.C.
Limestone
H. 18.4 cm, w. 11 cm, d. 6 cm
Egyptian Museum, Cairo, JE 53249

173. Seated man in the pre-Amarna style

Amarna, northern buildings
Dynasty 18, reign of Akhenaten,
1353–1336 B.C.
Limestone
H. 8.9 cm, w. (at seat) 2.7 cm, d. (of seat)
5.7 cm
Gift of the Egypt Exploration Society,
Brooklyn Museum, New York, 29.1310

Free-standing private statuary was exceedingly rare at Amarna.[1] Whatever exists is well under life-size[2] and appears to come from domestic contexts, perhaps even household shrines.[3] The larger of these two nonroyal statuettes shows a man with the elongated facial features, sinewy neck, pronounced collar bones, full breasts, and protruding belly that are hallmarks of the Amarna Period. The figure sits slightly forward in a relaxed pose on a high-back chair of the type common in the New Kingdom.[4] In contrast, the style of the smaller statuette harks back to an earlier era. Here the man sits stiffly upright on a plain cubic chair known since the Old Kingdom, and neither his facial features nor his body display Amarna's eccentricities. Nevertheless, the fact that he was found in Amarna and, like the larger statuette, clasps a lotus bud to his breast in a manner depicted only there,[5] leaves little doubt that he, too, is the product of an Amarna artisan. REF

1. Vandier 1958, p. 518.

2. Excepting the heads from the Thutmose studio, which were not intended as complete sculptures.

3. Frankfort and Pendlebury 1933, p. 43, pl. XXXVII.

4. Peter Der Manuelian in Brovarski, Doll, and Freed 1982, cat. 37.

5. Riefstahl 1951, p. 73.

174

174. Two men and a boy

Possibly from Gebelein
Dynasty 18, reign of Akhenaten,
1353–1336 B.C.
Limestone
H. 17 cm, w. 12.5 cm
Rogers Fund, 1911, The Metropolitan Museum of Art, New York, 11.150.21

Two men and a boy form a family group united by a slab that serves as back pillar for all three. This uninscribed group has frequently been described as three generations of male relatives.[1] However, a suggestion that it represents the same person at different ages cannot be excluded. The general composition of the group recalls both Old and Middle Kingdom prototypes, but the gestures were inspired by the small-scale representations of the royal family placed in shrines in private houses and worshipped as household gods.[2] Few Amarna private statues are known,[3] and since all of them were found in private houses along with royal statuettes, they may have been placed in domestic shrines in the way that private statues in Egypt had traditionally been donated to the temples. If

found in Gebelein, the statue might have been taken there by a family leaving Amarna. The style of the group suggests the late period of Amarna art. EP

1. Hayes 1959, p. 313, fig. 194; Aldred 1973, cat. 110; Aldred 1952, pp. 85–86, fig. 136; Vandier 1958, p. 445, pl. CXLVI; Hornemann 1966, no. 1403; Winlock 1937, fig. 15.

2. Aldred 1973, cat. 110.

3. Frankfort and Pendlebury 1933, pl. XXXVII.

172

173

175

175. Private stela

Amarna, outside walls of house R.44.2
Dynasty 18, reign of Akhenaten,
1353–1336 B.C.
Limestone
H. 19.7 cm, w. 17.2 cm, d. 4.9 cm
Gift of the Egypt Exploration Society, San
Diego Museum of Man, San Diego, 14881

In addition to the prominent officials
who enjoyed direct access to the king,
there were mid- and lower-level bureaucrats at Akhenaten's capital who remain
largely anonymous to us. One exception
is provided by this touching votive stela
from a house near the Great Temple. It
was packed in linen cloth prior to being
buried; this doubtless helped preserve
its colors. Two men, named Menena
and Yaya, sit on fairly elaborate
"turned leg" latticework stools, enjoy-
ing the attentions of two women,
named Tashety and Mery. Wine is being
poured and sipped, indicating the general theme of "making holiday." Aside
from the fine furniture and the elegant
flowing robes and the scented-ointment
cones on the heads of the women, no
information is provided about these
individuals' positions at Amarna, or
even their relationship to one another.[1]
PDM

1. For previous publications, see Aldred 1973,
cat. 141.

176. Monkey eating fruit

Amarna
Dynasty 18, reign of Akhenaten,
1353–1336 B.C.
Limestone
H. 7 cm, w. 6.5 cm, d. 0.9 cm
Courtesy of Petrie Museum of Egyptian
Archaeology, University College London,
UC. 025

177. Monkeys grooming

Amarna, house U.35.8
Dynasty 18, reign of Akhenaten,
1353–1336 B.C.
Limestone
H. 5.9 cm, w. 4.1 cm, d. 1.7 cm
Gift of the Egypt Exploration Society, San
Diego Museum of Man, San Diego, 14983

Painted-limestone statuettes depicting
men, women, and children engaged in
activities of daily life were popular during the Middle Kingdom (1980–1630
B.C.). Several of these small sculptures
were recovered from tombs where they
may have functioned as servant figures.[1]
Others, including monkey groups paro-
dying human behavior, appear more
playful and may have served as toys.[2]
   Monkey statuettes, some of which are
lively, complex compositions featuring
acrobats, boating crews, musicians, and
charioteers, were favorite novelty items
in Amarna homes.[3] Most common were
groups of two to three animals shown
eating, grooming, or tending the
young.[4] Sometimes the monkeys tender-
ly embrace—a gesture reminiscent of
the intimacy found in royal-family
sculpture and relief.
   These small, realistically rendered
sculptures are carved on both sides. The
majority incorporate a base for standing, while a few have borings near the
base. YJM

1. Reisner 1920, pp. 117–18, pl. XV.

2. Hayes 1953, p. 222, fig. 138.

3. Frankfort and Pendlebury 1933, p. 99. Similar
monkey statuettes were found at Medinet el-
Gurob. See Brunton and Engelbach 1927, pl.
XXVI.

4. Samson 1972, pp. 37–40.

176

177

178. Woman on a bed

Amarna, house N.49
Dynasty 18, reign of Akhenaten,
1353–1336 B.C.
Ceramic
Length 16.5 cm (bed), 12.5 cm (figure)
Gift of the Egypt Exploration Society,
Cincinnati Art Museum, Cincinnati,
1921.280-1

179. Woman and boy adoring Taweret

Amarna, house N.49.21
Dynasty 18, reign of Akhenaten,
1353–1336 B.C.
Limestone
H. 15.2 cm, w. 12.7 cm
Gift of the Egypt Exploration Society,
Cincinnati Art Museum, Cincinnati,
1921.279

The domestic deities that had been worshipped for centuries were neither
restricted nor abandoned in Amarna.
Images of household gods and goddesses continued to be worn as protective
amulets and worshipped at shrines in
the home. The protection of women
and children was a focal point of the
domestic religion, particularly with
regard to fertility, pregnancy, childbirth,
and early childhood. The terracotta
woman on a bed (separate pieces)
would likely have been used to help
ensure conception.[1] Similar figures of
women on beds include an image of a
child at the woman's side, frequently
nursing. Those figures would certainly
dispel theories that this type of female
image was intended as a concubine figure.[2] The stela of a woman and boy
worshipping Taweret,[3] the pregnant hippopotamus goddess, might indicate that
a child had been successfully born.
Cats. 178 and 179 were found together
in an Amarna house in a cabinet under
a staircase.[4] JLH

1. Anne K. Capel in Capel and Markoe 1996,
cat. 16.

2. Numerous parallels of women on beds include
an image of a child, incised, painted, or carved in
relief, always on the woman's left side, frequently
nursing. The Museum of Fine Arts, Boston,
posssesses seven such figures with children:
72.1616–72.1620; 03.1614; and 13.3834 Sheikh
Farag Tomb 189. Also see E 25.778 in the
Peabody Essex Museum, Salem, Massachusetts.
For other images, see Feucht 1995, p. 172, nn.
833–36.

3. Capel in Capel and Markoe 1996, cat. 16.

4. Peet and Woolley 1923, pp. 24–25, pls. XXII,
XIX; Capel in Capel and Markoe 1996, cat. 16.

178, 179

180. The goddess Taweret

Amarna, house O.49.1
Dynasty 18, reign of Akhenaten,
1353–1336 B.C.
Faience
H. 11 cm
Excavations of the Deutsche Orient-
Gesellschaft, 1911, Ägyptisches Museum
und Papyrussammlung, Berlin, 22272

181. The god Bes

Possibly from Amarna
Dynasty 18, reign of Akhenaten,
1353–1336 B.C.
Faience
H. 8.5 cm, w. 4 cm, d. 4 cm
Purchase 1912, Ägyptisches Museum und
Papyrussammlung, Berlin, 20484

182. Uraeus

Amarna, house P.48.2
Dynasty 18, reign of Akhenaten,
1353–1336 B.C.
Ceramic
H. 17.5 cm, w. 9.5 cm, d. 14 cm
Excavations of the Deutsche Orient-
Gesellschaft, 1912, Ägyptisches Museum
und Papyrussammlung, Berlin, 28759

Statuettes and stelae of traditional gods
have been found in many houses in
Amarna. Taweret,[1] in the shape of a
pregnant hippopotamus with human
arms and breasts and the legs of a lion,
was protector of pregnancy. Bes,[2] a
dwarf with the anthropomorphized gri-
mace of a lion, was responsible for
mother and child. The uraeus snake[3]
was an apotropaic deity, intended to
ward off the evil eye. All remained
indispensable popular divinities beside
the Aten. DW

1. Ägyptisches Museum 1967, cat. 893a.

2. Arielle P. Kozloff in Kozloff and Bryan 1992,
pp. 226–27.

3. Borchardt and Ricke 1980, p. 220, nos. 4, 47.

180

181

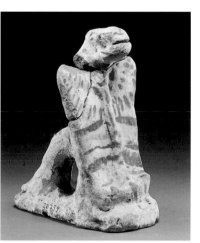

182

183. Unfinished statuette of a ram representing Amen

Amarna, house P.47.24
Dynasty 18, reign of Akhenaten,
1353–1336 B.C.
Limestone
H. 12 cm, w. 17 cm, d. 6.5 cm
Excavations of the Deutsche Orient-
Gesellschaft, Ägyptisches Museum und
Papyrussammlung, Berlin, 22253

The elite religion of the Aten was not
available to the average citizen, and the
Egyptians, even at Amarna, continued
their own personal worship. Prayers
written to Amen found in the Workmen's Village at Amarna[1] and images
from Amarna of Amen's sacred animal,
the ram,[2] show that even this cult was
present on some level. This unfinished
sculpture was no doubt intended as a
votive object. Perhaps these references
to Amen date to early in Akhenaten's
reign, when the worship of other gods
was not strictly prohibited. Later, sometime between years 8 and 12, Akhenaten became less tolerant and officially
banned the deities of the older religion.[3]
JLH

1. Grimal 1992, p. 230.

2. See, for example, a relief image of a ram from
Amarna in the Bolton Museum and Art Gallery,
Bolton, England, 22/139.

3. J. Allen 1996, p. 4.

183

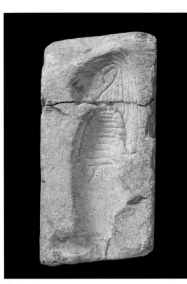

184

185

184. Mold with an image of the god Hapi

Amarna
Dynasty 18, reign of Akhenaten,
1353–1336 B.C.
Limestone
H. 7 cm, w. 3.6 cm, d. 2.1 cm
Courtesy of Petrie Museum of Egyptian Archaeology, University College London, UC. 24267

185. Statuette of Thoth and a Scribe

Amarna, house 0.47.16(a)
Dynasty 18, reign of Akhenaten,
1353–1336 B.C.
Steatite, limestone base
H. 14 cm, w. 6.8 cm, d. 11.2 cm
Egyptian Museum, Cairo, JE 59291

Ordinary people in Amarna had little choice but to continue observing the old funerary customs, which gave them the possibility of rebirth and eternal life. The Four Sons of Horus, Hapi among them, were an integral part of their Osirian religious beliefs. Cat. 184 would have been used to produce a flat image of the human-headed Hapi, customarily placed among the funerary trappings.

There was apparently no prohibition against worship of the minor deities. One of these was Thoth,[1] god of the moon, wisdom, and writing. Numerous two- and three-dimensional images of Thoth exist at Amarna, mostly in the form of a baboon. Statuettes of a scribe seated before Thoth in this form were extremely popular during the reign of Amenhotep III[2] and, as demonstrated by cat. 185,[3] a finely carved example, the type continued into the reign of Akhenaten. Since it was found in an Amarna house, this statuette was no doubt a votive piece from a domestic shrine. Unfortunately, it is uninscribed and cannot tell us about its owner. JLH

---

1. Hornung 1995, p. 97.

2. Peck 1978, p. 73; Betsy M. Bryan in Kozloff and Bryan 1992, cat. 41.

3. Adelheid Shunnar in Müller and Settgast 1976, cat. 45, which cites the findspot incorrectly as house O.46; Terrace and Fischer 1970, cat. 29.

4. Peck 1978, p. 73 notes that Ägyptisches Museum, Berlin, 22621, a scribe separated from its grouping, was excavated in house O.47.7. It is unusual to find two such objects in proximity.

186

186. Ear stela

Amarna
Dynasty 18, reign of Akhenaten,
1353–1336 B.C.
Faience
H. 4.5 cm, w. 3.1 cm, d. 1.6 cm
Courtesy of Petrie Museum of Egyptian Archaeology, University College London, UC. 722

This faience plaque in the shape of a human ear is impressed on both sides with images of ears. On the front there are ten ears in three rows divided by two register lines; the reverse has two ears.[1] New Kingdom plaques of faience in the shape of ears are known to be votive rather than amuletic.[2] Some votive plaques and stelae not in the shape of ears are also adorned with one or more human ears. These ear plaques or stelae seem to represent the ears of a god, into which the pious Egyptian could speak his prayers directly. Some were left as temple offerings.[3] Smaller ones are known to be pierced for suspension and were worn or carried by the devout.[4] The small size of this piece suggests that it could easily be carried or held. Another small personal ear stela pierced for suspension was found in a house in Amarna.[5] JLH

---

1. Pendlebury 1951, p. 229 and pl. CVIII.

2. Andrews 1994, p. 69.

3. Many derive from temple deposits: those with images of Ptah, from the Great Temple of Ptah in Memphis (Hayes 1959, p. 274); Hathor cows, from Deir el-Bahari (Hayes 1959, pp. 173–74); and the popular sphinx stela found at Giza (Lynn Holden in Brovarski, Doll, and Freed 1982, cat. 416).

4. Hayes 1959, pp. 173–74.

5. Frankfort and Pendlebury 1933, p. 52 and pl. XXXV, 5: limestone with ears painted in red and black pigment, about 9.5 by 5 cms. I would like to thank Yvonne Markowitz for this reference.

187. Votive bowl

Amarna
Dynasty 18, reign of Akhenaten,
1353–1336 B.C.
Ceramic
H. 10 cm, diam. 24 cm
Gift of the Egypt Exploration Fund through Peter Lacovara, Museum of Fine Arts, Boston, 1997.275

A number of these pottery bowls, with a distinctive sinusoidal (repeating sine curve) rim and the plastic figure of a snake in the bottom, were found in or near the Workmen's Village and chapels at Amarna.[1] The bowls are associated with the cobra-deity Renenutet, the goddess of the harvest,[2] and show that some of the more popular gods continued to be worshipped in the Aten's sacred city. PL

---

1. Kemp 1981, pp. 14–16.

2. Bomann 1991, p. 59.

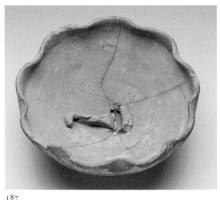

187

188. Hair ball

Amarna
Dynasty 18, reign of Akhenaten,
1353–1336 B.C.
Clay, hair
Diam. 4–4.5 cm each
The Board of Trustees of National
Museum & Galleries on Merseyside
(Liverpool Museum), Liverpool, 56.21.615

189. Hair ball

Amarna
Dynasty 18, reign of Akhenaten,
1353–1336 B.C.
Clay, hair
Diam. about 4.5 cm
The Board of Trustees of National
Museum & Galleries on Merseyside
(Liverpool Museum), Liverpool, 56.21.673

190. Model coffin with figure

Amarna
Dynasty 18, reign of Akhenaten,
1353–1336 B.C.
Clay
H. 3.9 cm, w. 9 cm, d. 6 cm
The Board of Trustees of National
Museum & Galleries on Merseyside
(Liverpool Museum), Liverpool,
56.21.893

188

189

190

Among the items recovered from private dwellings at Amarna were summarily made fetishes of clay. Some are clearly female fecundity figures, whereas others, rectangular in shape and decorated with impressed dots, only allude to the human form. More mysterious are clay balls containing clumps of hair that have been identified as human.[1] A number of these balls bear impressions on the surface made when the clay was still moist and plastic. These are typically hieroglyphic signs and symbols within ovals, with protective and/or rejuvenative meanings.

Another item from Amarna that falls into the folk-religion category is this clay model coffin with human figure. Although Flinders Petrie suggested that similar mud constructions were toys crafted by children,[2] it is likely that they, too, served a magical role. YJM

1. T. Eric Peet found a group of incised mud balls in an Old Kingdom burial context at Abydos. The cores of these balls are described as consisting of compacted vegetable fiber. The surface impressions, made with a reticulated seal, appear to be signs with unknown meanings. For a discussion of these items, see Peet 1915, pp. 8–9. For a description of two clay balls in the Manchester Museum that contain tufts of reddish-brown hair, see Crompton 1916, p. 128. For the symbolic and talismanic properties of hair, see Ritner 1993, pp. 210, 224–25.

2. Petrie 1927, p. 61, pl. LIII.

191

191. Fringed textile fragments

Amarna, Workmen's Village, no. 21/324
Dynasty 18, reign of Akhenaten,
1353–1336 B.C.
Linen
H. 29 cm, w. 19 cm, d. 0.2 cm
Gift of the Egypt Exploration Society,
1922, Bolton Museum and Art Gallery,
Bolton, England, 4.22.2.

This is undyed linen textile comprising one large fragment and three small detached fragments.[1] Woven in plain tabby weave, the cloth is fairly coarse and darkened by staining. The large fragment has a plain selvedge on one side and the warp threads at the bottom edge have been grouped and plaited to form a fringe There is an area of decoration or reinforcement where one undyed flax thread has been laid along the weft and couched down by stitching across the warps. There is no evidence that the selvedge was ever stitched as a plain seam, which would have been the case if this fragment had come from a bag tunic. It is perhaps from an item of household linen, such as a bedsheet, or a garment such as a shawl or sash. AT

1. Peet and Woolley 1923, p. 73.

192

192. Child's sandal

Amarna
Dynasty 18, reign of Akhenaten,
1353–1336 B.C.
Woven reed
Length 16.9 cm, w. 8.1 cm
Courtesy of Petrie Museum of Egyptian
Archaeology, University College London,
UC. 769

In the desert climate of Egypt, sandals were the preferred footwear.[1] Attached to the sole, which was shaped to the contours of the foot, was a strap running over the instep, with a thong that passed between the first two toes. Occasionally an ankle strap provided extra stability. Inexpensive pairs were manufactured of woven papyrus or rush, and more costly examples were made from leather. King Tutankhamen was buried with a variety of types,[2] ranging from simple, undecorated papyrus or rush to leather sandals ornamented with patterned beadwork or gold. His mummy was provided with sheet-gold sandals.

At Amarna, members of the royal family and their officials were represented in both relief and sculpture clad in sandals. Among the actual examples found in the excavations of the city[3] were sandals with wooden soles, which were for funerary use. Cat. 192 is a left-foot sandal with plaited sole. SD'A

1. See John McDonald in Brovarksi, Doll, and Freed 1982, cat. 201; John McDonald in A. Eggebrecht 1987; Green 1995–96.

2. Carter and Mace 1923, passim., pl. XXXIV; Reeves 1990a, pp. 155, 157.

3. Peet and Woolley 1923, pl. XX, 2.

193. Basket

Amarna
Dynasty 18, reign of Akhenaten,
1353–1336 B.C.
Vegetable fiber
H. 41.9 cm, w. 36.8 cm
Gift of the Egypt Exploration Society, San
Diego Museum of Man, San Diego, 14790

A popular domestic furnishing during the 18th Dynasty was the small, lidded basket. Used for storing food, ornaments, toiletries, and household goods, baskets were versatile containers of both practical and aesthetic value.[1]

Although several techniques were employed in ancient Egyptian basket manufacture, the coil method,[2] using native plants and fibers such as halfa grass, reed, and palm leaf, was the simplest and most widely used. It consists of a continuous coil of vegetable matter built up in successive revolutions and stitched with strips of palm leaf. The latter are cast over the coil and passed through the top of the underlying segment.[3] A coil-made lid, now missing, would have rested on an interior lip of this example. YJM

1. For a list of the varieties of personal belongings stored in small baskets during the New Kingdom, see Hayes 1959, p. 197.

2. The three main manufacturing techniques used in basketry were coiling, twining, and plaiting. For detailed definitions and examples from the Workmen's Village at Amarna, see Wendrich 1989, pp. 169–201.

3. McDonald 1982, p. 133.

194

194. Stirrup ring with a royal figure, possibly Akhenaten

Possibly from Amarna
Dynasty 18, reign of Akhenaten,
1353–1336 B.C.
Gold
Diam. of hoop 2.9 cm, w. of bezel 1.4 cm
The Trustees of the British Museum,
London, EA 32723

The ancient Egyptian stirrup ring is a type of finger ornament in which the bezel (central element) extends upward from the shoulders to form a signet. The latter, characterized by sunk-relief decoration in the form of symbols and/or text, derives from Middle Kingdom scarab rings that were occasionally used as seals.

By the New Kingdom, the amuletic properties of finger rings superseded any practical use. This is particularly evident at Amarna, where large numbers of mold-made faience rings with magical emblems were recovered by excavators. In addition, a new, honorific, role for the stirrup ring can be inferred from Amarna tomb scenes in which the king's favorites are rewarded with high-status goods, including various forms of jewelry.[1]

Images and cartouches of the royal couple are among the motifs found on the few gold stirrup rings that survive from the period.[2] In this example,[3] the royal figure, in all likelihood Akhenaten, is shown in profile, seated below a sun-disk with double uraei and above signs that translate, "Lord of the Two Lands," a standard kingly epithet. The king, who holds the feather of Truth, is flanked by an *ankh* and a feather associated with the god Shu. YJM

1. In his Amarna tomb, Ay and his wife are depicted standing beneath the Window of Appearances, where the royal family showers them with precious goods. Included are stirrup rings, *shebyu* collars, and vessels of precious metal. See N. de G. Davies 1903–8, vol. 6, pp. 21–22, pl. XXIX.

2. For a list of Amarna rings, see Wilkinson 1971, p. 129. For a fragment of a carnelian stirrup ring from the North Suburb (T.45, no. 30/44) with a seated, profile image of the king, see Frankfort and Pendlebury 1933, p. 46, pl. XL, 4.

3. For this and other rings of the period, see Andrews 1990, p. 165, pl. 148.

193

195

195. String of eye beads

Amarna, house N.51.3
Dynasty 18, reign of Akhenaten,
1353–1336 B.C.
Faience
Length 96 cm, w. of beads 2.5–3 cm
Ägyptisches Museum und
Papyrussammlung, Berlin, 21944

With the ban on traditional divinities
under Atenism, abstract amuletic forms
such as the *wedjat*, or sacred eye,
played a significant role in daily life at
Amarna. The popularity of this charm
is shown by the disproportionate number of faience ring bezels excavated at
the site that bear the eye motif.[1]

Although the power of the *wedjat*
referred historically to the magical
restoration of the injured eye of the fal-
con-god Horus, its protective and rejuvenative capacity was broadened over
time. The use of multiple eyes, either in
a series on a single object or as repeated
bead elements, compounded the amuletic effect.

Spherical eye beads of bichrome
faience first appear in Egypt during the
reign of Thutmose III (about 1479–
1425 B.C.) and may have been inspired
by stylized, hard-stone eye amulets from
western Asia.[3] The ancient Egyptians
would have interpreted these eye representations in the context of their own
beliefs—in essence, borrowing the form
but supplying the meaning.   YJM

1. Shaw 1984 pp. 124–25, fig. 9–1.

2. Eisen 1916, p. 3.

196. Bracelet fragment

Amarna, house N.48.1
Dynasty 18, reign of Akhenaten,
1353–1336 B.C.
Faience
H. 2.4 cm, w. 6.3 cm, d. 2.8 cm
Ägyptisches Museum und
Papyrussammlung, Berlin, 21900

197. Finger ring

Possibly from Amarna
Dynasty 18, reign of Akhenaten,
1353–1336 B.C.
Faience
H. 1 cm, w. 1.9 cm, d. 1.8 cm
Lent by the Syndics of the Fitzwilliam
Museum, Cambridge, EGA.6484.1943

198. Ear plugs

Amarna
Dynasty 18, reign of Akhenaten,
1353–1336 B.C.
Faience
H. 0.8 cm (1286), 1 cm (1287)
Courtesy of Petrie Museum of Egyptian
Archaeology, University College London,
UC. 1286, UC. 1287

Ornaments of multicolored faience were
popular items of adornment at Amarna.
Many of these decorations, such as the
bichrome faience bracelet fragment,
derive from precious-metal prototypes.[1]
In this case, a polished metal surface
has been replaced by a lively desert
landscape created by inlaying white
faience into a blue ground. The motifs—
stylized plants and antelope in various
states of activity—exemplify the Amarna penchant for the natural world.[2]

The white, blue, and red color scheme
used in the production of the mold-
made[3] finger ring and ear plugs illustrates the ability of faience to mimic
other materials.[4] The white, a substitute
for silver, was associated with the
moon, while the blue and red inlays,
used in lieu of lapis lazuli and carnelian,
were symbolic of the heavens and the
life-giving properties of blood. Faience
was also considered a magical material
its own right, a "dazzling" substance
with the capacity to rejuvenate.   YJM

196

197

198

1. The faience bracelet fragment may derive from
the *mesketu* bangle, a New Kingdom award
bestowed on civil servants. See Andrews 1990, p.
181–84, fig. 170.

2. For a detailed discussion of this fragment, see
Schoske, Kreissl, and Germer 1992, p. 69, no. 2.

3. For several rosette earring molds from
Amarna, see Petrie 1894, pl. XVIII.

4. For a similar ring, see Yvonne Markowitz and
Sheila Shear in Friedman 1998, cat. 105.

199

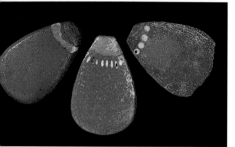

200

199. Lotus terminal with mold

Amarna
Dynasty 18, reign of Akhenaten,
1353–1336 B.C.
Faience
Mold: h. 5.2 cm, w. 5.5 cm, d. 1.9 cm
Lotus: h. 2.75 cm, w. 3.5 cm, d. 0.65 cm
Courtesy of Petrie Museum of Egyptian
Archaeology, University College London,
UC. 1713, UC. 1715

200. Petal inlays from a broad-collar

Amarna
Dynasty 18, reign of Akhenaten,
1353–1336 B.C.
Faience
H. 3.1 cm, w. 2 cm, d. 0.5 cm
H. 3.2 cm, w. 2.1 cm, d. 0.4 cm
H. 2.9 cm, w. 2.2 cm, d. 0.3 cm
Courtesy of Petrie Museum of Egyptian
Archaeology, University College London,
UC. 841, UC. 845, UC. 1589

The most popular neck ornament at
Amarna was the broadcollar (wesekh).
This multistrand adornment, based on
real garlands and worn by both sexes,
was often made of vibrantly colored
faience pendants in the form of fruits,
blossoms, and leaves.[1] The terminals, or
end pieces, of the necklace, commonly

in the shape of stylized blue lotus blossoms, were also made of polychrome
faience.[2] These elements were triangular
and pierced along the underside of the
broad, flat plane at the petal tips, where
the various strings were gathered to exit
the hole at the rounded apex.[3] Terminals, several of which were found by
Flinders Petrie, were made in reusable
open-face clay molds.[4]

Representations of *wesekh* collars in
statuary and relief were both painted
and enhanced by inlays of stone and
faience. Tear-drop-shaped petals of red
faience, graduated in size, would have
formed the bottom row of the ornament.[5] YJM

---

1. For a selection of the faience pendant forms,
see Frankfort and Pendlebury 1933, pl. XXVIII,
6; pl. XXIX, 5.

2. The body or background color of many
faience terminals was often selected to imitate the
precious metals, whereas the painted or inlaid
blossom elements were either naturalistically colored or meant to simulate semiprecious stones.

3. Yvonne Markowitz and Sheila Shear in
Friedman 1998, cat. 31.

4. For examples of both molds and terminals, see
Petrie 1894, pl. XIX.

5. Some of the red faience petal inlays recovered
by Petrie at Amarna were inlaid with white paste
at the tips—highlights suggestive of the precious-
metal horizontal bands found in sumptuous collars. See Petrie 1894, pl. XX, no. 503.

201

202

201. Ear studs

Amarna, Central City
Dynasty 18, reign of Akhenaten,
1353–1336 B.C.
Red glass
Diam. 2.5 cm, depth 2 cm
Courtesy of Petrie Museum of Egyptian
Archaeology, University College London,
UC. 22881

202. String of melon beads

Amarna
Dynasty 18, reign of Akhenaten,
1353–1336 B.C.
Glass
Length 12.7 cm
Gift of the Egypt Exploration Society,
Cincinnati Art Museum, Cincinnati,
1927.372

Glass ornaments were popular items of
adornment at Amarna. Many of the colors employed—yellow, white, red, blue,
turquoise, and green—simulated precious metals and semiprecious stones.
Materials had symbolic meaning in
ancient Egypt and were chosen for their
inherent properties, including color.
Glass, like faience, may have been considered magical because of the dramatic
transformation process that occurs during firing.[1] The dazzling, reflective surface would have had associations with
light and rebirth.

Beads[2] and ear ornaments were
worn by both sexes in ancient Egypt,
although kings are not depicted wearing
the latter. This is a curious convention,
since pharaohs are represented with sizable ear-lobe perforations, and several
New Kingdom royal mummies have
pierced ears. The number of elaborate
earrings found in Tutankhamen's tomb
is an indication of their popularity during the Amarna Period. YJM

---

1. For a discussion of the magical properties of
faience, see Patch 1998.

2. For an Amarna bead typology, see Frankfort
and Pendlebury 1933, pl. LI. For a selection of
faience and glass beads from Amarna, see Glenn
Markoe in Capel and Markoe 1996, cat. 27j-n.

203

204

203. Razor with handle

Amarna, no. 254.1928/29
Dynasty 18, reign of Akhenaten,
1353–1336 B.C.
Bronze
H. 13.5 cm, w. 15.5 cm, d. 1.5 cm
Gift of the Egypt Exploration Society,
Bolton Museum and Art Gallery, Bolton,
England, 28.29.4

204. Tweezers

Amarna, house Q.47.24
Dynasty 18, reign of Akhenaten,
1353–1336 B.C.
Bronze
Length 5 cm
Excavations of the Deutsche Orient-
Gesellschaft, 1913, Ägyptisches Museum
und Papyrussammlung, Berlin, 24699

To the ancient Egyptians, good personal hygiene was essential, and they employed razors for hair removal from the Predynastic Period onward.[1] In the New Kingdom, wealthier men and women kept their hair close-cropped and wore elaborate wigs for social occasions. The heads of priests were shaved. Men only rarely wore beards or mustaches. Razors of two different types were utilized during this period, and both types have been found at Amarna in domestic contexts; in one house, two razors wrapped in a piece of linen were found in the staircase.[2] The first type[3] has a simple scalpel shape. Cat. 203[4] is of the second, broader type, with a convex cutting edge opposite a tapered end. It was hafted onto a divided metal handle that was secured by rivets on both sides.

Tweezers were used as early as the Early Dynastic Period.[5] They took two forms, with rounded or pinched top, and may have served different functions, such as plucking hair or removing splinters.[6] Several pairs were found at Amarna.[7] SD'A

---

1. See W. V. Davies in Brovarski, Doll, and Freed 1982, pp. 189-91.

2. Frankfort and Pendlebury 1933, p. 16, pls. XXXII, 7 and XXXIV, 1. Cosmetic kits have also been found in 18th-Dynasty tombs; see Hayes 1959, p. 64.

3. See Glenn Markoe in Capel and Markoe 1996, cat. 21a; Patch 1990, cat. 33e; W. V. Davies in Brovarski, Doll, and Freed 1982, cat. 223; Hayes 1959, p. 64, fig. 33; Petrie 1917, p. 49, pls. LXII, LXIII.

4. See Patch 1990, cat. 33d; W. V. Davies in Brovarski, Doll, and Freed 1982, cats. 220-22; A. Thomas 1981, p. 65, pl. 21; Petrie 1917, pp. 49-50, pls. LX, LXI.

5. Petrie 1901, pl. XLIII, 15.

6. See Markoe 1996; Rita E. Freed in Brovarski, Doll, and Freed 1982, cat. 228; A. Thomas 1981, p. 66, pl. 21; Hayes 1959, p. 64, fig. 33; Petrie 1917, p. 51, pls. LXII, LIXV.

7. Pendlebury 1951, pls. LXXIX, 3, LXXII, 10; Frankfort and Pendlebury 1933, pls. XXXIV, 1, XLVII, 1; Peet and Woolley 1923, pp. 20, 23.

205. Hairpin with pomegranate-shaped terminal

Amarna
Dynasty 18, reign of Akhenaten, 1353–1336 B.C.
Wood
Length 10 cm
Gift of the Egypt Exploration Society, Cincinnati Art Museum, Cincinnati, 1921.299

206. Mirror with papyriform handle

Amarna, house U.35.17
Dynasty 18, reign of Akhenaten, 1353–1336 B.C.
Bronze, wood
H. 26.8 cm, diam. 13 cm (disk)
Gift of the Egypt Exploration Society, The Manchester Museum, University of Manchester, 8598

207. Spoon with papyrus-stalk handle

Amarna, house R.46.3
Dynasty 18, reign of Akhenaten, 1353–1336 B.C.
Bronze
H. 15.5 cm, w. 4.4 cm, d. 0.4 cm
Ägyptisches Museum und Papyrussammlung, Berlin, 22090

The mirror, hairpin and spoon found in the remains of Amarna houses are evidence of the time and attention that the Egyptians devoted to personal grooming. The bronze disk of the mirror would have been polished to a high shine. The elegant handle, representing a column shaped like a bundle of papyrus plants, has incised details that were once filled with blue pigment.[1]

The use of straight hairpins is known from Predynastic times. Ancient Egyptians used them in their elaborate coiffures, which were made up of wigs or their own hair embellished with false braids and curls. In the 18th Dynasty, upper-class women's hairstyles changed from one reign to the next, with the greatest range of styles in the Amarna Period.[2] This long, tapering wooden hairpin is topped with a carved pomegranate and, just below it, a series of incised chevron lines.[3] A similar hairpin is shown holding a lock of hair in a famous Middle Kingdom tomb scene of a hairdresser.[4]

205

206

This bronze spoon (cat. 207)[5] is one of two found in an Amarna house. Although the majority of spoons, made of wood or metal, were found in tombs, some derive from private houses and palaces.[6] They were commonly referred to as cosmetic or unguent spoons, but may also have had a ritual use in temple ceremonies. JLH and SD'A

---

1. Christine Lilyquist in Brovarski, Doll, and Freed 1982, cat. 217. For another Amarna mirror, see Peet and Woolley 1923, pl. XX.

2. Haynes 1977, passim.

3. Glenn Markoe in Capel and Markoe 1996, cat. 21h.

4. Fazzini 1975, cat. 33a.

5. Wallert 1967, pp. 17, 80; Hermann 1932, p. 100, pl. 11, 2; compare A. Thomas 1981, cat. 379, pl. 16, Brunner-Traut, Brunner, and Zick-Nissen 1984, cat. 46.

6. Wallert 1967, p.53.

207

208

209

208. Dwarf holding a jar

Possibly from Amarna
Dynasty 18, reign of Akhenaten,
1353–1336 B.C.
Boxwood
H. 5.9 cm, w. 1.8 cm, d. 2.6 cm
Helen and Alice Colburn Fund, Museum
of Fine Arts, Boston, 48.296

209. Servant bearing a vessel

Amarna
Dynasty 18, reign of Akhenaten,
1353–1336 B.C.
Wood
H. 21 cm, w. 4.3 cm, d. 9.1 cm
The Board of Trustees of National
Museums & Galleries on Merseyside
(Liverpool Museum), Liverpool, M 13519

These two objects belong to a genre of
figures of servants bearing jars, all dating to the 18th Dynasty. Wooden, stone,
or faience cosmetic vessels,[1] they most
likely contained unguents. A similar
motif is found on cosmetic spoons.[2]
Cat. 209[3] represents a male servant
bending forward under the weight of
his enormous jar. He wears a long kilt,
and the hole in his hand indicates that
he once held an object, possibly a stick[4]
with which to apply the vessel's contents. The dwarf (cat. 208)[5] bends to
the side to compensate for his heavy
load. His jar is inscribed crudely with
the names of Akhenaten and Nefertiti.
Dwarves were featured in Egyptian art
from the Early Dynastic Period onward,
as servants or craftsmen. At Amarna,[6]
they appear in tomb reliefs, often
accompanying Nefertiti's sister. SD'A

1. See, for example, Arielle P. Kozloff in Kozloff
and Bryan 1992, cats. 87–88; Rita E. Freed in
Brovarski, Doll, and Freed, cats. 238–39; Müller
and Settgast 1976, cat. 35; Vandier d'Abbadie
1972, cat. 393; Hayes 1959, fig. 198, p. 316;
Bothmer 1949; Roeder 1939; Davis et al. 1990,
p. 43, pl. III.

2. See Wallert 1967, pls. 24–25; Page-Gasser and
Wiese 1997, cat. 82.

3. Bienkowski 1994.

4. Ibid., pp. 60–61, fig. 3.

5. Dasen 1993, cat. 198, pl. 35, 2; Rita E. Freed
in T. Phillips 1995, cat. 1.46, with references.

6. Dasen 1993, pp. 147–50, 268–69. For other
general discussions of dwarves in ancient Egypt,
see el-Aguizy 1987 and Dasen 1988.

210. Ointment jar

Amarna
Dynasty 18, reign of Akhenaten,
1353–1336 B.C.
Calcite
H. 9.5 cm, diam. 7.4 cm
Loaned by the University of Pennsylvania
Museum of Archaeology and
Anthropology, Philadelphia, E 652

211. Footed *tazze*

Amarna
Dynasty 18 reign of Akhenaten,
1353–1336 B.C.
Calcite
H. 5.4 cm, diam. 15.9 cm
Gift of the Egypt Exploration Society,
Cincinnati Art Museum, Cincinnati,
1921.316

Translucent, easily polished calcite
(alabaster) was the most popular stone
for cosmetic containers in the New
Kingdom. Both of these vessels represent classic styles of ointment containers. The pear-shaped vessel with flat
bottom and ledge rim is first seen early
in Dynasty 18 and used until the end of
the New Kingdom.[1] The footed dish or
tazze is shown in tomb paintings holding the scented unguents that were to be
placed on the heads of those attending
festival banquets.[2] This two-ribbed version appears under Thutmose III with

210

little or no foot; later a separate foot
was added. This style, with two to four
ribs, can be found until the time of
Ramesses II. Numerous scenes of offering ointments are depicted at Amarna.
JLH

1. Janine Bourriau in Brovarski, Doll, and Freed
1982, cat. 121. A similar vessel was found in
Amarna house O.48.6 (6/12/1911 #526).

2. Bourriau 1982, cat. 120.

211

212

212. Fish vessel

Amarna, house immediately east of
N.49.20
Dynasty 18, reign of Akhenaten,
1353–1336 B.C.
Glass
H. 7 cm, length 14.5 cm
The Trustees of the British Museum,
London, 55193

The *bolti* (genus *Tilapia*) was the most
frequently depicted fish in ancient
Egypt. An inhabitant of shallow waters
and sheltered bays, this common Nilotic
fish was valued as an important source
of food. It was also a symbol with talismanic properties, its breeding and feeding associated with bounty, transformation, and rebirth.[1]

At Amarna, the *bolti* (its Arabic name)
was included in lively and naturalistic
pond scenes painted on the floors of
palaces. A popular three-dimensional
example of this form was the fish vessel—a specialized container for precious
substances such as unguents and scented
oils. This particular fish vessel of core-
formed, polychrome glass is exceptional
in that it represents fluid movement

frozen in time and a degree of craftsmanship unsurpassed in the ancient
world. Part of a cache beneath the floor
of a private house in the Central City,
the flask was found in several fragments
and later restored.[2] YJM

---

1. For further information on the habits and
symbolism of the *bolti* fish, see Brewer and
Friedman 1989, pp. 77–79.

2. Cooney 1976, p. 146.

213. Vessel with handles

Amarna
Dynasty 18, reign of Akhenaten,
1353–1336 B.C.
Glass
H. 8.2 cm, w. 6.2 cm
Musées Royaux d'Art et d'Histoire,
Brussels, E.6354

214. Globular vessel

Possibly from Amarna
Dynasty 18, reign of Akhenaten,
1353–1336 B.C.
Glass
H. 8.1 cm, diam. 5.7 cm
Bequest of Edward C. Moore, 1891, The
Metropolitan Museum of Art, New York,
91.1.1365

213

Jewel-like polychrome glass vessels were
a specialty of Amarna's skilled craftsmen. These precious containers were
formed around a sandy core and often
decorated with applied glass threads
that were marvered into the matrix (see
the essay "Crafts and Industries at
Amarna"). Fabricated in a variety of
shapes and colors, they were among the
prized possessions of the city's elite.

The discovery of the remnants of
a glassworks factory at Amarna by
Flinders Petrie provides evidence of
an indigenous glass industry. The raw
materials needed for production were
largely available in Egypt and some artisans were undoubtedly recruited from
established glass-manufacturing centers
such as existed at Malqata or Medinet
el-Gurob.

One of the few complete vessels recovered from Amarna is a *krateriskoi* (cat.
213), with angular handles, a wide
neck, and barber-pole trim on the rim
and foot.[1] Cat. 214, a pear-shaped jar, is
of unknown provenance, but possibly
from Amarna. Although its shape parallels an excavated vessel dating to the
early years of Amenhotep III's reign,[2]
the complex pattern of festoons with
loops and feather design is also common
among glass fragments found at
Amarna. YJM

214

---

1. The vessel was found in fragments among the
plundered remains of a large estate in the northwestern quarter of the North Suburb in a room
east of the front hall. See Frankfort and
Pendlebury 1933, pp. 40–41, pl. XII, 4.

2. This vessel, recovered from the Theban tomb
of Cha, is taller, wider, and lidded. The applied
glass threads were pulled to form multiple rows
of simple festoons. See Nolte 1977, pp. 26–27.

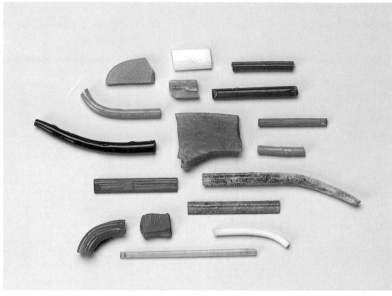

Although the Amarna letters point to the importation of raw glass, archaeological evidence suggests that glass was made in Egypt. Among the artifacts found by excavators and identified as related to glass production were furnaces,[1] slag, crucible fragments, melting pans, frit, clumps of raw glass, and monochrome rods in various lengths, shapes, and opacities. Some of the rods found by Flinders Petrie bear pincer marks, a result of heating and pulling on the tip.[2]

A specialty of the Amarna glass industry was the decorated, polychrome, core-formed vessel. Only fragments of stratified "eye" vessels[3] have been recovered from the city. They are varied in color and in the number of concentric rings around the black center. All are dramatic examples of highly skilled artisanry.

The eye decoration, found in personal adornment, probably derived from the sacred eye symbol and was believed to offer protection to the owner. YJM

1. During their 1996–97 season at Amarna, Paul Nicholson and Caroline Jackson of the Egypt Exploration Society's Amarna Glass Project replicated the furnaces found at site O.45.1, an area south of the Great Palace that may have been a royal faience- and glass-production center. Using timber as fuel, they achieved temperatures of around 1100°C and produced frit, blue glass, and other by-products similar to those found in earlier excavations. See Kemp and Nicholson 1997, p. 12. For a discussion of glassmaking evidence, see Nicholson 1995, pp. 11–19.

2. A typical grouping of rods and tubes from Amarna, some with tool marks, is in the collection of the Toledo Museum of Art. See Grose 1989, pp. 52–53, fig. 27.

3. The prefabricated eyes were added to the surface of the vessel while it was still in the molten state, and pressed into the body by rolling on a flat surface. See Cooney 1976, cat. 661.

215. Glass rods

Amarna
Dynasty 18, reign of Akhenaten,
1353–1336 B.C.
Glass
Length 6.5 cm (max.), w. 2.1 cm (max.)
Gift of the Egypt Exploration Society, San Diego Museum of Man, San Diego, 1900-27-9

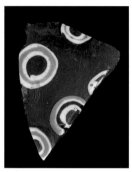

216. Fragment of a blue-bodied vessel with "eyes"

Amarna
Dynasty 18, reign of Akhenaten,
1353–1336 B.C.
Glass
H. 3.52 cm, w. 2.47 cm
The Trustees of the British Museum, London, EA 68392

217. Fragment of a yellow-bodied vessel with "eyes"

Amarna
Dynasty 18, reign of Akhenaten,
1353–1336 B.C.
Glass
H. 3.67 cm, w. 2.67 cm
The Trustees of the British Museum, London, EA 68393

218. Fragment from Akhenaten's sarcophagus with the head of Nefertiti

Amarna, Royal Tomb
Dynasty 18, reign of Akhenaten,
1353–1336 B.C.
Granite
H. 29 cm, w. 14 cm, d. 18 cm
Purchased 1900, Ägyptisches Museum und Papyrussammlung, Berlin, 14524

Akhenaten's sarcophagus was found in the Royal Tomb east of Amarna, smashed into hundreds of fragments. Because Akhenaten's monotheism excluded other gods, its corners[1] show four relief figures of Nefertiti. Later, on the sarcophagi of several kings of late Dynasty 18 (see cat. 250), the four traditional protective goddesses—Isis, Nephthys, Selket, and Neith—assume this position. DW

1. Martin 1974, 1989, vol. 1, cat. 2; Arnold 1996, pp. 94–96; fig. 85.

218

219. Upper part of a *shabti* of Akhenaten wearing a long wig

Probably from Amarna, Royal Tomb
Dynasty 18, reign of Akhenaten,
1353–1336 B.C.
Quartzite
H. 14.7 cm, w. 8.4 cm, d. 5.5 cm
Rogers Fund, 1947, The Metropolitan
Museum of Art, New York, 47.57.2

220. Upper part of a *shabti* of Akhenaten wearing a bag wig

Probably from Amarna, Royal Tomb
Dynasty 18, reign of Akhenaten,
1353–1336 B.C.
Faience
H. 11.3 cm, w. 7.6 cm, d. 5.2 cm
Purchase, Fletcher Fund, and The Guide
Foundation, Inc., Gift, 1966, The
Metropolitan Museum of Art, New York,
66.99.37

221. *Shabti* of Akhenaten with a bag wig

Probably from Amarna, Royal Tomb
Dynasty 18, reign of Akhenaten,
1353–1336 B.C.
Red granite
H. 27 cm
Gift of Mr. and Mrs. Jack A. Josephson,
1982, The Metropolitan Museum of Art,
New York, 1982.50

222. Head and shoulder of a *shabti* of Akhenaten wearing a *nemes* headdress

Probably from Amarna, Royal Tomb
Dynasty 18, reign of Akhenaten,
1353–1336 B.C.
Quartzite
H. 11.4 cm, w. 8.6 cm, d. 8.3 cm
Courtesy of the Trustees of the National
Museums of Scotland, Edinburgh,
A 1972.94

Judging from the fragmentary remains
that are thought to derive from the
Royal Tomb, Akhenaten was provided
with many items of the customary
funerary assemblage, modified to
accommodate his new religion. Such
was the case with the multitude of
shabti figures of the king. The *shabti*
spell from the Book of the Dead, with
its connotations of the god Osiris, has
been replaced by the king's titulary and
epithets in a single column. However,
the form of the *shabti*s is the familiar
mummifed figure. They vary in material, type of headdress or wig, and objects
held in the hands.

The four examples shown here are a
good representative sample. They wear
different types of headdresses, from the
simple long wig of cat. 219[1] to the more
elaborate bag wig *(khat)* with pigtail in
the back (cats. 220, 221)[2] or *nemes*
headdress (cat. 222).[3] Two carry *ankh*
("life") signs, though they are held differently, and cats. 221[4] (the only intact
shabti of the king known to date) and
222 once held a crook and a flail, two
of the traditional insignia of kingship.
Their physiognomies also differ, suggesting that they were manufactured at
various points in Akhenaten's reign and
reflect the stylistic changes well documented in his monuments.   SD'A

1. Martin 1974, 1989, vol. 1, cat. 190, pl. 40;
Aldred 1973, cat. 169.

2. Martin 1974, 1989, vol. 1, cat. 59, pl. 26;
Aldred 1973, cat. 170.

3. Martin 1974, 1989, vol. 1, cat. 193a, pl. 42;
Aldred 1973, cat. 175.

4. Peter F. Dorman in Metropolitan Museum of
Art 1982, pp. 6–7; Martin 1974, 1989, vol. 1,
pp. 6–7, cat. 87.

219

220

221

222

223

224

Because the Royal Tomb at Amarna was hewn from extremely hard rock, the workmen carved the sunk-relief decoration and inscriptions into a thick coating of plaster applied to the walls. These two plaster relief fragments are from one of the rooms subsidiary to the part of the tomb designated for the king's burial; the identity of the intended occupant is not known.[1] The servants bowing to the king across an Aten ray and the group of men and children worshipping the Aten were part of a scene of the royal family performing the morning ritual for the Aten[2]; the pair of horses drawing a chariot probably belonged to the entourage shown attending the royal family during the evening ritual for the setting sun.[3] The overlapping figures on both fragments impart a liveliness to the composition that is enhanced by the remaining paint. MEC

1. Martin 1974, 1989, vol. 2, pp. 37–41.

2. Bouriant, Legrain, and Jéquier 1903, pl. I; Martin 1974, 1989, vol. 1, cat. 456; vol. 2, pp. 28–30.

3. Bouriant, Legrain, and Jéquier 1903, pl. IV; Martin 1974, 1989, vol. 1, cat. 454; vol. 2, pp. 33–36.

225. Finger ring with a frog bezel

Reportedly from Amarna, Royal Tomb
Dynasty 18, reign of Akhenaten,
1353–1336 B.C.
Gold
H. 2.8 cm, w. 2.5 cm, d. 1.2 cm
Courtesy of the Trustees of the National Museums of Scotland, Edinburgh,
A 1883.49.2

226. Finger ring with a *wedjat-eye* bezel

Reportedly from Amarna, Royal Tomb
Dynasty 18, reign of Akhenaten,
1353–1336 B.C.
Gold, carnelian
H. 2.2 cm, w. 2.2 cm, d. 0.4 cm
Courtesy of the Trustees of the National Museums of Scotland, Edinburgh,
A 1883.49.8

227. Stirrup ring inscribed for Nefertiti

Reportedly from Amarna, Royal Tomb
Dynasty 18, reign of Akhenaten,
1353–1336 B.C.
Gold
H. 2.4 cm, w. 2.4 cm, d. 0.5 cm
Courtesy of the Trustees of the National Museums of Scotland, Edinburgh,
A 1883.49.1

228. Stirrup ring with Bes images

Reportedly from Amarna, Royal Tomb
Dynasty 18, reign of Akhenaten,
1353–1336 B.C.
Gold
H. 2.4 cm, w. 2.4 cm, d. 0.5 cm
The Board of Trustees of National Museums & Galleries on Merseyside (Liverpool Museum), Liverpool, 56.20.576

A popular ring form in ancient Egypt consisted of a wire hoop with amuletic bezel. A variant of the type has a hollow shank with tapered ends threaded through the bezel and wrapped around the shoulder. Both of these examples— one with a gold frog scaraboid in a granulated bezel mount, the other with a carnelian *wedjat* bezel[1]—are reported to have come from the Royal Tomb.[2] The frog scaraboid[3] has the inscription "Mut, Mistress of Heaven" on the underside, an interesting invocation of a goddess ostensibly banned at Amarna.[4]

The precious-metal stirrup ring is a New Kingdom innovation that evolved from Middle Kingdom scarab rings with a rigid bezel.[5] Typically cast in multipart molds, these ornaments often have sunk-relief bezels featuring royal figures, cartouches, and deities. One of the traditional gods that maintained a popular following at Amarna was Bes, protector of women and children. YJM

1. The sacred eye is the most common image found on the ubiquitous faience ring bezels excavated at Amarna. See Shaw 1984, pp. 124–26.

2. Martin 1974, 1989, vol. 1, pp. 76–77. For an account of the jewelry hoard discovered in the 1880s, see cat. 229 in the present volume. It is interesting, however, to compare the finger rings found in Tutankhamen's tomb with this group. Tutankhamen's ornaments are decidedly more elaborate and distinctive, qualities consistent with the status and resources of 18th-Dynasty royals. See Aldred 1971, pl. 91, p. 217.

3. The frog, an animal form of the protective childbirth goddess Heket, and the inscription dedicated to the goddess Mut, suggest a female owner. See Andrews 1990, p. 175.

4. For a similar ring dated to the reign of Amenhotep III, see Arielle P. Kozloff in Kozloff and Bryan 1992, pp. 449–50. For an excavated frog ring in faience (house T.54) see Frankfort and Pendlebury 1933, p. 57, no. 30/149.

5. Andrews 1990, pp. 164–66.

223. Relief of horses

Amarna, Royal Tomb, probably from room *alpha,* wall D
Dynasty 18, reign of Akhenaten,
1353–1336 B.C.
Painted plaster
H. 22 cm, w. 35.1 cm
Charles Edwin Wilbour Fund, Brooklyn Museum of Art, New York, 54.186

224. Relief of bowing figures

Amarna, Royal Tomb, from room *alpha,* wall A
Dynasty 18, reign of Akhenaten,
1353–1336 B.C.
Painted plaster
H. 16 cm, w. 26.8 cm
Charles Edwin Wilbour Fund, Brooklyn Museum of Art, New York, 54.188.5

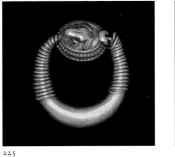

225

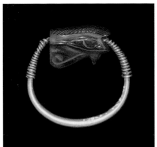

226

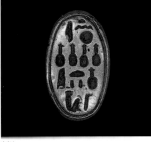

227

228

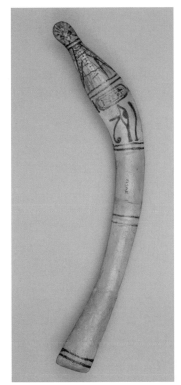

230

231

229. Elements from a broadcollar

Reportedly from Amarna, Royal Tomb
Dynasty 18, reign of Akhenaten,
1353–1336 B.C.
Gold, glass
Length 12.1 cm, w. 2.6 cm
Courtesy of the Trustees of the National
Museums of Scotland, Edinburgh,
A 1883.49.13

In the early 1880s, villagers living near
the Amarna ruins reported discovering
a cache of jewelry in a tomb identified
as belonging to Akhenaten. The ornaments, nineteen in number, quickly
reached the antiquities market and were
purchased by a London dealer for the
Royal Scottish Museum, Scotland.[1]

During the 1950s the jewelry was
examined by Egyptologist Cyril Aldred,
who noted that several items in the
group were Roman in date. He concluded that the hoard represented the plunder of ancient tomb robbers, who had
removed the jewels from the Royal
Tomb and concealed the booty nearby.
The treasure had apparently been mixed
with the remains of a later burial.[2]

The gold broadcollar elements in the
hoard are made of sheet-metal parts
assembled and soldered into three-
dimensional forms. Broadcollars were
worn by both sexes during the 18th
Dynasty.[3] YJM

1. For the original account of this fascinating
story, see Blackman 1917, p. 45. For a contemporary analysis of the find, see Martin 1974,
1989, vol. 1, pp. 4–5, 75–80.

2. It may be that several gold ear ornaments,
Hellenistic in style, were added to the group to
enhance its value.

3. Andrews 1990, pp. 109–11.

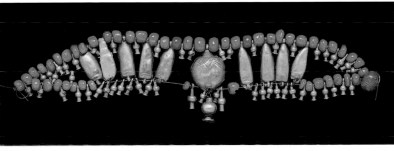

229

230. Model throw stick

Probably from Amarna, Royal Tomb
Dynasty 18, reign of Akhenaten,
1353–1336 B.C.
Faience
Length 38.5 cm, w. 4.4 cm, d. 1.7 cm
Purchased 1882, Trustees of the British
Museum, London, EA 34213

To judge from scenes on tomb and temple walls, from the time of the Old
Kingdom until the early New Kingdom,
throw sticks were used by bird hunters
in Egypt's marshes to stun their prey.
Although wooden examples survive
which could indeed have been thrown,
faience throw sticks like this one,
invariably bearing the name of a ruler
of the 18th or 19th Dynasty, are far
more likely to have had a ritual purpose. Akhenaten's nomen cartouche
occurs on one face and his prenomen
on the other, before a *wedjat*-eye and
above the lotus flower that fills the
broadest part of the stick. The only
novel element is the shallowness of the
curve, apparently an invention of the
Amarna Period.[1] CA

1. Diana Craig Patch in Friedman 1998, cat. 32.

231. Miniature situla inscribed for Princess Meketaten

Provenance not known
Dynasty 18, reign of Akhenaten,
1353–1336 B.C.
Gold
H. 4.5 cm, diam. 1.5 cm
Theodore M. Davis Collection, Bequest of
Theodore M. Davis, 1915, The
Metropolitan Museum of Art, New York,
30.8.372

This situla was presumably among the
funerary gifts to princess Meketaten,
the second daughter of Akhenaten,[1]
who was at most ten years old when
she died. It could have originally been
placed in her burial chamber (room
gamma) in the Royal Tomb at
Amarna.[2] The situla is inscribed for
"the King's Daughter Meketaten."
Made of two pieces of gold—a solid
bottom with thin gold foil attached—
this tiny situla imitates bronze vessels
used for offering sacred liquids. The
small size strongly suggests that this is
a model. As there is no residual material inside, it must have been placed in
the tomb empty, as a symbolic source
that could provide offerings forever. EP

1. Hayes 1959, p. 296; Arnold 1996, pp. 11,
115, fig. 6.

2. Martin 1974, 1989, vol. 2, pp. 38–48.

232

233

232. Tomb relief of Ay receiving a reward

Amarna, tomb of Ay
Dynasty 18, reign of Akhenaten,
1353–1336 B.C.
Limestone
H. 27.5 cm, w. 54 cm, d. 8.5 cm
Egyptian Museum, Cairo, JT 10/11/26/1

233. Relief of the head of Ay

Amarna, tomb of Ay
Dynasty 18, reign of Akhenaten,
1353–1336 B.C.
Limestone
H. 34 cm, w. 22.5 cm, d. 4.5–6 cm
Austin S. and Sarah C. Garver Funds,
Worcester Art Museum, Worcester,
1949.42

A nonroyal individual who became
pharaoh late in life, Ay constructed two
tombs, one at Amarna[1] and a later one
in the remote West Valley of the Kings.[2]
His unfinished Amarna tomb, in the
northern group, was the largest of the
private tombs, with a main chamber
that was intended to contain twenty-
four papyriform columns. The tomb is
thought to have been begun shortly
after the move to Amarna, and features
the more restrained style of this period.
The relief fragment (cat. 233)[3] is part of
a kneeling figure of Ay holding a fan (an
insignia of office) that accompanied an
extensive prayer. Prominently featured
in the tomb was a scene of Ay and his
wife being rewarded by the king (cat.
232).[4] Both wear wigs with fillets surmounted by scented ointment cones,
and are laden with gold collars. In the
larger scene, an onlooker comments that
they have become "people of gold," and
Ay proudly records in a tomb inscription that the king "doubled rewards for
me like the number of sands while I
was first of the officials in front of the
subjects."[5] SD'A

1. N. de G. Davies 1903–8, vol. 6, pp. 16–24,
passim.

2. Schaden 1984; Schaden 1992; Piankoff 1958;
see also Reeves and Wilkinson 1996, pp. 128–29.

3. Peterson 1964, p. 25, fig. 9; Milkovich 1963,
p. 155 and cover; Worcester Art Museum 1973,
p. 17; N. de G. Davies 1903–8, vol. 6, p. 18, pl.
XXXIX. The profile around the eyes, nose, and
cheeks has been substantially reworked, as has
the top of the fan.

4. Schaden 1992; Aldred 1988, fig. 4; Müller and
Settgast 1976, cat. 49; N. de G. Davies 1903–8,
vol. 6, p. 21, pl. XXIX.

5. Murnane 1995b, p. 117.

234. Canopic jar

Thebes, Valley of the Kings, tomb KV 55
Dynasty 18, reign of Akhenaten,
1353–1336 B.C.
Calcite
H. 37 cm, diam. 22 cm
Bequest of Theodore M. Davis, 1915,
Theodore Davis Collection, Gift of
Theodore M. Davis, 1907, The
Metropolitan Museum of Art, New York,
07.226.1

235. Lid of a canopic jar

Thebes, Valley of the Kings, tomb KV 55
Dynasty 18, reign of Akhenaten,
1353–1336 B.C.
Calcite, obsidian, blue glass, unidentified
stones
H. 18.2 cm, diam. 16.3 cm
Bequest of Theodore M. Davis, 1915, The
Metropolitan Museum of Art, New York,
30.8.54

The exquisitely rendered head on the
canopic jar lid is a representation of—
whom? This question has occupied
scholars for more than ninety years,
since the discovery of tomb KV 55 in
1907 (see the essay "Preparing for
Eternity"). Canopic jars were used to
house the viscera removed during mummification, and this jar was one of four
found in a niche in the tomb. The
inscriptions have been erased, but the
jars have been attributed over the years
to several members of the royal family,
from Queen Tiye to Akhenaten himself.
The consensus of the most recent research, however, is that Akhenaten's
secondary wife Kiya was the original
owner of the jars, though it has been
suggested that they were not originally
matched to the lids.[1] The lids portray
an individual in a Nubian wig, worn by
royal women and courtiers during the
Amarna Period, and include the royal
uraeus, which was broken off, presumably during the subsequent desecration
of the tomb. SD'A

1. For a recent discussion of the jars, see Arnold
1996, pp. 116–17, fig. 116; Ertman 1995;
Dodson 1994a, pp. 57–59; and Martin 1985. For
a fragment of a canopic jar belonging to an
unidentified Amarna queen, see Reeves 1994.

234, 235

236

237. Stela of Ptahmay with prayers to Aten and Ra-Horakhty

Probably from Memphis
Dynasty 18, reign of Akhenaten,
1353–1336 B.C.
Limestone
H. 71.5 cm, w. 49.5 cm, d. 14 cm
The Trustees of the British Museum,
London, EA 324

This elaborate door-shaped stela, topped by torus molding and a cavetto cornice, contains two scenes. In the upper register, seated on lion-footed chairs, are the stela's owner, a Guardian of the Treasury called Ptahmay, and his wife Takhert. Before them their son Paatenemheb and daughter Meryt offer prayers. In the lower register a man called Huy and his wife Wabt are seated on stools beside two young children, a boy labeled "his son Hat" and a girl "his daughter Wadjyt." Two further adults seated at right are named "his son Ramessu" and "his daughter Iwy." The relationship between the figures in the lower register and Ptahmay is not clear.

Carved around the edges of the stela are two mirror-image offering formulae. One asks the Aten for the usual bread and beer, flesh and fowl on Ptahmay's behalf; the other is an appeal to Ra, with various epithets, to grant a vision of his beauty to the deceased. The style dates the piece to the reign of Akhenaten, and the late form of the name of the Aten in the inscription suggests that it was made in year 9 or after.[1] CA

1. Assmann 1976, col. 957 and n. 18; D. Redford 1984, p. 186.

237

236. Pyramidion of a Servant of Aten

Provenance not known
Dynasty 18, reign of Akhenaten,
1353–1336 B.C.
Limestone
H. 60 cm, w. 29 cm, d. 28 cm
Purchased 1898, Ägyptisches Museum und Papyrussammlung, Berlin, 14123

Aside from the tombs of the courtiers at Amarna, nonroyal monuments from the reign of Akhenaten—such as stelae or statues—are rare. One of the few examples is this pyramidion,[1] probably from a tomb. Reliefs on its four sides represent the family of someone possibly named Neb-Ra, a functionary at one of the Aten temples at Amarna. The offering formula is addressed to the living Aten, whose sun-disk was perhaps fixed atop the pyramidion. DW

1. Porter and Moss 1934, p. 235; Roeder 1924, pp. 234–35.

238. *Shabti* of Isis, Chantress of Aten

Provenance not known
Dynasty 18, reign of Akhenaten,
1353–1336 B.C.
Limestone
H. 21.3 cm, w. 7 cm, d. 5.9 cm
Purchase, Fletcher Fund and The Guide Foundation, Inc., The Metropolitan Museum of Art, New York, 66.99.38

239. *Shabti* of Hatsheret, Chantress of Aten

Provenance not known
Dynasty 18, reign of Akhenaten,
1353–1336 B.C.
Ebony
H. 22.8 cm, w. 6.5 cm, d. 4.7 cm
The Trustees of the British Museum,
London, EA 8644

Private individuals continued to be provided with *shabti* figures during the Amarna Period,[1] and a few have been identified with known tomb owners at the site. The fact that the majority have not, however, hints at the existence of undocumented tombs of the period at Amarna or elsewhere. That *shabti*s were provided at all is interesting, since their customary function was to perform manual labor in the fields of an afterlife that was very much the realm of the old god Osiris.

Each of these *shabti*s[2] belongs to a Chantress of Aten, or temple singer. The number of Osiride attributes of the figures is striking, including the mummiform stance, the name Isis (the wife of Osiris), and the epithet "true of voice," which translates as "justified" in the traditional religion. The beautiful ebony *shabti* is inscribed with the conventional *shabti* spell from the Book of the Dead naming "the Osiris, Hatsheret." In the traditional religion, the deceased was called "an Osiris." SD'A

1. Geoffrey Martin has identified five classes of inscribed and uninscribed *shabti*s; see Martin 1986, pp. 110–11. See also Schneider 1977, pp. 289–92, and Aubert and Aubert 1974, pp. 53–57.

2. Martin 1986, nos. 7-8, pp. 115–16 and pls. 11–12, with additional references cited there.

238

239

The Legacy

240

241

240. Tutankhamen wearing a *nemes* headdress

Provenance not known
Dynasty 18, reign of Tutankhamen,
1332–1322 B.C.
Sandstone
H. 29.6, w. 26.5
Gift of Miss Mary S. Ames, Museum of
Fine Arts, Boston, 11.1533

241. Tutankhamen wearing a blue crown

Provenance not known
Dynasty 18, reign of Tutankhamen,
1332–1322 B.C.
Indurated limestone
H. 15.2 cm, w. 23 cm
Rogers Fund, 1950, The Metropolitan
Museum of Art, New York, 50.6

Tutankhamen, né Tutankhaten at
Amarna, ruled there for approximately
two years before abandoning the city. It
is therefore not surprising that many of
his images should bear great resemblance to Amarna Period works. Both
these heads have naturalistic eyes that
are large and almond shaped, and the
full, sensuous lips that are hallmarks of
Amarna.

With its round, cherubic face, the
head of the king in the blue crown
recalls images of the royal family from
late in the Amarna Period. It was originally part of a dyad, and the much larger hand atop the king's crown was most
likely that of Amen, whose primacy
Tutankhamen restored. A gesture of
coronation, it was attested earlier only
in relief representations.[1] (For a similar
composition, see cat. 243.)

In the other image, the king wears a
nemes and the lower part of the combined crown of Upper and Lower
Egypt, which still bears traces of red
paint. It is possible that the rest of the
crown was made of another piece of
stone, now lost.[2] The vertical slit above
the brow was for insertion of the hood
of a uraeus, which would have been
made of a different material. REF

1. Hayes 1959, p. 300.

2. Borchardt 1925, p. 153, or el-Saghir 1991, p.
57.

242. Amen with gold inlays

Provenance not known
Dynasty 18, reign of Tutankhamen,
1332–1322 B.C.
Bronze, gold
H. 22 cm (with present mount)
The Walters Art Gallery, Baltimore,
54.401

Few metal sculptures survive from the
Amarna Period, but those from the
reign of Tutankhamen indicate the quality of the pieces now lost. This figure
depicts the god Amen with the features
of Tutankhamen,[1] including large,
arched eyes, a broad nose, full lips, and
a somewhat rounded belly. The figure
wears a *rishi*, or feathered corselet, a
garment associated with kings and
divine beings. The details of the costume are rendered in gold inlay and the
eyes would probably have been inlaid in
glass. The traditional plumes of Amen's
crown are missing, but a channel remains in the headdress where the stylized feathers would have been set.

Bronze figures were often temple vo-
tives, and this magnificent piece would
have been dedicated by someone of very
high rank. PL

1. Steindorff 1946, p. 119, pl. 78, no. 477.

242

245

243

245. Head of Amen

Provenance not known
Dynasty 18, reign of Tutankhamen,
1332–1322 B.C.
Diorite
H. 44 cm, w. 38.5 cm, d. 41.5 cm
Rogers Fund, 1907, The Metropolitan
Museum of Art, New York, 07.228.34

This head belonged to a larger-than-life-
size statue of the god Amen.[1] The distinctive crown, once surmounted by tall
twin plumes, and the braided beard
were part of the god's iconography. The
facial features of the god—the full
mouth with a slightly drooping lower
lip, and almond-shaped, slanted eyes
with a deep depression between the eyes
and eyebrows—are those of Tutankhamen. The well-defined contours of the

eyes and mouth and the restrained
modeling give the face a cold, distant
expression that is evidence of the post-
Amarna style. A number of Amen's statues with facial features of the young
king were carved for Karnak as part
of the restoration program for Amen's
monuments undertaken by Tutankhamen.[2] This statue might be part of that
program. EP

1. Hayes 1959, p. 300, fig. 185; Lythgoe 1907, p.
195; Brinkmann 1967, p. 17; Spanel 1988, p. 98.

2. James Romano in Luxor Museum 1979, pp.
127, 137; Reeves 1990a, pp. 26-29.

243. Amen and Tutankhamen

Karnak
Dynasty 18, reign of Tutankhamen,
1332–1322 B.C.
Granodiorite
H. 220 cm, w. 44 cm, d. 78.5 cm
Musée du Louvre, Paris, E 11609

As a tangible demonstration of his
closeness to his deity, Tutankhamen
commissioned a number of statues of
himself with Amen. Here the god, easily
identifiable by his two tall plumes,
holds a smaller statue of the king in
a gesture of protection. The king is
dressed in a panther-skin garment, signifying that he is serving as Amen's
highest priest. Although the face of the
god does not show as much Amarna
influence as other contemporary representations (cats. 240, 241), the softness
of both torsos still harks back to those
years. The matte surface of the god's
plumes, beard, and collar suggests that
they were once covered in gold.[1]

As with many of Tutankhamen's statues, a later king, probably Horemheb,[2]
defaced the young king's name on the
back pillar. Fortunately for later generations, his agents missed two tiny cartouches on the skirt,[3] leaving no doubt
as to the original owner of the statue.
This statue was excavated by Auguste
Mariette in 1857–58, in expectation of
a visit to Egypt by Prince Napoleon.[4]
REF

1. Christiane Ziegler in Humbert, Pantazzi, and
Ziegler 1994, p. 516.

2. W. R. Johnson 1995, p. 1.

3. Bénédite 1920, p. 50.

4. Ziegler in Humbert, Pantazzi, and Ziegler
1994, p. 516.

244

244. Triad

Karnak cachette
Dynasty 18, reigns of Thutmose I,
1493–1479, and Tutankhamen,
1332–1322 B.C.
Calcite
H. 69 cm, w. 38 cm, d. 27 cm
Egyptian Museum, Cairo, JE 37394
(CG 42052)

A seated figure of Amen, god of Thebes,
is flanked by a king on his right and a
queen on his left. Hieroglyphic inscriptions carved on the throne base read,
"The Good God Aa-kheperu-Ra
(Thutmose I), beloved of Amen-Ra"
and "The Royal Wife Ahmose, beloved
of Amen-Ra." However, the facial features of the three figures bear no relation to those of the early 18th-Dynasty
figures named. Rather, they reflect the
post-Amarna style. Close examination
reveals that the upper and lower parts
of the triad were made of different
stones. In all likelihood, the original
upper section and the legs of Amen
were totally destroyed by Akhenaten's
priests during his reign and then
restored during the reign of Tutankhamen.[1] AAM

1. Seidel 1996, p. 125.

246

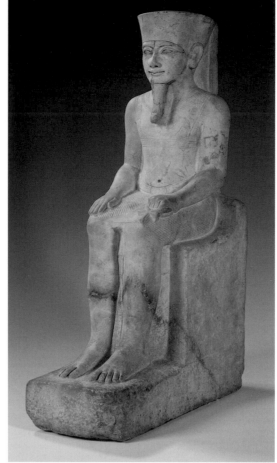

247

248. Head of Ay (?)

Asfun
Dynasty 18, reign of Ay (?),
1322–1319 B.C.
Limestone
H. 10 cm, w. 7 cm, d. 7.5 cm
Egyptian Museum, Cairo, JE 37930

The rendering of advanced age, nowhere better represented than in the life-size private heads found in the Thutmose workshop (cat. 139), was a part of Amarna's experimentation with naturalism that continued into the next dynasty.[1] Here on a much smaller scale is a master study of age that exhibits some qualities found in the finest Amarna works: the eyes, with pronounced inner canthi, and the delicate cosmetic lines hollowed out to receive inlays, are comparable to features of the famous Nefertiti bust.[2] The slightly open mouth, however, with its hint of a frown and its drooping lower lip, is unique to this individual.

Clues to the subject's identity are provided by the headgear. A uraeus has been added to what was originally a close-fitting skullcap, by cutting back the surface of the cap beside the hood of the snake.[3] The number of private individuals who became king is limited to two: Ay and Horemheb. Since Horemheb is neither attested at Amarna nor represented elsewhere in true Amarna style, the subject of this head must be Ay. REF

1. For a representation of an aged Ramesses II, see Freed 1987, cover.

2. Müller and Settgast 1976, frontispiece.

3. Gilbert 1941, pp. 45, 47.

246. Amen with soft features

Reportedly from Karnak
Dynasty 18, reign of Tutankhamen,
1332–1322 B.C.
Limestone
H. 111 cm
Badisches Landesmuseum, Karlsruhe,
65/15

247. Amen with formal features

Deir el-Bahari
Dynasty 18, reign of Tutankhamen,
1332–1322 B.C.
Limestone
H. 86 cm, w. 23 cm (with base), d. 49 cm
(with base)
Kestner-Museum, Hannover, lent by Fritz-
Behrens-Stiftung

As part of his restoration of Amen's power and prestige, Tutankhamen commissioned statues of the god in unprecedented numbers. Although uninscribed, these two statues of Amen were most likely part of that program. Virtually identical in material, pose, garments, and size (with the exception of the base), they were most likely carved at the same time and in the same place.[1] Nevertheless, they are strikingly different in facial modeling and body form, and appear to have been made by two different artists.

With its round face, relaxed features, fleshy breasts, and flaccid abdomen, cat. 246, like a number of statues of Tutankhamen from his tomb, is reminiscent of Amarna Period works.[2] In contrast, cat. 247 exhibits a leaner face and body, more removed from the Amarna style although still in keeping with other representations of Tutankhamen.[3]

The Amen with formal features was never quite finished. Red grid lines are still visible on both sides of the body, and finger- and toenails are not indicated. Each Amen originally wore a tall, two-feather crown (see cat. 243). REF and RD

1. Marianne Eaton-Krauss, oral communication.

2. Edwards 1976, pl. 23, for example.

3. Ibid., pl. 22, for example.

248

249. Relief of the god Hapi from a throne base

Probably from Medinet Habu
Dynasty 18, reign of Ay, 1322–1319 B.C.
Limestone
H. 45.5 cm, w. 36.5 cm
Gift of Edward W. Forbes, Museum of
Fine Arts, Boston, 50.3789

The god Hapi, with his pendulous
breasts and headdress of papyrus or lily,
represented the fecundity of the Nile
inundation. He is often sculpted in pairs
on the sides of royal thrones,[1] binding
symbolic plants of Upper and Lower
Egypt in a unifying gesture.

This fragment[2] derives from the mortuary temple begun by Ay and completed by Horemheb at Medinet Habu in
Thebes.[3] It belonged to a pair of colossal seated figures of Ay flanking the
entrance to the broad, columned hall.
The god has the features of the king,
rendered in a more traditional style.
Hapi's appearance on the throne base
also points forward to the restoration
of religious orthodoxy. SD'A

---

1. See, for example, the Middle Kingdom throne
base of Sesostris I. Lange and Hirmer 1968, pl.
89.

2. Schaden 1992, n. 115; Myśliwiec 1976, pp.
86–87, fig. 189; Eaton 1942.

3. Hölscher 1939, pp. 65–114, especially p. 105;
compare pl. 50.

249

250

250. Fragment from the sarcophagus of Ay

Thebes, West Valley, tomb of Ay
Dynasty 18, reign of Ay, 1322–1319 B.C.
Red granite
H. 39 cm, w. 27.5 cm, d. 7.6 cm
Purchase 1909, Ägyptisches Museum und
Papyrussammlung, Berlin, 19524

The sarcophagus of Ay[1] bears the four
traditional protective goddesses in the
places Nefertiti occupied on the sarcophagus of Akhenaten (see cat. 218).
This fragment from the foot end[2] shows
the head of Selket, surmounted by a
scorpion. Below her shoulders the wings
of her feathered arms can be seen.
Selket's face reflects the late Amarna
style. DW

---

1. The sarcophagus, including a cast of the Berlin
fragment, was recently returned from the
Egyptian Museum, Cairo (JE 72131) to the tomb
of Ay in the West Valley (Thebes).

2. Porter and Moss 1964, p. 551; Schäfer 1931,
pl. 57.

251. General Horemheb as a scribe

Possibly from Memphis
Dynasty 18, reign of Tutankhamen,
1332–1322 B.C.
Grey granite
H. 116.8 cm
Gift of Mr. and Mrs. V. Everit Macy, 1923,
The Metropolitan Museum of Art, New
York, 23.10.1

By the end of Tutankhamen's reign,
there was a concerted attempt to under-
mine and repress innovations associated
with Amarna. Pivotal in the return of
power to traditional institutions was
Horemheb, Commander-in-Chief of the
Army, royal scribe, and deputy to King
Tutankhamen.

Horemheb is presented here in the traditional posture of a scribe. He holds on
his lap a papyrus scroll inscribed with a
hymn to Thoth, the god of writing. His
official role is further highlighted by
scribal palettes on his chest, back, and
knee.[1]

Horemheb's sensitive, subdued, and
dreamy expression is characteristic of
the late Amarna style found at Memphis.[2] His eyes are heavy-lidded and his
lips delicate and full. There is considerable detailing of the long, heavy wig,
diaphanous shirt, and pleated kilt. An
image of the recently restored god Amen
in sunk relief decorates the right forearm. Carved along the base is an
inscription with the titles, duties, and
accomplishments of this important figure who would later become king. YJM

---

1. Peter Dorman in Metropolitan Museum
of Art 1987, p. 66, no. 46.

2. Martin 1989, p. 108, pls. 151–52.

251

253

As a general, Horemheb's mission to reassert Egyptian control over the empire was successful, at least according to reliefs and inscriptions elsewhere in the tomb.[2] For this the king and queen decorated him with the massive gold collars[3] shown in cat. 253, from the south wall of the second courtyard of the tomb's above-ground chapel.[4] The pilaster (cat. 252) from the same location[5] depicts Horemheb with a fan over his shoulder and his arms upraised in adoration before a prayer to the sun-god Ra.[6] The uraeus was added to both reliefs after Horemheb became king, although the tomb itself was abandoned in favor of the sepulcher he built in the Valley of the Kings at Thebes.

The ability to capture a single moment in time, the sensitivity to detail, and the naturalism expressed in these reliefs would not have been possible without the background of Amarna. It is likely that some of the artisans who left that city following Akhenaten's death continued their work at Saqqara. REF

1. Martin 1989, pp. 2–6.

2. Martin 1991, pp. 56–58, 62, and figs. 35–42, 44–45, 48–49.

3. Marianne Eaton-Krauss in Brovarski, Doll, and Freed 1982, cat. 316.

4. Martin 1989, pp. 84, 87–92, and pls. 106–7.

5. Ibid., pp. 84, 92–93, and pls. 109–10.

6. Ibid., pp. 92–93.

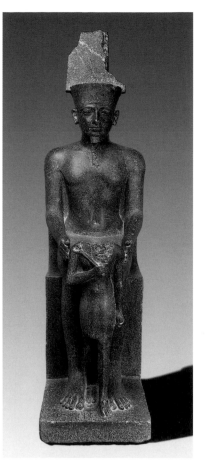

254

252

252. Door-jamb of General Horemheb

Saqqara, south of the Djoser Precinct
Dynasty 18, reign of Tutankhamen,
1332–1322 B.C.
Limestone
H. 175 cm, w. 42 cm
Purchased from Giovanni Anastasi, 1839,
The Trustees of the British Museum,
London, EA 552

253. General Horemheb receiving an award

Saqqara, south of the Djoser Precinct
Dynasty 18, reign of Tutankhamen,
1332–1322 B.C.
Limestone
H. 86 cm, w. 109 cm, d. 19.5 cm
Rijksmuseum van Oudheden, Leiden,
H.III.PPPP

Before he became king, Horemheb served as commander of Tutankhamen's army, and during that time he built a tomb at Saqqara, the necropolis of Memphis. These two reliefs were among the many removed from that tomb in the nineteenth century. Subsequently covered by desert sands, the tomb was not rediscovered until 1975.[1]

254. Amen and Horemheb

Karnak, Luxor temple cachette
Dynasty 18, reign of Horemheb,
1319–1292 B.C.
Diorite
H. 141 cm, w. 40.5 cm, d. 79.5 cm
Luxor Museum, Luxor, 834

This statue and a second similar to it[1] were part of one of the most exciting finds in recent history. Beginning in January 1989, Egyptian excavators at Luxor uncovered twenty-six statues ranging in date from Thutmose III of Dynasty 18 through Taharqa of Dynasty 25.[2]

Horemheb continued in the sculptural tradition begun by Tutankhamen (cats. 241 and 243), having himself depicted on a small scale in front of a much larger image of Amen, who blesses him or affixes his crown. The entwined plants of Upper and Lower Egypt, symbolizing the unification of the country, decorate the sides of the god's throne. On the back pillar is the king's titulary, and his name is also found on the base, in front of his feet. Neither bears any trace of recarving.

Amen's face—the king's would have been similar—is leaner, more aloof, and more formally modeled than faces of the god and king during Tutankhamen's reign (compare cats. 240–41, 243, 246–47). Even more noticeable is the difference in the rendering of the bodies. The god's triangular torso, with its taut pectoral muscles, trim waist, flat belly, and median line, bears a closer resemblance to torsos of the Thutmoside Period (cat. 1) and earlier than it does to works of the Amarna Period or immediately after. It clearly shows the diminishment of Amarna's influence, particularly at Thebes, and the return to classical body forms. REF

1. el-Saghir 1991, pp. 65–68.

2. el-Saghir 1991.

255. Block statue of Yii

Dahamsha (ancient Sumenu)
Dynasty 18, reign of Tutankhamen,
1332–1322 B.C., or Ay, 1322–1319 B.C.
Indurated limestone
H. 47.2 cm, w. 25.1 cm, d. 31 cm
Charles Edwin Wilbour Fund, Brooklyn
Museum of Art, New York, 66.174.1

Early 12th-Dynasty artists invented the
block statue, which showed the subject—almost always male—seated on
the ground, knees drawn to his chest,
arms crossed, and body enveloped by a
long cloak. The cloak alludes to mummiform images of Osiris, god of the
dead, and represents the deceased's wish
to be reborn, like Osiris, after death.[1]
The seated attitude and crossed arms
convey subservience.[2] Block statues
placed in temples served as an eternal
audience passively observing the never-
ending cycle of rituals performed for the
gods.[3]

Block statues enjoyed considerable
popularity in early Dynasty 18, particularly with elite officials. However, only
one Amarna example is known.[4] The
block statue regained its favored status
in the post-Amarna period. This exam-

ple represents Yii, who served as Second
Prophet of Amen, First Prophet of Mut,
King's Scribe, and Steward in the House
of a Queen (Tiye or Tiy) in the House
of Amen.[5] A cartouche containing Ay's
prenomen on the sculpture's upper right
arm suggests that it was made during
that king's brief reign.[6] Recently, however, a scholar interpreted the cartouche
as a later addition and proposed that
the statue dates to Tutankhamen.[7]

Viewed from the front, the figure of
Yii conforms to all the canons of the
block statue. When seen from behind,
however, the sculpture shows thick rolls
of fat girding Yii's waist, as if the carver
wished to convey a sense of the subject's
true appearance. JFR

1. Schulz 1992, vol. 2, pp. 728-35.

2. Ibid., pp. 721-42.

3. Ibid., pp. 763-67.

4. Berlin, Stiftung Preussischer Kulturbesitz–
Ägyptisches Museum 4/65: Ägyptisches Museum
1967, cat. 765 (illus.); Schulz 1992, vol. 1, pp.
83–84, no. 22 and vol. 2, pl. 7a–d.

5. Sauneron 1968, pp. 66–78; James 1974, cat.
425; Helck 1975, p. 142, no. 150.

6. This dating has been accepted by most scholars who have cited the sculpture: for example,
Bothmer 1966–67, pp. 84–85; Vandier 1968, p.
341; Fischer 1973, pl. 26, n. 34; Helck 1984, p.
215, n. 12; Thirion 1985, p. 141; Richard A.
Fazzini in Fazzini et al. 1989, cat. 56; Schulz
1992, vol. 1, p. 108; van Dijk 1993, p. 61; and
Sowada 1994, p. 142.

7. Wente 1989–90, p. 171, n. 6.

256

255

256. Maya and Meryt

Saqqara
Dynasty 18, reign of Horemheb,
1319–1292 B.C.
Limestone
H. 158 cm, w. 90 cm, d. 120 cm
Purchased 1828 (Anastasi Collection),
Rijksmuseum van Oudheden, Leiden,
AST 3

Maya was one of the highest officials
during the reigns of Tutankhamen and
Horemheb. As Overseer of the Treasury
and Director of Works, he supervised
the repair of Egypt's temples, which had
suffered neglect and iconoclastic attacks
under Akhenaten. He was also responsible for the burial of Tutankhamen.
Maya's own tomb was one of the

largest monuments in the necropolis
at Saqqara. Rediscovered in 1986,[1] it
demonstrates that Maya was able to
mobilize teams of excellent sculptors.
This statue, which was taken from
Maya's tomb in the nineteenth century,
is undoubtedly one of the finest sculptures of the period. With an exquisite
mixture of Amarna-style naturalism
and a new monumentality, it depicts the
deceased seated next to his wife, Meryt.
Two other seated statues in the Leiden
museum portray the husband and wife
separately. MJR

1. Martin 1991, pp. 147-88.

257

258

259

257. Stela of Ipu

Saqqara
Dynasty 18, reign of Tutankhamen,
1332–1322 B.C.
Limestone
H. 128 cm, w. 85 cm, d. 15 cm
Purchased 1828 (Anastasi Collection)
Rijksmuseum van Oudheden, Leiden, AP 9

According to the inscriptions on this stela, Ipu was a "Royal Butler, Pure of Hands, of the Lord of the Two Lands." The style of the relief figures, with their large heads and thin limbs, is characteristic of figural art produced during the period of Tutankhamen.[1] Ipu must have served the pharaoh in his Memphite palace, since on the stela he prays for "a beautiful burial in the West of Memphis."

The representation in the upper register shows the court official, with the Gold of Honor around his neck, offering to the god Ptah-Sokar-Osiris. The lower register depicts a family reunion around Ipu's parents. On the plinth, we see a realistic scene of women lamenting at the tomb's entrance, while servants carry provisions for use in the hereafter. MJR

1. Berlandini 1982, p. 202; Gessler-Löhr 1989, pp. 28–29.

258. Amenmose and Depet, parents of General Amenemonet

Saqqara, tomb of Amenemonet
Late Dynasty 18, about 1332–1292 B.C.
Limestone
H. 56 cm
Musée du Louvre, Paris, B 6

259. Stela of the scribe Amenemonet

Provenance not known
Dynasty 18, reign of Horemheb,
1319–1292 B.C.
Limestone
H. 49.5 cm, w. 32.5 cm, d. 4.5 cm
Collection of Thomas H. Lee, Boston

Although the Saqqara tomb of Amenemonet has only recently been rediscovered, it is doubtful that the Amenemonets (meaning "Amen is in the Valley") on these two monuments represent one and the same man. What the relief and the stela do share, however, are the elaborate costumes and sensitive modeling of first-rate craftsmanship. In the round-topped stela's upper right, the "Scribe Who Counts the Grain of the Temple of Amen," Amenemonet, raises his arms in adoration before the seated figure of Osiris, god of the underworld. The Goddess of the West (that is, the funerary realm), stands behind. The seven individuals seated below are Amenemonet's family members, and a three-column hymn at the lower left praises his character.

The larger-scale couple in the relief are probably another Amenemonet's parents, named Amenmose and Depet. The flaring sleeves, sumptuous wigs with delicate curls, and even the form of the sunk-relief hieroglyphs all point to post-Amarna relief style.[1] PDM

1. For previous publication of the relief, see Ziegler 1990, p. 55.

260

260. Head of an older man

Saft el-Hinna
Late Dynasty 18, about 1332–1292 B.C.
Granite
H. 14 cm, w. 12 cm, d. 9 cm
Purchased 1979, Staatliche Sammlung
Ägyptischer Kunst, Munich, ÄS 6296

One of the most impressive examples of sculpture in the post-Amarna period is this head[1] showing the face of an old man. Its hollow cheeks, the pouches under the eyes, and the wrinkled brow are characteristic of the portrait of old age. In contrast to the broad and peaceful expanse of the face, the wig, with its very detailed, hastily scratched lines, gives an impression of anxiety that has close parallels in the Memphite relief of this epoch.

At the back of the head the wig is divided into two large hanks of hair, like the wig of the scribe statue of Horem-heb (cat. 251). The head—broken off in antiquity—belongs to a statue of a man seated between two standing women, which was excavated at Saft el-Hinna in the eastern Nile Delta and is now in the Egyptian Museum, Cairo.[2] The statue was reused in the Third Intermediate Period (1075–656 B.C.), when it also lost the original inscriptions, which revealed the identity of the man. SS

1. Wildung 1980; Schoske 1993, pp. 35f.; Wildung 1995a, pp. 78–80.

2. Daressy 1920.

261

262

261. Aged man

Probably from Saqqara
Dynasty 18, reign of Tutankhamen
through Sety I, 1332–1279 B.C.
Limestone
H. 31.3 cm, w. 14.4 cm
Charles Edwin Wilbour Fund, Brooklyn
Museum of Art, New York, 47.120.1

The rather small size of this sunk-relief figure,[1] together with his gesture of salutation, suggests that he was addressing a superior, most likely the owner of the tomb for which the relief was carved. The formal wig and wide-sleeved shirt show that he was himself a man of high rank,[2] while his elderly features denote a specific individual of great seniority.[3] Although the heavy eyelid, the creases between the nose and mouth, and the fleshy jaw had long been used to indicate age in representations of important men,[4] the forehead wrinkles and jutting collarbones show Amarna influence.[5] The flaccid but sinewy arm, and the hand, with its creased palm and expressive fingers, have no exact parallels,[6] but they serve to dramatize this conventional gesture in a manner strikingly reminiscent of Amarna art.[7] ERR

1. Riefstahl 1951; Martin 1987, cat. 14, pp. 11–12, pl. 5; Fazzini 1975, cat. 70, pp. 86, 136.

2. The same costume worn by Horemheb: see cat. 251.

3. Comparable figure in Horemheb's tomb: Martin 1989, scene 21, pp. 41–43 pls. 32, 34.

4. Already in representations of Khaibausoker, Dynasty 3: Cherpion 1980, pls. 1, 5 (Egyptian Museum, Cairo, CG 1385).

5. Forehead lines: Catharine Roehrig in Metropolitan Museum of Art 1992, pp. 28–29 (MMA, New York, 1985.328.13); Collarbones: cat. 135; Aldred 1973, cats. 49, 117.

6. For lined palms, see Baines 1992. Other examples in this period: cat. 136; Martin 1989, scenes 21, 76, pls. 32, 111; Amarna precursors: Roeder 1969, no. 482-VII, pl. 4.

7. For example, Metropolitan Museum of Art 1992, no. 33, p. 57 (MMA 1985.328.1); Roehrig in Metropolitan Museum of Art 1992, pp. 25, 26 (MMA 1985.328.2, 1982.449).

262. Three foreigners

Probably from Saqqara
Dynasty 18, reign of Tutankhamen,
1332–1322 B.C.
Limestone
H. 20.3 cm, w. 50 cm, d. 5 cm
Collection of Jack A. Josephson, New
York, 120.79

This fragmentary block depicts the heads of three foreigners in its lower, more complete register, and portions of two feet in the upper register. The forward man is a Libyan, identifiable by the two feathers in his hair and a side lock. He is followed by two Western Asiatics, one with a bald or shaved head, the other with a cloth head wrapping. They are undoubtedly prisoners, as evidenced by the cruelly bound wrists of the bald man and the torn earlobes of both, their earrings presumably forcibly removed. Although Geoffrey Martin believes all three are captives, the status of the Libyan is debatable.[1] He could have been a mercenary in the service of the pharaoh, carrying a weapon in his missing hand. The arrogant expression on his face contrasts dramatically with the downcast looks of the other two. The complete scene in the lower register would have shown a procession of captives facing a large representation of a king or an army general. The upper register almost certainly portrayed a line of infantry. The foot on the right is the forward foot of a striding soldier. The big toe and part of the instep from the back foot of the warrior stepping out ahead of him appears on the left.[2] Slight traces of black and red paint survive on the block's surface and modern plaster repairs are visible, particularly on the face of the Libyan. JJ

1. Martin 1987, p.18.

2. Strouhal 1992, p. 207, fig. 220.

263

264

265

263. Small anthropoid bust

Possibly from Deir el-Medina
Dynasty 18, reign of Akhenaten,
1353–1336 B.C.
Wood
H. 7.8 cm
Charles Edwin Wilbour Fund, Brooklyn
Museum of Art, New York, 53.246

264. Large anthropoid bust

Possibly from Deir el-Medina
Late Dynasty 18–early Dynasty 19,
1336–1279 B.C.
Limestone
H. 26.2 cm, w. 15.5 cm
Charles Edwin Wilbour Fund, Brooklyn
Museum of Art, New York, 54.1

Ten New Kingdom sites have each
yielded one or more anthropoid busts.[1]
They are made of granite, limestone,
sandstone, wood, faience, and clay, and
range widely in scale.[2] The heads usually wear tripartite wigs. Some are bald;
others have cropped hair. The amor-
phous torso grows wider as it extends
downward, and its flat surface gives no
indication of arms. Among the approximately 150 surviving busts, several
retain traces of original polychrome
decoration. The most common design
is the broad floral collar, sometimes
embellished with pendant lotus buds
and blossoms. Both women and men
wore the tripartite wig and broadcollar
in the New Kingdom, which makes it
difficult to determine the sex of most
of these busts, if such a distinction was
ever intended.

Because so few were discovered in
datable contexts, these sculptures must
be dated using stylistic analysis. The
earliest seems to have been produced
around the time of Amenhotep II[3]; several have been assigned a general late-
18th-Dynasty date[4]; at least three were
found at Amarna and presumably date
to Akhenaten's reign when, according
to John Cooney, the wooden bust
exhibited here was also carved[5]; the
larger bust is one of many attributed
to the late 18th–early 19th Dynasties.[6]

The bust's form seems to derive from
anthropoid coffins cut off just below the
waist.[7] At least some of these busts represented the *akh*, the spiritual aspect of
the deceased that received offerings.[8]

Keeping generalized images of the
ancestors' *akh*s within their homes,
Egyptians could honor the dead by
depositing food and other gifts on offering tables placed before the busts. They
thus discharged their familial responsibilities without leaving the house. In
exchange for the offerings, the *akh*
guarded the threshold of the house. JFR

1. Keith-Bennett 1981, pp. 47–71.

2. Metropolitan Museum of Art, New York,
66.99.29: Cooney 1953, pp. 8–9, pl. XXIII.

3. Egyptian Museum, Cairo, JE 35885: Keith-
Bennett 1981, no. As 1, p. 54, figs. 4–6.

4. For example, Christos G. Bastis Collection,
New York: Bothmer 1987, cat. 7.

5. Keith-Bennett 1981, nos. Am 1–Am 3, pp. 52-
54, 63, fig. 1; Brooklyn Museum of Art 1956,
cat. 11B, pp. 11-12, pl. 25.

6. Lynn Holden in Brovarski, Doll, and Freed
1982, cat. 409.

7. Chevrier 1935, p. 117.

8. Friedman 1985, p. 84.

265. Situla with erased cartouche

Provenance not known
Dynasty 18, reign of Akhenaten,
1353–1336 B.C.
Faience
H. 30.7 cm, diam. 11.2 cm
The Walters Art Gallery, Baltimore,
48.456

The situla, made in a variety of materials and shapes, was an important
class of ritual vessel during the New
Kingdom.[1] By the mid-18th Dynasty,
situlae were featured in Theban tomb
scenes as part of a milk ritual in which
drops of the sacred liquid were sprinkled on the earth before an advancing
coffin. The vessels were also included
among the food offerings on funerary
stelae as well as in ritual purification
scenes.

At Amarna, situlae are well represented in temple treasuries.[2] In addition,
several bronze examples, inscribed for
Akhenaten, Nefertiti, and Aten, were
found by Pendlebury in the sanctuary
of the Great Temple.[3] A faience example,[4] with the name of Akhenaten erased
from its cartouche, demonstrates the
continued use of the vessel after the
rejection of Atenism. YJM and PL

1. For a detailed discussion of the history and
function of the Egyptian situla, see Lichtheim
1947, pp. 169–70.

2. For example, in the sanctuary of the temple
represented in the Amarna tomb of Meryra I are
two stands with four vessels each that appear to
be situlae. See N. de. G. Davies 1903–8, vol. 1,
pl. XI. For information on the five situlae recovered from the Great Temple, see Pendlebury
1951, pp. 12, 188–89 and pl. LX.

3. Pendlebury 1951, pl. LX.

4. New Kingdom situlae of bichrome faience
were also decorated with painted motifs such as
lotus blossoms. See Elvira D'Amicone in A.
Eggebrecht 1987, cat. 252.

Catalogue authors

CA	Carol Andrews
MEC	Madeleine E. Cody
SD'A	Sue D'Auria
RD	Rosemarie Drenkhahn
ME	Marc Etienne
RAF	Richard A. Fazzini
REF	Rita E. Freed
JLH	Joyce L. Haynes
MJ	Mogens Jørgensen
JJ	Jack Josephson
TK	Timothy Kendall
PL	Peter Lacovara
AAM	Adel A. Mahmoud
PDM	Peter Der Manuelian
YJM	Yvonne J. Markowitz
EP	Elena Pischikova
MJR	Maarten J. Raven
JFR	James F. Romano
ERR	Edna R. Russmann
MS	Mohammed Saleh
SS	Sylvia Schoske
DPS	David P. Silverman
AT	Angela Thomas
MT	May Trad
EV	Eleni Vassilika
DW	Dietrich Wildung

Glossary

A note on spelling and translation

Spelling conventions vary for Egyptian words rendered in English, since hieroglyphs and hieratic indicate only consonant sounds. Quotations from other texts may therefore differ from the spellings used in this book (for example, "Re" instead of "Ra").

Within quotations, words in parentheses are those supplied by the translator to help the sense of the sentence; words in square brackets are those now lost but assumed to have been present in the text; words between "less than" and "greater than" signs (<>) are those apparently left out by the scribe.

We have respected authors' preferences regarding variant translations and the use of the definite article with "Aten" and "Pharaoh."

The numerical designations of pharaohs were not used by the ancient Egyptians, but introduced by Egyptologists to distinguish among kings with the same name. Likewise the designations of Meryra I and II, who were both officials under Akhenaten.

A

Abydos. Center of worship of Osiris, god of death and resurrection, and the most important religious site in ancient Egypt. It included the royal tombs of Dynasty 1, cemeteries, cenotaphs, and several temples.

Akhet. Egyptian word for "horizon," represented in hieroglyphs as a sun-disk between two hills. The ancient name of Amarna was Akhetaten, "Horizon of Aten."

Amen. Theban god, known as "the Hidden One," who became the supreme state god of the New Kingdom and was depicted as a man with a double-plumed crown or a ram with curved horns. Amen was proscribed during the Amarna Period, his image and name erased from the monuments of Egypt.

Ankh. Hieroglyphic sign meaning "life." It was often shown being held by a god before the nose of the king, who was thus given "the breath of life." At Amarna, the entire city was believed to be enlivened by the power of Aten, but only members of the royal family were offered "life" by the hands of Aten's rays.

Atum. Early creator god of Heliopolis, the center of the sun cult during the Old Kingdom. Believed to have risen self-created from the primeval waters, Atum was the foremost god of the Ennead, the nine cosmic deities responsible for the creation of the world. His children were Shu, god of air, and Tefnut, goddess of moisture.

B

Ba. One of the aspects of the human spirit that existed after death, represented by a human-headed bird. The *ba* was believed to travel to and from the tomb.

Bes. Composite household god depicted as a dwarf with a feathered headdress, protruding tongue, shaggy beard, and lion's mane. His image is often found on objects of daily life and, despite the ousting of traditional gods under Atenism, he remained popular at Amarna.

C

Canopic chest. Wood or stone chest, divided into four compartments, used to hold the viscera of a mummified body. The chest sometimes held a set of canopic jars or, for Tutankhamen, minature coffins ("coffinettes").

Cartouche. Oval loop in which the prenomen or nomen of a king was written. The cartouche, the hieroglyph for the verb "to encircle," indicated that the king ruled all that was encompassed by the sun. (For examples, see "Cast of Characters," page 288.)

Cuneiform. System of writing, distinguished by wedge-shaped characters, that was used in the ancient Near East. It was the international form of written communication during the Amarna Period.

D

Double crown. King's crown worn to symbolize the unity of the Two Lands. It combined the White Crown of Upper Egypt and the Red Crown of Lower Egypt

E

Epithet. Descriptive name or title of an individual, such as the Royal Butler Parennefer's: "Clean of Hands."

F

Faience. Nonclay ceramic composed of quartz, lime, and alkali, widely used in Egypt. When combined with water, it can be modeled by hand or shaped in a mold. Upon heating, a reflective, vitreous glaze, described by the ancients as "dazzling," forms on the surface. Faience was often used for decorative architectural elements, amulets, and jewelry.

G

Geb. God who personified Earth. He was the husband of the sky-goddess Nut and the father of Osiris and Isis. Geb was represented anthropomorphically and sometimes colored green to represent vegetation.

Gempaaten. Structures in the temple complex at Karnak and at Amarna dedicated to Aten and built by Akhenaten. A town at Kawa in Nubia was also given this name, which means "Aten is Found."

H

Hapi. God of the Nile's annual inundation. Hapi was portrayed as a corpulent man with pendulous breasts, wearing a headdress of aquatic plants that represented the bounty of the Nile.

Harim. Household of the king's lesser wives, which existed to supply the king with heirs. At Amarna, as elsewhere, the *harim* was a large and lively institution, with its own agricultural lands, overseers, teachers, and entertainers, as well as a contingent of foreign princesses.

Hathor. Goddess of love, music, and motherhood, known as "the Golden One," represented as a woman with a horned sun-disk or as a cow. Associated with her cult was the sistrum, a musical instrument with a column-shaped handle surmounted by a double-sided Hathor mask and a headdress in the form of a shrine, with rods that jingled.

Heb-sed. Festival of the renewal of kingship, usually held after thirty years of a king's reign, and thereafter at more frequent intervals. The king performed a series of rituals in his role as ruler of Upper and Lower Egypt, including offering to various deities. Akhenaten celebrated at least one *heb-sed*, early in his reign.

Hieratic. Cursive form of writing in ancient Egypt, based on hieroglyphs. It was a simpler and quicker means of recording text on papyrus.

Hieroglyphic. Early form of ancient Egyptian writing, composed of ideograms (pictorial signs) and phonograms (sound signs). It is found primarily on monuments, temples, tombs, stelae, and statuary.

Horus. Sun-god manifested by the reigning king, symbolized by a falcon. The son of Osiris and Isis, Horus was awarded the throne of Egypt after a long struggle against Seth, his father's brother and murderer.

Hyksos. Name applied to several Western Asiatic groups that entered the Egyptian Delta at the end of the Middle Kingdom. These foreigners eventually ruled Egypt from their capital in the north and were later expelled by Theban leaders who established the 18th Dynasty. The period of Hyksos rule is also known as the Second Intermediate Period.

I

Isis. Goddess who was the wife of Osiris and the mother of Horus. She was represented in human form wearing a headdress with the throne hieroglyph or sun-disk with horns.

J

Jubilee. See *Heb-sed.*

K

Ka. One of the spiritual components of an individual, symbolized by upraised arms. The *ka*, sometimes translated as "life-force," was created at a person's birth and survived his or her death, residing in the tomb as the recipient of offerings left for the deceased.

Khat headdress. Also known as the bag wig or *afnet*, popular during the Amarna Period. Worn by Akhenaten, Tiye, and Nefertiti, it covered the hair completely and could be topped by other crowns.

Kush. Name used by the ancient Egyptians, Assyrians, and Hebrews for Nubia, Egypt's neighbor to the south, which encompassed the area between modern Aswan and Khartoum.

M

Maat. Goddess depicted as a woman wearing a headdress made of a single ostrich feather. She embodied cosmic order, truth, harmony, and justice.

Mortuary temple. Temple in the royal funerary complex where rituals were celebrated for the cult of the dead king. In the 18th Dynasty, these were constructed on the west bank at Thebes, physically separated from the royal tombs. Akhenaten's mortuary temple, if it existed, has not been identified.

Mummification. The ancient Egyptian method of preserving the body through desiccation. The eviscerated body was immersed in and packed with the mineral salt natron for forty days, then wrapped in linen.

Mut. Member of the Theban sacred triad, consort of Amen and mother of Khonsu. The goddess was typically represented as a woman wearing a vulture headdress topped by the double crown. During the New Kingdom, she was known as "the eye of Ra" and was sometimes depicted as a lioness-headed woman.

N

Nemes headdress. Worn by kings, it was a striped headcloth with lappets in front, and tied in the back.

Nephthys. See Selket.

Nomen. Part of the king's name (titulary) equivalent to the family name. It was often preceded by *sa ra* ("son of Ra") and enclosed in a cartouche.

Nut. Sky goddess, daughter of the first couple (Shu and Tefnut), wife of Geb, and mother of Isis and Osiris. She was represented as a woman whose body curves over the earth.

O

Opet festival. Annual celebration in which barks containing the statues of Amen, Mut, and Khonsu (the Theban holy triad) were carried in procession about a mile and a half, from the Karnak Amen temple to the sanctuary of the Luxor Amen temple, to recharge the king with divine power.

Osiris. God of the underworld, husband of Isis, and father of Horus. He was murdered by his brother Seth and resurrected with the help of Isis. He was usually portrayed as a mummified human wearing a tall crown.

P

Prenomen. The part of the king's name received upon accession to the throne. It typically followed the title *ny sut bity* ("He Who Belongs to the Sedge and the Bee"), was compounded with the name "Ra" ("Aten" during the Amarna Period), and was enclosed within a cartouche.

Ptah. Creator god of Memphis, capable of bringing forth life through words. A patron of craftsmen, he was usually shown as a man in mummy wrappings holding a *was* scepter (see below).

Ptah-Sokar-Osiris. Composite deity represented as a mummiform figure with a tall feather crown. He combined the revitalizing powers of Ptah with the gods of the necropolis (death and resurrection) Sokar and Osiris.

Pylon. Monumental entrance gateway to an Egyptian temple, consisting of two trapezoidal towers. The outer façades were often decorated with large-scale reliefs of the king and gods.

Pyramidion. Small stone pyramid that served as the capstone of a brick pyramid-shaped chapel associated with some New Kingdom private tombs.

R

Ra. Creator/sun god of Heliopolis whose cult gained prominence late in the Old Kingdom (Dynasties 5–6), as manifested by sun temples and the inclusion of the god's name in the titulary of the king. Later, other gods enhanced their divinity by assimilating with this powerful deity.

Ra-Atum. Solar gods of Heliopolis whose amalgamation re-established an early myth in which the creator emerges on a mound of earth from a watery chaos called *Nun.*

Ra-Horakhty. Composite of the sun-god Ra and Horakhty ("Horus of the Horizon"), the sun-god when he rises in the east and is "reborn." Ra-Horakhty was represented as a falcon-headed man.

S

Sakhmet. Goddess of war, daughter of the sun-god Ra, portrayed with the head of a lioness and the body of a woman. More than seven hundred seated statues of the goddess were erected at Thebes, primarily at the Karnak Amen temple.

Scarab. Sacred beetle, believed to possess the powers of self-creation and rejuvenation and thought to represent the god Khepri, who combined the beetle's powers with characteristics of the sun-god Ra.

Sed-festival. See *Heb-sed*.

Selket. One of the four protective goddesses of the deceased. Along with Isis, Nephthys, and Neith, she was mentioned in the Book of the Dead and featured on New Kingdom funerary equipment. Selket's emblem, the scorpion, derived from her association with the desert.

Sem priest. A priest who served as officiant at the Opening of the Mouth ceremony, a symbolic revitalization of the deceased.

Seth. Originally a beneficent god, later viewed as a manifestation of evil. According to myth, he murdered his brother Osiris. He was represented as an unidentifiable animal, with a long muzzle and pointed ears.

Shabti. Mummiform figurine placed in the tomb to work as the representative of the deceased in the fields of the afterlife. *Shabti*s were sometimes provided with model agricultural implements.

Shu. God of sunlight and air, son of the Heliopolitan creator-god Atum. He is often shown as a human with upraised arms, signifying his role as separator of the earth (Geb) and sky (Nut). Akhenaten described Shu as dwelling in the sun's disk (Aten).

Sokar. God of death and patron of the necropolis at Memphis, portrayed as a mummy with the head of a falcon. He was later combined with the gods Ptah and Osiris and worshipped as the composite deity Ptah-Sokar-Osiris.

Stela. Round-topped commemorative tablet. Funerary and votive stelae were placed in tomb chapels and temples. At Amarna, Akhenaten had boundary stelae erected to delineate his plans for the city's construction.

T

Talatat. Building block used during the Amarna Period, with a standard size of 52 by 26 by 24 centimeters (20 by 10 by 10 inches). The name comes from either the Italian *tagliata* ("cut masonry") or the Arabic for "threes."

Tefnut. Primeval goddess, representing moisture, whose twin brother and mate was Shu, god of air. Tefnut was the mother of Geb and Nut and was portrayed as a human with the head of a lioness.

Taweret. Composite goddess, both hippopotamus and woman, with leonine paws and a crocodile tail. She was a popular household divinity protective of women and children.

U

Upper/Lower Egypt. The two traditional geographical divisions of Egypt. Because the Nile flows from south to north, the southern part of the country is designated as Upper Egypt, while the north, including the Delta, is Lower Egypt.

V

Valley of the Kings. Ravine in the cliffs on the west bank of Thebes, chosen by the kings of the New Kingdom for their rock-cut tombs.

Votive chapels. Cult structures built by nonroyal people, in which votive offerings were left and ceremonial meals took place. They had both religious and funerary functions, serving as chapels to various deities, tomb chapels, or chapels for ancestor cults. At Amarna, votive chapels were erected adjacent to the Workmen's Village.

W

Was scepter. A staff split at the bottom and surmounted by a foxlike head. Often held by deities, it became a general symbol of well-being and prosperity.

Cast of Characters

Akhenaten

Neferkheprura Amenhotep IV/
Neferkheprura-Waenra Akhenaten

Pharaoh after Amenhotep III; initiated the Amarna revolution; husband of Nefertiti and Kiya, father of at least six daughters and possibly one son, Tutankhaten/Tutankhamen

Nefertiti

Nefertiti/
Nefernefruaten-Nefertiti/
Ankhkheprura Nefernefruaten

Chief queen of Akhenaten; possibly same individual as Smenkhkara; may have ruled as pharaoh after Akhenaten

Tutankhamen

Nebkheprura Tutankhaten/
Nebkheprura Tutankhamen

Possibly son of Akhenaten and either Nefertiti or Kiya; eventual successor to Akhenaten (after brief reign of Nefertiti/Smenkhkara); husband of Ankhesenpaaten/Ankhesenamen

---

Amenhotep III (Nebmaatra Amenhotep)
Pharaoh; husband of Queen Tiye; father of Amenhotep IV/Akhenaten

Ankhesenpaaten/Ankhesenamen
Third daughter of Akhenaten and Nefertiti; wife of Tutankhaten/Tutankhamen

Ankhesenpaaten-tasherit
Daughter of Akhenaten and (possibly) Ankhesenpaaten or Kiya

Ay (Kheperkheprura Ay)
Probably son of Yuya and Tjuyu and brother of Tiye; Chief of Chariotry under Akhenaten; pharaoh after Tutankhamen

Baketaten
Daughter of Amenhotep III and Tiye; sister of Akhenaten

Horemheb (Djeserkheprura-Setepenra Horemheb)
Commander-in-Chief of the Army under Tutankhamen; pharaoh after Tutankhamen and Ay

Kiya
Secondary wife of Akhenaten; possibly mother of Tutankhamen

Meketaten
Second daughter of Akhenaten and Nefertiti

Meretaten
Eldest daughter of Akhenaten and Nefertiti

Meretaten-tasherit
Daughter of Akhenaten and (possibly) Meretaten or Kiya

Mutbenret
Daughter of Ay; sister of Nefertiti; mother not identified

Nefernefruaten-tasherit
Fourth daughter of Akhenaten and Nefertiti

Nefernefrura
Fifth daughter of Akhenaten and Nefertiti

Setepenra
Sixth daughter of Akhenaten and Nefertiti

Smenkhkara (Ankhkheprura Smenkhkara)
Successor to Akhenaten as pharaoh; possibly Meretaten's husband; may have been Nefertiti under a new name

Tiye
Daughter of Yuya and Tjuyu; chief queen of Amenhotep III

The Exploration of Amarna

1714
French Jesuit priest Claude Sicard describes the first known boundary stela.

1798-99
Napoleon's savants make the first map of Amarna, which is published in a series of volumes called *Description de l'Égypte*, between 1821 and 1830.

1824
Sir John Gardiner Wilkinson explores and maps the city.

1843-45
A Prussian mission under the leadership of Richard Lepsius records monuments and topography. The results are published in *Denkmaeler aus Ægypten und Æthiopien* between 1849 and 1913.

1887
An Amarna woman discovers a cache of nearly four hundred clay tablets inscribed in cuneiform—diplomatic correspondence from the fourteenth century B.C.

1891-92
The Egypt Exploration Fund of London undertakes the first scientific excavation of Amarna, under the directorship of Sir William Matthew Flinders Petrie. Petrie's work is primarily in the Central City.

1903-8
Norman de Garis Davies publishes descriptions of Amarna's private tombs and boundary stelae, with drawings and photographs.

1907-14
The Deutsche Orient-Gesellschaft, under the leadership of Ludwig Borchardt, excavates the North and South suburbs, including the workshop of the sculptor Thutmose, findspot of the Nefertiti bust now at the Ägyptisches Museum, Berlin.

1921-36
T. E. Peet, Sir Leonard Woolley, Henri Frankfort, and J. D. S. Pendlebury, working for the Egypt Exploration Society (formerly the Egypt Exploration Fund), focus on religious and royal structures.

1960s
The Egyptian Antiquities Organization, now Egypt's Supreme Council of Antiquities, excavates at Amarna.

1977 to present
The Egypt Exploration Society resumes work at Amarna under the leadership of Barry Kemp. In 1980, a second mission, led by Geoffrey Martin, describes and copies reliefs from the Royal Tomb, subsequently publishing its findings along with descriptions of objects believed to have come from the tomb.

About the Authors

Sue H. D'Auria, Research Fellow in the Department of Ancient Egyptian, Nubian, and Near Eastern Art at the Museum of Fine Arts, Boston, is an Egyptologist with a specialty in archaeology. She has published numerous articles, organized several exhibitions, and edited a museum catalogue of Egyptian funerary arts.

John L. Foster, former Professor and Chair of the Department of English at Roosevelt University, has been editor of the *Journal of the American Research Center in Egypt* since 1984. He is well-known for his sensitive and lyrical translations of Egyptian texts, some of which can be found in *Hymns, Prayers, and Songs: An Anthology of Ancient Egyptian Lyric Poetry.*

Rita E. Freed is curator of the exhibition and Norma-Jean Calderwood Curator in the Department of Ancient Egyptian, Nubian, and Near Eastern Art at the Museum of Fine Arts, Boston. She has excavated in Egypt, written and lectured extensively on the art of ancient Egypt, and organized several traveling exhibitions on the subject.

W. Raymond Johnson is Director of the Epigraphic Survey, Oriental Institute, University of Chicago, and a specialist in the art and architecture of the late 18th Dynasty. He has written numerous articles on the reign of King Amenhotep III.

Timothy Kendall, Vice-President of the International Society of Nubian Studies, is a specialist in both Ancient Near Eastern and Nubian art and archaeology. He has directed field work at Gebel Barkal (Sudan) and has written numerous articles on warfare in western Asia.

Peter Lacovara is Curator of Ancient Art at the Michael C. Carlos Museum, Emory University, in Atlanta, Georgia. An archaeologist with field experience at Giza, Deir el-Ballas, and the Valley of the Kings, he has also organized exhibitions and published numerous articles and books, including *The New Kingdom Royal City.*

Michael Mallinson is an award-winning architect (Mallinson Architects, London) with experience in museum installations and historic conservation. A former member of the Egypt Exploration Society Expedition team, he participated in recent survey and restoration work in the Central City at Amarna.

Peter Der Manuelian is a Research Fellow in the Department of Ancient Egyptian, Nubian, and Near Eastern Art at the Museum of Fine Arts, Boston. He has published monographs on the New Kingdom and Late Period and is co-editor of The Giza Mastabas series, on the Old Kingdom cemeteries surrounding the Giza Pyramids.

Yvonne J. Markowitz, the Suzanne E. Chapman Artist in the Department of Ancient Egyptian, Nubian, and Near Eastern Art at the Museum of Fine Arts, Boston, is an Egyptologist and jewelry historian with a special interest in ancient Egyptian crafts. She is editor of *Jewelry: Journal of the American Society of Jewelry Historians.*

William J. Murnane is Professor of Ancient History at the University of Memphis. An Egyptologist, he is Director of the Amarna Boundary Stelae Project and the Karnak Hypostyle Hall Project. His books *Ancient Egyptian Coregencies* and *Texts from the Amarna Period* are invaluable references for all in the field.

Donald B. Redford is Professor of Classics, Ancient Mediterranean Studies, and History at Pennsylvania State University. He serves as Director of the Akhenaten Temple Project at Karnak and is a leading Amarna scholar whose books on the subject include *The Akhenaten Temple Project: East Karnak Expedition 1986-1987* and *Akhenaten: The Heretic King.*

Nicholas Reeves is Director of the Amarna Royal Tombs Project in the Valley of the Kings. He is Honorary Fellow at the Oriental Museum, Durham, and Honorary Research Fellow at the Institute of Archaeology in London. His books include *Valley of the Kings: Decline of a Royal Necropolis, The Complete Tutankhamun,* and *The Complete Valley of the Kings.* A new study on the Amarna pharaohs is forthcoming.

David P. Silverman is Professor of Egyptology and Chair of the Department of Asian and Middle Eastern Studies at the University of Pennsylvania. He has excavated at several sites in Egypt, curated Egyptian exhibitions, and written on a variety of subjects, including Egyptian religion, language, and art.

Bibliography

Abbreviations

ADAIK = Abhandlungen des Deutschen Archäologischen Instituts Kairo

AJA = American Journal of Archaeology

AO = Acta Orientalia

ASAE = Annales du Service des Antiquités de l'Égypt

BÄBA = Beiträge zur Ägyptischen Bauforschung und Altertumskunde

BES = Bulletin of the Egyptological Seminar

BIFAO = Bulletin de l'Institut Français d'Archéologie Orientale

BiOr = Bibliotheca Orientalis

BMFA = Bulletin of the Museum of Fine Arts

BMMA = Bulletin of the Metropolitan Museum of Art

BSEG = Bulletin, Société d'Égyptologie

BSFE = Bulletin de la Société Française d'Égyptologie

CdE = Chronique d'Égypte

CHB = Chicago House Bulletin

CRIPEL = Cahier de Recherches de l'Institut de Papyrologie et d'Égyptologie de Lille

DE = Discussions in Egyptology

EA = Egyptian Archaeology

GM = Göttinger Miszellen

HÄB = Hildesheimer Ägyptologische Beiträge

JARCE = Journal of the American Research Center in Egypt

JBM = Jahrbuch der Berliner Museen

JCS = Journal of Cuneiform Studies

JEA = Journal of Egyptian Archaeology

JNES = Journal of Near Eastern Studies

JPK = Jahrbuch Preussischer Kulturbesitz

JPKu = Jahrbuch der Preussischen Kunstsammlungen

JSSEA = Journal of the Society for the Study of Egyptian Antiquities

KMT = KMT, A Modern Journal of Ancient Egypt

LÄ = Lexikon der Ägyptologie

MÄS = Müncher Ägyptologische Studien

MDAIK = Mitteilungen des Deutschen Archäologischen Instituts

MeB = Medelhavsmuseet Bulletin

MonPiot = Monuments et mémoires, Fondation Eugène Piot

MNCG = Meddelelser fra Ny Carlsberg Glyptotek

OMRO = Oudheidkundige Mededelingen uit het Rijksmuseum van Oudheden te Leiden

RdE = Revue d'Égyptologie

SAK = Studien zur altägyptischen Kultur

WA = World Archaeology

ZÄS = Zeitschrift für ägyptische Sprache

Adams 1977
William Y. Adams. *Nubia: Corridor to Africa*. Princeton, 1977.

el-Aguizy 1987
Ola el-Aguizy. "Dwarfs and Pygmies in Ancient Egypt." *ASAE* 71 (1987), pp. 53–60.

Ägyptisches Museum 1967
Ägyptisches Museum, Berlin. *Ägyptisches Museum, Berlin. Staatliche Museen (West Berlin)*. Berlin, 1967.

Ägyptisches Museum 1985
Ägyptisches Museum, Berlin. *Egyptian Museum*. Staatliche Museen Preussischer Kulturbesitz. Berlin, 1985.

Aldred 1952
Cyril Aldred. *The Development of Ancient Egyptian Art, from 3200 to 1315 B.C.* London, 1952.

Aldred 1957
Cyril Aldred. "The End of the El-'Amarna Period." *JEA* 43 (1957), pp. 30–41.

Aldred 1971
Cyril Aldred. *Jewels of the Pharaohs*. London, 1971.

Aldred 1973
Cyril Aldred. *Akhenaten and Nefertiti*. Exh. cat., The Brooklyn Museum. New York, 1973.

Aldred 1976
Cyril Aldred. "The Horizon of the Aten." *JEA* 62 (1976), p. 184.

Aldred 1982
Cyril Aldred. "El Amarna." In *Excavating in Egypt: The Egypt Exploration Society 1882–1982*, ed. T. G. H. James, pp. 89–106. Chicago and London, 1982.

Aldred 1988
Cyril Aldred. *Akhenaten, King of Egypt*. London, 1988.

J. Allen 1982
James P. Allen. "Synthetic and Analytic Tenses in the Pyramid Texts." In *L'Égyptologie en 1979: Colloques internationaux du Centre National de la Recherche Scientifique*. No. 595, pp. 19–32. Paris, 1982.

J. Allen 1988a
James P. Allen. *Genesis in Egypt: The Philosophy of Ancient Egyptian Creation Accounts*. New Haven, 1988.

J. Allen 1988b
James P. Allen. "Two Altered Inscriptions of the Late Amarna Period." *JARCE* 25 (1988), pp. 117–26.

J. Allen 1989
James P. Allen. "The Natural Philosophy of Akhenaten." In *Religion and Philosophy in Ancient Egypt*, Yale Egyptological Studies 3, ed. William Kelly Simpson, pp. 89–102. New Haven, 1989.

J. Allen 1991
James P. Allen. "Akhenaten's 'Mystery' Coregent and Successor." *Amarna Letters* 1 (1991), pp. 74–85.

J. Allen 1994
James P. Allen. "Nefertiti and Smenkh-ka-re." *GM* 141 (1994), pp. 7–17.

J. Allen 1996
James P. Allen. "The Religion of Amarna." In Dorothea Arnold, *The Royal Women of Amarna: Images of Beauty from Ancient Egypt*, pp. 3–5. Exh. cat., The Metropolitan Museum of Art. New York, 1996.

S. Allen 1997
Susan Allen. "Spinning Bowls: "Representation and Reality." In *Ancient Egypt, the Aegean, and the Near East: Studies in Honour of Martha Rhoads Bell,* ed. Jacke Phillips, pp. 17–38. San Antonio, 1997.

Andrews 1990
Carol Andrews. *Ancient Egyptian Jewellery.* London, 1990.

Andrews 1994
Carol Andrews. *Amulets of Ancient Egypt.* Austin, 1994.

Arnold 1996
Dorothea Arnold. *The Royal Women of Amarna: Images of Beauty from Ancient Egypt,* with contributions by James P. Allen and L. Green. Exh. cat., The Metropolitan Museum of Art. New York, 1996.

Arnold and Bourriau 1993
Dorothea Arnold and Janine Bourriau. *An Introduction to Ancient Egyptian Pottery.* Mainz am Rhein, 1993.

Asselbergs 1923
Henri Asselbergs. "Ein merkwürdiges Relief Amenophis IV im Louvre-Museum." *ZÄS* 58 (1923), pp. 36–38.

Assmann 1975
Jan Assmann. *Ägyptische Hymnen und Gebete.* Zurich, 1975.

Assmann 1976
Jan Assmann. "Harachte." *LÄ* 2 (1976), cols. 956–61.

Assmann 1984
Jan Assmann. "Das Grab mit gewundnem Abstieg: Zum Typenwandel des Privat-Felsgrabes im Neuen Reich." *MDAIK* 40 (1984), pp. 277–90.

Assmann 1992
Jan Assmann. "Akhanyati's Theology in Light and Time." *Proceedings of the Israel Academy of Sciences and Humanities,* VII 4, pp. 143–76. Jerusalem, 1992.

Assmann 1995
Jan Assmann. *Egyptian Solar Religion in the New Kingdom: Re, Amun and the Crisis of Polytheism,* trans. Anthony Alcock. London, 1995.

Assmann 1997
Jan Assmann. *Moses the Egyptian: The Memory of Egypt in Western Monotheism.* London, 1997.

Aubert and Aubert 1974
Jacques Aubert and Liliane Aubert. *Statuettes Égyptienne: Chaouabtis, ouchebtis.* Paris, 1974.

Badawy 1968
Alexander Badawy. *A History of Egyptian Architecture: The Empire (the New Kingdom), from the End of the Eighteenth Dynasty to the End of the Twentieth Dynasty, 1580–1085 B.C.* Berkeley and Los Angeles, 1968.

Bailey 1997
Donald Bailey. "Animal-Shaped Weights of the Late Bronze Age in the British Museum." In *Ancient Egypt, the Aegean, and the Near East: Studies in Honour of Martha Rhoads Bell,* ed. Jacke Phillips, pp. 67–80. San Antonio, 1997.

Baines 1985
John Baines. *Fecundity Figures: Egyptian Personification and the Iconography of a Genre.* Wiltshire, 1985.

Baines 1992
John Baines. "Open Palms." In *Atti Sesto Congresso Internazionale di Egittologia.* Vol. 1, pp. 29–32. Turin, 1992.

Baines 1996
John Baines. "Classicism and Modernism in the Literature of the New Kingdom." In *Ancient Egyptian Literature, History and Forms,* ed. Anthony Loprieno, pp. 157–75. Leiden, 1996.

Baines 1998
John Baines. "The Dawn of the Amarna Age." In *Amenhotep III: Perspectives on His Reign,* ed. David O'Connor and Eric H. Cline, pp. 271–312. Ann Arbor, 1998.

Baines and Málek 1980
John Baines and Jaromir Málek. *Atlas of Ancient Egypt.* Oxford, 1980.

Barber 1991
E. J. Barber. *Prehistoric Textiles.* Princeton, 1991.

Beckwith and Saitoti 1980
Carol Beckwith and Teplit O. Saitoti, *Maasai.* New York, 1980.

L. Bell 1985
Lanny Bell. "Luxor Temple and the Cult of the Royal Ka." *JNES* 44 (1985), pp. 251–94.

L. Bell 1986
Lanny Bell. "La parenté de Toutankhamon." *Les Dossiers: Histoire et Archéologie* (1986), pp. 47–49.

L. Bell 1997
Lanny Bell. "Two Ceremonial Manacles from Ancient Egypt." In *Ancient Egypt, the Aegean, and the Near East: Studies in Honour of Martha Rhoads Bell,* ed. Jacke Phillips, pp. 81–86. San Antonio, 1997.

M. Bell 1990
Martha Bell. "An Armchair Excavation of KV 55." *JARCE* 27 (1990), pp. 97–137.

Bénédite 1920
Georges Bénédite. "Amon et Toutânkamon." MonPiot 24, pp. 47–68. Paris, 1920.

Bennett 1939
John Bennett. "The Restoration Stela of Tut'ankhamūn." *JEA* 25 (1939), pp. 8–15.

Berlandini 1982
Jocelyne Berlandini. "Les tombes amarniennes et d'époque Toutânkhamon à Sakkara: Critières stylistiques." In *L'Égyptologie en 1979: Colloques internationaux du Centre National de la Recherche Scientifique.* No. 595, pp. 195–212. Paris, 1982.

Berman and Letellier 1996
Lawrence M. Berman and Bernadette Letellier. *Pharaohs: Treasures of Egyptian Art from the Louvre.* Cleveland, 1996.

Bickel 1997
Susanne Bickel. *Untersuchungen im Totentempel des Merneptah in Theben, unter der Leitung von Horst Jaritz III: Tore und andere wiederverwendete Bauteile Amenophis' III.* BÄBA 16. Stuttgart, 1997.

Bickel and Jaritz 1994
Susanne Bickel and Horst Jaritz. "Une porte monumentale d'Amenhotep III: Second rapport préliminaire sur les blocs réemployés dans le temple de Merenptah à Gurna." *BIAFO* 94 (1994), pp. 277–85.

Bienkowski 1994
Piotr B. Bienkowski. "A Servant in the Land of Egypt." In *The Unbroken Reed: Studies in the Culture and Heritage of Ancient Egypt in Honour of A. F. Shore,* ed. Christopher Eyre, Anthony Leahy, and Lisa Montagno Leahy, pp. 53-64. London, 1994.

Blackman 1917
Aylward M. Blackman. "The Nugent and Haggard Collections." *JEA* 4 (1917), pp. 39–46.

Blackman 1937
Aylward M. Blackman. "Preliminary Report on the Excavations at Sesebi, Northern Province, Anglo-Egyptian Sudan, 1936–37." *JEA* 23 (1937), pp. 145–51, pls. 12–19.

Blankenberg-van Delden 1969
C. Blankenberg-van Delden. *The Large Commemorative Scarabs of Amenhotep III.* Leiden, 1969.

Bomann 1991
Ann H. Bomann. *The Private Chapel in Ancient Egypt: A Study of the Chapels in the Workmen's Village at El Amarna with Special Reference to Deir el Medina and Other Sites.* London and New York, 1991.

Borchardt 1925
Ludwig Borchardt. *Catalogue général des antiquités égyptiennes du Musée du Caire: Statuen und Statuetten von Königen und Privatleuten.* Berlin, 1925.

Borchardt and Ricke 1980
Ludwig Borchardt and Herbert Ricke. *Die Wohnhäuser in Tell el-Amarna.* Berlin, 1980.

Borowski 1998
Oded Borowski. *Every Living Thing: Daily Use of Animals in Ancient Israel.* Walnut Creek, Calif., 1998.

Bothmer 1949
Bernard V. Bothmer. "The Dwarf as Bearer." *BMFA* 47 (1949), pp. 9–11.

Bothmer 1966–67
Bernard V. Bothmer. "Private Sculpture of Dynasty XVIII in Brooklyn." *Brooklyn Museum Annual* 8 (1966–67), pp. 55–89.

Bothmer 1978
Bernard V. Bothmer. "On Photographing Egyptian Art." *SAK* 6 (1978), pp. 51–53.

Bothmer 1987
Bernard V. Bothmer. "Egyptian Antiquities." In *Antiquities from the Collection of Christos G. Bastis*, ed. Emma Swan Hall, pp. 1–106. New York, 1987.

Bothmer 1990
Bernard V. Bothmer. "Eyes and Iconography in the Splendid Century: King Amenhotep III and His Aftermath." In *The Art of Amenhotep III: Art Historical Analysis*, ed. Lawrence M. Berman, pp. 84–92. Cleveland, 1990.

Bothmer and Keith 1970
Bernard V. Bothmer and Jean L. Keith. "Brief Guide to the Department of Ancient Art," The Brooklyn Museum. Brooklyn, 1970.

Bothmer and Keith 1974
Bernard V. Bothmer and Jean L. Keith. "Brief Guide to the Department of Egyptian and Classical Art." The Brooklyn Museum. Brooklyn, 1974.

Bouriant, Legrain, and Jéquier 1903
Urbain Bouriant, Georges Legrain, and Gustave Jéquier. *Monuments pour servir à l'étude du culte d'Atonou en Égypte I: Les tombes de Khouitatonou*. Cairo, 1903.

Bourriau 1981
Janine Bourriau. *Umm El-Ga'ab: Pottery from the Nile Valley before the Arab Conquest*. Cambridge, 1981.

Boyce 1989
Andrew Boyce. "Notes on the Manufacture and Use of Faience Rings at Amarna." *Amarna Reports* 5 (1989), pp. 160–68.

Boyce 1995
Andrew Boyce. "Reports on the Excavation of House P.46.33: The Finds." *Amarna Reports* 6 (1995), pp. 44–136.

Breasted 1934
James Henry Breasted. *The Dawn of Conscience*. New York and London, 1934.

Brewer and Friedman 1989
Douglas Brewer and Renée Friedman. *Fish and Fishing in Ancient Egypt*. Warminster, 1989.

Brier 1998
Bob Brier. *The Murder of Tutankhamen*. New York, 1998.

Brinkmann 1967
E. M. Brinkmann. "Die Statue des Gottes Amun im Badischen Landesmuseum." *Jahrbuch der Staatlichen Kunstsammlungen in Baden-Württemberg* 4 (1967), pp. 7–18.

Brock 1995
Lyla Pinch Brock. "Theodore Davis and the Rediscovery of Tomb 55." In *Valley of the Sun Kings: New Explorations in the Tombs of the Pharaohs*, ed. Richard H. Wilkinson, pp. 34–46. Tucson, 1995.

Brock 1997
Lyla Pinch Brock. "The Final Clearance of KV 55." In *Ancient Egypt, the Aegean, and the Near East: Studies in Honour of Martha Rhoads Bell*, ed. Jacke Phillips, pp. 121–36. San Antonio, 1997.

Brooklyn Museum of Art 1956
Five Years of Collecting Egyptian Art, 1951–1956. Exh. cat., The Brooklyn Museum. Brooklyn, 1956.

Brooklyn Museum of Art 1993
"Akhenaten and His Family." Brooklyn Museum West Wing Gallery Guides. Brooklyn, 1993.

Brooklyn Museum of Art 1999
Art for Eternity: Masterworks from Ancient Egypt. Exh. cat., Brooklyn Museum of Art. Brooklyn, 1999.

Brovarski 1983
Edward Brovarski. "Sokar." *LÄ* 5 (1983), cols. 1055–74.

Brovarski, Doll, and Freed 1982
Edward Brovarski, Susan K. Doll, and Rita E. Freed. *Egypt's Golden Age: The Art of the New Kingdom 1558–1085 B.C.* Exh. cat., Museum of Fine Arts, Boston. Boston, 1982.

Brunner 1979
Hellmut Brunner. "Sokar im Totentempel Amenophis' III." In *Festschrift Elmar Edel*, ed. Manfred Görg and Edgar Pusch, pp. 60–65. Bamberg, 1979.

Brunner-Traut 1975
Emma Brunner-Traut. "Farben." *LÄ* 2 (1986), cols. 117–28.

Brunner-Traut 1986
Emma Brunner-Traut. "Tanz." *LÄ* 6 (1986), cols. 215–31.

Brunner-Traut, Brunner, and Zick-Nissen 1984
Emma Brunner-Traut, Hellmut Brunner, and Johanna Zick-Nissen. *Osiris, Kreuz und Halbmond*. Mainz am Rhein, 1984.

Brunton and Engelbach 1927
Guy Brunton and Reginald Engelbach. *Gurob*. London, 1927.

Bryan 1991
Betsy M. Bryan. *The Reign of Thutmosis IV*. Baltimore, 1991.

Bryce 1990
Trevor R. Bryce. "The Death of Niphururiya and Its Aftermath." *JEA* 76 (1990), pp. 97–105.

Capel and Markoe 1996
Anne K. Capel and Glenn E. Markoe, eds. *Mistress of the House, Mistress of Heaven: Women in Ancient Egypt*. New York, 1996.

Carter and Mace 1923
Howard Carter and A. C. Mace. *The Tomb of Tut-ankh-amen* 1. London, 1923.

Chappaz 1983
Jean-Luc Chappaz. "Le premier édifice d'Aménophis IV à Karnak." *BSEG* 8 (1983), pp. 13–45.

Cherpion 1980
Nadine Cherpion. "Le mastaba de Khabaousokar (MM A₂): Problèmes de chronologie." *Orientalia Lovaniensia Periodica* 11 (1980), pp. 79–90.

Chevrier 1926
Henri Chevrier. "Rapport sur les travaux de Karnak (mars–mai 1926)." *ASAE* 26 (1926), pp. 119–30.

Chevrier 1927
Henri Chevrier. "Rapport sur les travaux de Karnak (novembre–mai 1927)." *ASAE* 27 (1927), pp. 134–53.

Chevrier 1935
Henri Chevrier, "Rapport sur les travaux de Karnak (1934–1935)." *ASAE* 35 (1935), pp. 97–121.

Chevrier 1938
Henri Chevrier. "Rapport sur les travaux de Karnak (1937–1938)." *ASAE* 38 (1938), pp. 567–608.

Connolly, Harrison, and Ahmed 1976
R. C. Connolly, R. G. Harrison, and Soheir Ahmed. "Serological Evidence for the Parentage of Tut'ankhamun and Smenkhkare." *JEA* 62 (1976), pp. 184–86.

Cooney 1953
John D. Cooney. "Egyptian Art in the Collection of Albert Gallatin." *JNES* 12 (1953), pp. 1–19.

Cooney 1965
John D. Cooney. *Amarna Reliefs from Hermopolis in American Collections*. Brooklyn, 1965.

Cooney 1976
John D. Cooney. *Catalogue of Egyptian Antiquities in the British Museum: IV, Glass*. London, 1976.

Crompton 1916
Winifred Crompton. "Two Clay Balls in the Manchester Museum." *JEA* 3 (1916), p. 128, pl. XVI.

Daniel 1971
Laurent Daniel. "Reconstruction d'une paroi du temple d'Aton à Karnak." *Kêmi* 21 (1971), pp. 151–54.

Daressy 1903
Georges Daressy. "Le palais d'Aménophis III et le Birket Habou." *ASAE* 4 (1903), pp. 165–70.

Daressy 1920
Georges Daressy. "Un groupe de Saft el Henneh." *ASAE* 20 (1920), pp. 123–28.

Dasen 1988
Véronique Dasen. "Dwarfism in Egypt and Classical Antiquity: Iconography and Medical History." *Medical History* 32 (1988), pp. 253–76.

Dasen 1993
Véronique Dasen. *Dwarfs in Ancient Egypt and Greece.* Oxford, 1993.

Daumas 1977
François Daumas. "Hathor." *LÄ* 2 (1977), cols. 1024–33.

B. G. Davies 1992
Benedict G. Davies, trans. *Egyptian Historical Records of the Later Eighteenth Dynasty,* Fascicle IV. Warminster, 1992.

N. de G. Davies 1903–8
Norman de Garis Davies. *The Rock Tombs of El Amarna.* 6 vols. London, 1903–8.

N. de G. Davies 1923
Norman de Garis Davies. "Akhenaten at Thebes." *JEA* 9 (1923), pp. 132–52.

N. de G. Davies 1941
Norman de Garis Davies. *The Tomb of the Vizier Ramose.* London, 1941.

N. de G. Davies 1943
Norman de Garis Davies. *The Tomb of Rekh-mi-Rēʿ.* Vol. 2. New York, 1943.

W. V. Davies 1982
W. V. Davies. "The Origin of the Blue Crown." *JEA* 68 (1982), pp. 69–76.

W. V. Davies 1987a
W. V. Davies. *Catalogue of Egyptian Antiquities in the British Museum: VII, Tools and Weapons.* Vol. 1. London, 1987.

W. V. Davies 1987b
W. V. Davies. *Egyptian Hieroglyphs.* Berkeley and London, 1987.

Davis et al. 1907
Theodore M. Davis, Gaston Maspero, and Percy Newberry. *The Tomb of Iouiya and Touiyou.* London, 1907.

Davis et al. 1910
Theodore M. Davis, Gaston Maspero, G. Elliot Smith, Edward Ayrton, and George Daressy. *The Tomb of Queen Tîyi.* London, 1910.

Davis et al. 1912
Theodore M. Davis, Gaston Maspero, and Georges Daressy. *The Tombs of Harmhabi and Toutânkhamanou.* London, 1912.

Davis et al. 1990
Theodore M. Davis, Gaston Maspero,

G. Elliot Smith, Edward Ayrton, Georges Daressy, and Nicholas Reeves. *The Tomb of Queen Tîyi.* 2nd ed. San Francisco, 1990.

De Meulenaere 1976
Herman De Meulenaere, ed. *Égypte éternelle: Chefs-d'oeuvre du Brooklyn Museum.* Exh. cat., Musées Royaux d'Art et d'Histoire. Brussels, 1976.

Dewachter 1984
Michel Dewachter. "Les 'Premiers fils royaux d'Amon': Compléments et remarques." *RdE* 35 (1984), pp. 83–94.

Dodson 1990
Aidan Dodson. "Crown Prince Djhutmose and the Royal Sons of the Eighteenth Dynasty." *JEA* 76 (1990), pp. 87–96.

Dodson 1994a
Aidan Dodson. *The Canopic Equipment of the Kings of Egypt.* London, 1994.

Dodson 1994b
Aidan Dodson. "Kings' Valley Tomb 55." *Amarna Letters* 3 (1994), pp. 92–103.

Doll 1982a
Susan K. Doll. "The Farm and Barnyard." In *Egypt's Golden Age: The Art of the New Kingdom 1558–1085. B.C.,* ed. Edward Brovarski, Susan K. Doll, and Rita E. Freed. Exh. cat., Museum of Fine Arts, Boston. Boston, 1982.

Doll 1982b
Susan K. Doll. "Weights and Measures." In *Egypt's Golden Age: The Art of the New Kingdom, 1558–1085. B.C.,* ed. Edward Brovarski, Susan K. Doll, and Rita E. Freed. Exh. cat., Museum of Fine Arts, Boston. Boston, 1982.

Drenkhahn 1989
Rosemarie Drenkhahn. *Ägyptische Reliefs im Kestner-Museum Hannover.* Hannover, 1989.

Dunham 1970
Dows Dunham. *The Barkal Temples.* Boston, 1970.

Eastwood 1985
Gilian M. Eastwood. "Preliminary Report on the Textiles." *Amarna Reports* 2 (1985), pp. 191–204.

Eaton 1942
Elizabeth S. Eaton. "Recent Discoveries in the Egyptian Department I: A Fragment from a Statue of King Eye." *BMFA* 40 (1942), pp. 42–45.

Eaton-Krauss 1976
Marianne Eaton-Krauss. "Concerning Standard-Bearing Statues." *SAK* 4 (1976), pp. 69–73.

Eaton-Krauss 1981
Marianne Eaton-Krauss. "Miscellanea Amarnensia." *CdE* 56 (1981) pp. 245–64.

Eaton-Krauss 1985
Marianne Eaton-Krauss. "Tutanchamun." *LÄ* 6 (1985), cols. 812–16.

Eaton-Krauss 1988
Marianne Eaton-Krauss. "Tutankhamen at Karnak." *MDAIK* 44 (1988), pp. 1–11.

Eaton-Krauss 1990
Marianne Eaton-Krauss. "Akhenaten versus Akhenaten." *BiOr* 47 (1990), pp. 541–59.

Eaton-Krauss 1992
Marianne Eaton-Krauss. Review of *Corpus der hieroglyphischen Inschriften aus dem Grab des Tutankhamen,* by Horst Beinlich. *JEA* 78 (1992), pp. 333–36.

Eaton-Krauss 1994
Marianne Eaton-Krauss. Review of *The Complete Tutankhamen: The King, the Tomb, the Royal Treasure,* by Nicholas Reeves. *JEA* 80 (1994), pp. 253–56.

Eaton-Krauss and Murnane 1991
Marianne Eaton-Krauss and William Murnane. "Tutankhamen, Ay, and the Avenue of Sphinxes between Pylon X and the Mut Precinct at Karnak." *BSEG* 15 (1991), pp. 31–38.

Edwards 1976
I. E. S. Edwards. *Treasures of Tutankhamun.* New York, 1976.

A. Eggebrecht 1987
Arne Eggebrecht, ed. *Ägyptens Aufstieg zur Weltmacht.* Exh. cat., Roemer-und-Pelizaeus-Museum. Hildesheim, 1987.

E. Eggebrecht 1976
Eva Eggebrecht. "Handschuhe." *LÄ* 2 (1976), cols. 948–49.

Eisen 1916
Gustavus Eisen. "The Characteristics of Eye Beads from the Earliest Times to the Present." *AJA* 20 (1916), pp. 1–27.

Emery, Smith, and Millard 1979
Walter B. Emery, H. S. Smith, and A. Millard. *The Fortress of Buhen: The Archaeo-logical Report.* London, 1979.

Epigraphic Survey 1980
Epigraphic Survey, Oriental Institute of the University of Chicago. *The Tomb of Kheruef.* Chicago, 1980.

Erman 1900
Adolf Erman. "Geschichtliche Inschriften aus dem Berliner Museum." *ZÄS* 38 (1900), pp. 112–26.

Ertman 1995
Earl L. Ertman. "Evidence of the Alterations to the Canopic Jar Portraits and Coffin Mask from KV 55." In *Valley of the Sun Kings: New Explorations in the Tombs of the Pharaohs,* ed. Richard H. Wilkinson, pp. 108–21. Tucson, 1995.

Eyre 1990
Christopher J. Eyre. "The Semna Stelae: Quotation, Genre, and Functions of Literature." In *Studies in Egyptology Presented to Miriam Lichtheim,* ed. Sarah I. Groll, pp. 134–65. Jerusalem, 1990.

Fairman 1938
Herbert W. Fairman. "Preliminary Report on the Excavations at Sesebi (Sudla) and 'Amārah West, Anglo-Egyptian Sudan, 1937–38." *JEA* 24 (1938), pp. 151–56, pls. 8–10.

Fairman 1949
Herbert W. Fairman. "Town Planning in Pharaonic Egypt." *Town Planning Review* 20 (1949), pp. 32–51.

Fairman 1972
Herbert W. Fairman. "Tutankhamun and the End of the Eighteenth Dynasty." *Antiquity* 46 (1972), pp. 15–18.

Fay 1986
Biri Fay. "Nefertiti Times Three." *JPK* 23 (1986), pp. 359–76.

Fazzini 1975
Richard A. Fazzini. *Images for Eternity: Egyptian Art from Berkeley and Brooklyn.* Exh. cat., Fine Arts Museums

of San Francisco. San Francisco and Brooklyn, 1975.

Fazzini et al. 1989
Richard A. Fazzini, Robert S. Bianchi, James F. Romano, and Donald B. Spanel, eds. *Egyptian Art in the Brooklyn Museum*. Brooklyn, 1989.

Fazzini 1997
Richard Fazzini. "The Wilbour Plaque at the Brooklyn Museum." *Antiques* (January 1997), pp. 218–21.

Feucht 1995
Erika Feucht. *Das Kind im Alten Ägypten*. Frankfurt am Main, 1995.

Fischer 1973
Henry G. Fischer. "An Eleventh Dynasty Couple Holding the Sign of Life." *ZÄS* 100 (1973), pp. 16–28.

Fischer 1980
Henry G. Fischer. "Proskynese." *LÄ* 4 (1980), cols. 1125–27.

Forman and Quirke 1996
Werner Forman and Stephen Quirke. *Hieroglyphs and the Afterlife in Ancient Egypt*. Norman, Okla., 1996.

Foster 1992
John L. Foster, trans. *Echoes of Egyptian Voices: An Anthology of Ancient Egyptian Poetry*. Norman, Okla., and London, 1992.

Foster 1995
John L. Foster, trans. *Hymns, Prayers, and Songs: An Anthology of Ancient Egyptian Lyric Poetry*, ed. Susan Tower Hollis. Atlanta, 1995.

Frankfort and Pendlebury 1933
Henri Frankfort and J. D. S. Pendlebury. *The City of Akhenaten* 2. London, 1933.

Freed 1987
Rita E. Freed. *Ramesses the Great and His Time*. Memphis, 1987.

Freud 1939
Sigmund Freud. *Der Mann Moses und die monotheistische Religion*. Amsterdam, 1939.

Friedman 1985
Florence Friedman. "On the Meaning of Some Anthropoid Busts from Deir el-Medîna." *JEA* 71 (1985), pp. 82–97.

Friedman 1986
Florence Friedman. "ꜣḫ [akh] in the Amarna Period." *JARCE* 23 (1986), pp. 99–106.

Friedman 1998
Florence Friedman, ed. *Gifts of the Nile: Ancient Egyptian Faience*. Exh. cat., Museum of the Rhode Island School of Design. Providence, 1998.

Fritz 1991
Walter Fritz. "Bemerkungen zum Datierungsvermerk auf der Amarnatafel Kn 27." *SAK* 18 (1991), pp. 207–14.

Gaballa 1976
G. A. Gaballa. *Narrative in Egyptian Art*. Mainz, 1976.

Gaballa 1977
G. A. Gaballa. "The Chief Worker in Fine Gold, Ptahmay—An Inquest." *GM* 26 (1977), pp. 13–16.

Gabolde 1990
Marc Gabolde. "Le droit d'aînesse d'Ankhesenpaaton (à propos de deux récents articles sur la stèle UC 410)." *BSEG* 14 (1990), pp. 33–47.

Gabolde 1992a
Marc Gabolde. "Baketaton fille de Kiya?" *BSEG* 16 (1992), pp. 27–40.

Gabolde 1992b
Marc Gabolde. *Le père divin Äy*. Ph.D. dissertation, University of Lyons II, 1992.

Gabolde 1993
Marc Gabolde. "La postérité d'Aménophis III." *Égyptes* 1 (1993), pp. 29–34.

Gardiner 1928
Alan H. Gardiner. "The Graffito from the Tomb of Pere." *JEA* 14 (1928), pp. 10–11.

Gardiner 1935
Alan H. Gardiner. *The Temple of King Sethos I at Abydos*. Vol. 2: *The Chapels of Amen-Re, Re-Harakhti, Ptah, and King Sethos*. London and New York, 1935.

Gardiner 1969
Alan H. Gardiner. *Egyptian Grammar*. 3rd ed. Oxford, 1969.

Germer 1984
Renate Germer. "Die angebliche Mumie de Tije: Probleme interdisziplinärer Arbeiten." *SAK* 11 (1984), pp. 85–90.

Gessler-Löhr 1989
Beatrix Gessler-Löhr. "Bemerkungen zu einigen wbꜣw njswt der nach-Amarnazeit." *GM* 112 (1989), pp. 27–34.

Gessler-Löhr 1995
Beatrix Gessler-Löhr. "Bemerkungen zur Nekropole des Neuen Reiches von Saqqara vor der Amarna-Zeit, I: Gräber der Wesire von Unterägypten." In *Gedenkschrift für Winifried Barta, Münchener Ägyptologische Untersuchungen* 4, ed. Dieter Kessler and Regine Schulz, pp. 133–57. Frankfurt, 1995.

Gessler-Löhr 1997
Beatrix Gessler-Löhr. "Bemerkungen zur Nekropole des Neuen Reiches von Saqqara vor der Amarna-Zeit, II: Gräber der Bürgermeister von Memphis." *OMRO* 77 (1997), pp. 31–71.

Gilbert 1941
Pierre Gilbert. "Contribution à l'iconographie du pharaon Aÿ." *CdE* 16 (1941), pp. 45–47.

Giles 1997
Frederick J. Giles. *The Amarna Age: Western Asia*. Warminster, 1997.

Gnirs 1989
Andrea Gnirs. "Haremhab—ein Staatsreformator? Neue Betrachtungen zum Haremhab-Dekret." *SAK* 16 (1989), pp. 83–110.

Gohary 1992
Jocelyn Gohary. *Akhenaten's Sed-Festival at Karnak*. London, 1992.

Gomaà 1973
Farouk Gomaà. "Chaemwese, Sohn Ramses' II: Und Hoherpriester von Memphis." *Ägyptologische Abhandlungen* 27. Wiesbaden, 1973.

Green 1993
Lyn Green. "The Origins of the Giant Lyre and Asiatic Influences on the Cult of the Aten." *JSSEA* 23 (1993), pp. 56–62.

Green 1995–96
Lyn Green. "Seeing through Ancient Egyptian Clothes." *KMT* 6 (Winter 1995–96), pp. 28–40.

Griffith 1906–7
Francis Llewellyn Griffith. "Excavations and Explorations." *Archaeological Reports* (1906–7), pp. 16–30.

Griffith 1918
Francis Llewellyn Griffith. "The Jubilee of Akhenaton." *JEA* 5 (1918), pp. 61–63.

Griffith 1922
Francis Llewellyn Griffith, addendum to Arthur Weigall. "The Mummy of Akhenaton." *JEA* 8 (1922), pp. 199–200.

Griffith 1926
Francis Llewellyn Griffith. "Stela in Honour of Amenophis III and Taya, from Tell el-'Amarnah." *JEA* 12 (1926), pp. 1–2.

Grimal 1992
Nicolas Grimal. *A History of Ancient Egypt*. London, 1992.

Grimm, Schoske, and Wildung 1997
Alfred Grimm, Sylvia Schoske, and Dietrich Wildung. *Pharao: Kunst und Herrschaft im alten Ägypten*. Munich, 1997.

Groll 1975–76
Sarah I. Groll. "The Literary and the Non-Verbal Systems in Late Egyptian." In *Miscellana in Honorem Josephi Vergote*, ed. Paul Naster, Herman De Meulenaere, and Jean Quaegebeur, pp. 237–46. Leuven, 1975–76.

Grose 1989
David Frederick Grose. *The Toledo Museum of Art: Early Ancient Glass*. New York, 1989.

Güterbock 1956
Hans G. Güterbock. "The Deeds of Suppiluliuma as Told by His Son, Mursili II." *JCS* 10 (1956), pp. 41–68, 75–98, 107–30.

Habachi 1956
Labib Habachi. "Amenwahsu Attached to the Cult of Anubis, Lord of the Dawning Land." *MDAIK* 14 (1956), pp. 52–62.

Habachi 1965
Labib Habachi. "Varia from the Reign of Akhenaten." *MDAIK* 20 (1965), pp. 70–92.

Habachi 1969
Labib Habachi. "Features of the Deification of Ramesses II." ADAIK 5. Glückstadt, 1969.

Habachi 1971
Labib Habachi. "Akhenaten in Heliopolis." BÄBA 12, pp. 35–45. Wiesbaden, 1971.

E. Hall 1986
Emma Swan Hall. *The Pharaoh Smites His Enemies*. Berlin, 1986.

R. Hall 1986
Rosalind Hall. *Egyptian Textiles*. Aylesbury, Bucks, 1986.

Hanke 1975
Rainer Hanke. "Änderungen von Bildern und Inschriften während der Amarna-Zeit." *SAK* 2 (1975), pp. 79–93.

Hanke 1978
Rainer Hanke. *Amarna-Reliefs aus Hermopolis: Neue Veröffentlichungen und Studien*. Hildesheim, 1978.

Hankey 1997
Vronwy Hankey. "Aegean Pottery at el-Amarna: Shapes and Decorative Motifs." In *Ancient Egypt, The Aegean, and the Near East: Studies in Honour of Martha Rhoads Bell*, ed. Jacke Phillips, pp. 193–216. San Antonio, 1997.

Hari 1965
Robert Hari. *Horembeb et la reine Moutnedjemet, ou La fin d'une dynastie*. Geneva, 1965.

Hari 1976
Robert Hari. "La reine d'Horemheb était-elle la sœur de Nefertiti?" *CdE* 51 (1976), pp. 39–46.

Hari 1984
Robert Hari. "La 'damnatio memoriae' amarnienne." In *Mélanges Gutbub*, pp. 95–102. Montpellier, 1984.

Hari 1984–85
Robert Hari. "Quelques remarques sur l'abandon d'Akhetaten." *BSEG* 9–10 (1984–1985), pp. 113–18.

J. E. Harris et al. 1978
James E. Harris, Edward F. Wente, Charles F. Cox, Ibrahim el-Nawaway, Charles Kowalski, Arthur T. Story, William R. Russell, Paul V. Ponitz, and

Geoffrey F. Walker. "Mummy of the 'Elder Lady' in the Tomb of Amenhotep II: Egyptian Museum Catalog Number 61070." *Science* 200 (9 June 1978), pp. 1149–51.

J. R. Harris 1973a
John R. Harris. "Nefernefruaten." *GM* 4 (1973), pp. 15–17.

J. R. Harris 1973b
John R. Harris. "Nefertiti Rediviva." *AO* 35 (1973), pp. 5–13.

J. R. Harris 1974a
John R. Harris. "Kiya." *CdE* 49 (1974), pp. 25–30.

J. R. Harris 1974b
John R. Harris. "Nefernefruaten Regnans." *AO* 36 (1974), pp. 11–21.

J. R. Harris 1975
John R. Harris. "Contributions to the History of the Eighteenth Dynasty." *SAK* 2 (1975), pp. 95–101

J. R. Harris 1976
John R. Harris. "Et nyt bevis på kongeparrets ligestilling i Amarnatiden." *MNCG* 33 (1976), pp. 78–84.

J. R. Harris 1977a
John R. Harris. "Akhenaten or Nefertiti?" *AO* 38 (1977), pp. 5–10.

J. R. Harris 1977b
John R. Harris. "A Fine Piece of Egyptian Faience." *Burlington Magazine* 119 (April–June 1977), pp. 340–33.

J. R. Harris 1992
John R. Harris. "Akhenaten and Nefernefruaten in the Tomb of Tut'ankhamun." In *After Tut'ankhamun: Research and Excavation in the Royal Necropolis at Thebes*, ed. Nicholas Reeves. Studies in Egyptology. London, 1992.

J. R. Harris 1993
John R. Harris. Manuscript of public lecture. Copenhagen, November 1993.

Harris and Manniche 1976
John R. Harris and Lise Manniche. "Amarna-tiden i nyt lys." *Louisiana Revy* 17:1 (October 1976), pp. 9–11.

Harris and Wente 1980
James E. Harris and Edward F. Wente, eds. *An X-Ray Atlas of the Royal Mummies*. Chicago, 1980.

Hart 1998
George Hart. Review of *The Murder of Tutankhamen—a 3000-Year-Old Murder Mystery*, by Bob Brier. *EA* 13 (1998), p. 11.

Hayes 1951
William C. Hayes. "Inscriptions from the Palace of Amenhotep III." *JNES* 10 (1951), pp. 35–56, 82–111, 156–83, 231–42.

Hayes 1953
William C. Hayes. *The Scepter of Egypt* 1. New York, 1953.

Hayes 1959
William C. Hayes. *The Scepter of Egypt* 2. Cambridge, Mass., 1959.

Haynes 1977
Joyce Haynes. "The Development of Women's Hairstyles in Dynasty Eighteen." *JSSEA* 8:1 (1977), pp. 18–24.

Helck 1969
Wolfgang Helck. "Die Tochterheirat ägyptischer Könige." *CdE* 44 (1969), pp. 22–26.

Helck 1975
Wofgang Helck. *Historische-Biographische Texte der 2. Zwischenzeit und neue Texte der 18. Dynastie*. Wiesbaden, 1975.

Helck 1981
"Probleme der Königsfolge in der Übergangzeit von 18. zu 19. Dyn." *MDAIK* 37 (1981), pp. 207–15.

Helck 1984
Wolfgang Helck. "Kijê." *MDAIK* 40 (1984), pp. 159–67.

Hermann 1932
Alfred Hermann. "Das Motiv der Ente mit zurückgewendetem Kopfe im ägyptischen Kunstgewerbe." *ZÄS* 68 (1932), pp. 86–105.

Hölscher 1939
Uvo Hölscher. *The Temples of the Eighteenth Dynasty: The Excavation of Medinet Habu*. Vol. 2. Chicago, 1939.

Honigsberg 1940
Paul Honigsberg. "Sanitary Installations in Ancient Egypt." *Journal of the Egyptian Medical Association* 23 (1940), pp. 199–246.

Hope 1991
Colin Hope. *Blue-painted and Polychrome Decorated Pottery from Amarna: A Preliminary Corpus*. Cahiers de la céramique égyptienne 2. Cairo, 1991.

Hornemann 1957
Bodil Hornemann. *Types of Ancient Egyptian Statuary* 3. Munksgaard, 1957.

Hornemann 1966
Bodil Hornemann. *Types of Ancient Egyptian Statuary* 4–5. Munksgaard, 1966.

Hornung 1971
Erik Hornung with F. Teichmann. *Das Grab des Horemhab im Tal der Könige*. Berne, 1971.

Hornung 1992
Erik Hornung. "The Rediscovery of Akhenaten and His Place in Religion." *JARCE* 29 (1992), pp. 43–49.

Hornung 1995
Erik Hornung. *Echnaton. Die Religion des Lichtes*. Zurich, 1995.

Hoving 1996
Thomas Hoving. *The Hunt for Big-Time Art Fakes*. New York, 1996.

Hulin 1985
Linda Hulin. "Chapels 570 and 571 and Adjacent Ground." *Amarna Reports* 2 (1985), pp. 29–38.

Humbert, Pantazzi, and Ziegler 1994
Jean-Marcel Humbert, Michael Pantazzi, and Christiane Ziegler, eds. *Egyptomania: L'Égypte dans l'art occidental 1730–1930*. Paris 1994.

Hussein and Harris 1988
Fawzia Hussein and James E. Harris. "The Skeletal Remains from Tomb No. 55." *Fifth International Congress of Egyptologists, Cairo, October 29–November 3, 1988, Abstracts of Papers*, pp. 140–41. Cairo, 1988.

Ikram 1989
Salima Ikram. "Domestic Shrines and the Cult of the Royal Family at el-Amarna." *JEA* 75 (1989), pp. 89–101.

James 1974
T. G. H. James. *Corpus of Hieroglyphic Inscriptions in The Brooklyn Museum I: From Dynasty I to the End of*

Dynasty XVIII. Wilbour Monographs 6. Brooklyn, 1974.

James 1984
T. G. H. James. *Pharaoh's People: Scenes from Life in Imperial Egypt.* Chicago, 1984.

James 1985
T. G. H. James. *Egyptian Painting and Drawing in the British Museum.* London, 1985.

G. Johnson 1992
George B. Johnson. "Norman de Garis Davies and the Rock Tombs of El-Amarna." *Amarna Letters* 2 (1992), pp. 56–69.

G. Johnson 1998
George B. Johnson. "Who Owned What in Tomb 55?" *KMT* 4 (Spring 1998), pp. 57–66.

W. R. Johnson 1990.
W. Raymond Johnson. "Images of Amenhotep III in Thebes: Styles and Intentions." In *The Art of Amenhotep III: Art Historical Analysis*, ed. Lawrence M. Berman, pp. 26–48. Cleveland, 1990.

W. R. Johnson 1994
W. Raymond Johnson. "Hidden Kings and Queens of the Luxor Temple Cachette." *Amarna Letters* 3 (1994), pp. 128–149.

W. R. Johnson 1995
W. Raymond Johnson. "The Year of the Goddess." *CHB* 7:1 (1995), pp. 1–4.

W. R. Johnson 1996
W. Raymond Johnson. "Amenhotep III and Amarna: Some New Considerations." *JEA* 82 (1996), pp. 65–82.

Jørgensen 1988
Mogens Jørgensen. "Et portræt af Kija i Ny Carlsberg Glyptotek." *MNCG* 44 (1988), pp. 7–26.

Jørgensen 1992
Mogens Jørgensen. "En Palimpsest fra el-Amarna." *MNCG* 48 (1992), pp. 5–13.

Jørgensen 1998
Mogens Jørgensen. *Egypt.* Vol. 2. Ny Carlsberg Glyptotek. Copenhagen, 1998.

Junge 1984
Friedrich Junge. "Sprache." *LÄ* 5 (1984), cols. 1178–1211.

Junge 1996
Friedrich Junge. *Einführung in die Grammatik Neuägyptisch.* Wiesbaden, 1996.

Kampp 1995
Friederike Kampp. "Zur Konzeption doppelter Bestattungsanlagen." In *Thebanische Beamtennekropolen*, ed. Jan Assmann, Eberhard Dziobek, Christian Guksch, and Friederike Kampp, pp. 205–18. Heidelberg, 1995.

Kampp 1996
Friederike Kampp. *Die thebanische Nekropole: zum Wandel des Grabgedankens von der XVIII. bis zur XX. Dynastie.* 2 vols. Mainz am Rhein, 1996.

Karig and Zauzich 1976
Joachim Karig and Karl-Theodor Zauzich, eds. *Ägyptische Kunst aus dem Brooklyn Museum.* Exh. cat., Ägyptisches Museum der Staatlichen Museen Preussischer Kulturbesitz. Berlin, 1976.

Kees 1960
Hermann Kees. "Webpriester der 18. Dynastie im Trägerdienst bei Prozessionen." *ZÄS* 85 (1960), pp. 45–56.

Keith-Bennett 1981
Jean L. Keith-Bennett. "Anthropoid Busts: II, Not From Deir el Medineh Alone." *BES* 3 (1981), pp. 43–71.

Kemp 1976
Barry J. Kemp. "The Window of Appearance at El-Amarna and the Basic Structure of this City." *JEA* 62 (1976), pp. 81–99.

Kemp 1977a
Barry J. Kemp. " A Building of Amenophis III at Kôm el 'Abd." *JEA* 63 (1977), pp. 71–82.

Kemp 1977b
Barry J. Kemp. "The City of El Amarna as a Source for the Study of Urban Archaeology in Ancient Egypt." *WA* (1977), pp. 123–39.

Kemp 1981
Barry J. Kemp. "Preliminary Report on the El-Amarna Expedition 1980." *JEA* 67 (1981), pp. 5–20.

Kemp 1987
Barry J. Kemp. "The Amarna Workmen's Village in Retrospect." *JEA* 73 (1987), pp. 21–50.

Kemp 1989
Barry J. Kemp. *Ancient Egypt: Anatomy of a Civilization.* London and New York, 1989.

Kemp 1993
Barry J. Kemp. "Amarna's Other Period." *EA* 3 (1993), pp. 13–14.

Kemp 1995
Barry J. Kemp, "Outlying Temples at Amarna." *Amarna Reports* 6 (1995), pp. 411–62.

Kemp 1997
Barry J. Kemp. "Amarna's Textile Industry." *EA* 11 (1997), pp. 7–9.

Kemp and Nicholson 1997
Barry J. Kemp and Paul T. Nicholson. "Fieldwork, 1996–7: Tell el-Amarna." *JEA* 83 (1997), pp. 8–13.

Kendall 1982
Timothy Kendall. "The House." In *Egypt's Golden Age: The Art of Living in the New Kingdom 1558–1085 B.C.*, ed. Edward Brovarski, Susan K. Doll, and Rita E. Freed, pp. 25–34. Exh. cat, Museum of Fine Arts, Boston. Boston, 1982.

Kendall 1989
Timothy Kendall. "Ethnoarchaeology in Meroitic Studies." In *Studia Meroitica 1984: Proceedings of the Fifth International Conference for Meroitic Studies, Rome 1984*, ed. Sergio Donadoni and Steffen Wenig. Meroitica 10 (1989), pp. 625–745.

Kendall 1994
Timothy Kendall. "A New Map of the Gebel Barkal Temples." In *Études nubiennes, Conférence de Genève: Actes du VIIe Congrès international d'études nubiennes, 3–8 septembre*, ed. Charles Bonnet. Vol. 2, pp. 139–145. Geneva, 1994.

Kendall 1997
Timothy Kendall. "Do Ancient Dances Survive in Present-Day Sudan?" In *The Spirit's Dance in Africa*, ed. Esther Dagan, pp. 306–9. Montreal, 1997.

el-Khouly and Martin 1987
Aly el-Khouly and Geoffrey T. Martin. *Excavations in the Royal Necropolis at El-'Amarna 1984.* Cairo, 1987.

Killean 1980
Carolyn Killean. "Demonstrative Variation in Oral Media Arabic in Egypt." *Studies in Arabic Linguistics: Special Volume of Studies in Linguistic Sciences* 10, no. 2 (1980), pp. 165–78.

Kozloff and Bryan 1992
Arielle P. Kozloff and Betsy M. Bryan, with Lawrence M. Berman. *Egypt's Dazzling Sun: Amenhotep III and His World.* Exh. cat., Cleveland Museum of Art. Cleveland, 1992.

Krauss 1978
Rolf Krauss. *Das Ende der Amarnazeit: Beiträge zur Geschichte und Chronologie des Neuen Reiches.* HÄB 7. Hildesheim, 1978.

Krauss 1983
Rolf Krauss. "Der Bildhauer Thutmose in Amarna." *JPK* 20 (1983), pp. 119–32.

Krauss 1986a
Rolf Krauss. "Kija — ursprüngliche Besitzerin der Kanopen aus KV 55." *MDAIK* 42 (1986), pp. 67–80.

Krauss 1986b
Rolf Krauss. "Der Oberbildhauer Bak und sein Denkstein in Berlin." *Jahrbuch der Berliner Museen* 28 (1986), pp. 5–46.

Krauss 1989
Rolf Krauss. "Neues zu den Stelenfragmenten UC London 410 + Kairo JE 64959." *BSEG* 13 (1989), pp. 83–87.

Krauss 1990
Rolf Krauss. "Einige Kleinfunde mit Namen von Amarnaherrschern." *CdE* 65 (1990), pp. 206–18.

Krauss 1991a
Rolf Krauss. "Die Amarnazeitliche Familienstele Berlin 14145 unter besonderer Berücksichtigung von Massordnung und Komposition." *JBM* 33 (1991) pp. 7–36.

Krauss 1991b
Rolf Krauss. "Nefertiti—A Drawing-Board Beauty?" *Amarna Letters* 1 (1991), pp. 46–49.

Krauss 1993
Rolf Krauss. Review of *The Royal Tomb at El-'Amarna II*, by Geoffrey Martin. *JEA* 79 (1993), pp. 300–302.

Krauss 1996
Rolf Krauss. "Nochmals die Bestattungszeit Tutanchamuns und ein Exkurs über das Problem der Perseareife." *SAK* 23 (1996), pp. 227–54.

Krauss 1997a
Rolf Krauss. "Zur Chronologie der Nachfolger Achenatens unter Berücksichtigung der DOG-Funde in Amarna." *Mitteilungen der Deutschen Orient-Gesellschaft* 129 (1997), pp. 225–50.

Krauss 1997b
Rolf Krauss. "Nefertitis Ende." *MDAIK* 53 (1997), pp. 209–19.

Krauss and Ullrich 1982
Rolf Krauss and Detlef Ullrich. "Ein gläserner Doppelring aus Altägypten." *JPK* 19 (1982), pp. 199–212.

Kroeber 1970
Burkhardt Kroeber. *Die Neuägyptizismen vor der Amarnazeit.* Ph.D. dissertation, Tübingen University, 1970.

Kruchten 1981
Jean-Marie Kruchten. *Le décret d'Horemheb.* Brussels, 1981.

Laboury 1998
Dimitri Laboury. *La statuaire de Thoutmosis III: Essai d'interprétation d'un portrait royal dans son contexte historique.* Aegyptiaca Leodiensia 5. Liège, 1998.

Lacovara 1997
Peter Lacovara. *The New Kingdom Royal City.* London and New York, 1997.

Lange and Hirmer 1968
Kurt Lange and Max Hirmer. *Egypt.* London and New York, 1968.

Lansing 1940
Ambrose Lansing. *Ancient Egyptian Jewelry.* New York, 1940.

Leahy 1978
M. Anthony Leahy. *Excavations at Malkata and the Birket Habu 1971–1974: The Inscriptions.* Warminster, 1978.

Legrain 1903
Georges Legrain. "Fragments de canopes." *ASAE* 4 (1903), pp. 138–49.

Legrain 1904
Georges Legrain. "Notes d'inspection, XV: Seconde note sur des fragments de canopes." *ASAE* 5 (1904), pp. 139–41.

Lichtheim 1947
Miriam Lichtheim. "Oriental Institute Museum Notes—Situla No. 11395 and Some Remarks on Egyptian Situlae." *JNES* 6 (1947), pp. 169–79.

Lilyquist and Brill 1993
Christina Lilyquist and R. H. Brill. *Studies in Early Egyptian Glass.* New York, 1993.

Lipinska 1966
Jadwiga Lipinska. "The Portraits of Tuthmosis III Newly Discovered at Deir el-Bahri." In *Mélanges Offerts à Kazimierz Michalowski*, pp. 129–38. Warsaw, 1966.

Littauer 1969
Mary A. Littauer. "Bits and Pieces." *Antiquity* 43 (1969), pp. 289–300.

Littauer and Crouwel 1985
Mary A. Littauer and J. H. Crouwel. *Tut'ankhamūn's Tomb Series, VIII: Chariots and Related Equipment from the Tomb of Tut'ankhamūn.* Oxford, 1985.

Lloyd 1933
Seton Lloyd. "Model of a Tell el-Amarnah House." *JEA* 19 (1933), pp. 1–7.

Loeben 1986
Christian Loeben. "Eine Bestattung der grossen königlichen Gemahlin Nofretete in Amarna?" *MDAIK* 42 (1986), pp. 99–107.

Loeben 1991
Christian Loeben. "No Evidence of Coregency: Zwei getilgte Inschriften aus dem Grab von Tutanchamun." *BSEG* 15 (1991), pp. 81–90.

Loeben 1994
Christian Loeben. "No Evidence of Coregency: Two Erased Inscriptions from Tutankhamen's Tomb." *Amarna Letters* 3 (1994), pp. 104–9.

Löhr 1970
Beatrix Löhr. "Ein memphitisches Grab vom Ende der 18. Dynastie (um 1320 v. Chr)" *Pantheon* 28 (1970), pp. 467–74.

Löhr 1975
Beatrix Löhr. "Ahanjati in Memphis." *SAK* 2 (1975), pp. 139–87.

Lorton 1983
David Lorton. Review of *Der Ägyptische Mythos von der Himmelskuh: Eine Ätiologie des Unvollkommenen*, by Erik Hornung. *BiOr* 40 (1983), pp. 609–16.

Lucas 1939
Alfred Lucas. "Glass Figures." *ASAE* 39 (1939), pp. 227–43.

Lucas and Harris 1962
Alfred Lucas and John R. Harris. *Ancient Egyptian Materials and Industries.* 4th ed. London, 1962.

Luxor Museum 1979
The Luxor Museum of Ancient Egyptian Art Catalogue. Cairo, 1979.

Lythgoe 1907
Albert M. Lythgoe. "Recent Egyptian Aquisitions." *BMMA* 2 (1907), pp. 193–96.

MacAdam 1955
M. F. Laming MacAdam. *The Temples of Kawa, II: History and Archaeology of the Site.* London, 1955.

Mace 1922
Arthur C. Mace. "Loom Weights in Egypt." *Ancient Egypt* (1922), pp. 75–76.

el-Mallakh and Brackman 1978
Kamal el-Mallakh and Arnold C. Brackman. *The Gold of Tutankhamen.* New York, 1978.

Mallinson 1995
Michael Mallinson. "Excavation and Survey in the Central City, 1988–92." *Amarna Reports* 6 (1995), pp. 169–215.

Manniche 1971
Lise Manniche. "Les scènes de musique sur les talatat du IX pylône de Karnak." *Kêmi* 21 (1971), pp. 155–64.

Manniche 1975a
Lise Manniche. *Ancient Egyptian Musical Instruments.* MÄS 34 (1975).

Manniche 1975b
Lise Manniche. "The Wife of Bata." *GM* 18 (1975), pp. 33–38.

Manniche 1976
Lise Manniche. *Musical Instruments from the Tomb of Tut'ankhamūn.* Tut'ankhamūn's Tomb Series 6. Oxford, 1976.

Manniche 1978
Lise Manniche. "Symbolic Blindness." *CdE* 53 (1978), pp. 13–21.

Manniche 1987a
Lise Manniche. *City of the Dead: Thebes in Egypt.* Chicago, 1987.

Manniche 1987b
Lise Manniche. *Sexual Life in Ancient Egypt.* London, 1987.

Manniche 1991a
Lise Manniche. *Music and Musicians in Ancient Egypt.* London, 1991.

Manniche 1991b
Lise Manniche. "Music at Court of the Aten." *Amarna Letters* 1 (1991), pp. 62–65.

Manuelian 1994
Peter Der Manuelian. "The Giza Mastaba Niche and Full Frontal Figure of Redi-nes." In *For this Ka: Essays Offered in Memory of Klaus Baer*, ed. David Silverman, pp. 55–78. Chicago, 1994.

Manuelian 1999
Peter Der Manuelian. "Semi-literacy in Egypt: Some Erasures from the Amarna Period." In *Gold of Praise: Studies on Ancient Egypt in Honor of Edward F. Wente*, ed. Emily Teeter and John A. Larson. Chicago, 1999, forthcoming.

Markoe 1996
Glenn E. Markoe. "Hair Ornaments and Accessories." In *Mysteries of the House, Mysteries of Heaven: Women in Ancient Egypt*, ed. Anne K. Capel and Glenn E. Markoe, p. 75. New York, 1996.

Martin 1974
Geoffrey T. Martin. Review of *Amarna, City of Akhenaten and Nefertiti: Key Pieces from the Petrie Collection*, by Julia Samson. *JEA* 60 (1974), pp. 267–69.

Martin 1974, 1989
Geoffrey T. Martin. *The Royal Tomb at El-'Amarna.* 2 vols. London, 1974, 1989.

Martin 1985
Geoffrey T. Martin. "Notes on a Canopic Jar from Kings' Valley Tomb 55." In *Mélanges Gamal Eddin Mokhtar*. Vol. 2, pp. 111–24. Cairo, 1985.

Martin 1986
Geoffrey T. Martin. "Shabtis of Private Persons in the Amarna Period." *MDAIK* 42 (1986), pp. 109–29.

Martin 1987
Geoffrey T. Martin. *Corpus of Reliefs of the New Kingdom from the Memphite Necropolis and Lower Egypt.* Vol. 1. London, 1987.

Martin 1989
Geoffrey T. Martin. *The Memphite Tomb of Ḥoremḥeb, Commander in Chief of Tutʿankhamūn.* Vol. 1: *The Reliefs, Inscriptions, and Commentary.* London, 1989.

Martin et al. 1988
Geoffrey T. Martin, Maarten J. Raven, Barbara Greene Aston, and Jacobus van Dijk. "The Tomb of Maya and Meryt: Preliminary Report on the Saqqâra Excavations, 1987–8." *JEA* 74 (1988), pp. 1–14.

Masali and Chiarelli 1972
Melchiorre Masali and Brunetto Chiarelli. "Demographic Data on the Remains of Ancient Egyptians." *Journal of Human Evolution* 1 (1972), pp. 161–69.

McDonald 1982
John K. McDonald. "Baskets and Basketry." In *Egypt's Golden Age: The Art of Living in the New Kingdom 1558–1085 B.C.,* ed. Edward Brovarski, Susan Doll, and Rita Freed, pp. 133–39. Exh. cat., Museum of Fine Arts, Boston. Boston, 1982.

Meggs 1992
Philip B. Meggs. *A History of Graphic Design.* New York, 1992.

Mekhitarian 1978
Arpag Mekhitarian. *Egyptian Painting.* Geneva, 1978.

Meltzer 1989
Edmund S. Meltzer. "Herodotus on Akhenaten?" *DE* 15 (1989), pp. 51–56.

Merrillees 1968
R. S. Merrillees. *The Cypriote Bronze Age Pottery Found in Egypt.* Studies in Mediterranean Archaeology 18. Sölvegatan, Denmark, 1968.

Metropolitan Museum of Art 1982
The Metropolitan Museum of Art. Notable Acquisitions 1981–82. New York, 1982.

Metropolitan Museum of Art 1987
The Metropolitan Museum of Art. *Egypt and the Ancient Near East.* New York, 1987.

Metropolitan Museum of Art 1992
"Ancient Art: Gifts from the Norbert Schimmel Collection." *BMMA* 49 (Spring 1992), pp. 1–64.

Meyers 1981
Elizabeth L. Meyers. *A Program of Political Theology in Amarna Tomb Art: Imagery as Metaphor.* Ph.D. dissertation, University of Pennsylvania, 1981.

Meyers 1985
Elizabeth L. Meyers. "Component Design as a Narrative Device in Amarna Tomb Art." *Studies in the History of Art* 16 (1985), pp. 35–51.

Milkovich 1963
Michael Milkovich. "Ancient Art in the Worcester Art Museum." *Archaeology* 16 (1963), pp. 154–55.

Millet 1988
Nicholas B. Millet. "Some Canopic Inscriptions of the Reign of Amenhotep III." *GM* 104 (1988), pp. 91–93.

Möller 1965
Lise Lotte Möller. *Ägyptische Kunst aus der Zeit des Königs Echnaton.* Exh. cat., Museum für Kunst und Gewerbe. Hamburg, 1965.

Moran 1992
William L. Moran, ed. and trans. *The Amarna Letters.* Baltimore and London, 1992.

Moret 1902
Alexandre Moret. *Du caractère religieux de la royauté pharaonique.* Paris, 1902.

Morkot 1986
Robert Morkot. "Violent Images of Queenship and the Royal Cult." *Wepwawet* 2 (Summer 1989), pp. 1–9.

H. Müller 1964
Hans Wolfgang Müller. *Ägyptische Kunstwerke, Kleinfunde und Glas in der Sammlung E. und M. Kofler-Truniger, Luzern.* MÄS 5 (1964).

M. Müller 1988
Maya Müller. *Die Kunst Amenophis' III. und Echnatons.* Basel, 1988.

Müller and Settgast 1976
Hans Müller and Jürgen Settgast, eds. *Nofretete–Echnaton.* Exh. cat., Ägyptisches Museum. Berlin, 1976.

Munro 1986
Irmtraut Munro. "Zusammenstellung von Datierungskriterien für Inschriften der Amarna-Zeit nach J. J. Perepelkin, *Die Revolution Amenophis' IV, Teil 1* (russ.), 1967." *GM* 94 (1986), pp. 81–87.

Munro 1987
Irmtraut Munro. Review of *The Revolution of Amenhotep IV* (in Russian), by Y. Y. Perepelkin. *BiOr* 44 (1987), cols. 137–43.

Münzen und Medaillen 1974
Münzen und Medaillen A.G. *Werke Ägyptischer Kunst,* Auktion 49. 27 June 1974. Basel.

Murnane 1977
William J. Murnane. *Ancient Egyptian Coregencies.* Chicago, 1977.

Murnane 1981
William J. Murnane. "Opetfest." *LÄ* 4 (1981), cols. 574–79.

Murnane 1990
William J. Murnane. *The Road to Kadesh.* Studies in Oriental Civilization 42. 2nd ed., revised. Chicago, 1990.

Murnane 1995a
William J. Murnane. "The History of Ancient Egypt: An Overview." In *Civilizations of the Ancient New East,* ed. Jack M. Sasson. Vol. 2, pp. 691–734. New York, 1995.

Murnane 1995b
William J. Murnane. *Texts from the Amarna Period in Egypt.* Society of Biblical Literature, Writings from the Ancient World Series 5. Atlanta, 1995.

Murnane and van Siclen 1993
William J. Murnane and Charles C. van Siclen III. *The Boundary Stelae of Akhenaten.* London, 1993.

Muscarella 1974
Oscar White Muscarella, ed. *Ancient Art: the Norbert Schimmel Collection.* Mainz am Rhein, 1974.

Mysliwiec 1976
Karol Mysliwiec. *Le portrait royal dans le bas-relief du Nouvel Empire.* Warsaw, 1976.

Newberry 1928
Percy E. Newberry. "Akhenaten's Eldest Son-in-Law 'Ankhkheprurēʿ.'" *JEA* 14 (1928), pp. 3–9.

Newton 1924
Francis G. Newton. "Excavations at El-ʿAmarnah, 1923–1924." *JEA* 10 (1924), pp. 289–98.

Nicholson 1993
Paul T. Nicholson. *Egyptian Faience and Glass.* Buckinghamshire, 1993.

Nicholson 1995
Paul T. Nicholson. "Glassmaking and Glassworking at Amarna: Some New Work." *Journal of Glass Studies* 37 (1995), pp. 11–19.

Nicholson 1998
Paul T. Nicholson. "Materials and Technology." In *Gifts of the Nile: Ancient Egyptian Faience,* ed. Florence Friedman, pp. 50–64. Providence, 1998.

Nicholson, Jackson, and Trott 1997
Paul T. Nicholson, Caroline M. Jackson, and Katharine M. Trott. "The Ulu Burun Glass Ingots, Cylindrical Vessels and Egyptian Glass." *JEA* 83 (1997), pp. 143–53.

Noblecourt 1963
Christiane Desroches Noblecourt. *Tutankhamen: Life and Death of a Pharaoh.* New York, 1963.

Noblecourt 1967
Christiane Desroches Noblecourt. *Toutankhamon et son temps.* Exh. cat., Réunion des Musées Nationaux (Petit Palais). Paris, 1967.

Noblecourt 1968
Christiane Desroches Noblecourt. "La cueillette du raisin à la fin de l'époque amarnienne." *JEA* 54 (1968), pp. 82–88.

Noblecourt 1974
Christiane Desroches Noblecourt. "La statue colossale fragmentaire d'Aménophis IV offerte par l'Éypte à la France (Louvre E. 27112)." MonPiot 59, pp. 1–44. Paris, 1974.

Nolte 1977
Birgit Nolte. "An Egyptian Glass Vessel in The Metropolitan Museum of Art." *Ancient Egypt in The Metropolitan Museum Journal: Vols. 1–11 (1968–1976)*, pp. 25–29. New York, 1977.

O'Connor 1987–88
David O'Connor. "Demarcating the Boundaries: An Interpretation of a Scene in the Tomb of Mahu at El-Amarna." BES 9 (1987–88), pp. 41–52.

O'Connor 1989
David O'Connor. "City and Palace in New Kingdom Egypt." CRIPEL 11, pp. 73–87. Lille, 1989.

Owen and Kemp 1994
"Craftsmen's Work Patterns in Unfinished Tombs at Amarna." *Cambridge Archaeology Journal* 4 (April 1994), pp. 121–46.

Page-Gasser and Wiese 1997
Madeleine Page-Gasser and André B. Wiese. *Ägypten: Augenblicke der Ewigkeit*. Mainz, 1997.

Pardey 1998
Eva Pardey. "The Royal Administration and its Organization." In *Egypt: The World of the Pharaohs*, ed. Regine Schulz and Matthias Seidel, pp. 357–63. Cologne, 1998.

Patch 1990
Diana Craig Patch. *Reflections of Greatness: Ancient Egypt at The Carnegie Museum of Natural History*. Pittsburgh, 1990.

Patch 1998
Diana Craig Patch. "By Necessity or Design: Faience Use in Ancient Egypt." In *Gifts of the Nile: Ancient Egyptian Faience*, ed. Florence Friedman, pp. 32–45. Providence, 1998.

Peck 1978
William H. Peck. *Egyptian Drawings*. London, 1978.

Peet 1915
T. Eric Peet. "A Remarkable Burial Custom of the Old Kingdom." *JEA* 2 (1915), pp. 8–9.

Peet 1921
T. Eric Peet. "Excavations at Tell el-Amarna." *JEA* 7 (1921), pp. 169–85.

Peet and Woolley 1923
T. Eric Peet and C. Leonard Woolley. *The City of Akhenaten* 1. London, 1923.

Pendlebury 1931
J. D. S. Pendlebury. "Preliminary Report of Excavations at Tell El-'Amarnah, 1930–31." *JEA* 17 (1931), pp. 233–44.

Pendlebury 1933a
J. D. S. Pendlebury. "A 'Monotheistic Utopia' of Ancient Egypt." *The Illustrated London News*, 6 May 1933, pp. 629–33.

Pendlebury 1933b
J. D. S. Pendlebury. "Preliminary Report of the Excavations at Tell El-'Amarnah, 1932–33." *JEA* 19 (1933), pp. 113–18.

Pendlebury 1935
J. D. S. Pendlebury. *Tell el-Amarna*. London, 1935.

Pendlebury 1951
J. D. S. Pendlebury. *The City of Akhenaten* 3. 2 vols. London, 1951.

Perepelkin 1967, 1984
Yuri Y. Perepelkin. *Perevorot Amenkhotpa IV*. 2 vols. Moscow, 1967, 1984.

Perepelkin 1978
G. (Yuri Y.) Perepelkin. *The Secret of the Gold Coffin*. Moscow, 1978.

Peterson 1964
Bengt J. Peterson. "Two Royal Heads from Amarna." *MeB* 4 (1964), pp. 13–29.

Petrie 1894
W. M. F. Petrie. *Tell el Amarna*. London, 1894.

Petrie 1901
W. M. F. Petrie. *The Royal Tombs of the Earliest Dynasties* 2. London, 1901.

Petrie 1910
W. M. F. Petrie. *Meydum and Memphis* 3. London, 1910.

Petrie 1917
W. M. F. Petrie. *Tools and Weapons*. London, 1917.

Petrie 1927
W. M. F. Petrie. *Objects of Daily Use*. London, 1927.

Petrie 1937
W. M. F. Petrie. *Funeral Furniture and Stone Vases*. London, 1937.

J. Phillips 1991
Jacke Phillips. "Sculpture Ateliers of Akhenaten." *Amarna Letters* 1 (1991), pp. 31–40.

J. Phillips 1994
Jacke Phillips. "The Composite Sculpture of Akhenaten." *Amarna Letters* 3 (1994), pp. 58–71.

T. Phillips 1995
Tom Phillips, ed. *Africa: The Art of a Continent*. Exh. cat., Royal Academy of Arts. London, 1995.

Piankoff 1958
Alexandre Piankoff. "Les peintures dans la tombe du roi Aï." *MDAIK* 16 (1958), pp. 247–51.

Pillet 1929
Maurice Pillet. "Quelques bas-reliefs inédits d'Amenhotep IV-Akhenaten." *Revue de l'Égypte ancienne* (1929), pp. 136–43.

Polz 1995
Felicitas Polz. "Die Bildnisse Sesostris' III. und Amenemhets III. Bemerkungen zur königlichen Rundplastik der späten 12. Dynastie." *MDAIK* 51 (1995), pp. 227–54, pls. 48–52.

Porter and Moss 1929
Bertha Porter and Rosalind L. B. Moss. *Topographical Bibliography of Ancient Egyptian Hieroglyphic Texts, Reliefs, and Paintings II: Theban Temples*. Oxford, 1929.

Porter and Moss 1934
Bertha Porter and Rosalind L. B. Moss. *Topographical Bibliography of Ancient Egyptian Hieroglyphic Texts, Reliefs, and Paintings IV: Lower and Middle Egypt*. Oxford, 1934.

Porter and Moss 1964
Bertha Porter and Rosalind L. B. Moss. *Topographical Bibliography of Ancient Egyptian Hieroglyphic Texts, Reliefs, and Paintings I: The Theban Necropolis, Part 2*. 2nd ed. Oxford, 1964.

Porter and Moss 1972
Bertha Porter and Rosalind L.B. Moss. *Topographical Bibliography of Ancient Egyptian Hieroglyphic Texts, Reliefs, and Paintings II: Theban Temples*. 2nd ed. Oxford, 1972.

Powell 1995
Catherine Powell. "The Nature and Use of Ancient Potter's Wheels." *Amarna Reports* 6 (1995), pp. 309–35.

Priese 1991
Karl-Heinz Priese, ed. *Ägyptisches Museum: Museumsinsel Berlin*. Mainz, 1991.

Quibell 1908
James E. Quibell. *The Tomb of Yuaa and Thuiu*. Cairo, 1908.

Raven 1994
Maarten J. Raven. "A Sarcophagus for Queen Tiy and Other Fragments from the Royal Tomb at el-Amarna." *OMRO* 74 (1994), pp. 7–20.

D. Redford 1967
Donald B. Redford. *History and Chronology of the Eighteenth Dynasty of Egypt: Seven Studies*. Toronto, 1967.

D. Redford 1973
Donald B. Redford. "Studies on Akhenaten at Thebes 1. A Report on the Work of the Akhenaten Temple Project of the University Museum, University of Pennsylvania." *JARCE* 10 (1973), pp. 77–94.

D. Redford 1975
Donald B. Redford. "Reconstructing the Temples of a Heretical Pharaoh." *Archaeology* 28 (1975), pp. 16–22.

D. Redford 1977
Donald B. Redford. "Preliminary Report of the First Season of Excavation in East Karnak." *JARCE* 14 (1977), pp. 9–32.

D. Redford 1978
Donald B. Redford. "The Razed Temple of Akhenaten." *Scientific American* (December 1978), pp. 136–47.

D. Redford 1979a
Donald B. Redford. "The Akhenaten Temple Project and Karnak Excavations." *Expedition* 21 (Winter 1979), pp. 54–59.

D. Redford 1979b
Donald B. Redford. "Once Again the Filiation of Tutankhamun." *JSSEA* 9:3 (1979), pp. 111–15.

D. Redford 1983
Donald B. Redford. "Interim Report on the Excavations at East Karnak (1981–1982 Seasons). Stratigraphy and Architecture." *JSSEA* 13:4 (1983), pp. 203–23.

D. Redford 1984
Donald B. Redford. *Akhenaten: The Heretic King.* Princeton, 1984.

D. Redford 1986
Donald B. Redford. *Pharaonic King-Lists, Annals and Day-Books.* Missassauga, Ont., 1986.

D. Redford 1994
Donald B. Redford. "East Karnak and the Sed-Festival of Akhenaten." In *Hommages à Jean Leclant I: Études pharaoniques,* pp. 485–92. Cairo, 1994.

D. Redford 1995
Donald B. Redford. "The Concept of Kingship During the Eighteenth Dynasty." In *Ancient Egyptian Kingship,* ed. David O'Connor and David P. Silverman, pp. 157–84. Leiden, 1995.

S. Redford 1995
Susan Redford. "Two Field Seasons in the Tomb of Parennefer, No. 188 at Thebes." *KMT* 6 (Spring 1995), pp. 62–70.

S. Redford 1997
Susan Redford. "The 1997 Field Campaign to the Tomb of Parennefer (T.T. 188)." *The Akhenaten Temple Project Newsletter* (September 1997), pp. 1–4.

Reeves 1978
C. Nicholas Reeves. "A Further Occurrence of Nefertiti as *ḥmt nsw 'ȝt.*" *GM* 30 (1978), pp. 61–69.

Reeves 1988
C. Nicholas Reeves. "New Light on Kiya from Texts in the British Museum." *JEA* 74 (1988), pp. 91–101.

Reeves 1990a
Nicholas Reeves. *The Complete Tutankhamun.* London, 1990.

Reeves 1990b
C. Nicholas Reeves. *Valley of the Kings: The Decline of a Royal Necropolis.* London, 1990.

Reeves 1994
C. Nicholas Reeves. "A Fragment from the Canopic Jar of an Amarna Queen." *RdE* 45 (1994), pp. 198–200.

Reeves 1996
C. Nicholas Reeves. "A New Portrait of Amenhotep IV-Akhenaten." *Minerva* 7 (January-February 1996), pp. 36–37.

Reeves 1997
Nicholas Reeves. Public Lecture, London, May 1997.

Reeves forthcoming
Nicholas Reeves. "A Canopic Jar of Mutnodjmet, the *Shabti*s of Tiye, and the Coregency of Amenhotep III and Akhenaten."

Reeves and Wilkinson 1996
Nicholas Reeves and Richard H. Wilkinson. *The Complete Valley of the Kings.* London, 1996.

Reisner 1918
George A. Reisner. "The Barkal Temples in 1916." *JEA* 5 (1918), pp. 99–112, pls. 11–17.

Reisner 1920
George A. Reisner. "Note on the Statuette of a Blind Harper in the Cairo Museum." *JEA* 6 (1920), pp. 117–18, pl. XV.

Reisner and Reisner 1933
George A. Reisner and Mary B. Reisner. "Inscribed Monuments from Gebel Barkal." *ZÄS* 69 (1933), pp. 24–39.

Ricke 1932
Herbert Ricke. *Der Grundriss des Amarna-Wohnhauses.* Leipzig, 1932.

Ricke 1981
Herbert Ricke. "Der Totentempel Amenophis III. Baureste und Ergänzung." In *Untersuchungen im Totentempel Amenophis' III,* ed. Gerhard Haeny, pp. 3–37. BÄBA 11. Wiesbaden, 1981.

Riefstahl 1951
Elizabeth Riefstahl. "An Egyptian Portrait of an Old Man." *JNES* 10 (1951), pp. 65–73.

Ritner 1993
Robert K. Ritner. *The Mechanics of Ancient Egyptian Magical Practice.* Studies in Ancient Oriental Civilizations 54. Chicago, 1993.

Robins 1981a
Gay Robins. "*ḥmt nsw wrt* Meritaton." *GM* 52 (1981), pp. 75–81.

Robins 1981b
Gay Robins. "The Value of the Estimated Ages of the Royal Mummies at Death as Historical Evidence." *GM* 45 (1981), pp. 63–68.

Robins 1993
Gay Robins. "The Representation of Sexual Characteristics in Amarna Art." *JSSEA* 23 (1993), pp. 29–41.

Robins 1994
Gay Robins. *Proportion and Style in Ancient Egyptian Art.* Austin, 1994.

Robins 1997a
Gay Robins. *The Art of Ancient Egypt.* London, 1997.

Robins 1997b
Gay Robins. "The Feminization of the Male Figure in New Kingdom Two-Dimensional Art." In *Chief of Seers: Egyptian Studies in Memory of Cyril Aldred,* ed. Elizabeth Goring, Nicholas Reeves, and John Ruffle, pp. 251–65. London, 1997.

Roeder 1924
Günther Roeder. *Ägyptische Inschriften aus den Staatlichen Museen zu Berlin.* Leipzig, 1924.

Roeder 1939
Günther Roeder. "Freie Plastik aus Ägypten in dem Rijksmuseum van Oudheden." *OMRO* 20 (1939), pp. 1–23.

Roeder 1941
Günther Roeder. "Lebensgrosse Tonmodelle aus einer altägyptischen Bildhauerwerkstatt." *JPKu* 62 (1941), pp. 145–70.

Roeder 1969
Günther Roeder. *Amarna Reliefs aus Hermopolis.* Hildesheim, 1969.

Romer 1984
John Romer. *Ancient Lives: Daily Life in Egypt of the Pharaohs.* New York, 1984.

Russmann 1980
Edna R. Russmann. "The Anatomy of an Artistic Convention: Representation of the Near Foot in Two Dimensions through the New Kingdom." *BES* 2 (1980), pp. 57–81.

Russmann 1989
Edna R. Russmann. *Egyptian Sculpture: Cairo and Luxor.* Austin, 1989.

Russmann 1995
Edna R. Russmann. "A Second Style in Egyptian Art of the Old Kingdom." *MDAIK* 51 (1995), pp. 269–79.

Saad 1976
Ramadan Saad. "The Ninth Pylon and Its Talatat." In Ray Winfield Smith and Donald B. Redford, *The Akhenaten Temple Project I: Initial Discoveries,* pp. 68–75. Warminister, 1976.

Sa'ad 1970
Rany Sa'ad. "Les travaux d'Aménophis IV au IIIe pylône du temple d'Amon Rê à Karnak." *Kemi* 20 (1970), pp. 187–93.

el-Saghir 1991
Mohammed el-Saghir. *The Discovery of the Statuary Cachette of Luxor Temple.* Mainz, 1991.

Saleh and Sououzian 1986
Mohamed Saleh and Hourig Sourouzian. *Das Ägyptisches Museum, Kairo.* Mainz, 1986.

Saleh and Sourouzian 1987
Mohamed Saleh and Hourig Sourouzian. *The Egyptian Museum Cairo.* Cairo, 1987.

Samson 1972
Julia Samson. *Amarna, City of Akhenaten and Nefertiti: Key Pieces from the Petrie Collection.* London, 1972.

Samson 1973
Julia Samson. "Amarna Crowns and Wigs." *JEA* 59 (1973), pp. 47–59.

Samson 1976
Julia Samson. "Royal Names in Amarna History." *CdE* 51 (1976), pp. 30–38.

Samson 1978
Julia Samson. *Amarna, City of Akhenaten and Nefertiti: Nefertiti as Pharaoh.* Warminster, 1978.

Sandman 1938
Maj Sandman. *Texts from the Time of Akhenaten.* Bibliotheca Aegyptiaca 8. Brussels, 1938.

Sauneron 1968
Serge Sauneron. "Quelques monuments de Soumenou au Musée de Brooklyn." *Kêmi* 18 (1968), pp. 57–78.

Schaden 1977
Otto Schaden. *The God's Father Ay.* Ph.D. dissertation, University of Minnesota, 1977.

Schaden 1984
Otto J. Schaden. "Clearance of the Tomb of King Ay (WV 23)." *JARCE* 21 (1984), pp. 39–64.

Schaden 1992
Otto J. Schaden. "The God's Father Ay." *Amarna Letters* 2 (1992), pp. 92–115.

Schäfer 1931
Heinrich Schäfer. *Amarna in Religion und Kunst.* Leipzig, 1931.

Schmitz 1976
Bettina Schmitz. *Untersuchungen zum Titel s3 njswt, Königssohn.* Halbelts Dissertationdrucke, Reihe Ägyptologie, Heft 2. Bonn, 1976.

Schneider 1974
Hans D. Schneider. "Maya, l'amateur de statues: À propos de trois statues fameuses du Musée de Leyde et d'une sépulture oubliée à Saqqarah." *BSFE* 69 (1974), pp. 20–48.

Schneider 1977
Hans D. Schneider. *Shabtis.* 3 vols. Leiden, 1977.

Schneider 1996
Hans D. Schneider. *The Memphite Tomb of Horemheb, Commander-in-Chief of Tut'ankhamūn II: A Catalogue of the Finds.* Leiden and London, 1996.

Schneider and Raven 1981
Hans D. Schneider and Maarten J. Raven. *Die Egyptische Oudheid.* Gravenhage, 1981.

Schoske 1990
Sylvia Schoske. *Schönheit—Abglanz der Göttlichkeit: Kosmetik im alten Ägypten.* Exh. cat., Staatliche Sammlung Ägyptischer Kunst. Munich, 1990.

Schoske 1993
Sylvia Schoske. *Egyptian Art in Munich.* Munich, 1993.

Schoske, Kreissl, and Germer 1992
Sylvia Schoske, Barbara Kreissl, and Renate Germer. *"Anch," Blumen für das Leben: Pflanzen im alten Ägypten.* Munich, 1992.

Schulman 1964
Alan R. Schulman. "Some Observations on the Military Background of the Amarna Period." *JARCE* 3 (1964), pp. 51–69.

Schulman 1965
Alan R. Schulman. "The Berlin 'Trauerrelief' (No. 12411) and some Officials of Tut'ankhamūn and Ay." *JARCE* 4 (1965), pp. 55–68.

Schulman 1978
Alan R. Schulman. "'Ankhesenamūn, Nofretity and the Amka Affair." *JARCE* 15 (1978), pp. 43–48.

Schulz 1992
Regine Schulz. *Die Entwicklung und Bedeutung des kuboiden Statuentypus; Eine Untersuchung zu den sogenannten 'Würfelhockern.'* 2 vols. HÄB 33–34 Hildesheim, 1992.

Seidel 1996
Matthias Seidel. *Die königlichen Statuengruppen.* Gerstenberg, 1996.

Sethe and Helck 1927–58
Kurt Sethe and Wolfgang Helck, trans. *Urkunden der 18. Dynastie.* Leipzig and Berlin, 1927–58.

Seyfried 1987
Karl Seyfried. "Bemerkungen zur Erweiterung der unterirdischen Anlagen einiger Gräber des Neuen Reiches in Theben—Versuch einer Deutung." *ASAE* 71 (1987), pp. 229–49.

Shaw 1984
Ian Shaw. "Ring Bezels at el-Amarna." *Amarna Reports* 1 (1994), pp. 124–32.

Silverman 1981
David P. Silverman. "Plural Demonstrative Constructions in Ancient Egyptian." *RdE* 33 (1981), pp. 59–65.

Silverman 1990
David P. Silverman. *Language and Writing in Ancient Egypt.* The Carnegie Series on Egypt. Pittsburgh, 1990.

Silverman 1991a
David P. Silverman. "Divinities and Deities in Ancient Egypt." In *Religion in Ancient Egypt*, ed. Byron E. Shafer, pp. 7–87. Ithaca, 1991.

Silverman 1991b
David P. Silverman. "Texts from the Amarna Period and Their Position in the Development of Ancient Egyptian." *Lingua Aegyptia* 1. Göttingen, 1991.

Silverman 1995
David P. Silverman. "The Nature of Egyptian Kingship." In *Ancient Egyptian Kingship*, ed. David O'Connor and David P. Silverman, pp. 49–94. Leiden, 1995.

Silverman 1997
David P. Silverman, ed. *Ancient Egypt.* London, 1997.

Simpson 1963
William Kelly Simpson. *Heka-nefer and the Dynastic Material from Toshka and Arminna.* New Haven, 1963.

Simpson 1974
William Kelly Simpson. "A Commemorative Scarab of Amenophis III of the Irrigation Basin/Lake Series from the Levant in the Museum of Fine Arts, Boston, and Remarks on Two Other Commemorative Scarabs." *JEA* 60 (1974), pp. 140–41, pl. 33, 1–3.

Simpson 1977
William Kelly Simpson. *The Face of Egypt: Permanence and Change in Egyptian Art.* Exh. cat., Katonah Gallery and Dallas Museum of Fine Arts. Katonah, N. Y., 1977.

R. Smith 1970
Ray Winfield Smith. "Computer Helps Scholars Re-Create an Egyptian Temple." *National Geographic* 138:5 (November 1970), pp. 634–55.

S. Smith 1992
Stuart Tyson Smith. "Intact Tombs of the Seventeenth and Eighteenth Dynasties from Thebes and the New Kingdom Burial System." *MDAIK* 48 (1992), pp. 193–231.

W. Smith 1965
William Stevenson Smith. *The Art and Architecture of Ancient Egypt.* Harmondsworth, Middlesex, 1965.

Smith and Redford 1976
Ray W. Smith and Donald B. Redford. *The Akhenaten Temple Project I: Initial Discoveries.* Warminster, 1976.

Smith and Smith 1976
Harry S. Smith and Alexandrina Smith. "A Reconsideration of the Kamose Texts." *ZÄS* 103 (1973), pp. 48–76.

Sourouzian 1994
Hourig Sourouzian. "Inventaire iconographique des statues en manteau jubilaire de l'époque thinite jusqu'à leur disparition sous Amenhotep III." *Hommages à Jean Leclant*, vol. 1, ed. Catherine Berger, Gisèle Clerc, and Nicolas Grimal, pp. 499–530. Bibliothèque d'Étude 106. Cairo, 1994.

Sowada 1994
Karin Sowada. "A Late Eighteenth Dynasty Statue in the Nicholson Museum, Sydney." *JEA* 80 (1994), pp. 137–43.

Spanel 1988
Donald Spanel. *Through Ancient Eyes: Egyptian Portraiture, An Exhibition.* Birmingham Museum of Art. Birmingham, Ala., 1988.

Spencer 1989
A. Jeffrey Spencer. *Excavations at el-Ashmunein II: The Temple Area.* London, 1989.

Steindorff 1946
Georg Steindorff. *Catalogue of Egyptian Sculpture in the Walters Art Gallery.* Baltimore, 1946.

Stricker 1944
Bruno H. Stricker. "De Indeeling der Egyptische taalgeschiedenis." *OMRO* 25 (1944), pp. 12–51.

Strouhal 1992
Eugen Strouhal. *Life of the Ancient Egyptians.* Norman, Okla., 1992.

Strudwick 1994
Nigel Strudwick. "Change and Continuity at Thebes: The Private Tomb after Akhenaten." In *The Unbroken Reed: Studies in the Culture and Heritage of Ancient Egypt in Honour of A. F. Shore.*, ed. Christopher Eyre, Anthony Leahy, and Lisa Montagno Leahy, pp. 321–36. London, 1994.

Tait 1963
G. A. D. Tait. "The Egyptian Relief Chalice." *JEA* 49 (1963), pp. 93–146.

Tawfik 1973
Sayed Tawfik. "Aton Studies." *MDAIK* 29 (1973), pp. 77–86.

Tawfik 1975
Sayed Tawfik. "Aton Studies." *MDAIK* 31 (1975), pp. 159–68.

Taylor and Boyce 1986
John Taylor and Andrew Boyce. "The Late New Kingdom Burial Beside the Main Chapel." *Amarna Reports* 3 (1986), pp. 118–19.

Terrace 1962
Edward L. B. Terrace. "Limestone Relief: Bowing Figures." In W. S. Smith, "Some Recent Accessions." *BMFA* 60 (1962), p. 135.

Terrace 1964
Edward L. B. Terrace. "Recent Acquisitions in the Department of Egyptian Art." *BMFA* 62 (1964), pp. 48–63.

Terrace and Fischer 1970
Edward L. B. Terrace and Henry G. Fischer. *Treasures of Egyptian Art from the Cairo Museum.* London, 1970.

Thiron 1985
Michelle Thiron. "Notes d'onomastique, contribution à une révision de Ranke PN." *RdE* 36 (1985), pp. 125–43.

A. Thomas 1981
Angela P. Thomas. *Gurob: A New Kingdom Town.* 2 vols. Warminster, 1981.

A. Thomas 1994
Angela P. Thomas. "The Other Woman at Akhetaten, Royal Wife Kiya." *Amarna Letters* 3 (1994), pp. 73–81.

N. Thomas 1995
Nancy Thomas, ed. *The American Discovery of Ancient Egypt.* Exh. cat., Los Angeles County Museum of Art and the American Research Center in Egypt. Los Angeles, 1995.

Tietze 1985
Christian Tietze. "Amarna: Analyse der Wohnhäuser und soziale Struktur der Stadtbewohner." *ZÄS* 112 (1985), pp. 48–84.

Tietze 1986
Christian Tietze. "Amarna (Teil II). Analyse der ökonomischen Beziehungen der Stadtbewohner." *ZÄS* 113 (1986), pp. 55–78.

Tobin 1986
Vincent A. Tobin. *The Intellectual Organization of the Amarna Period.* Ph.D. dissertation, Hebrew University of Jerusalem, 1986.

Traunecker 1986
Claude Traunecker. "Aménophis IV et Nefertiti: Le couple royal d'après les talatates du IXe pylône de Karnak." *BSFE* 107 (octobre 1986), pp. 17–44.

Troy 1986
Lana Troy. *Patterns of Queenship in Ancient Egyptian Myth and History.* Uppsala, 1986.

Turner 1954
W. E. S. Turner. "Studies in Ancient Glasses and Glassmaking Processes, Part I: Crucibles and Melting Temperatures Employed in Ancient Egypt at about 1370 B.C." *Journal for the Society of Glass Technology* 38 (1954), pp. 436–44.

Turner 1956
W. E. S. Turner. "Studies in Ancient Glasses and Glassmaking Processes, Part IV: The Chemical Composition of Ancient Glasses." *Journal for the Society of Glass Technology* 40 (1956), pp. 162–86.

Tytus 1903
Robb de P. Tytus. *A Preliminary Report on the Re-excavation of the Palace of Amenhotep III.* New York, 1903.

van den Boorn 1988
G. P. F. van den Boorn. *The Duties of the Vizier: Civil Administration in the Early New Kingdom.* London, 1988.

van den Hout 1994
Theo P. J. van den Hout. "Der Falke und das Kücken: der neue Pharao und der hethitische Prinz?" *Zeitschrift für Assyriologie* 84 (1994) pp. 60–88.

van Dijk 1988
Jacobus van Dijk. "The Development of the Memphite Necropolis in the Post-Amarna Period." In *Memphis et ses nécropoles au Nouvel Empire*, ed. Alain-Pierre Zivie. Paris, 1988.

van Dijk 1993
Jacobus van Dijk. *The New Kingdom Necropolis at Memphis: Historical and Iconographical Studies.* Groningen, 1993.

van Dijk 1995
Jacobus van Dijk. "Kiya Revisited." In *Seventh International Congress of Egyptologists, Cambridge, 3–9 September 1995, Abstracts of Papers*, ed. Christopher Eyre, p. 50. London, 1995.

van Siclen 1973
Charles C. van Siclen III. "The Accession Date of Amenhotep III and the Jubilee." *JNES* 32 (1973), pp. 290–300.

Vandersleyen 1993
Claude Vandersleyen. "Les scènes de lamentation des chambres alpha et gamma dans la tombe d'Akhénaton." *RdE* 44 (1993), pp. 192–94.

Vandersleyen 1995
Claude Vandersleyen. *L'Égypte et la Vallée du Nil.* Vol. 2, *De la fin de l'Ancien Empire à la fin du Nouvel Empire.* Paris, 1995.

Vandier 1958
Jacques Vandier. *Manuel d'archéologie égyptienne* 3. Paris, 1958.

Vandier 1968
Jacques Vandier. "La statue d'un grand prêtre de Mendès." *JEA* 54 (1968), pp. 89–94.

Vandier d'Abbadie 1972
J. Vandier d'Abbadie. *Catalogue des objets de toilette égyptiens.* Paris, 1972.

Vassilika 1995
Eleni Vassilika. *Egyptian Art.* Cambridge, 1995.

Vercoutter 1976
Jean Vercoutter. "The Iconography of the Black in Ancient Egypt: From the Beginnings to the Twenty-fifth Dynasty." In *The Image of the Black in Western Art*, ed. Ladislas Bugner. Vol. 1: *From the Pharaohs to the Fall of the Roman Empire*, pp. 33–88. Cambridge, Mass., 1976.

Vergnieux and Gondran 1997
Robert Vergnieux and Michel Gondran. *Aménophis IV et les pierres du soleil: Akhénaten retrouvé.* Paris, 1997.

Vergote 1961
Jean Vergote. *Toutankhamon dans les archives hittites.* Istanbul, 1961.

Vogelsang-Eastwood 1992
Gillian Vogelsang-Eastwood. *The Production of Linen in Pharaonic Egypt.* Leiden, 1992.

Vogelsang-Eastwood 1995
Gillian Vogelsang-Eastwood. *Die Kleider des Pharaos: Die Verwendung von Stoffen im Alten Ägypten.* Hannover/Amsterdam, 1995.

von der Way 1996.
Thomas von der Way. "Überlegungen zur Jenseitsvorstellung in der Amarnazeit." *ZÄS* 123 (1996) pp. 157–64.

Wainwright 1925
G. A. Wainwright. "Antiquities from Middle Egypt and the Fayûm." *ASAE* 25 (1925), pp. 144–48.

Walker 1991
Edward James Walker. *Aspects of the Primeval Nature of Egyptian Kingship: Pharaoh as Atum.* Ph.D. dissertation, University of Chicago, 1991.

Wallert 1967
Ingrid Wallert. *Der Verzierte Löffel.* Weisbaden, 1967.

Watanabe and Iseke 1986
Yasutada Watanabe and Kazuaki Iseke. *The Architecture of Kom el-Samak at Malkata South: A Study of Architectural Restoration.* Tokyo, 1986.

Weatherhead 1995
Fran Weatherhead. "Two Studies on Amarna Pigments." *Amarna Reports* 6 (1995), pp. 384–98.

Weatherhead and Buckley 1989
Fran Weatherhead and Andrew Buckley. "Artists' Pigments from Amarna." *Amarna Reports* 5 (1989), pp. 202-22.

Webb 1995
Peter John Webb. "The Ushabti Treasures of Chiddingstone Castle." *KMT* 6 (Spring 1995), pp. 56-57.

Weinstein et al. 1998
James M. Weinstein, Eric H. Cline, Kenneth A. Kitchen, and David O'Connor. "The World Abroad." In *Amenhotep III: Perspectives on His Reign*, ed. David O'Connor and Eric H. Cline, pp. 223-70. Ann Arbor, 1998.

Wendrich 1989
Willemina Wendrich. "Preliminary Report on the Amarna Basketry and Cordage." *Amarna Reports* 5 (1989), pp. 169-201.

Wente 1989-90
Edward F. Wente. "A Taxing Problem." *BES* 10 (1989-90), pp. 169-76.

Wente and Harris 1992
Edward F. Wente and James E. Harris. "Royal Mummies of the Eighteenth Dynasty: A Biologic and Egyptological Approach." In *After Tut'ankhamun: Research and Excavation in the Royal Necropolis at Thebes*, ed. Nicholas Reeves. Studies in Egyptology. London, 1992.

Werner 1986
Edward K. Werner. "Montu and the 'Falcon Ships' of the Eighteenth Dynasty." *JARCE* 23 (1986), pp. 107-23.

Wildung 1976
Dietrich Wildung, ed. *Staatliche Sammlung Ägyptischer Kunst*. Munich, 1976.

Wildung 1977
Dietrich Wildung. *Egyptian Saints*. New York, 1977.

Wildung 1980
Dietrich Wildung. "Neuerwerbungen Staatliche Sammlung Ägyptischer Kunst." *Münchner Jahrbuch der bildenden Kunst* 31 (1980), pp. 259-63.

Wildung 1992
Dietrich Wildung. "Einblicke: Zerstörungsfreie Untersuchungen an altägyptischen Objekten." *JPK* 29 (1994), pp. 133-56.

Wildung 1995a
Dietrich Wildung. "Headhunters." In *Staatliche Sammlung Ägyptischer Kunst München*, ed. Sylvia Schoske, pp. 74-80. Mainz, 1995.

Wildung 1995b
Dietrich Wildung. "Metamorphosen einer Königin: Neue Ergebnisse zur Ikonographie des Berliner Kopfes der Teje mit Hilfe der Computertomographie." *Antike Welt* 26 (1995), pp. 245-49.

Wildung 1997a
Dietrich Wildung. "Ein folgenreicher Todesfall." *Antike Welt* 28 (1997), pp. 27-32.

Wildung 1997b
Dietrich Wildung, ed. *Sudan: Ancient Kingdoms of the Nile*. Paris and New York, 1997.

Wildung 1998
Dietrich Wildung. "Le frère aîné d'Ekhnaton: Réflexions sur un décès prématuré." *BSFE* 143 (octobre 1998), pp. 10-18.

Wilkinson 1971
Alix Wilkinson. *Ancient Egyptian Jewellery*. London, 1971.

Williams 1930
C. R. Williams. "Two Egyptian Torsos from the Main Temple of the Sun at el 'Amarna." *Metropolitan Museum Studies* 3 (1930), pp. 81-99.

Williams and Ogden 1994
Dyfri Williams and Jack Ogden. *Greek Gold*. New York, 1994.

Winlock 1922
Herbert Winlock. "A Gift of Egyptian Antiquities." *BMMA* 8 (1922), pp. 170-73.

Winlock 1937
Herbert Winlock. *Egyptian Statues and Statuettes*. New York, 1937.

Wolf 1931
Walther Wolf. *Das Schöne Fest von Opet: Die Festzugdarstellung im grossen Säulengange des Tempels von Luksor*. Leipzig, 1931.

Worcester Art Museum 1973
A Handbook to the Worcester Art Museum. Worcester, Mass., 1973.

Wreszinski 1923
Walter Wreszinski. *Atlas zur Altaegypischen Kulturgeschichte* 1. Leipzig, 1923.

Wreszinski 1935
Walter Wreszinski. *Atlas zur Altaegyptischen Kulturgeschichte* 2. Leipzig, 1935.

Ziegler 1990
Christiane Ziegler. *The Louvre: Egyptian Antiquities*. London, 1990.

A. Zivie 1988
Alain-Pierre Zivie. "Aper-el et ses voisins." In *Memphis et ses nécropoles au Nouvel Empire*, ed. Alain-Pierre Zivie, pp. 103-12. Paris, 1988.

A. Zivie 1990
Alain-Pierre Zivie. *Découverte à Saqqarah: Le vizir oublié*. Paris, 1990.

A. Zivie 1998
Alain-Pierre Zivie. "The Tomb of the Lady Maïa, Wet-nurse of Tutankhamen." *ES* 13 (1998), pp. 7-8.

C. Zivie 1975
Christiane Zivie. "À propos de quelques reliefs du Nouvel Empire au Musée du Caire." *BIFAO* 75 (1975), pp. 285-310.

Index

Queen Tiye and, 47, 203, *215*
Hatshepsut, 42, 47–48
Hatsheret (Chantress of Aten), *shabti* figure, *271*
Hatti, 158, 181, 182
Hattusha, 161
hawk-headed god (Pe), *210*
headdresses
  afnet (khat), 207, *215*, 245, *246, 267*
  nemes, 27, *200*, 204, *205*, 267, *274*
  types of, 267
headrest, *253*
heads (plaster). *See also* masks
  depictions of
    at Amarna, *25*, 123–26
    nonroyal, 125–26, *247*
    royal, 123–25, *215*
heart scarab, 174*n*33
heb-sed. See jubilee festivals
Heh (god), *233*
Heliopolis, 234
Henuttaneb, 82, 85
herdsman, depiction of (with goat), *249*
Hermopolis, 117
hes vase, *235*
hieratic script, 151, 158
hieroglyphs, 151
  ostracon with, *248*
  referring to Amen, 149
Hittites, 160–61, 181–83. *See also* Shuppiluliuma
  prince solicited by Ankhesenamen, 36
  prince solicited by Nefertiti, 91
Horakhty. *See also* Ra-Horakhty; Ra-Horakhty-Atum
  hymns to, 98
Horemheb, 36, 53, 109, 117, 161, 178, 207, 275
  depictions of, 187–88
    with Amen, *193, 278*
    receiving award, *176, 177, 278*
    as scribe, *190, 191, 277*
    as Standard Bearer for Amen, *194*, 195
  door-jamb of, *278*
  influence of Amarna on, 192–95
  opposition to, 183
  reforms of, 149
  reign of, 183, 192–95
  repudiation of Aten by, 183, 185, 187–88, 192–93
  restoration of Amen by, 187–88, *278*
  titles of, 180
  tomb of, 174, 190
horizon *(akhet)*, 75, 78

horses
  depictions of
    with chariot, *241, 242*
    head, *156, 157, 241*
    relief, *268*
  harness, *242*
  uses of, *252*
Horus (god), 107, 231, 261
household shrines, 254
House of Rejoicing, 62, 76
House of the Correspondence of the Pharaoh. *See under* Amarna
House of the Sun-Disk, 62
housing, 28–29
  building materials, 28
  depiction on canal, *250*
  design of, 29
  layout of, 28–29
  plans for, *70, 71*
  private, 28, 29, 70–71
  size, 28–29
  for workmen, 61, 69
human figure, depictions of
  under Akhenaten, 22–23, 112–16, 195
  corpulent, 46, 47, 112, 203, 204
  with elongated features, 55, *208*
  at Karnak, 112–14
  naturalistic treatment of, 27
  Old Kingdom art styles, 39
  proportion standards, 113, 188, 191
Hutbenben, 57, 87, 115
Huy, *271*
Huya
  shrine of, 172
  tomb of, 171, 172–73
    relief depicting Huya's workshop, *132*
Hyksos, 18, 41, 142
"Hymn of Suty and Hor," 98–99
hymns, 97–99. *See also* "Great Hymn to Aten"

I

infant burials, 166
inlays
  in faience, 138
  use of, 223
instruments, musical. *See also* musicians; harps; lutes; lyre
  clappers, *235*
intimacy, depictions of, 28, 92, 119, *120, 121, 220*, 247
Ipu, on stela, *280*
Ipuy, on stela, *206*
Ipy, tomb of, 173
irrigation system, 28

Ishtar (goddess), 204
Isis (Chantress of Aten), *shabti* figure, *271*
Isis (goddess), 82, 85, 97, 107, 234, 266
Iuty (sculptor), *132*
Iwy, *271*

J

Jackson, Caroline, 139
jewelry, 135
  beads
    "eyes" on, 140
    melon, *262*
    wedjat (sacred eye), 140, *261*
  bracelet, *261*
  broadcollars, *262, 269. See also* collars
  ear ornaments, 135, *258, 261, 262*
  "eye" necklace, 140, *261*
  neck ornaments, 43, 45, 234, *262*
  menat, 234
  rings
    faience, 138, *261*
    with frog bezel, *268, 269*
    glass, *94*
    gold and silver, 135
    stirrup (signet), *85, 234, 260, 268, 269*
    with *wedjat*-eye bezel, 135, *268, 269*
jubilee festivals *(heb-sed*, or *sed*-festivals)
  Akhenaten, 31, 53, 56–57
  Amenhotep III, 43, 53, 72, 81, 204
  depictions of, *56, 207, 208, 209*
  Karnak, 86
  Tiye and, 88
  tradition of, 56–57

K

ka, 162, 166, 172, *251*
Kadesh, 181–82
Kahun, 68
Kamose, 18
Karnak. *See also* Gempaaten (Karnak); Rewedmenu; Tenimenu
  Amen-Ra temple, 18, 41
  building program, 22–23
  depictions
    Akhenaten, 112–14
    Aten, 22, 114, 116
    distorted, of human figure, 112–14
    Nefertiti, 112–14
    Osiris, 113
    Shu, 113
    smiting, 110, *112*

Ishtar...
Tefnut, 113
East Karnak, 56
Ninth Pylon, 50, *52*, 53, 210
  plan of, *53*
  sed-festivals, 86
  shrines to Nefertiti, 87–88
  temples, 50, 59, 75, 112–16
  Tenth Pylon, 53, 207
  Third Pylon, 22
Kassite Babylonia, 158
Kemp, Barry, 25, 64, 66, 68, 139
kenbet, 146, 149
Khaemhat, tomb of, *80, 81*
khat. See under headdresses
khepresh (blue) crown. *See under* crowns
Kheruef, 83, 146
  tomb of, *165*, 202
Khnum (god), 72, 97
Khonsu (god), 20, 107
  Opet festival and, 72
Khor, 102
kilts, 43
King's Estate (Amarna), 65
King's House (Amarna), 27, 65, 67, 78
Kiya, 17, 33, 34, 86–87, *87*, 94*n*66, 174, *178*, 218, *270*
  burial of, 92
  canopic jar with lid, 162, *163*
  depictions of, *125*
    defacement of, 92
    head, 92
    kissing daughter, 92
    purification of, 232
    relief reworked for Meretaten, 221
  disappearance of, 92
  role of, 91–92
knife, *251*
Kom el-Nana, 64
Kush. *See* Nubia
Kushites. *See* Nubians

L

lamp, *253*
language
  adjectives, possessive, 153
  articles, definite, 151, 153
  of Amarna letters, 158
  changes in, 151–54
  divinity of Akhenaten and, 154
  plural signs, destruction of, 23, 107
  spoken, 151, 153
  study of, 155*n*7
  vernacular, 151, 153
latrine seat, *253*
lattice stool, *141, 253*
Leiden Hymns, 104–5, 109

Figure identification

Fig. 4 Colossal statue of Amenhotep IV/Akhenaten from Karnak (detail shown, fig. 66)
Karnak, Gempaaten
Dynasty 18, reign of Amenhotep IV/Akhenaten, 1353–1336 B.C. (years 2–5)
Sandstone
H. 400 cm
Egyptian Museum, Cairo, JE 49529

Fig. 5 Colossal statue, possibly Nefertiti, from Karnak
Karnak, Gempaaten
Dynasty 18, reign of Amenhotep IV/Akhenaten, 1353–1336 B.C. (years 2–5)
Sandstone
H. 400 cm
Egyptian Museum, Cairo, JE 55938

Fig. 13 Akhenaten kissing a child
Amarna, sculptor's studio
Dynasty 18, reign of Akhenaten, 1353–1336 B.C.
Limestone
H. 39.5 cm, w. 16 cm, l. 21.5 cm
Egyptian Museum, Cairo, JE 44866

Fig. 17 Grieving scene from the Royal Tomb at Amarna
Geoffrey T. Martin, *The Royal Tomb of El-'Amarna*, vol. 2 (London: Egypt Exploration Society, 1989), pl. 68.

Fig. 26 Detail of Amenhotep III on a sledge
Luxor temple cachette
Dynasty 18, reign of Amenhotep III, 1390–1353 B.C.
Quartzite
H. 249 cm
Luxor Museum, Luxor, M 838

Fig. 33 Plan of Karnak
Drawing by Donald Redford

Fig. 39 Bowing foreigners
Karnak
Dynasty 18, reign of Amenhotep IV/Akhenaten, 1353–1336 B.C. (years 2–5)
Sandstone
H. 22 cm, w. 54 cm, d. 6 cm
Egyptian Museum, Cairo, SR 13439

Fig. 41 Plan of the Great Temple
J. D. S. Pendlebury, *The City of Akhenaten* 3 (London: Egypt Exploration Society, 1951), pl. IV.

Fig. 45 Plan of the North Palace
William Stevenson Smith, *The Art and Architecture of Ancient Egypt* (New York: Penguin, 1981), fig. 304.

Fig. 46 Aerial view of the Central City
J. D. S. Pendlebury, *The City of Akhenaten* 3 (London: Egypt Exploration Society, 1951), pl. XXIV.

Fig. 47 Reconstruction of a chapel outside the Workmen's Village
Watercolor by Fran Weatherhead

Fig. 48 Plan of Amarna house T.36.11
Seton Lloyd, "Model of an Amarnah house," *Journal of Egyptian Archaeology* 19 (1933), fig. 3.

Fig. 51 Plotting out the city
Computer graphic by Michael Mallinson

Fig. 52 Small Temple computer reconstruction
Computer reconstruction by Michael Mallinson

Fig. 54 Detail from a relief of Amenhotep III, tomb of Khaemhat
Theban Tomb 57
Dynasty 18, reign of Amenhotep III, 1390–1353 B.C.
Limestone
H. 31.5 cm
Ägyptisches Museum und Papyrussammlung, Berlin, 14503

Fig. 57 Bust of Queen Nefertiti
Amarna, house P.47.2
Dynasty 18, reign of Akhenaten, 1353–1336 B.C.
Limestone
H. 50 cm.
Ägyptisches Museum und Papyrussammlung, Berlin, 21300

Fig. 60 The reception of foreign tribute, from the tomb of Meryra II
Norman de Garis Davies, *The Rock Tombs of El Amarna* 2 (London: Egypt Exploration Society, 1905), pl. XXXVII.

Fig. 61 Canopic coffinette from the tomb of Tutankhamen
Thebes, Valley of the Kings
Dynasty 18, reign of Tutankhamen, 1332–1322 B.C.

Gold inlaid with carnelian and paste
H. 39.5 cm, w. 45.2 cm
Egyptian Museum, Cairo, JE 60691

Fig. 63 Relief of Kiya kissing her daughter
Amarna, found at Hermopolis
Dynasty 18, reign of Akhenaten, 1353–1336 B.C.
Limestone
H. 23.2 cm, w. 45.2 cm, d. 3.4 cm
Charles Edwin Wilbour Fund, Brooklyn Museum of Art, New York, 60.197.8

Fig. 64 Detail of a painting fragment showing two princesses
Amarna, King's House
Dynasty 18, reign of Akhenaten, 1353–1336 B.C.
Painted plaster
L. 36 cm
Ashmolean Museum, Oxford, 1893.1-41 (267)

Fig. 65 Glass ring with the names of Ay and Ankhesenamen
Provenance not known
Dynasty 18, reign of Ay, 1322–1319 B.C.
Glass
Bezel l. 1.9 cm, diam. 1.6 cm
Ägyptisches Museum und Papyrussammlung, Berlin, 34316

Fig. 70 Painted limestone stela of the royal family
Amarna
Dynasty 18, reign of Akhenaten, 1353–1336 B.C.
Limestone
H. 43.5 cm.
Egyptian Museum, Cairo, JE 44865

Fig. 82 Family intimacy: Fragment showing Akhenaten and Nefertiti
Amarna
Dynasty 18, reign of Akhenaten, 1353–1336 B.C.
Limestone
H. 12 cm
Ägyptisches Museum und Papyrussammlung, Berlin, 14511

Fragment showing Nefertiti and daughters on Akhenaten's lap
Amarna
Dynasty 18, reign of Akhenaten, 1353–1336 B.C.
Limestone
H. 24.7 cm, w. 34 cm
Musée du Louvre, Paris, E 11624

Fig. 83 "Green Room" wall painting (facsimile)
Amarna, North Palace
(copy of a mural painting from the northeast court)
Watercolor by Nina de Garis Davies
H. 105.5 cm, w. 425 cm
(1:1 scale with original)
Egyptian Expedition of The Metropolitan Museum of Art, Rogers Fund, 1930, The Metropolitan Museum of Art, New York, 30.4.136

Fig. 84 Ground floor of the Thutmose workshop
Computer reconstruction by Barry Girsh for The Metropolitan Museum of Art, New York

Fig. 90 Statue of an aging Nefertiti
Amarna, workshop of Thutmose, P.47.2
Dynasty 18, reign of Akhenaten, 1353–1336 B.C.
Limestone
H. 40 cm
Ägyptisches Museum und Papyrussammlung, Berlin, 21263

Fig. 93 Atelier of the sculptor Iuty, from the tomb of the Steward Huya
Drawing by Yvonne Markowitz, adapted from Norman de Garis Davies, *The Rock Tombs of El Amarna* 3 (London: Egypt Exploration Society, 1905), pl. XVIII.

Fig. 97 Polychrome faience: Daisy tile
Amarna
Dynasty 18, reign of Akhenaten, 1353–1336 B.C.
Faience
L. 16.5 cm, w. 11.1 cm, d. 0.7 cm
Gift of the Egypt Exploration Society, Brooklyn Museum of Art, New York, 35.2001

Fig. 105 Vertical loom as represented in the Theban tomb of Djehutynefer
Drawing by Yvonne Markowitz.

Fig. 107 Tradition and innovation
Norman de Garis Davies, *The Tomb of the Vizier Ramose* (London: Egypt Exploration Society, 1941), pls. XXIX, XXXIII.

Fig. 108 Stamped brick
Amarna, records office
Dynasty 18, reign of Akhenaten, 1353–1336 B.C.
Clay

L. 30 cm, w. 15 cm
Gift of the Egypt Exploration Fund
through the Honorable Robert Bass,
Museum of Fine Arts, Boston, 37.10.

**Fig. 120 Painted papyrus illustrating a
battle scene**
Amarna
Dynasty 18, reign of Akhenaten,
1353–1336 B.C.
Papyrus
H. 10.3 cm, w. 10 cm (fragment shown)
British Museum, London, EA 74100

Line drawing
Richard Parkinson, "Akhenaten's
Army," *Egyptian Archaeology: The
Bulletin of the Egypt Exploration
Society* 3 (1993), p. 34.

**Fig. 123 Plan and isometric rendering
of the tomb of Amenhotep III**
Drawing by Yvonne Markowitz after
Philip Winton in *The Complete Valley
of the Kings*, by Nicholas Reeves and
Richard H. Wilkinson (London:
Thames and Hudson, 1996), p. 111.

**Fig. 124 Plan of an 18th Dynasty T-
shaped private tomb**
Drawing by Yvonne Markowitz.

**Fig. 127 Plan of the Royal Tomb at
Amarna**
Drawing by Yvonne Markowitz after
Philip Winton in *The Complete Valley
of the Kings*, by Nicholas Reeves and
Richard H. Wilkinson (London:
Thames and Hudson, 1996), p. 118.

**Fig. 131 The rewarding of the
deceased, tomb of Meryra II**
Norman de Garis Davies, *The Rock
Tombs of El Amarna* 2 (London: Egypt
Exploration Society, 1905), pl. XXXIII.

Fig. 134 Stela from the tomb of Any
Amarna
Dynasty 18, reign of Akhenaten,
1353–1336 B.C.
Limestone
H. 27 cm, w. 23.4 cm
Egyptian Museum, Cairo, JE 34177

Fig. 135 Coffin lid from tomb KV 55
Thebes
Dynasty 18, reign of Akhenaten,
1353–1336 B.C.
Wood with inlay
L. 183 cm, w. 57 cm
Egyptian Museum, Cairo, JE 39627

**Fig. 137 Granite sculpture of
Tutankhamen**
Karnak, Amen temple cachette
Dynasty 18, reign of Tutankhamen,
1332–1322 B.C.
Granite
H. 153 cm
Egyptian Museum, Cairo, CG 42091

**Fig. 138 Limestone stela with two
royal figures**
Amarna
Dynasty 18, reign of Akhenaten,
1353–1336 B.C.
Limestone
H. 21 cm, w. 16 cm
Ägyptisches Museum und
Papyrussammlung, Berlin, 17813

**Fig. 139 Back panel of Tutankhamen's
throne** (detail)
Thebes, Valley of the Kings, tomb of
Tutankhamen
Dynasty 18, reign of Tutankhamen,
1332–1322 B.C.
Wood, gold sheet, semiprecious stones
H. 102 cm, w. 54 cm
Egyptian Museum, Cairo, JE 62028

**Fig. 140 Restoration Stela of
Tutankhamen**
Karnak, Great Hypostyle Hall
Dynasty 18, reign of Tutankhamen,
1332–1322 B.C.
Quartzite
H. 129 cm
Egyptian Museum, Cairo, JE 34183

**Fig. 152 King Horemheb (?) as a
Standard Bearer of Amen**
Karnak
Dynasty 18, reign of Horemheb (?),
1319–1292 B.C.
Black granite
H. 80 cm, w. 35 cm, d. 34 cm
Egyptian Museum, Cairo, CG 603

Map credits

**Page 14: Egypt and the Near East
during the Amarna Period**
Left: Map by Peter Der Manuelian
after B. G. Trugger, B. J. Kemp, D.
O'Connor, and A. B. Lloyd, *Ancient
Egypt: A Social History* (London:
Cambridge University Press, 1983),
fig. 3.5.

Right: Map by Peter Der Manuelian.

**Page 15: The City of Amarna
(Akhetaten)**
Map by Peter Der Manuelian after
Barry Girsh in *The Royal Women of
Amarna*, by Dorothea Arnold (New
York: Metropolitan Museum of Art,
1996), fig. 13.

Photography credits

All photographs of objects in the exhibition were provided courtesy of the lender, except as noted. Additional photographs and illustrations were provided courtesy of the individuals and institutions credited below.

Ägyptisches Museum und Papyrussammlung, Berlin: figs. 65, 82; Chr. Begall: cat. 137; Margarete Büsing: fig. 3, 14, 15, 55, 56, 57, 73, 81, 86, 91, 112, cats. 15, 36, 39, 42, 44, 47, 51, 53, 93, 99, 100, 131, 164, 180, 182, 183, 195, 196, 236; Saburō Kitai: cat. 132; Jürgen Liepe: figs. 54, 121, 138, cats. 104, 114, 171.

Ashmolean Museum, Oxford: fig. 64.

British Museum, London: fig. 120 (papyrus fragment).

Brooklyn Museum of Art, New York: figs. 63, 97.

© CNRS/CFEETK. Fonds Chevrier: fig. 34; A. Chéné: fig. 74.

Sue D'Auria: fig. 125.

Egypt Exploration Society, London: figs. 17, 41, 46, 48, 53, 60, 67, 107, 128, 129, 130, 131, 133.

Rita Freed: figs. 2, 10, 76.

W. Raymond Johnson: fig. 26.

© Justin Kerr, New York: fig. 61.

© Könemann GmbH, Köln. Andrea Jemolo: figs. 106, 139.

© LotosFilm, Kaufbeuren: fig. 6.

Michael Mallinson: figs. 51, 52.

Yvonne Markowitz: figs. 93, 105, 123, 124, 127.

© Metropolitan Museum of Art, New York: figs. 83, 84; Bruce White: figs. 7, 9, 79, 90, cats. 19, 41, 45, 48, 56, 139, 231, 245; Schecter Lee: fig. 12, cat. 241.

William Murnane: figs. 114, 141.

Museum of Fine Arts, Boston: fig. 108; Mohamed Gabr: figs. 4, 5, 66, 137, 140, cat. 1; Sharif Sonbol: figs. 27, 28, 30, 31, 35, 36, 39, 78, 89, 134, 135, 150, 151, 152, cats. 11, 12, 22, 23, 26, 30, 33, 34, 40, 71, 134, 172, 185, 232, 244, 248, 254.

Gwil Owen, Cambridge University: figs. 109, 132, 143.

Richard Parkinson: fig. 120 (line drawing).

© Philipp von Zabern GmbH, Munich. Jürgen Liepe: figs. 13, 70, 113, cat. 72.

© PhotoArchive Jürgen Liepe, Berlin: cat. 18.

Donald Redford: fig. 33.

© RMN, Paris: figs. 1, 21, 82, 92, cats. 78, 85, 258; Chuzeville: figs. 38, 146, cats. 21, 243; C. Larrieu: cat. 95; H. Lewandowski: figs. 8, 18, cats. 49, 46.

Matthias Seidel: fig. 32.

Sylvia Sarner: figs. 25, 77, 142, cats. 6, 27, 63, 64, 75, 262.

Thea Weistreich Art Advisory Services, New York: cat. 259.

Fran Weatherhead: fig. 47.